POVERTY AND SHARED PROSPERITY 2016

TAKING ON INEQUALITY

TAKING ON
INEQUALITY

WORLD BANK GROUP

ISBN (paper): 978-1-4648-0958-3
ISBN (electronic): 978-1-4648-0979-8
DOI: 10.1596/978-1-4648-0958-3

Cover design: Patricia Hord Graphik Design

Library of Congress Cataloging-in-Publication Data has been applied for.

Contents

Foreword — ix
Acknowledgments — xi
About the Core Team and the Contributors — xiii
Abbreviations — xvii

Overview — **1**
Notes — 19
References — 20

1 Poverty and Shared Prosperity: Setting the Stage — **23**
Concepts, measurement, and data — 23
A special focus in 2016: taking on inequality — 29
Notes — 32
References — 33

2 Global Poverty — **35**
Monitoring global poverty — 35
A profile of the poor in the developing world — 42
Annex 2A Historical global and regional poverty estimates — 46
Annex 2B Technical note: global poverty measurement using 2013 data — 47
Notes — 50
References — 51

3 Shared Prosperity — **53**
Shared prosperity: where we stand — 53
The bottom 40 in relative terms: the shared prosperity premium — 56
Incomes of the bottom 40 and the top 10: the Palma premium — 57
Who are the bottom 40? — 57
Is the poverty goal attainable at current levels of growth and shared prosperity? — 59
Conclusions: continued progress, but no room for complacency — 62

Annex 3A Shared prosperity estimates based on the latest surveys, by country, circa 2008–13   64

Notes   66

References   67

4   Inequality   69

Inequality matters   69

Separating fact from myth: what is the evidence on inequality?   75

Concluding remarks   87

Annex 4A Data construction   89

Global inequality database   89

Database of within-country Gini indexes   89

Notes   91

References   95

5   Reductions in Inequality: A Country Perspective   101

Introduction   102

Brazil: multiple policies aligned to redress record inequality   103

Cambodia: new earning opportunities emerging from impressive growth   107

Mali: a vulnerable economy favored by the vagaries of agriculture   110

Peru: equalizing investment despite informality and low human capital   114

Tanzania: sharing prosperity in the midst of diversification   117

Concluding remarks: learning from country experiences   120

Notes   122

References   124

6   Reductions in Inequality: A Policy Perspective   129

Introduction   130

Early childhood development and nutrition   131

Health care and education   135

Conditional cash transfers   140

Rural infrastructure   145

Taxation   148

Concluding remarks   152

Notes   154

References   159

Boxes

1.1 The Welfare Aggregate: Income versus Consumption   25

2.1 Measuring Global Poverty and Purchasing Power Parities   37

2.2 Projecting Poverty Rates   43

3.1 The Bottom 40 versus the Poor   59

3.2 Simulating Poverty Trajectories   61

4.1 Cross-Country Studies of the Effect of Inequality on Growth   71

4.2 Perceptions of Inequality in the Middle East and North Africa   73

4.3 Absolute versus Relative Inequality   78

4.4 Comparison of Levels and Trends in Income and Consumption Inequality   79

4.5 Comparing Trends in Inequality: Household Surveys and Administrative Records   80

6.1 Tax Reform and Fiscal Consolidation   150

Figures

O.1 Distribution of the Extreme Poor, the Nonpoor, the Bottom 40, and the Top 60, 2013   2

O.2 World and Regional Trends, Poverty Headcount Ratio, 1990–2013   5

O.3 Trends in the Global Poverty Headcount Ratio and the Number of the Global Poor, 1990–2013   5

O.4 Where Are the Global Poor Living? The Global Poor, by Region, 2013   6

O.5 Profile of the Poor, by Characteristics and Region, 2013   6

O.6 Age Profile of the Poor, 2013   7

O.7 Shared Prosperity, 83 Countries, 2008–13   8

O.8 Boosting Shared Prosperity and Ending Poverty, 10-Year Scenario, 2013–30   9

O.9 Global Inequality, 1820–2010   9

O.10 Global Inequality, 1988–2013   10

O.11 Average Within-Country Inequality, 1988–2013   10

O.12 Trends in the Average National Gini, by Region, 1988–2013   11

O.13 The National Income Share of the Richest 1 Percent, Selected Economies   12

O.14 Available Country Poverty Estimates, Number, by Region and Year   19

1.1 Available Country Poverty Estimates, by Region and Year   28

1.2 Availability of Poverty Data, by All Possible 10-Year Periods, 1990–2013   28

1.3 Double and Triple Dips in Growth, Selected Economies, 2006–15   30

2.1 The Global Poverty Headcount Ratio and the Number of the Extreme Poor, 1990–2013   36

2.2 Where Are the Global Poor Living? The Global Poor, by Region, 2013   37

2.3 Regional and World Trends, Number of the Extreme Poor, 1990–2013   38

2.4 Regional and World Trends, Extreme Poverty Headcount Ratio, 1990–2013   39

2.5 Poverty Headcount Ratios and Number of the Poor, by Country Income, 2013   40

2.6 Poverty Headcount Ratios, Top 10 Countries, 2013   41

2.7 Number of the Poor, Top 10 Countries, 2013   41

2.8 Trends in the Poverty Gap and the Global Headcount Ratio, 1990–2013   42

2.9 Profile of the Poor, by Characteristics and Region, 2013   44

2.10 Profile of the Extreme and Moderate Poor, by Selected Characteristics, 2013   44

2.11 Age Profile of the Poor, 2013   45

3.1 Shared Prosperity, 83 Countries, 2008–13   55

3.2 The Bottom 40, Brazil, India, and the United States, Circa 2013   58

B3.1.1 Distribution of the Extreme Poor, the Nonpoor, the Bottom 40, and the Top 60, 2013   59

3.3 Income Group Composition, the Bottom 40, Selected Countries, Circa 2013   60

3.4 Boosting Shared Prosperity and Ending Poverty, 2013–30   62

4.1 Growth of the Bottom 40 versus Growth at the Mean, 2008–13   72

B4.2.1 Actual versus Anticipated Feelings of Well-Being, Middle East and North Africa   74

4.2 The Top 1 Percent Income Share, Selected Economies   76

4.3	Global Income Inequality, 1820–2010	76
4.4	Long-Run Changes in the Gini Index, Selected Developing Countries, 1980–2014	77
B4.3.1	Comparing Absolute and Relative Gains across the Distribution	78
B4.4.1	Levels of Income and Consumption, Gini Indexes, 2013	79
B4.4.2	Trends in Income and Consumption, Gini Indexes, Circa 2008–13	79
B4.5.1	Comparison of Top Incomes and the Gini Index, Brazil, 2006–12	80
4.5	Global Inequality, 1988–2013	81
4.6	Average Within-Country Inequality, 1988–2013	83
4.7	Trends in the Average Gini, by Region, 1988–2013	83
4.8	The Gini Index, 101 Countries, 2013	84
4.9	Distribution of the Gini Index, 2013	85
4.10	Trends in the Within-Country Gini Index, 1993–2013	86
5.1	Trends in the Gini Index, Brazil, 1981–2014	104
5.2	Growth Incidence Curve, Brazil, 2004–14	104
5.3	Contributions of Growth and Redistribution Effects to Poverty Reduction, Brazil, 2004–14	105
5.4	Trends in the Gini Index, Cambodia, 2007–13	107
5.5	Growth Incidence Curve, Cambodia, 2012–13	108

5.6	Contributions of Growth and Redistribution Effects to Poverty Reduction, Cambodia, 2008–12	108
5.7	Trends in the Gini Index, Mali, 2001–10	111
5.8	Growth Incidence Curve, Mali, 2001–10	112
5.9	Contributions of Growth and Redistribution Effects to Poverty Reduction, Mali, 2006–09	112
5.10	Trends in the Gini Index, Peru, 2004–14	115
5.11	Growth Incidence Curve, Peru, 2004–14	115
5.12	Contributions of Growth and Redistribution Effects to Poverty Reduction, Peru, 2004–14	115
5.13	Trends in the Gini Index, Tanzania, 2001–12	117
5.14	Growth Incidence Curve, Tanzania, 2007–12	118
5.15	Contributions of Growth and Redistribution Effects to Poverty Reduction, Tanzania, 2007–12	118
6.1	The Mental Development of Stunted Children, Jamaica, 1986–87	132
6.2	Median Coverage, Selected Health Care Interventions, by Wealth Quintile, Low- and Middle-Income Countries, Circa 2005–13	136
6.3	Mathematics Scores, by Household Income Level, Selected Countries, Circa 2007–11	139
6.4	Simulated Gini Point Reduction in the Gini Index Attributable to CCTs, Circa 2013	141

Tables

O.1	World and Regional Poverty Estimates, 2013	4
2.1	World and Regional Poverty Estimates, 2013	36
2A.1	Historical Trends, World Extreme Poverty Estimates, 1990–2013	46
2A.2	Historical Trends, Regional Poverty Headcount Ratios, 1990–2013	46
2A.3	Historical Trends, Number of Extreme Poor, by Region, 1990–2013	46
2B.1	Poverty Estimates Based on China's Old Survey Methodology, 2013	49
3.1	Shared Prosperity, Circa 2008–13	54

3A.1	Shared Prosperity Estimates, Circa 2008–13	64
4.1	Countries with an Increasing or Decreasing Gini Index and the Average Gini	86
4A.1	Population Coverage of the Data Used in the Global Inequality Estimates	89
4A.2	Population Coverage of the Data Used in the Analysis	90
5.1	Annualized per Capita GDP Growth and Reductions in Inequality, Selected Countries	103
5.2	Typology of Poverty and Inequality Levels, Selected Countries, Circa 2013	103

Foreword

The World Bank Group's goals are clear—we are committed to ending extreme poverty by 2030 and boosting shared prosperity of the bottom 40 percent of populations in every country. If we are to reach our goals, it's crucial to report on both the progress and the barriers to improving people's lives.

We have created the *Poverty and Shared Prosperity* annual flagship series to do just that, providing the latest and most accurate statistics and analysis on extreme poverty and shared prosperity.

As we work toward the end-poverty goal in 2030, it's important to remember that the developing world has made unprecedented progress in reducing extreme poverty. Since 1990, nearly 1.1 billion people have lifted themselves out of extreme poverty. In areas ranging from child survival to primary school enrollments, the improvements to people's lives have advanced with a momentum that few could have imagined when the World Bank was founded more than 70 years ago.

But today we face a powerful threat to progress around the world: Inequality.

High income inequality is hardly new in human history. But today, inequality is constraining national economies and destabilizing global collaboration in ways that put humanity's most critical achievements and aspirations at risk. This includes the goal of ending extreme poverty by 2030.

That is why this first *Poverty and Shared Prosperity* report took a deeper look at inequality—making the case for action by explaining the benefits for countries in closing persistent gaps. More equal countries tend to have healthier people and be more economically efficient than highly unequal countries. And countries that invest smartly in reducing inequality today are likely to see more prolonged economic growth than those that don't. Less inequality can benefit the vast majority of the world's population.

The last part of this report describes the successful strategies that many countries are already using to fight inequality. World Bank Group economists have conducted a comprehensive review of policies that can raise the incomes of the poor, analyzed a vast body of evidence, and singled out some of the policies that are well known to work best. Their results offer policy options that can be relevant for most countries in the world.

Whether you're a government leader, an entrepreneur, an activist, or a frontline service provider, my hope is that this report will inform your decisions and inspire you to make your actions count.

Thank you for your work to build a fairer, *more equal,* and more prosperous future for all.

Jim Yong Kim
President, World Bank Group

Acknowledgments

Dedicated to the loving memory of Martin Andres Cuesta Lopez.

This report has been prepared by a team led by José Cuesta and Mario Negre and comprising Timm Bönke, Soumya Chattopadhyay, Shaohua Chen, Will Durbin, María Eugenia Genoni, Aparajita Goyal, Christoph Lakner, Terra Lawson-Remer, Maura K. Leary, Renzo Massari, Jose Montes, David Newhouse, Stace Nicholson, Espen Beer Prydz, Maika Schmidt, and Ani Silwal.

The work has been carried out under the general supervision of Francisco H. G. Ferreira and Ana Revenga and the guidance of Kaushik Basu and Jan Walliser. World Bank President Jim Yong Kim was an invaluable source of encouragement to the team.

Kathleen Beegle, Branko Milanović, Ambar Narayan, and Sudhir Shetty served as peer reviewers. Robert Zimmermann edited the document, and Susan Graham was the production editor. The report's publishing was supervised by Patricia Katayama. Venkat Gopalakrishnan, Phil Hay, Mary D. Lewis, and Mikael Ello Reventar contributed to dissemination. Additional support was provided by Anna Regina Rillo Bonfield, Pamela Gaye C. Gunio, Estella Malayika, Nelly Obias, and Clara Serraino.

The team would like to thank François Bourguignon, Branko Milanović, and Matthew Wai-Poi for sharing data. The team would also like to acknowledge the following people for insightful discussions, including Omar Arias, João Pedro Azevedo, Benu Bidani, Andrés Castañeda, Luc Christiansen, Andrew Dabalen, Klaus Deininger, Dung Doan, Martin C. Evans, Deon Filmer, Alan Fuchs, Emanuela Galasso, Xavier Gine, Stephane Hallegatte, Ruth Hill, Leora Klapper, Jose R. Lopez-Calix, Carolina Mejia-Mantilla, Rinku Murgai, Luis F. López-Calva, Minh Cong Nguyen, Pedro Olinto, Maria Beatriz Orlando, Carlos Rodríguez-Castelán, Halsey Rogers, Julie Rozenberg, Carlos Silva-Jauregui, Emmanuel Skoufias, Pablo Suárez-Becerra, Hiroki Uematsu, Adam Wagstaff, and Yukata Yoshino. Comments to previous versions of the report were provided by Pedro Alba, Maurizio Bussolo, Jose Familiar Calderon, Anna Chytla, Amit Dar, Augusto de la Torre, Shanta Devarajan, Marianne Fay, Erik Feyen, Norbert Fiess, Lisa Finneran, Haisan Fu, Ejaz Ghani, Aart Kraay, Cyril Muller, Mamta Murthi, Alberto Ninio, Martin Rama, Sheila Redzepi, Jose G. Reis, Joanna Silva, Philip Schellekens, Richard Scobey, Radwan Shaban, Nikola Spatafora, Hans Timmer, Yvonne Tsikata, Laura Tuck, Jos Verbeek, and Xiaoqing Yu.

The report benefited from substantial support from the German Development Institute/ *Deutsches Institut für Entwicklungspolitik (DIE)*.

About the Core Team and the Contributors

The Core Team

José Cuesta, co-director of the report, is a World Bank senior economist with a PhD in economics from Oxford University. He is also an affiliated professor at Georgetown University's McCourt School of Public Policy. Cuesta was previously an assistant professor in development economics at the Institute of Social Studies in The Hague. He also worked as a research economist and social sector specialist for the Inter-American Development Bank and as an economist for the United Nations Development Programme in Honduras. His research interests revolve around poverty and conflict economics, specifically the distributive analysis of social policies, intrahousehold allocation, social protection, and labor distortions. He also studies the interaction among poverty, conflict, and culture. A Spanish national, Cuesta has experience in countries in Africa, Asia, and Latin America. He is currently an associate editor for the *European Journal of Development Research* and the *Journal of Economic Policy Reform,* and the editor of the World Bank's quarterly *Food Price Watch.*

Mario Negre, co-director of the report, is a senior economist in the World Bank Development Economics Research Group, where he is seconded by the German Development Institute. He is a nonresidential research fellow at Maastricht School of Management. He has worked at the European Parliament, first as an adviser to the chairman of the Development Committee and then for all external relations committees. Since 2012, he has been a senior researcher at the German Development Institute. His fields of specialization are pro-poor growth, inclusiveness, inequality, and poverty measurement, as well as development cooperation policy, particularly in Europe. Mario holds a BSc in physics from the University of Barcelona, an MA in development policies from the University of Bremen, and a PhD in development economics from the Jawaharlal Nehru University, India.

Soumya Chattopadhyay is a research fellow in the Growth, Poverty, and Inequality Programme at the Overseas Development Institute. His research interests include assessing the impact on subjective well-being of macro conditions and policy interventions using household surveys, identifying the vulnerable and the marginalized, and the issues revolving around infrastructure investment and service delivery. Previously, he worked at the World Bank. He was a senior research associate in the Global Economy and Development Program at the Brookings Institution, and taught at the School of Public Policy at the University of Maryland. Soumya holds a BA in economics from the University of Delhi and the University of Cambridge, a masters in public management, and a PhD in international economic policy from the University of Maryland.

Shaohua Chen is a lead statistician in the Development Economics Research Group of the World Bank. Her main research interests over the past 20 years have been on poverty and inequality measurement. She has managed the global poverty monitoring and online computational tool PovcalNet at the World Bank since 1991. She is also responsible for the measurement and projection of global poverty for the major reports of the World Bank, such as *World Development Indicators* and the *Global Monitoring Report*. Before joining the World Bank, Shaohua was a lecturer at Huazhong University of Science and Technology. Her research findings have been published in major economic and statistical journals, including the *Journal of Development Economics*, the *Journal of Public Economics*, *The Quarterly Journal of Economics*, and *The Review of Economics and Statistics*. She received her MSc in statistical computing from the American University.

María Eugenia Genoni is a senior economist at the Poverty and Equity Global Practice at the World Bank. Her fields of specialization are survey design, poverty and inequality, migration, and risk management. At the World Bank, she has led the poverty and equity programs in Bolivia and Peru. She has also contributed to the poverty work in Argentina and Central America and to the Regional Gender Impact Evaluation Initiative. Before joining the World Bank, María worked in the research department at the Inter-American Development Bank and the Ministry of Finance of the Province of Buenos Aires in Argentina. She holds a PhD in economics from Duke University.

Christoph Lakner is an economist in the Development Research Group at the World Bank (Poverty and Inequality Team). He previously worked in the World Bank's Poverty Practice on Poverty and Inequality issues in Argentina. His research interests include inequality, poverty, and labor markets in developing countries. In particular, he has been working on global inequality, the relationship between inequality of opportunity and growth, the implications of regional price differences for inequality, and the income composition of top incomes. He holds a BA, MPhil, and DPhil in economics from the University of Oxford.

Maura K. Leary is the communications lead for the World Bank Group's Poverty and Equity Global Practice, where she manages strategic communications and outreach on poverty reduction, equity, shared prosperity, and inequality. From 2011 to 2013, she was the partnerships and communications specialist on the Gender and Development team. Prior to joining the World Bank in 2011, she worked at George Washington University and Tufts University, managing academic programs in France and the United States for high school, university, graduate, and adult students. She holds a BA in French from Connecticut College and a master's degree in international affairs from the Elliott School of International Affairs at the George Washington University.

José Montes is a data scientist in the Poverty and Equity Global Practice of the World Bank. He has been working for more than 10 years in poverty and inequality measurement and helping national statistics offices improve the quality, consistency, and documentation of their household surveys. Since 2013, he has been part of Europe and Central Asia Team Statistics Development, and since 2016, part of the core team of the Global Team Statistics Development. Prior to the World Bank, he worked at the Inter-American Development Bank as a household survey specialist in the Poverty and Advisory Unit. He was also a lecturer at the Universidad del Pacífico. José holds a BA in economics from the Universidad del Pacífico and an MSc in economics and an MSc in statistics from Texas A&M University.

Espen Beer Prydz is an economist in the World Bank's Development Economics Research Group. His research interests include issues of poverty, inequality, and survey methods. He has worked in Cambodia, Indonesia, and South Sudan on poverty, social protection, and economic policy. Prior to joining the World Bank, Espen undertook research on poverty, labor markets, and gender with the Development Centre of the Organisation for Economic Co-operation and Development and the Abdul Latif Jameel Poverty Action Lab. Prydz is a Norwegian national who holds a BS from the London School of Economics and an MPA in international development from the John F. Kennedy School of Government at Harvard University.

Maika Schmidt is a consultant in the World Bank's Development Economics Research Group. Her research interests are poverty, inequality, and pro-poor growth with a focus on measurement issues, specifically multidimensional indicators. Maika has worked for the Deutsche Gesellschaft für Internationale Zusammenarbeit. She holds a BSc in economics from the University of Mannheim, a master's from the Barcelona Graduate School of Economics, and a master of research from Pompeu Fabra University, Barcelona. She is currently pursuing her PhD in development economics from the University of Sussex.

Ani Silwal is a consultant in the World Bank's Development Economics Research Group. He holds a BA from Swarthmore College, an MSc from the University of Maryland, and a PhD in economics from the University of Sussex. He has also worked on international migration and remittances. His research interest is the constraints that households face in escaping poverty.

The Contributors

Timm Bönke is assistant professor of public economics at the School of Business and Economics at Freie Universität Berlin. His research interests revolve mainly around inequality and the distribution of income and wealth, the inclusiveness of growth, the design and incentives of state welfare institutions, and redistribution and insurance through tax-benefit systems. Since 2015, he has been associate editor of the *Journal of Income Distribution* and scientific board member of the Research Institute Economics of Inequality at Vienna University of Economics and Business. In addition, he is a regular reviewer for scientific foundations and acts as a scientific and political consultant. Timm holds a masters and a PhD in economics from Freie Universität Berlin.

Will Durbin studied ethics, politics, and economics as an undergraduate at Yale University and international development for a master's degree at the Woodrow Wilson School of Public and International Affairs, Princeton University. He previously worked on climate change and environmental policy and currently focuses on poverty reduction.

Aparajita Goyal is a senior economist in the Poverty and Equity Global Practice of the World Bank. Her work focuses on microeconomic issues of development, with an emphasis on technological innovation in agriculture, access to markets, and intellectual property rights. Her research has been published in leading academic journals, such as *American Economic Review*, *Journal of Human Resources*, and *Journal of Development Economics*, and has been featured in the popular press, including *Frontline*, *Economist*, and *Wall Street Journal*. Within the World Bank, she has previously worked in the Development Economics Research Group, Office of the Chief Economist for the Latin America and Caribbean Region, and Agriculture Global Practice after joining the Young Professionals Program. She holds a BA in economics from St. Stephen's College, University of Delhi, India, an MSc from the London School of Economics, and a PhD in economics from the University of Maryland.

Renzo Massari is a consultant in the World Bank's Development Economics Research Group. His research interests include developing and applying econometric and machine learning methods to poverty and inequality measurement, the use of big data in development, imputation methods, and survey methodology. Previously, he worked at the Labor and Social Protection Unit at the Inter-American Development Bank and as a consultant in empirical regulatory and policy issues in Peru and in the United States. He holds a certification in data science and a PhD in economics from Duke University.

Terra Lawson-Remer's work addresses the determinants and consequences of sustainable development, poverty and inequality, and social and economic rights fulfillment within and across generations. Her expertise includes health care, education, international economic law, legal empowerment, natural resource governance, global trade and transnational investment, extractive industries, democratic transitions, civil society, property rights, and business and human rights. She is the author of dozens of academic books and articles, including, most recently, *Fulfilling Social and Economic Rights* (with Sakiko Fukuda-Parr and Susan Randolph), published by Oxford University Press. Terra earned her BA in ethics, politics, and economics from Yale University; her JD from New York University School of Law, where she was a Dean's Merit Scholar; and her PhD in political economy from the Law and Society Institute, New York University.

David Newhouse is a senior economist in the Poverty and Equity Global Practice. He currently leads the Bank's engagement on poverty in Sri Lanka, as well as on projects that aim to understand the nature of global poverty and incorporate satellite imagery into poverty measurement. He was formerly a labor economist in the Social Protection and Labor Practice, where he helped lead efforts to analyze labor markets and the policy response in the wake of the 2008 financial crisis. He first joined the Bank in August 2007 and co-led the Indonesian Jobs Report. Previously, he worked in the Fiscal Affairs Department of the International Monetary Fund providing policy advice on energy and food subsidies. David holds a PhD in economics from Cornell University. He has co-authored a book and several journal articles on a wide range of issues relating to labor, health, and education in developing countries.

Stace Nicholson is a senior program officer for international economic and financial affairs at the Japan International Cooperation Agency's U.S. office. In this position, he conducts and oversees research that supports credit risk assessment of the agency's concessional loan portfolio and serves as the agency's junior liaison with multilateral financial institutions based in Washington. His work includes tracking macroeconomic developments across a range of emerging and frontier, or developing economies, facilitating research partnerships and project co-financing on an ad hoc basis, and reporting on development finance trends. Prior to joining the agency, Stace interned with the Ghana Center for Democratic Development and undertook field research in Uganda as a microfinance client assessment fellow for the Foundation for International Community Assistance. He is a summa cum laude graduate (political science) of Manchester College and holds a master's degree in global finance, trade, and economic integration from the Josef Korbel School for International Studies, University of Denver.

Abbreviations

BRICS	Brazil, Russian Federation, India, China, and South Africa
CCT	conditional cash transfer
CPI	consumer price index
ECD	early childhood development
EU	European Union
GDP	gross domestic product
IQ	intelligence quotient
OECD	Organisation for Economic Co-operation and Development
PPP	purchasing power parity
SEDLAC	Socio-Economic Database for Latin America and the Caribbean
UNESCO	United Nations Educational, Scientific, and Cultural Organization
VAT	value added tax
WDI	World Development Indicators

Note: All dollar amounts are U.S. dollars (US$) unless otherwise indicated.

For a list of the 3-letter country codes used by the World Bank, please go to: https://datahelpdesk.worldbank.org/knowledgebase/articles/906519-world-bank-country-and-lending-groups.

Overview

Two complementary goals to leave no one behind

On April 20, 2013, the Board of Executive Directors of the World Bank adopted two ambitious goals: end global extreme poverty and promote shared prosperity in every country in a sustainable way. This implies reducing the poverty headcount ratio from 10.7 percent globally in 2013 to 3.0 percent by 2030 and fostering the growth in the income or the consumption expenditure of the poorest 40 percent of the population (the bottom 40) in each country. These two goals are part of a wider international development agenda and are intimately related to United Nation's Sustainable Development Goals 1 and 10, respectively, which have been adopted by the global community.

Each goal has an intrinsic value on its own merits, but the two goals are also highly complementary. Take the example of a low-income Sub-Saharan African country with a high poverty headcount ratio and an upper-middle-income country in Eastern Europe or Latin America with low levels of extreme poverty, but rising concerns about inequality. Ending extreme poverty is especially relevant in the former, while expanding shared prosperity is especially meaningful in the latter. The complementarity of the two goals also derives from the composition of the world's poor and bottom 40 populations. At a global scale, while 9 in every 10 of the extreme poor were among the national bottom 40 in 2013, only a quarter of the bottom 40 were among the extreme poor (both cases refer to the orange area in figure O.1).

This complementarity has three important implications. First, by choosing these two goals, the World Bank focuses squarely on improving the welfare of the least well off across the world, effectively ensuring that everyone is part of a dynamic and inclusive growth process, no matter the circumstances, the country context, or the time period. Second, monitoring the two goals separately is necessary to understand with precision the progress in achieving better living conditions among those most in need. Third, policy interventions that reduce extreme poverty may or may not be effective in boosting shared prosperity if the two groups—the poor and the bottom 40—are composed of distinct populations.

To understand more clearly the progress toward the achievement of the goals, the World Bank is launching the annual *Poverty and Shared Prosperity* report series, which this report inaugurates. The report series will inform a global audience comprising development practitioners, policy makers, researchers, advocates, and citizens in general with the latest and most accurate estimates on trends in global poverty and shared prosperity. Every year, it will update information on the global number of the poor, the poverty headcount ratio worldwide, the regions that have been more successful or that have been lagging in advancing toward the goals, and the enhancements in monitoring and measuring poverty. In addition, it will feature a special

FIGURE 0.1 Distribution of the Extreme Poor, the Nonpoor, the Bottom 40, and the Top 60, 2013

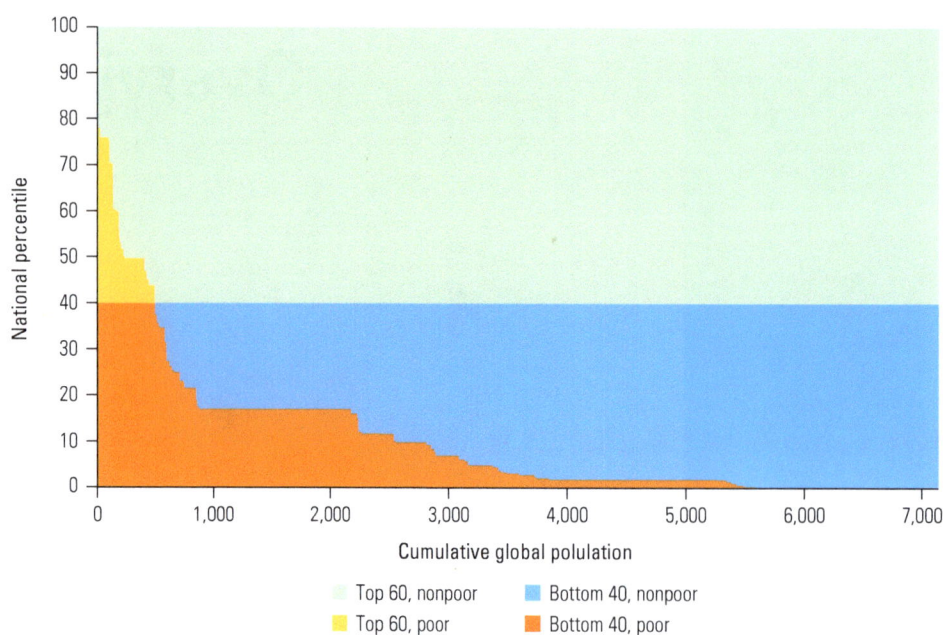

Source: Inspired by Beegle et al. 2014 and updated with 2013 data.
Note: The figure has been constructed from vertical bars representing countries sorted in descending order by extreme poverty headcount ratio (from left to right). The width of each bar reflects the size of the national population. The figure thus illustrates the situation across the total global population.

focal theme. This year, the focal theme is inequality.

Inequality matters for achieving the goals, but also for other reasons

Despite decades of substantial progress in boosting prosperity and reducing poverty, the world continues to suffer from substantial inequalities. For example, the poorest children are four times less likely than the richest children to be enrolled in primary education across developing countries. Among the estimated 780 million illiterate adults worldwide, nearly two-thirds are women. Poor people face higher risks of malnutrition and death in childhood and lower odds of receiving key health care interventions.[1]

Such inequalities are associated with high financial cost, affect economic growth, and generate social and political burdens and barriers. But leveling the playing field is also an issue of fairness and justice that resonates across societies on its own merits.

These substantive considerations highlight the importance of directing attention to the problem of inequality.

There are other reasons too. Sustaining the rapid progress in reducing poverty and boosting shared prosperity that has been achieved over the last 25 years is at risk because of the struggles across economies to recover from the global financial crisis that started in 2008 and the subsequent slowdown in global growth. The goal of eliminating extreme poverty by 2030—which is likely to become more difficult as we approach more closely to it—might not be achieved without accelerated economic growth or reductions in within-country inequalities, especially among those countries with large concentrations of the poor. Generally speaking, poverty can be reduced through higher average growth, a narrowing in inequality, or a combination of the two.[2] Achieving the same poverty reduction during a slowdown in growth therefore requires a more equal income distribution. It follows that, to reach the goals, efforts to foster growth need to be complemented by equity-enhancing policies and interventions.

Some level of inequality is desirable to maintain an appropriate incentive structure in the economy or simply because inequality also reflects different levels of talent and effort among individuals. However, the substantial inequality observed in the world today offers ample room for taking on inequality. Doing so without compromising growth is not only possible, but can be beneficial for poverty reduction and shared prosperity if done smartly. A trade-off between efficiency and equity is not inevitable. The evidence that equity-enhancing interventions can also bolster economic growth and long-term prosperity is wide-ranging. To the extent that such interventions interrupt the intergenerational reproduction of inequalities of opportunity, they address the roots and drivers of inequality, while laying the foundations for boosting shared prosperity and fostering long-term growth. Reducing inequalities of opportunity among individuals, economies, and regions may also be conducive to political and societal stability and social cohesion. In more cohesive societies, threats arising from extremism, political turmoil, and institutional fragility are less likely.

The key question the report addresses: what can be done to take on inequality?

This report addresses the issue of inequality by documenting trends in inequality, identifying recent country experiences in successfully reducing inequality and boosting shared prosperity, examining key lessons, and synthesizing the evidence on public policies that lessen inequality by reducing poverty and promoting shared prosperity.

Inequality exists in many dimensions, and the question "inequality of what?" is essential. The report focuses on inequalities in income or consumption expenditures, but it also analyzes the deprivations among the extreme poor and the well-being of the bottom 40. However, it does not address all types of inequality, for example, inequality related to ownership of assets. This does not mean that such forms of inequality do not deserve attention. According to Oxfam, 62 individuals in 2015 had the same wealth as the bottom half of the world's population; within the African continent, this statistic is even more extreme.[3] However, the report looks into inequality in income, in outcomes such as in health care and education, and inequality in opportunities. Income inequality and unequal opportunities are intimately related. This report aims to dispel myths around income inequality. Reflecting on what has worked in addressing this profound problem is key to taking on inequality more successfully.

The report makes four main contributions. First, it presents the most recent numbers on poverty, shared prosperity, and inequality. Second, it stresses the importance of inequality reduction in ending poverty and boosting shared prosperity by 2030, particularly in a context of weaker growth. Third, it highlights the diversity of within-country inequality reduction episodes and synthesizes the experiences of several countries and policies in addressing the roots of inequality without compromising economic growth. Along the way, the report shatters some myths and sharpens our knowledge of what works in reducing inequalities. Finally, it also advocates for the need to expand and improve data collection—availability, comparability, and quality—and rigorous evidence on inequality impacts. This is essential for high-quality poverty and shared prosperity monitoring and the policy decisions such an exercise ought to support.

Extreme poverty is shrinking worldwide, but is still widespread in Africa

In 2013, the year of the latest comprehensive data on global poverty, 767 million people are estimated to have been living below the international poverty line of US$1.90 per person per day (table O.1). Almost 11 people in every 100 in the world, or 10.7 percent of the global population, were poor by this standard, about 1.7 percentage points down from the global poverty headcount ratio in 2012. Although this

TABLE 0.1 World and Regional Poverty Estimates, 2013

Region	Headcount ratio (%)	Poverty gap (%)	Squared poverty gap (%)	Poor (millions)
East Asia and Pacific	3.5	0.7	0.2	71.0
Eastern Europe and Central Asia	2.3	0.6	0.3	10.8
Latin America and the Caribbean	5.4	2.6	1.8	33.6
Middle East and North Africa[a]	—	—	—	—
South Asia	15.1	2.8	0.8	256.2
Sub-Saharan Africa	41.0	15.9	8.4	388.7
Total, six regions	12.6	3.8	1.8	766.6
World	10.7	3.2	1.5	766.6

Source: Latest estimates based on 2013 data using PovcalNet (online analysis tool), World Bank, Washington, DC, http://iresearch .worldbank.org/PovcalNet/.

Note: Poverty is measured using the US$1.90-a-day 2011 purchasing power parity (PPP) poverty line. The six-region total includes all developing regions. World includes all developing regions, plus industrialized countries. Definitions of geographical regions are those of PovcalNet. — = not available.

a. Estimates on the Middle East and North Africa are omitted because of data coverage and quality problems. The population coverage of available household surveys is too low; the share of the total regional population represented by the available surveys is below 40 percent. There are also issues in the application of the 2011 PPP U.S. dollar to the region. These issues revolve around the quality of the data in several countries experiencing severe political instability, breaks in the consumer price index (CPI) series, and measurement or comparability problems in specific household surveys. These caveats suggest that further methodological analyses and the availability of new household survey data are both needed before reliable and sufficiently precise estimates can be produced.

represented a noticeable decline, the poverty rate remains unacceptably high given the low standard of living implied by the $1.90-a-day threshold.

The substantial decline is mostly explained by the lower number of the extreme poor in two regions, East Asia and Pacific (71 million fewer poor) and South Asia (37 million fewer poor), that showed cuts in the extreme poverty headcount ratio of 3.6 and 2.4 percentage points, respectively. The former is explained in large part by lower estimates on China and Indonesia, whereas the decrease in South Asia is driven by India's growth. The number of the poor in Sub-Saharan Africa fell by only 4 million between 2012 and 2013, a 1.6 percentage point drop that leaves the headcount ratio at a still high 41.0 percent. Eastern Europe and Central Asia's headcount ratio shrank by about a quarter of a percentage point, down to 2.3 percent, while, in Latin America and the Caribbean, the ratio declined by 0.2 percentage points, to 5.4 percent (figure O.2).

Both the extreme poverty headcount ratio and the total number of the extreme poor have steadily declined worldwide since 1990 (figure O.3). The world had almost 1.1 billion fewer poor in 2013 than in 1990, a period in which the world population grew by almost 1.9 billion people. Overall, the global extreme poverty headcount ratio dropped steadily over this period. Despite more rapid demographic growth in poorer areas, the forceful trend in poverty reduction culminated with 114 million people lifting themselves out of extreme poverty in 2013 alone (in net terms).

The geography of global extreme poverty is changing as poverty declines

As extreme poverty declines globally, the regional poverty profile has been changing. This is a direct result of uneven progress, mainly at the expense of Sub-Saharan Africa, which has the world's largest headcount ratio (41.0 percent) and houses the largest number of the poor (389 million), more than all other regions combined. This is a notable shift with respect to 1990, when half of the poor were living in East Asia and Pacific, which, today, is home to only 9.3 percent of the global poor. South Asia has another third of the poor, while Latin America and the Caribbean, along with Eastern Europe and Central Asia, complete the global count with 4.4 percent and 1.4 percent, respectively (figure O.4).[4]

FIGURE O.2 World and Regional Trends, Poverty Headcount Ratio, 1990–2013

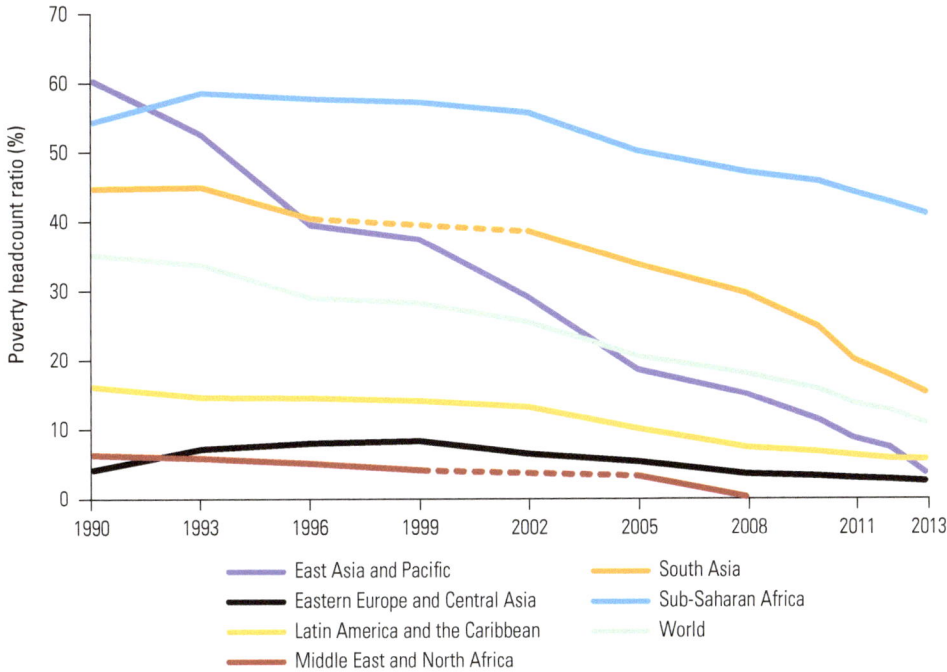

Source: Latest estimates based on 2013 data using PovcalNet (online analysis tool), World Bank, Washington, DC, http://iresearch .worldbank.org/PovcalNet/.
Note: Poverty is measured using the US$1.90-a-day 2011 PPP poverty line. Breaks in trends arise because of a lack of good-quality data.

Who are the poor?

Exploring the characteristics of the poor is key to a better understanding of the circumstances and contexts surrounding poverty. A large database of household surveys in 89 developing countries provides insights into this issue by facilitating a demographic profile of the poor at the US$1.90 poverty line.[5] This poverty profile reveals that the global poor are predominantly rural, young, poorly educated, mostly employed in the agricultural sector, and live in larger households with more children. Indeed, 80 percent of the worldwide poor live in rural areas; 64 percent work in agriculture; 44 percent are 14 years old or younger; and 39 percent have no formal education at all. The data also confirm wide regional variations in the distribution of the poor across these characteristics (figure O.5).

When looking at the incidence of poverty across different population groups, poverty headcount ratios are more than three times higher among rural residents

FIGURE O.3 Trends in the Global Poverty Headcount Ratio and the Number of the Global Poor, 1990–2013

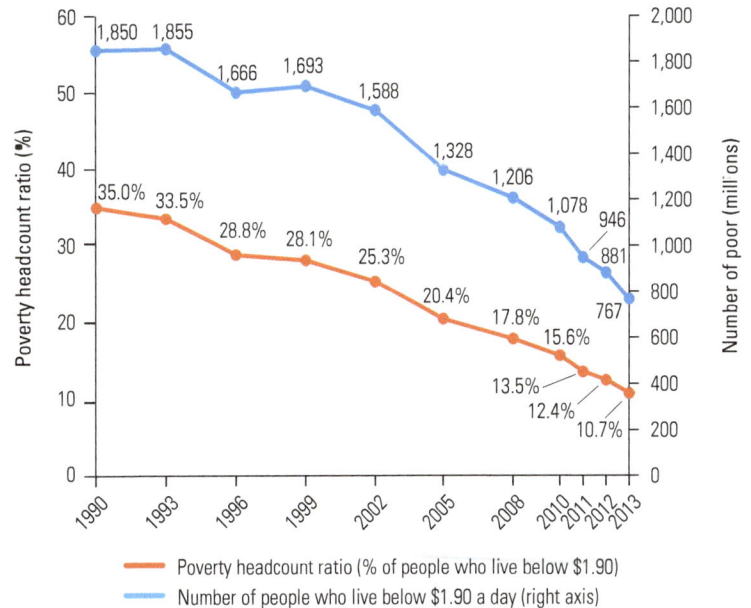

Source: Latest estimates based on 2013 data using PovcalNet (online analysis tool), World Bank, Washington, DC, http://iresearch.worldbank.org/PovcalNet/.
Note: Poverty is measured using the US$1.90-a-day 2011 PPP poverty line.

FIGURE 0.4 **Where Are the Global Poor Living? The Global Poor, by Region, 2013**

Share of global poor by region (%)

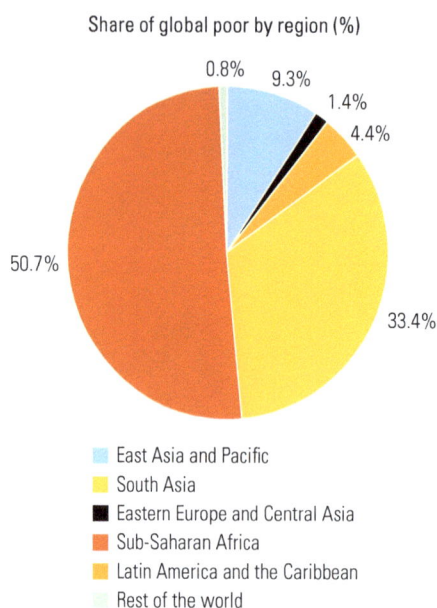

- East Asia and Pacific
- South Asia
- Eastern Europe and Central Asia
- Sub-Saharan Africa
- Latin America and the Caribbean
- Rest of the world

Source: Latest estimates based on 2013 data using PovcalNet (online analysis tool), World Bank, Washington, DC, http://iresearch.worldbank.org/PovcalNet/.

FIGURE 0.5 **Profile of the Poor, by Characteristics and Region, 2013**

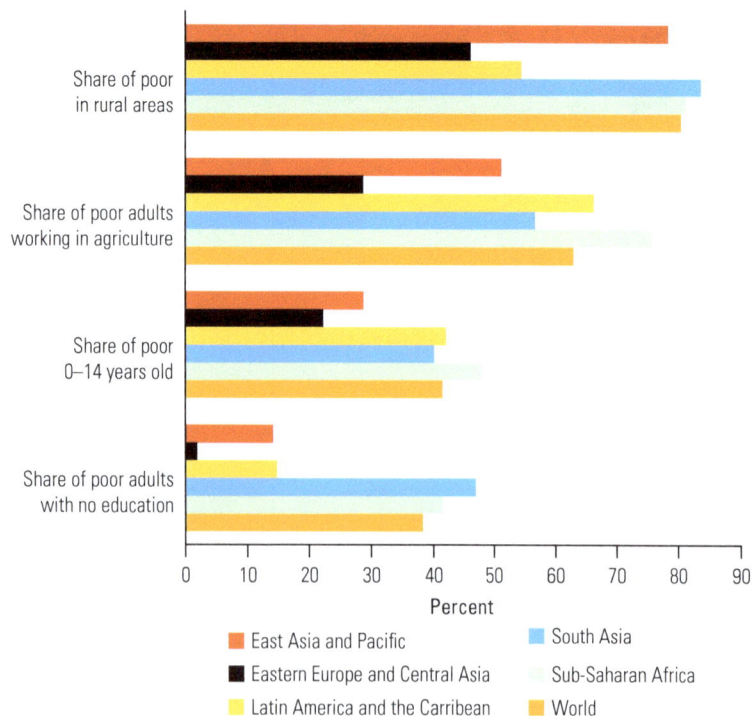

- East Asia and Pacific
- Eastern Europe and Central Asia
- Latin America and the Carribean
- South Asia
- Sub-Saharan Africa
- World

Source: Castañeda et al. 2016.
Note: Poverty is measured using the US$1.90-a-day 2011 PPP poverty line.

than among urban dwellers: 18.2 percent versus 5.5 percent, respectively. Agricultural workers are over four times more likely than people employed in other sectors of the economy to be poor. Educational attainment is inversely correlated with poverty. A small share of primary-school graduates are living in poverty: fewer than 8.0 percent of people who completed primary school, but not secondary school, are living below the US$1.90 poverty line. Among individuals who have attended university, the share is less than 1.5 percent.[6] Similar differences are observed if poverty incidence is measured relative to the US$3.10-a-day poverty line.

Age profiles confirm that children are more likely than adults to be poor. Children under 18 account for half the global poor in 2013, but less than a third of the sample population (32 percent) (figure O.6). Younger children (ages 0–14) contribute especially heavily to the poverty headcount, much more than their share in the world's population.

Progress in boosting shared prosperity worldwide is uneven

Shared prosperity is measured as the growth in the average income or consumption of the bottom 40. The larger the growth rate in the income of the bottom 40, the more quickly prosperity is shared with the most disadvantaged sectors in society.

To the extent that greater economic growth is associated with rising incomes among the poor and the bottom 40, more rapid growth will lead to greater shared prosperity and poverty reduction. Likewise, a more rapid increase in shared prosperity and in the narrowing of inequality typically accelerates the decline in poverty at any given rate of growth.

Progress on this indicator is examined in this report using the latest information available on each country, currently circa 2008–13. To take into account the share of prosperity going to groups other than the bottom 40, the report also monitors the *shared prosperity premium*, defined as the difference between the growth in the income of the bottom 40 and the growth in income at the mean in each country. A pos-

FIGURE O.6 **Age Profile of the Poor, 2013**

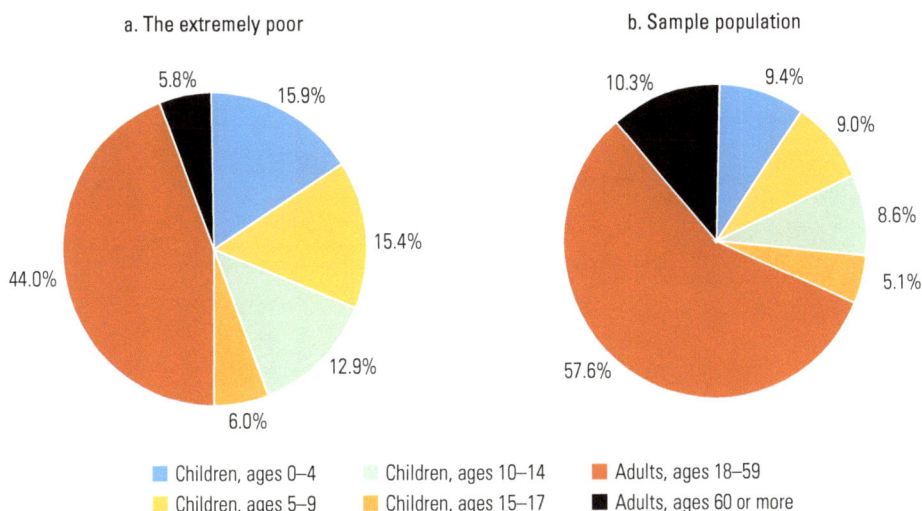

a. The extremely poor

5.8%
15.9%
15.4%
44.0%
12.9%
6.0%

b. Sample population

10.3%
9.4%
9.0%
8.6%
5.1%
57.6%

■ Children, ages 0–4   ■ Children, ages 10–14   ■ Adults, ages 18–59
■ Children, ages 5–9   ■ Children, ages 15–17   ■ Adults, ages 60 or more

Source: Newhouse et al. 2016.

itive premium indicates that the growth in the income or consumption of the bottom 40 exceeds that of the mean, and by implication, that of the rest of the population. A higher or lower premium indicates the extent to which distributional changes favor the bottom 40 relative to the top 60.

The bottom 40 benefited from solid economic growth in many countries in 2008–13. Overall, the bottom 40 in 60 of the 83 countries monitored experienced positive income growth, representing 67 percent of the world's population and 89 percent of the population represented by the surveys (figure O.7). A total of 49 countries reported a positive shared prosperity premium: income growth among the bottom 40 exceeded that of the mean (and therefore, that of the top 60). However, there is no room for complacency: in 23 countries, the incomes of the bottom 40 declined during the period.

There are wide regional differences in shared prosperity and the shared prosperity premium. The best performers were in East Asia and Pacific and in Latin America and the Caribbean, while high-income industrialized countries performed the least well. Greece, a high-income country, experienced an annualized contraction of 10.0 percent in the income of the bottom 40, while the Democratic Republic of Congo recorded a rise of 9.6 percent. In Latin America and

the Caribbean, the income of the bottom 40 grew by 8.0 percent in Paraguay, while in Honduras, income contracted by about 2.5 percent annually during the same spell.

A source of concern is the small value of the shared prosperity premium. While the average annualized growth in the income or consumption of the bottom 40 was 2.0 percent worldwide circa 2008–13 (a population-weighted 4.6 percent), the average shared prosperity premium was only 0.5 percentage points during the same period (a population-weighted 0.4 percentage point). Is this sufficient to expect large reductions in inequality and poverty so as to achieve the World Bank goals by 2030?

A more rapid decline in inequality is needed to end poverty

Figure O.8 makes it clear that the goal of ending poverty by 2030 cannot be reached at current levels of economic growth. It shows the trajectory of the global poverty headcount ratio under various assumptions about distributional changes and under the assumption that every country will grow at its rate of the last 10 years. These changes are modeled by means of alternative shared prosperity premiums in each country. Thus, in the scenario of a premium labeled

FIGURE 0.7 Shared Prosperity, 83 Countries, 2008–13

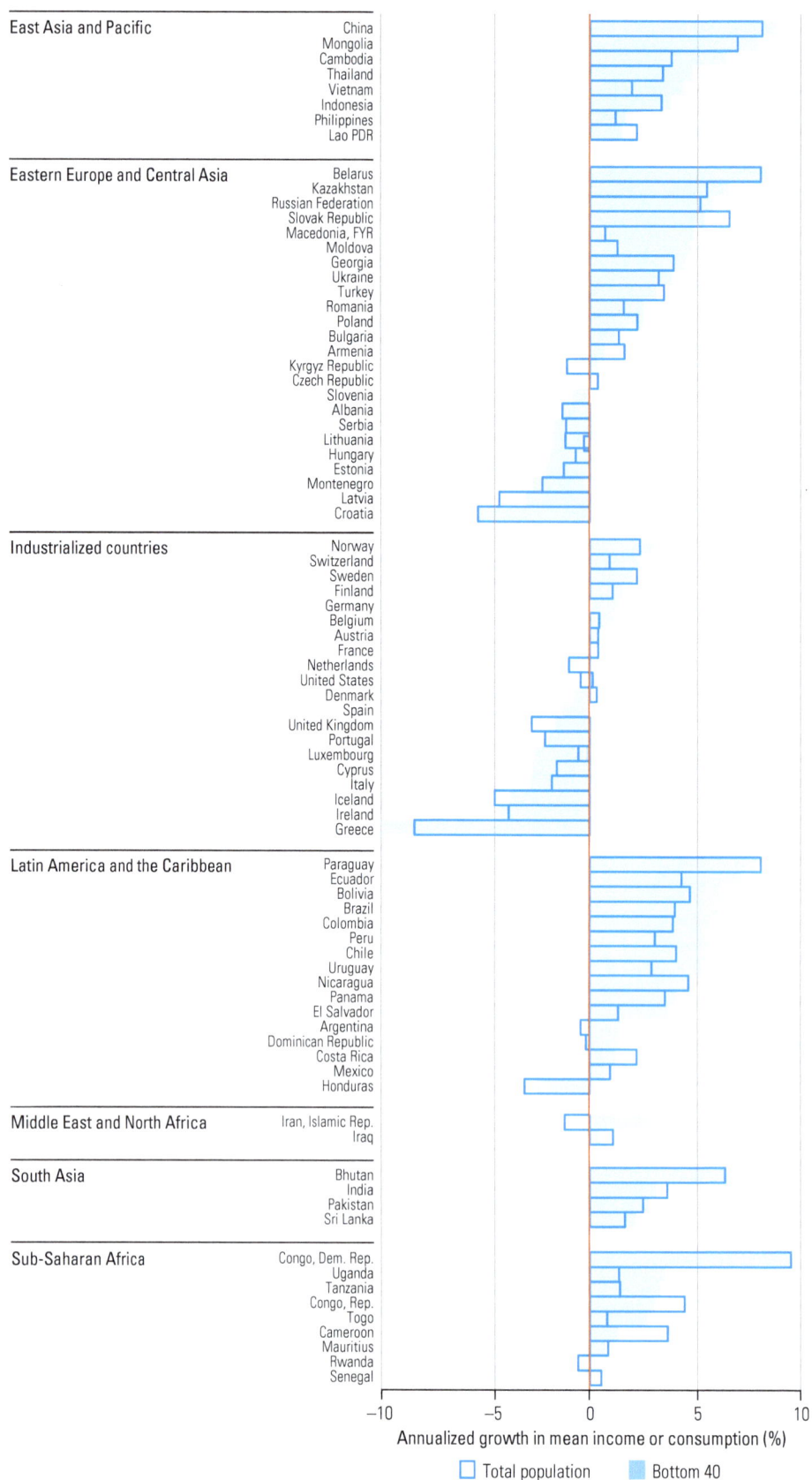

Source: GDSP (Global Database of Shared Prosperity), World Bank, Washington, DC, http://www.worldbank.org/en/topic/poverty
/brief/global-database-of-shared-prosperity.
Note: The data show the annualized growth in mean household per capita income or consumption according to surveys.

FIGURE 0.8 Boosting Shared Prosperity and Ending Poverty, 10-Year Scenario, 2013–30

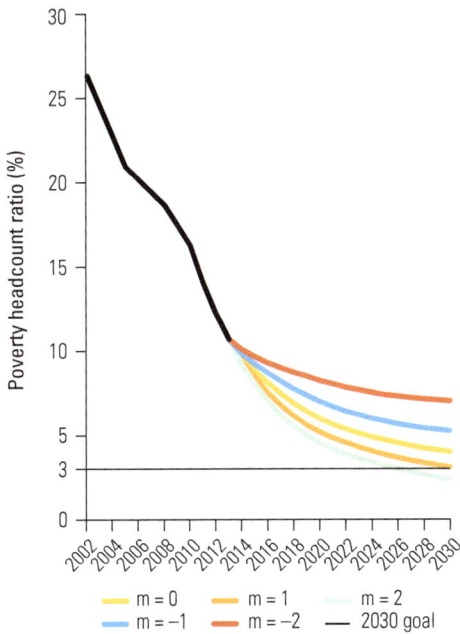

Source: Updated results based on Lakner, Negre, and Prydz 2014.
Note: m = the assumed shared prosperity premium, that is, the growth in income or consumption among the bottom 40, minus the growth in income or consumption at the mean. Thus, for example, m = 2 indicates that the growth in income among the bottom 40 exceeds the growth in income at the mean by 2 percentage points in each country. Poverty is measured using the US$1.90-a-day 2011 PPP poverty line.

m = 1, the growth in the income of the bottom 40 in each country is assumed to exceed the growth rate in the mean by 1 percentage point. Meanwhile, in the scenario m = 0, growth is distributionally neutral: the income of the bottom 40 and the mean grow at the same pace. Under these scenarios, the poverty goal would only be reached if the shared prosperity premium is in excess of 1 percentage point, which is double the simple average premium countries are able to achieve today (0.5 percentage points). Thus, income or consumption needs to grow more quickly among the bottom 40 than at the mean, and at a more rapid pace than today, especially in countries with substantial numbers of the poor.

This is the analytical result of a set of simulations. In practice, this does not mean that every country worldwide must improve its income distribution to achieve the pov-

erty goal by 2030. However, it illustrates that under current average growth rates, reductions in inequality will be key to reaching the poverty goal by 2030. This is so under specific assumptions about how economic growth will occur until 2030. If the poverty goal is to be accomplished by 2030, the income distribution must improve, especially among countries in which there are high numbers of poor, relatively wide inequality levels, and weak economic growth.

Globally, the narrowing in inequality since the 1990s is an historical exception to a rising trend

Data since the 1990s show a substantial narrowing in inequality in income or consumption worldwide, irrespective of residence. This is the first such reduction since the industrial revolution (figure O.9). This unprecedented decline occurred during a period of increasing global integration. From 1820 to the 1990s, global inequality steadily rose. Then, the Gini index fell to 62.5 in 2013, most markedly beginning in 2008, when the Gini was 66.8 (the blue line in figure O.10).

FIGURE 0.9 Global Inequality, 1820–2010

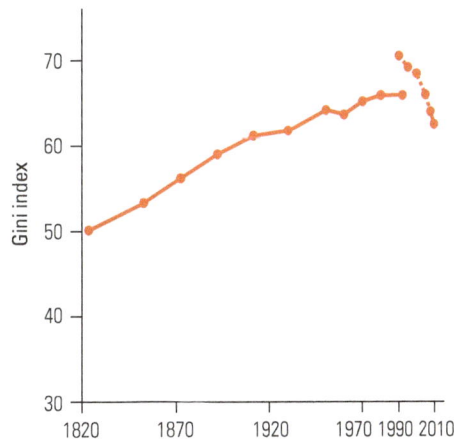

Source: Based on figure 1 (p. 27) of *The Globalization of Inequality* by Francois Bourguignon (Princeton University Press 2015). Used with permission.
Note: The discontinuity in the series represents the change in the base year of the purchasing power parity (PPP) exchange rates from 1990 to 2005. The figure uses GDP per capita in combination with distributional statistics from household surveys. Figure O.10 uses income (or consumption) per capita directly from household surveys (in 2011 PPP exchange rates).

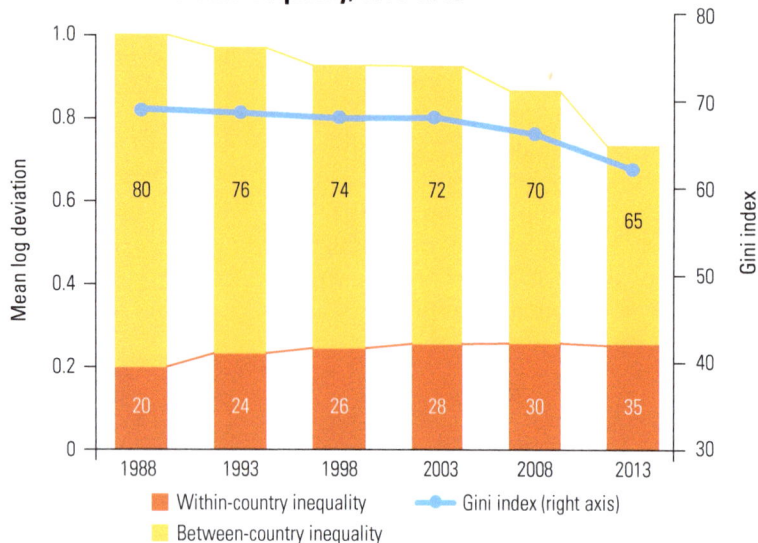

FIGURE O.10 Global Inequality, 1988–2013

Sources: Lakner and Milanović 2016; Milanović 2016; World Bank calculations based on PovcalNet (online analysis tool), World Bank, Washington, DC, http://iresearch.worldbank.org/PovcalNet/.
Note: For each country, household income or consumption per capita is obtained directly from house-hold surveys and expressed in 2011 PPP exchange rates. Each country distribution is represented by 10 decile groups. The line (measured on the right axis) shows the level of the global Gini index. The height of the bars indicates the level of global inequality as measured by GE(0) (the mean log deviation). The red bars show the corresponding level of population-weighted inequality within countries. The level of between-country inequality, which captures differences in average incomes across countries, is shown by the yellow bars. The numbers in the bars refer to the relative contributions (in percent) of these two sources to total global inequality.

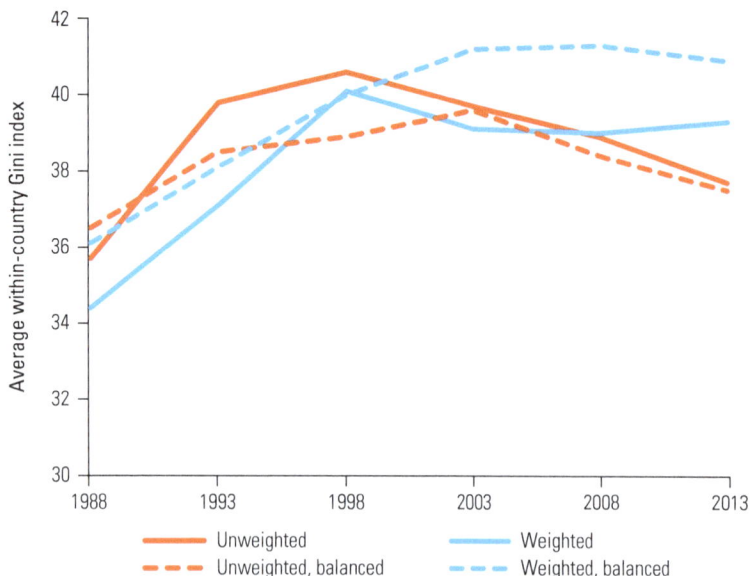

FIGURE O.11 Average Within-Country Inequality, 1988–2013

Source: World Bank calculations based on data in Milanović 2014; PovcalNet (online analysis tool), World Bank, Washington, DC, http://iresearch.worldbank.org/PovcalNet/; WDI (World Development Indicators) (database), World Bank, Washington, DC, http://data.worldbank.org/data-catalog/world-development -indicators.
Note: The solid lines show the trend in the average within-country Gini index with and without population weights in the full sample (an average of 109 countries per benchmark year). The dashed lines refer to the balanced sample, that is, using only the set of 41 countries on which data are available in every bench-mark year.

This unprecedented drop in global inequal-ity was driven by a convergence in average incomes across countries that was spurred by rising incomes in populous countries such as China and India. As a result, between-country inequality declined. In contrast, within-country inequality, the other com-ponent of global inequality, took on a greater role in global inequality (explaining a third of the total variation) (figure O.10).

Despite recent progress, average within-country inequality is greater now than 25 years ago

The population-weighted Gini index cap-tures within-country inequality relative to the average person across the countries on which data are available (figure O.11). This indicator rose steeply, by 6 points, from 34 to 40 between 1988 and 1998. Since then, inequality has declined more moderately, by almost 1 point, to a Gini of 39 in 2013. Thus, within-country inequality for the av-erage person in the world was wider in 2013 than 25 years previously.

The population-weighted result on within-country inequality is largely robust to other specifications, such as population-unweighted estimates or estimates draw-ing on different country samples. As shown in figure O.11, the unweighted Gini index of within-country inequality worldwide also rose during the 1990s, but by a smaller amount than the population-weighted index. The simple average Gini increased by around 5 points, from 36 in 1988 to 41 ten years later, before declining steadily thereaf-ter, reaching 38 in 2013.

The levels and trends in average in-equality are quite different across regions, although the most recent decline is broad-based (figure O.12). Developing countries tend to exhibit wider within-country in-equality relative to developed countries. Latin America and the Caribbean, as well as Sub-Saharan Africa, stand out as high-inequality regions. The former is also the region most successful in reducing inequal-ity. Sub-Saharan Africa has likewise steadily narrowed inequality since the early 1990s, although this progress hides wide-ranging variations within the continent.[7] In Eastern Europe and Central Asia, average inequality rose sharply after the fall of the Berlin Wall, but has since been on a declining trend. The average industrialized country saw an increase in the Gini index from 30 to 33 between 1988 and 2008. In the five years leading up to 2013, average within-income inequality appears to have fallen in all regions except in the Middle East and North Africa and in South Asia.

Providing a simple explanation behind regional inequality trends is particularly challenging because the patterns may be distinctive and the drivers specific to the trends exhibited by countries within a region. Rather than providing a simplistic explanation, it may therefore be useful to examine closely the country variations within regions to understand the extent to which the common drivers behind inequality—gaps in human capital accumulation, varying access to jobs and income-generating opportunities, and government interventions to address market-based inequalities—are relevant in each country.

Indeed, between 2008 and 2013, the number of countries experiencing declining inequality was twice the number exhibiting widening inequality. This shows that within-country inequality can widen or narrow. Despite the progress, stark inequalities persist. For example, Haiti and South Africa are the most unequal countries in the world (for which data are available), with a Gini exceeding 60 points in 2013. Another Sub-Saharan African country (Rwanda) and another seven Latin America and Caribbean countries (Brazil, Chile, Colombia, Costa Rica, Honduras, Mexico, and Panama) make up the top 10 most unequal countries in the world, with Gini indexes in excess of or close to 50.

In many economies, the income share of the top income groups is expanding

In many economies in which information on the top 1 percent of the income distri-

FIGURE O.12 Trends in the Average National Gini, by Region, 1988–2013

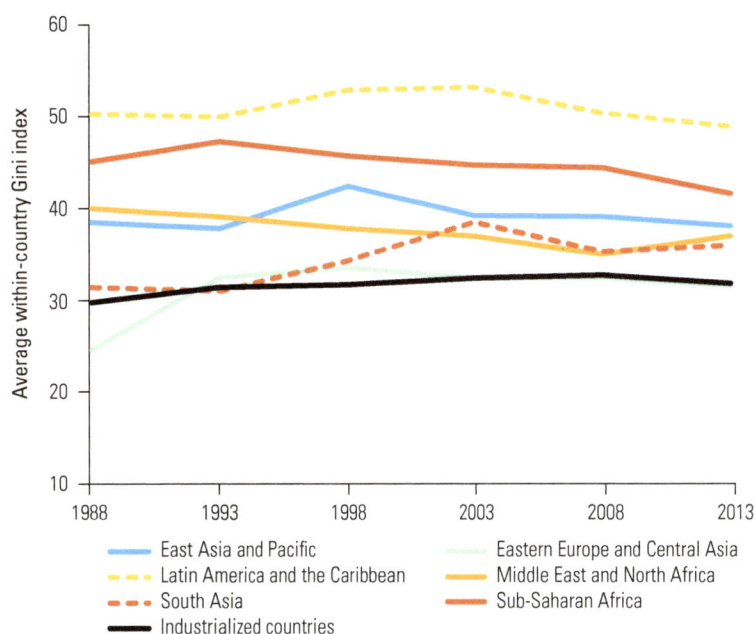

Source: World Bank calculations based on data in Milanović 2014; PovcalNet (online analysis tool), World Bank, Washington, DC, http://iresearch.worldbank.org/PovcalNet/.
Note: The lines show the average within-country Gini index by region. It is the simple average in the full sample without weighting countries by population. Industrialized countries are a subset of high-income countries. See chapter 2, annex 2B, for the list of industrialized countries.

bution is available, such as Argentina; India; the Republic of Korea; South Africa; Taiwan, China; and the United States, the share of the top 1 percent in total income has been increasing. In South Africa, the top income share roughly doubled over 20 years to levels comparable with those observed in the United States (figure O.13).

Inequality reduction is not limited to a few countries, settings, and policy choices

Some countries have performed remarkably well in reducing inequality and boosting shared prosperity. Others have not. Among the constellation of policies that have been implemented, what have been the key levers in boosting shared prosperity and narrowing inequality among countries?

The report focuses on the experiences of five low- and middle-income countries, covering Asia, Latin America and the Caribbean, and Sub-Saharan Africa. The countries

FIGURE 0.13 The National Income Share of the Richest 1 Percent, Selected Economies

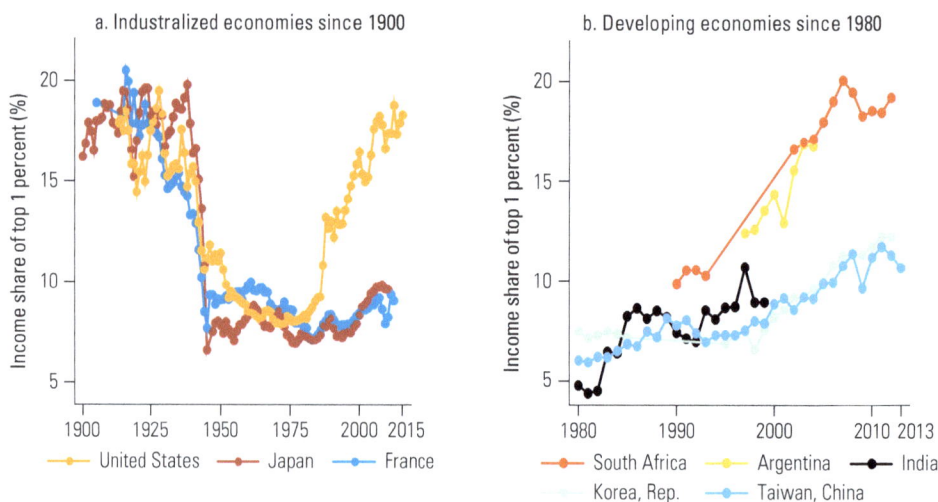

a. Industrialized economies since 1900 — *United States, Japan, France*

b. Developing economies since 1980 — *South Africa, Argentina, India, Korea, Rep., Taiwan, China*

Source: Calculations based on data of WID (World Wealth and Income Database), Paris School of Economics, Paris, http://www.parisschoolofeconomics.eu/en/research/the-world-wealth-income-database/.
Note: The income share excludes capital gains. These measures are typically derived from tax record data. For South Africa, the income share refers to adults.

analyzed are Brazil, Cambodia, Mali, Peru, and Tanzania. These are among the best performers, showing good shared prosperity premiums and strong records in narrowing income inequality and reducing extreme poverty. They are also sufficiently diverse to embody different development strategies and historical circumstances.

The five countries exercised judicious macroeconomic management, appropriately dealt with external shocks, and implemented more or less protracted and coherent economic and social sector reforms. They also benefited from favorable external conditions in the form of cheap and abundant international credit, high commodity prices, and booming trade. Decision making and the context allowed rapid, sustainable, and inclusive growth. The countries also highlight the importance of labor markets in translating economic growth into inequality reduction by increasing job opportunities and earnings, reintegrating individuals who have been excluded from economic opportunities, and narrowing gaps across workers because of gender, residence, or sector of employment. Notwithstanding these common factors, country-specific choices and economic developments—deliberate or not—

also play a role in reducing inequalities. For example, the minimum wage and safety nets have been crucial in allowing Brazil to lessen inequality, while diversification from agriculture into light manufacturing and services in Cambodia opened job opportunities to the poor.

Overall, these country cases also highlight that success in reducing inequality and boosting shared prosperity in a given period does not necessarily translate into similar success on other economic, social, or political fronts, nor into sustainable reductions in inequality over time. Indeed, conflict emerged in Mali after the period of inequality reduction, in large part because of protracted flaws in governance.[8] The marked differences in the most recent policy choices between Brazil and Peru on fiscal consolidation and the control of inflation largely explain the stark differences in their most recent growth patterns: gradual recovery in Peru, recession in Brazil. Meanwhile, long-standing barriers constraining productivity and investments in agriculture in Cambodia and an unfinished transition to a market-based economy in Tanzania call into question the sustainability of inequality reduction in these two countries.[9]

The common elements and country-specific peculiarities are summarized below.

Brazil, 2004–14: policies aligned to redress record inequality

In 1989, Brazil's Gini index was 63, the second highest in the world. However, the incomes of the less well off in Brazil surged between 2004 and 2014 amid rapid economic growth. The Gini dropped to 51 in 2014, while income growth among the bottom 40 averaged 6.8 percent a year, well above the average 4.5 percent among all Brazilians.

Multiple drivers underlie Brazil's success. The 1988 Constitution laid the foundations for tackling historical inequalities by guaranteeing basic social rights such as free public education, free universal health care, pensions, and social assistance. A macroeconomic framework established in the 1990s allowed inflation to be curbed, promoted the prudent management of fiscal balances, and created an enabling environment for policies to address inequality. During the 2000s, the boom in commodity prices generated positive terms of trade. Macroeconomic stability, combined with this favorable external context, propelled economic growth. Labor market dynamics—including increasing wage premiums for the less skilled, more formal jobs, and a rising minimum wage—and the expansion of social policies helped boost the incomes of the poor. These two factors accounted for approximately 80 percent of the decline in inequality in 2003–13: 41 percent of the Gini decline in these years stemmed from labor incomes, and 39 percent from nonlabor income sources such as government transfers.[10] According to some estimates, Bolsa Família, Brazil's flagship conditional cash transfer (CCT) program, alone explains between 10 percent and 15 percent of the narrowing income inequality observed in the 2000s.[11]

Cambodia, 2004–14: earning opportunities emerging from growth

Cambodia's annual economic growth averaged 7.8 percent between 2004 and 2014, placing the country among the most rapidly growing economies in the world. Poor Cambodians harnessed the opportunities created by this growth. They seized jobs in labor-intensive industries and services, diversifying their incomes away from subsistence agriculture and reaping higher returns from traditional agricultural activities. Annual consumption growth among the bottom 40 averaged 6.3 percent between 2008 and 2013, twice the consumption growth of the top 60.

A proliferation of employment opportunities followed expansions in the garment, tourism, and real estate sectors.[12] Relative to other sectors, wages in the garment industry tended to be higher and more stable, while the gender gap tended to be narrower. Meanwhile, the agricultural sector's vitality at a time of historically high international prices explains how farm incomes from paddy rice farming more than doubled between 2004 and 2009.[13] Indeed, rural areas largely drove the country's success in inequality and poverty reduction. Nonetheless, obstacles are evident in the inadequate pace of job creation, given Cambodia's young demographic and structural constraints that weigh on leading sectors.

Mali, 2001–10: vagaries of agriculture rescue a weak economy

Before the outbreak of conflict in the country's northern region in 2012, Mali had made important strides in reducing inequality. Between 2001 and 2010, GDP growth averaged 5.7 percent a year. During the period, the Gini index fell 7 points. The income of the bottom 40 grew, while the mean contracted.

Agriculture has been a key driver behind the improvement in living conditions among the poor. Approximately 73 percent of Malians and 90 percent of the poor live in rural areas. For those involved in farming activities, own-account production typically does not permit self-sufficiency, and income has to be supplemented with casual labor and private transfers. Higher cereal production in the 2000s benefited the labor income of the poor by raising both farm production and off-farm labor income through greater demand for wage labor by commercial cereal producers. In the latter half of the first decade of the 2000s, while manufacturing was contracting, agricultural production, favored by good weather conditions, boomed, resulting in reduced inequality.[14] Since 2012, however, the conflict in the north has put the brakes on the progress of the previous decade. The crisis has disrupted education and health care services in the north, and displaced populations are exerting pressure on service delivery in the south. This resurgence of conflict comes after two decades of relative stability, including multiparty elections, and is associated with a long-term deterioration in governance, the expanding presence of political pay-offs and co-optation, and an army with limited capacity to face increasing security threats.[15]

Peru, 2004–14: equalizing growth through capital investment

The improvement in living conditions among the poor and the bottom 40 in Peru has been remarkable. The Gini index fell from 51 in 2004 to 44 in 2014, and poverty rates dropped from 12 percent in 2004 to 3 percent in 2014. The outstanding growth of the economy (6.6 percent annually during the period) in a context of macroeconomic stability, favorable external conditions, and important structural reforms was responsible for this progress. In the early 2000s, prudent macroeconomic policies and high commodity prices attracted foreign direct investment into the economy, particularly in the mining sector. Capital accumulation became the main driver of growth, accounting for more than two-thirds of total growth after 2001. The labor market was the main pathway for the translation of the country's impressive growth into less inequality and poverty, explaining about 80 percent of the reduction in the Gini and three-quarters of the reduction in extreme poverty during the last decade.[16] Critical to this success were a closing wage gap between formal and informal workers, high labor force participation rates, and low unemployment.

Challenges remain. Analysts question the quality of public spending, notably in education. Despite significant gains in enrollments, Peru lags comparator countries in international assessments of education quality outcomes, such as student test scores. This is a serious consideration because the favorable external conditions that have underpinned Peru's growth have recently begun to recede. Maintaining the impressive gains in a much less favorable environment will require policy reforms that address the limited productivity resulting from the low quality of human capital and the high rates of informality.

Tanzania, 2004–14: sharing prosperity amid diversification

Tanzania maintained robust and stable economic growth between 2004 and 2014, averaging 6.5 percent a year. The national poverty headcount ratio fell from 34.4 percent in 2007 to 28.2 percent in 2012. The Gini index declined from around 39 to 36 over the same period. Annual consumption growth among the bottom 40, at 3.4 percent, was more than three times the growth among the top 60, at 1.0 percent.

Since the early 2000s, the country's economic expansion has been driven primarily by rapidly growing sectors, especially communications, financial services, and construction. However, the growth in these sectors has not been translated into substantive improvements in the living conditions of the poor, the less well educated, or rural residents. After 2007, there was a surge in retail trade and manufacturing, particularly agroprocessing in products such as food, beverages, and tobacco, which has allowed the inclusion of less highly skilled workers in the economy.[17] Among policies explicitly aimed at rendering the income distribution more equitable, the Tanzania Social Action Fund stands out. It encompasses a CCT program, public works, and a community savings component that is expected to enable the poorest segments of the population to increase their savings and their investments in livestock and to become more resilient.[18] Despite this progress, much remains to be done to trim regional disparities and expand access to basic services in a context of rapid urbanization. Indeed, today's economy is still characterized by a lack of competition in the private sector and the absence of growth, as well as a strongly regulated economic environment.

There are some common building blocks behind successful inequality reductions

The experiences of five countries cannot supply precise policy prescriptions that are valid everywhere and in all circumstances. However, they demonstrate that narrowing inequality and sharing prosperity are possible in many settings, including low- and middle-income countries; rural economies; more highly diversified, modern economies; and countries benefiting from external booms, but also countries facing unfavorable conditions, such as a history of conflict or substantial, long-term inequality. The building blocks of success have been prudent macroeconomic policies, strong growth, functioning labor markets, and coherent domestic policies focusing on safety nets, human capital, and infrastructure.

As the building blocks get in place, many approaches to narrowing inequality are possible. However, sustaining this success may require similar approaches. The accumulation of good-quality human capital, diversification in the income-earning opportunities available to the poor, safety nets capable of protecting the poorest from risk, and enhanced infrastructure to connect lagging regions to economically more vibrant ones are all potentially desirable approaches to sharing prosperity and reducing inequality.

Thus, the experiences of Cambodia, Mali, and Tanzania underscore the need to expand safety nets, which have not been sufficient to protect the poorest in these countries. The experiences of Brazil and Tanzania point to the need to realign fiscal systems to produce a greater impact in reducing inequality. Infrastructure is apparently still a significant obstacle in Cambodia, while in Mali, in addition to conflict, dependence on external factors, from donor flows to the vagaries of weather, threaten sustained improvement. In Peru, the quality of education is below regional standards and represents a barrier to maintaining and enhancing economic productivity should favorable external conditions disappear.

Countries willing to make the appropriate policy choices are more likely to narrow inequality. Those that are not willing to make these choices might continue to suffer the disadvantages of growing inequality.

Taking on inequality involves human capital accumulation, income generating opportunities, consumption smoothing, and redistribution

The report assesses what we know about key domestic policy interventions that are effective in reducing inequality, the benefits they generate, the choices that need to be made concerning their design and implementation, and the trade-offs with which they are associated. It is not meant to provide an exhaustive or comprehensive review of every intervention that could reduce inequality, nor does it seek to supply universal prescriptions. Instead, it focuses on a few policy areas on which a body of rigorous evidence allows lessons to be drawn with confidence. The policies, if well designed, have favorable effects not only on inequality reduction, but also on poverty reduction without major efficiency and equity trade-offs. The policy areas are early childhood development (ECD), universal health care, universal access to good-quality education, CCTs, investments in new or improved rural roads and electrification, and taxation, mainly on personal income and consumption.

There are many pathways through which policy interventions can affect inequality, whether this effect is intended or unintended. The impacts can be large or small, short term or lifelong, and they may narrow disparities in income, well-being, or opportunity. For example, taxes can have direct and deliberate redistributive effects, reaching up to 20 points of the Gini index of market incomes in some European Union (EU) economies.[19] In contrast, investments in rural roads and electrification influence income generation opportunities, employment, and even perceptions of gender roles. Expanding ECD, health care coverage, and good-quality education often reduces cognitive, nutritional, and health status gaps, thereby narrowing inequalities in human capital development and future income opportunities. By smoothing consumption among the most deprived, especially during shocks, CCTs help prevent the widening of inequality.

Evidence of the benefits of such interventions is encouraging. For example, in 1986, a Jamaican intervention sought to support toddlers ages 9–24 months who suffered from stunting.[20] The intervention consisted of weekly visits to the households of the toddlers by community health workers to teach parenting skills aimed at fostering cognitive and socioemotional development among the children. It also provided nutrition supplements and psychosocial stimulation. Researchers followed up among the participants 20 years after the intervention and found that the groups of children receiving stimulation (with or without the nutrition supplements) had, as adults, 25 percent higher earnings than the control group. The greater earnings had allowed individuals in the stimulation program to enjoy livelihoods at a similar level as the members of a nonstunted comparison group, effectively eliminating the inequality in incomes between the groups.

Thailand's Universal Coverage Scheme enhances equity by bringing a large uninsured population under the umbrella of a national insurance program, thereby greatly reducing catastrophic health care payments and improving access to essential health services among the poor. Within a year of its launch, the scheme was covering 75 percent of the population, including 18 million previously uninsured people.[21]

Recent assessments in developed and developing countries highlight the important consequences of successful experiences in improving the quality of teaching. For example, estimates in the United States indicate that pupils taught by teachers who are at the 90th percentile in effectiveness are able to learn 1.5 years' worth of material in a single academic year, while pupils taught by teachers at the 10th percentile learn only a half-year's worth of material.[22] Increased schooling has been linked to more productive nonfarm activities in China, Ghana, and Pakistan.[23]

In Bangladesh, the Shombob Pilot Program reduced the incidence of wasting among 10- to 22-month-old infants by 40 percent.[24] Mexico's Prospera Program has helped lower infant mortality and maternal mortality by as much as 11 percent.[25] The Nahouri Pilot Project in Burkina Faso is credited with raising primary and secondary enrollment rates by 22 percent among boys.[26] In Pakistan, CCTs made available only in favor of girls led to increases in enrollment in the range of 11–13 percentage points.[27]

Also in Bangladesh, the Rural Development Program and the Rural Roads and Markets Improvement and Maintenance Program have boosted employment and wages in agricultural and nonagricultural activities, as well as aggregate harvest outputs. Per capita annual spending across households in the program areas has risen by about 10 percent.[28] In rural Vietnam, school enrollment rates among children in households on the electricity grid were 9.0 percentage points higher among girls and 6.3 percentage points higher among boys relative to children in households not on the grid. Electrification was also associated with almost an extra year in the average years of schooling among girls and an extra 0.13 year among boys.[29] Similarly, access in rural areas to *telenovelas* (television soap operas) resulted in lower fertility rates in Brazil, which may be related to the empowerment of women through the imitation of role models of emancipated women and the representation of smaller families.[30]

Such evidence demonstrates that interventions can be designed successfully in a variety of settings. Yet, the long road ahead argues against any complacency and against the fallacy of sweeping prescriptions. The challenges and uncertainties are diverse and complicated, as follows:

Despite progress, intolerable disparities in well-being still exist that concrete policy interventions could confront directly. In many low- and middle-income countries, preschool enrollment rates among the poorest quintile are less than a third of the rates among the richest quintile. Mothers in the bottom 40 across developing countries are 50 percent less likely to receive antenatal care. The poorest children are four times less likely than the richest children to be enrolled in primary education and systematically record lower test scores than children in the richest households. Among the estimated 780 million illiterate adults worldwide, nearly two-thirds are women. Only one-quarter of the poorest quintile are covered by safety nets, and the share is even smaller in Sub-Saharan Africa and South Asia.[31]

Trade-offs in implementation should not be overlooked because of excessive attention to efficiency and equity trade-offs. Investments in ECD, universal health care, and good-quality education have both equity and efficiency benefits given the current gaps in access. Connecting poor farmers to urban markets can positively affect the income of farm households as well as reduce their income gaps with the rest of the population. In reducing inequality, many policy choices are less often restricted by an imbalance in the equity-efficiency trade-off than by an imbalance in the trade-offs between expanding the coverage of an intervention and increasing the benefits, between enhancing the quality of services and increasing access to services through the construction of facilities such as schools or clinics, between expanding the coverage of electrification in rural areas and ensuring program financial viability, between cash or in-kind resource transfers, and between conditionality and the lack of conditionality.

The fine points of policy design absolutely matter in ensuring that interventions are equalizing without compromising efficiency. Different choices in Chile and Mexico in recent tax reforms with the same objectives led to different impacts. The ultrarich bore the brunt of the income tax component of the reform in Chile, while in Mexico, the middle class also largely shared the cost of the reform.[32] ECD programs are most effective if they are aimed at the first 1,000 days of the lives of children, continue during childhood, and integrate stimulation, parenting, and nutrition components. In many contexts, incentivizing higher quality in teaching, while making social transfers conditional on school completion may have a greater impact than constructing new schools.

Avoid unexamined reliance on universal prescriptions and unique models of success. Evidence strongly suggests that the implementation of such prescriptions and models does not automatically ensure a reduction in inequality. Nonetheless, some initiatives are more likely than others to generate inequality reductions and improvements in the well-being of the poorest. For example, integrated interventions are more likely to succeed than isolated, monolithic interventions. Composition influences the degree of success. If CCTs are combined with other safety net interventions, such as transfers of productive assets, skills training, and access to credit and finance, they have been shown to generate wide-ranging benefits. Investments in rural roads that attract additional investments in public services, such as electrification, agricultural extension services, and enhanced water and sanitation services, improve not only the connectivity of people to economic opportunities, but also security, productivity, and the quality of services. Simplicity and flexibility often drive success. Thus, the ability of the safety net system in the Philippines to scale up to reach hundreds of thousands of beneficiaries after catastrophic events is in part explained by the flexibility of the system in the face of emergency situations. Exclusive and prolonged breastfeeding is another example of a simple and extraordinarily cost-efficient intervention to improve ECD.[33]

Equalizing interventions are not a luxury reserved for middle- and high-income countries, nor an option only available during periods of prosperity. There are numerous instances of the implementation of successful interventions in ECD, universal health care coverage, CCTs, investment in rural infrastructure, and redistributive tax schemes across low-income countries. This evidence should dispel the notion that only middle- and high-income countries can afford equalizing policies. Of course, context always matters: weak capacity, lack of political will, restricted fiscal space, vulnerability to external crises or climate change, internal conflict, and challenging geography are among the obstacles to the reduction of inequality worldwide. These obstacles are not insurmountable, however. This is also the case during periods of crisis. Examples of CCTs integrated in safety nets that effectively protect the most vulnerable against natural disasters demonstrate that a crisis is not an excuse for inaction, but an incentive for the adoption of equalizing interventions.

The poor must be able to participate in and benefit from interventions: good policy choices benefit the poorest. Evidence on ECD programs, initiatives to promote universal health care coverage, and efforts to foster good-quality teaching proves that the most underprivileged children often benefit the most.[34] Yet, this outcome should not be taken for granted. Thus, the more well off households among the targeted population, that is, households with children with higher baseline levels of development and more well educated mothers, are typically more likely to send their children to preschool or to take part in parenting programs. Many rural electrification initiatives are associated with high connection costs to keep electrification campaigns financially feasible, but this often means the poorest households must opt out.[35] Policy design needs to take such outcomes into account up front and explicitly.

More knowledge! Despite the growing evidence on the impacts of policy interventions, improving the evidence base on initiatives that successfully narrow inequality requires more investment in filling data gaps and enhancing the understanding of the specific pathways—whether intended or unintended—through which programs affect inequality. For example, rigorous evaluations have played a critical role in fine-tuning the design of CCTs and advocating for CCT desirability. Monitoring ECD programs for decades has made the quantification of the long-term effects of such programs possible. Yet, the road ahead is still long and steep. Especially important is the long-term generation of more microeconomic household data, more compelling evidence on the benefits of the integration of multiple interventions, and more information on the potential distributional effects of policy interventions aimed at addressing long-term challenges such as climate change.[36]

Data need to allow for more comprehensive monitoring of specific changes in inequality, but also in poverty and shared prosperity. Substantial efforts are required to address the poor quality, comparability, and availability of data, especially in low-income countries. Figure O.14 shows the availability of poverty estimates by country and region. The availability is particularly limited in Sub-Saharan Africa and in the Middle East and North Africa. This report makes a strong case for expanding the availability of and access to data on inequality, poverty, and shared prosperity.

FIGURE 0.14 Available Country Poverty Estimates, Number, by Region and Year

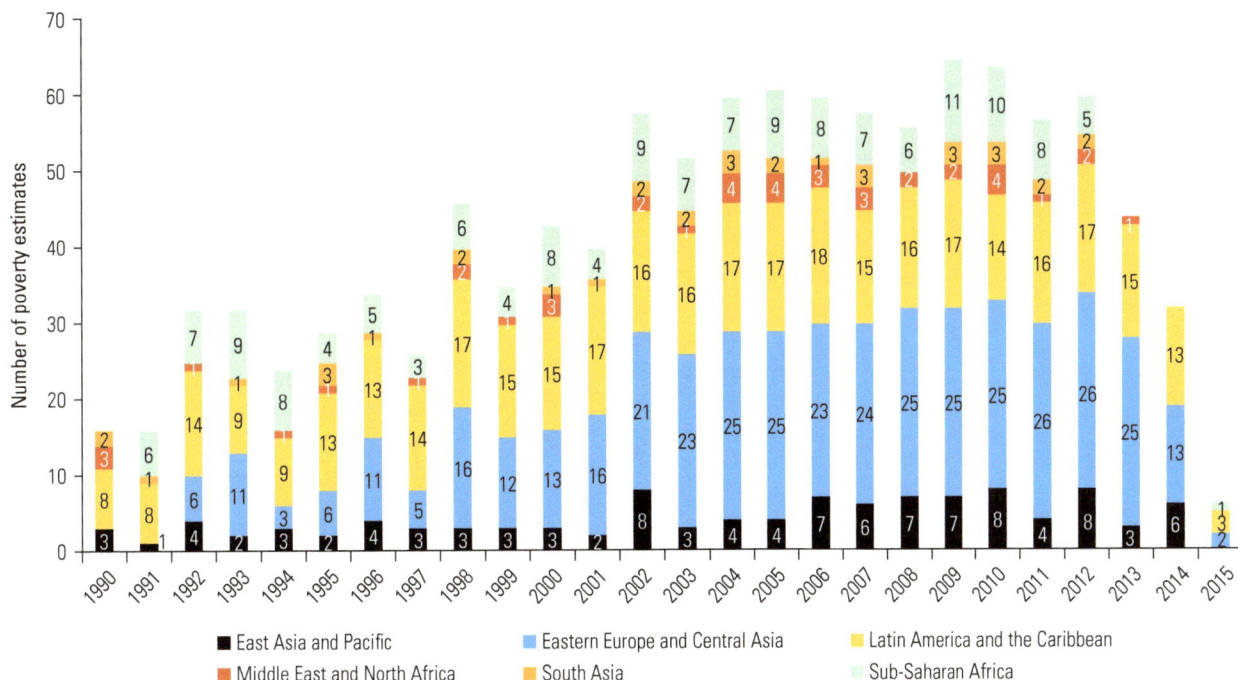

Source: Poverty and Equity Data (database), World Bank, Washington, DC, http://povertydata.worldbank.org/poverty/home/.
Note: The presentation follows the definition of the developing world of Serajuddin et al. (2015), which includes 150 countries and territories in the early 1990s and 155 in 2013. High-income countries such as the original members of the Organisation for Economic Co-operation and Development (OECD), where extreme poverty is assumed to be zero, are not considered in this sample.

Notes

1. WHO (2015).
2. For a formal decomposition, see Datt and Ravallion (1992), among others. In the general case, a reduction in inequality at a given growth rate leads to a reduction in poverty according to most poverty measures. Exceptions are, for instance, progressive distributional changes whereby some nonpoor fall under the poverty line over time, thus increasing the headcount ratio. Even in that case, other poverty measures with higher social welfare weights for lower percentiles tend to decrease.
3. See Oxfam (2016). Lakner (2015) estimates that the 10 wealthiest Africans own as much as the poorest half of the continent.
4. The countries classified as industrialized in this report are assumed to have zero poverty at the $1.90-a-day poverty line, an assumption that may change in the future because of the World Bank's implementation of the report of the Commission on Global Poverty on global poverty estimation. See "Commis-

sion on Global Poverty," World Bank, Washington, DC, http://www.worldbank.org/en /programs/commission-on-global-poverty.
5. Poverty and Equity Data (database), World Bank, Washington, DC, http://povertydata .worldbank.org/poverty/home/.
6. Castañeda et al. (2016) analyze the robustness of these results by comparing different lineup methods and different ways to adjust welfare aggregates, weights, and poverty lines. They find only minimal differences. They also check for fixed effects and sensitivity to missing data. The resulting demographic profile thus paints a robust picture of global poverty.
7. Beegle et al. (2016) and Cornia (2014) document a bifurcation in inequality trends in Sub-Saharan Africa, that is, within a set of African countries with at least two recent, strictly comparable surveys, there is an even split between countries with widening inequality and countries with narrowing inequality. The surveys are drawn from the first decade of the 2000s.
8. World Bank (2015a).

9. In Cambodia, these difficulties revolve around problems in land tenure, bottlenecks in fertilizer and seed markets, inadequate extension services and irrigation systems, and, among farmers, the lack of savings and access to credit. In addition, recent agricultural productivity gains from an expansion in the arable land under cultivation are not sustainable indefinitely and are thus unable to offset these problems. As a result, smallholders are generally vulnerable to swings in the international prices for rice. In Tanzania, the unfinished transition to a market-based economy translates into a private sector characterized by a lack of competition, an absence of growth, and a heavy regulatory burden associated with the public sector. See World Bank (2014, 2016a).

10. World Bank (2016b).

11. Barros et al. (2010); Osorio and Souza (2012).

12. ADB (2014).

13. World Bank (2009, 2014).

14. Josz (2013).

15. World Bank (2015a).

16. Genoni and Salazar (2015).

17. World Bank (2015b).

18. World Bank (2016c).

19. Avram, Levy, and Sunderland (2014); De Agostini, Paulus, and Tasseva (2015).

20. Gertler et al. (2014); Grantham-McGregor et al. (1991).

21. UNICEF (2016).

22. Araujo et al. (2016).

23. Fafchamps and Quisumbing (1999); Jolliffe (1998); Yang (1997).

24. Ferré and Sharif (2014).

25. Behrman and Hoddinott (2005); Gertler (2004).

26. Akresh, de Walque, and Kazianga (2013).

27. Fiszbein and Schady (2009).

28. Aggarwal (2015); Asher and Novosad (2016).

29. Khandker, Barnes, and Samad (2013).

30. La Ferrara, Chong, and Duryea (2012).

31. See the evidence presented in chapter 6.

32. Abramovsky et al. (2014); World Bank (2016d).

33. See the evidence presented in chapter 6.

34. See the evidence presented in chapter 6.

35. See the evidence presented in chapter 6.

36. Hallegate et al. (2016).

References

Abramovsky, Laura, Orazio Attanasio, Kai Barron, Pedro Carneiro, and George Stoye. 2014. "Challenges to Promoting Social Inclusion of the Extreme Poor: Evidence from a Large Scale Experiment in Colombia." IFS Working Paper W14/33, Institute for Fiscal Studies, London.

ADB (Asian Development Bank). 2014. Cambodia: Diversifying beyond Garments and Tourism, Country Diagnostic Study. November. Manila: Economics and Research Department, ADB.

Aggarwal, Shilpa. 2015. "Do Rural Roads Create Pathways Out of Poverty? Evidence from India." Working paper, Indian School of Business, Hyderabad, India.

Akresh, Richard, Damien de Walque, Harounan Kazianga. 2013. "Cash Transfers and Child Schooling: Evidence from a Randomized Evaluation of the Role of Conditionality." Policy Research Working Paper 6340, World Bank, Washington, DC.

Araujo, María Caridad, Pedro Carneiro, Yyannú Cruz-Aguayo, and Norbert Schady. 2016. "Teacher Quality and Learning Outcomes in Kindergarten." Quarterly Journal of Economics 125 (1): 175–214.

Asher, Sam, and Paul Novosad. 2016. "Market Access and Structural Transformation: Evidence from Rural Roads in India." Working paper (April 20), University of Oxford, Oxford.

Avram, Silvia, Horacio Levy, and Holly Sutherland. 2014. "Income Redistribution in the European Union." IZA Journal of European Labor Studies 3 (22): 1–29.

Barros, Ricardo Paes de, Mirela De Carvalho, Samuel Franco, and Rosane Mendonça. 2010. "Markets, the State, and the Dynamics of Inequality in Brazil." In Declining Inequality in Latin America: A Decade of Progress?, edited by Luis F. López-Calva and Nora Lustig, 134–74. New York: United Nations Development Programme; Baltimore: Brookings Institution Press.

Beegle, Kathleen, Luc Christiaensen, Andrew Dabalen, and Isis Gaddis. 2016. Poverty in a Rising Africa. Washington, DC: World Bank.

Beegle, Kathleen, Pedro Olinto, Carlos E. Sobrado, Hiroki Uematsu, and Yeon Soo Kim. 2014. "Ending Extreme Poverty and Promoting Shared Prosperity: Could There Be Trade-Offs between These Two Goals?" Inequality in Focus 3 (1): 1–6.

Behrman, Jere R., and John Hoddinott. 2005. "Programme Evaluation with Unobserved Heterogeneity and Selective Implementation:

The Mexican PROGRESA Impact on Child Nutrition." *Oxford Bulletin of Economics and Statistics* 67 (4): 547–69.

Bourguignon, François. 2015. *The Globalization of Inequality*. Translated by Thomas Scott-Railton. Princeton, NJ: Princeton University Press.

Castañeda, Andres, Dung Doan, David Newhouse, Minh C. Nguyen, Hiroki Uematsu, João Pedro Azevedo, and Data for Goals Group. 2016. "Who Are the Poor in the Developing World?" Policy Research Working Paper 7844, World Bank, Washington DC.

Cornia, Giovanni Andrea. 2014. "Income Inequality Levels, Trends, and Determinants in Sub-Saharan Africa: An Overview of the Main Changes." Università degli Studi di Firenze, Florence.

Datt, Gaurav, and Martin Ravallion. 1992. "Growth and Redistribution Components of Changes in Poverty Measures: A Decomposition with Applications to Brazil and India in the 1980s." *Journal of Development Economics* 38 (2): 275–95.

De Agostini, Paola, Alari Paulus, and Iva Valentinova Tasseva. 2015. "The Effect of Tax-Benefit Changes on the Income Distribution in 2008–2014." Euromod Working Paper EM11/15, Institute for Social and Economic Research, University of Essex, Colchester, United Kingdom.

Fafchamps, Marcel, and Agnes R. Quisumbing. 1999. "Human Capital, Productivity, and Labor Allocation in Rural Pakistan." *Journal of Human Resources* 34 (2): 369–406.

Ferré, Céline, and Iffath Sharif. 2014. "Can Conditional Cash Transfers Improve Education and Nutrition Outcomes for Poor Children in Bangladesh? Evidence from a Pilot Project." Policy Research Working Paper 7077, World Bank, Washington, DC.

Fiszbein, Ariel, and Norbert Schady. 2009. *Conditional Cash Transfers: Reducing Present and Future Poverty*. Washington, DC: World Bank.

Genoni, María Eugenia, and Mateo Salazar. 2015. "Steering toward Shared Prosperity in Peru." In *Shared Prosperity and Poverty Eradication in Latin America and the Caribbean*, edited by Louise Cord, María Eugenia Genoni, and Carlos Rodríguez-Castelán, 269–302. Washington, DC: World Bank.

Gertler, Paul J. 2004. "Do Conditional Cash Transfers Improve Child Health? Evidence from PROGRESA's Control Randomized Experiment." *American Economic Review* 94 (2): 336–41.

Gertler, Paul J., James J. Heckman, Rodrigo Pinto, Arianna Zanolini, Christel Vermeersch, Susan Walker, Susan M. Chang, and Sally Grantham-McGregor. 2014. "Labor Market Returns to an Early Childhood Stimulation Intervention in Jamaica." *Science* 344 (6187): 998–1001.

Grantham-McGregor, Sally M., Christine A. Powell, Susan P. Walker, and John H. Himes. 1991. "Nutritional Supplementation, Psychosocial Stimulation, and Mental Development of Stunted Children: The Jamaican Study." *Lancet* 338 (8758): 1–5.

Hallegatte, Stephane, Mook Bangalore, Laura Bonzanigo, Marianne Fay, Tomaro Kane, Ulf Narloch, Julie Rozenberg, David Treguer, and Adrien Vogt-Schilb. 2016. *Shock Waves: Managing the Impacts of Climate Change on Poverty*. Climate Change and Development Series. Washington, DC: World Bank.

Jolliffe, Dean. 1998. "Skills, Schooling, and Household Income in Ghana." *World Bank Economic Review* 12 (1): 81–104.

Josz, Christian. 2013. "Mali: Achieving Strong and Inclusive Growth with Macroeconomic Stability." African Development 13/08, International Monetary Fund, Washington, DC.

Khandker, Shahidur R., Douglas F. Barnes, and Hussain A. Samad. 2013. "Welfare Impacts of Rural Electrification: A Panel Data Analysis from Vietnam." *Economic Development and Cultural Change* 61 (3): 659–92.

La Ferrara, Eliana, Alberto Chong, and Suzanne Duryea. 2012. "Soap Operas and Fertility: Evidence from Brazil." *American Economic Review* 4 (4): 1–31.

Lakner, Christoph. 2015. "The Ten Richest Africans Own as Much as the Poorest Half of the Continent." *Let's Talk Development* (blog), March 11. http://blogs.worldbank.org /developmenttalk/ten-richest-africans-own -much-poorest-halfcontinent.

Lakner, Christoph, and Branko Milanović. 2016. "Global Income Distribution: From the Fall of the Berlin Wall to the Great Recession." *World Bank Economic Review* 30 (2): 203–32.

Lakner, Christoph, Mario Negre, and Espen Beer Prydz. 2014. "Twinning the Goals: How Can Shared Prosperity Help to Reduce Global Poverty?" Policy Research Working Paper 7106, World Bank, Washington, DC.

Milanović, Branko. 2014. "All the Ginis, 1950–2012 (updated in Autumn 2014)." November, World Bank, Washington, DC. http://go.worldbank.org/9VCQW66LA0.

———. 2016. *Global Inequality: A New Approach for the Age of Globalization.* Cambridge, MA: Harvard University Press.

Newhouse, David, Pablo Suarez-Becerra, Martin C. Evans, and Data for Goals Group. 2016. "New Estimates of Extreme Poverty for Children." Policy Research Working Paper 7845, World Bank, Washington, DC.

Osorio, Rafael Guerreiro, and Pedro H. G. Ferreira de Souza. 2012. "O Bolsa Família depois do Brasil Carinhoso: uma análise do potencial de redução da pobreza extrema." Institute for Applied Economic Research, Brasília.

Oxfam. 2016. "An Economy for the 1%: How Privilege and Power in the Economy Drive Extreme Inequality and How This Can Be Stopped." Oxfam Briefing Paper 210, Oxfam GB, Oxford.

Serajuddin, Umar, Hiroki Uematsu, Christina Wieser, Nobuo Yoshida, and Andrew Dabalen. 2015. "Data Deprivation: Another Deprivation to End." Policy Research Working Paper 7252, World Bank, Washington, DC.

UNICEF (United Nations Children's Fund). 2016. *The State of the World's Children 2016: A Fair Chance for Every Child.* June. New York: UNICEF.

WHO (World Health Organization). 2015. *World Health Statistics.* Geneva: WHO.

World Bank. 2009. "International Development Association Program Document, Kingdom of Cambodia: Proposed Smallholder Agriculture and Social Protection Support Operation." Report 48083-KH (June 19), World Bank, Washington, DC.

———. 2014. "Where Have All the Poor Gone? Cambodia Poverty Assessment 2013." Report ACS4545, World Bank, Washington, DC.

———. 2015a. "Republic of Mali, Priorities for Ending Poverty and Boosting Shared Prosperity: Systematic Country Diagnostic (SCD)." Report 94191-ML (June 22), World Bank, Washington, DC.

———. 2015b. "Tanzania Mainland: Poverty Assessment." Report AUS6819 v2, World Bank, Washington, DC.

———. 2016a. "Ngazi Ya Pili (To the Next Level): United Republic of Tanzania Systematic Country Diagnostics." Regional Operations Committee Decision Review Draft (June 2), World Bank, Washington, DC.

———. 2016b. *Brazil Systematic Country Diagnostic: Retaking the Path to Inclusion, Growth, and Sustainability.* Report 101431-BR, Washington, DC: World Bank.

———. 2016c. "International Development Association Project Paper, United Republic of Tanzania: Productive Social Safety Net (PSSN)." Report PAD1500 (May 20), World Bank, Washington, DC.

———. 2016d. "Chile: Distributional Effects of the 2014 Tax Reform," World Bank, Washington, DC.

Yang, Dennis. 1997. "Education and Off-Farm Work." *Economic Development and Cultural Change* 45 (3): 613–32.

Poverty and Shared Prosperity: Setting the Stage

Concepts, measurement, and data

The World Bank goals

On April 20, 2013, the Board of Executive Directors of the World Bank adopted two ambitious goals: end extreme poverty globally and promote shared prosperity in every country in a sustainable way.

Progress toward the first of these goals is measured by monitoring the rate of extreme poverty using the international poverty standard. The World Bank set a target of reducing the poverty headcount ratio from 12.4 percent globally in 2012 to 3.0 percent by 2030, and, to avoid overreliance on efforts toward the end of the period, the institution set an interim target of 9.0 percent by 2020, consistent with an annual reduction in global extreme poverty of a half percentage point over 2012–20.[1]

The second goal is not defined globally, but tracks progress at the level of countries. Despite not providing a single global target, the shared prosperity goal is universal because it includes developed countries that do not contribute to the global poverty count, but are still monitored in terms of shared prosperity. Progress on the shared prosperity goal is measured by the growth in the average income or consumption expenditure of the poorest 40 percent of the population distribution (the bottom 40) within each country.[2] This goal is not associated with a target in 2030, but it reflects the aim that every country should promote the welfare of its least privileged citizens.

Measuring the World Bank goals

Poverty

The first World Bank goal, ending poverty, is global, and measurement involves adding up the number of poor people in all countries. Three specific components are critical to this aggregation. The first component is cost-of-living comparability across countries. The key information for ensuring this comparability is data to gauge purchasing power parities (PPPs). The data are collected through the International Comparison Program, an independent worldwide statistical partnership that gathers data on prices and expenditures within economies. The comparison of incomes across households in different countries entails the use of exchange rates between local currencies, the units of value used by household surveys. However, the use of market exchange rates is not sufficient because market exchange rates do not accurately assess differences in purchasing power and are inaccurate in capturing the costs faced by the poor. Despite the limitations stemming from the complexity of a global exercise of this nature, the PPPs fill this gap by allowing income comparisons in real terms, while accounting for differences in prices across countries. Comparing prices across the world is a tricky endeavor because most products are not sold everywhere, or, even if they are, the quality may vary considerably country-by-country and region-by-region. Moreover, an everyday product in one country may be a luxury item in another. Likewise, prices may also vary widely within a single country; so, spatial price variations should also be taken into account where possible. Because relative prices evolve, updates of PPPs may be necessary so that PPP exchange rates are used reliably in price comparisons.

A second key component of the aggregation of the poor is the definition of an international poverty line in PPP terms. Countries determine their own poverty lines mostly by means of a basic needs standard that is linked to a predefined consumption basket of essential goods and services, or relative to an agreed position along the distribution of income or consumption (for example, 60 percent of the median national household income). The World Bank uses an international poverty line based on the national thresholds of some of the poorest countries.[3] To account for changes in relative prices across countries over time, the 2011 PPP was adopted in 2015 as the standard. This involved an upward adjustment of the international poverty line to US$1.90 a day in income or consumption expenditure so as to preserve the real value of the US$1.25-a-day line in 2005 PPP that was the previous international line. Global poverty incidence changes little as a result, and progress toward the global poverty target for 2030 is unaffected.[4]

The third element in a proper aggregation of the poverty count is the treatment of the lack of reliable data on some economies and a range of difficulties in the aggregation of existing and available data. Hence, for those countries lacking reliable income or consumption data or on which data are not available for analysis, a regional average poverty rate is used. In calculating this rate, available and reliable evidence is gathered on countries within the same region and then extrapolated onto the countries on which data are unavailable.[5]

These three ingredients permit the estimation of the global count of the poor. Yet, the global aggregation exercise rests on various assumptions. Most significantly, zero poverty is assumed in most high-income countries, that is, industrialized countries, although a nonnegligible share of households in these countries report incomes below the international poverty line. The United States is a good example. According to some estimates, 1 percent to 4 percent of the population there (measured by income) is living below a $2.00-a-day poverty line (in 2005 prices).[6] If welfare is measured by consumption, however, high-income countries typically report no poverty at all. This is because the poor in these countries generally have access to free public services and social transfers that are not accounted for in the income aggregate, but that ensure that the population's consumption levels are above the recognized poverty standards. Box 1.1 discusses key issues in the use of incomes and consumption as welfare aggregates.

Shared prosperity

To analyze both prosperity and equity dynamically, the World Bank focuses, in the second goal, on the growth experienced by people at the bottom of the income or consumption distribution within a country. In practice, this is defined as the growth in the average income or consumption of the bottom 40, which is measured through household surveys.[7] Although the choice of the bottom 40 is somewhat arbitrary, the bottom 40 has been a focus of poverty analysis for quite some time.[8] Indeed, the bottom 40 threshold reflects a commitment to focus on the least well off regardless of the actual poverty rate. In cases where the national poverty headcount is above 40 percent, the shared prosperity indicator centers on the poorest of the poor.

Why choose an income growth indicator that focuses only on the bottom of the distribution? One of the most widely used indicators of economic prosperity is growth in per capita gross domestic product (GDP). The economic health and development of countries are often judged on this basis. However, a per capita growth rate says little about how specific population groups benefit from economic progress. Similarly, standard indicators of inequality, such as the Gini index, do not offer information on the size of the pie being shared.

The shared prosperity indicator therefore represents a practical compromise between a

BOX 1.1 The Welfare Aggregate: Income versus Consumption

The global poverty headcount requires that the number of the poor within a country be measured by adding up the poor based on a welfare aggregate obtained through household surveys. In most countries, the aggregate of choice is per capita consumption. Indeed, 75 percent of the countries in the World Bank PovcalNet database—the official online repository of World Bank poverty data—use this aggregate.[a] The countries in the database that use incomes are mostly high-income countries and Latin America and Caribbean countries.

Are these two aggregates—income and consumption—the same? They are not. Conceptually, income is a measure of the potential set of all goods and services that an individual or a household could obtain based on their purchasing power. Meanwhile, consumption represents a direct measure of the goods and services that the individual or household has actually obtained. Therefore, consumption does not capture opportunities, but realized outcomes that directly determine an individual or household's well-being.

In practice, income is generally more volatile in the sense that it may be influenced greatly by seasonal factors or by a lack of regularity, particularly in agriculture and in the informal sector. It also has other important shortcomings, such as the frequent case of households that declare zero income on a survey, but exhibit a consumption level that is not zero. This may occur because the households lack income during a survey recall period, are dissaving, or are experiencing a spell of unemployment, or because the consumption of home-produced goods has not been correctly measured.

In contrast, consumption does not normally vary as widely; it displays a much smoother behavior. For this reason, consumption tends to be the preferred aggregate in measuring poverty in developing economies, which typically depend more on agriculture and have a larger informal sector.

Despite these differences, both aggregates are used indistinctively in the measurement of the World Bank goals to maximize the number of countries monitored. Although this creates issues of comparability in the measurement of poverty, it allows the coverage of the global goals to be expanded. The distinction may be more problematic, however, in the analysis of inequality. This is a result of the fact that the coverage of household surveys is generally incomplete among top earners, entrepreneurial and capital incomes are inadequately reported, and measures of consumption often underestimate the living conditions of the rich.

a. PovcalNet (online analysis tool), World Bank, Washington, DC, http://iresearch.worldbank.org /PovcalNet/.

---

prosperity indicator that fails to capture inequality and an equity indicator that fails to capture growth. By focusing on the growth in incomes of the bottom 40, the shared prosperity indicator incorporates a measure of prosperity and distributional dimensions. Furthermore, by choosing this indicator to measure one of its goals, the World Bank focuses squarely on improving the welfare of the least well off within every country across the world, ensuring that everyone is part of a dynamic and inclusive growth process, no matter the circumstances, the country context, or the time period.[9]

Linking shared prosperity and inequality: the shared prosperity premium

Tracking the growth rate of the average income of the poorest two-fifths of the population is crucial for assessing the inclusive nature of growth. However, taking this measure a step further and comparing it to the performance of the mean provides important additional insights. Whether the income or consumption of the bottom 40 grows more quickly or more slowly than the average determines whether or not the bottom 40 disproportionately benefit from growth relative to the average individual in society. If incomes among the bottom 40 grow at a rate above the rate at the mean, this implies that the incomes of the bottom 40 are rising more rapidly than the incomes among the rest of the population, that is, the top 60.

This concept has been embodied in the shared prosperity premium, an indicator that is defined as the difference between the growth in the incomes or the consumption of the bottom 40 and the growth in the incomes or consumption of the mean.[10]

The shared prosperity goal thus possesses an inequality dimension even though it is not an inequality indicator. This dimension can be readily assessed by comparing growth among the bottom 40 with growth at the mean. The difference is positive if the former grows more quickly than the latter and negative otherwise. The indicator can easily be used to provide a rough assessment of the magnitude of changes in inequality. One may also decompose the sources of the growth measured: the growth of the bottom 40 may derive from growth in the mean income (or consumption) of the overall population, or it may arise from changes in the share of overall income that accrues to the bottom 40 according to the following accounting relationship:[11]

$$g_{40} = g_{mean} + g_{shareB40}, \qquad (1.1)$$

where g_{40} is the income growth of the bottom 40; g_{mean} is the growth of the mean; and $g_{shareB40}$ is the growth in the income share of the bottom 40.

The growth in income or consumption among the bottom 40 may therefore be associated with participation in average growth, with a rising share of the bottom 40 in total income or consumption, or, ideally, with both so that achievements through one channel are not offset by poor performance in the other. Such a decomposition synthesizes the distributional character of the shared prosperity indicator, although the indicator, strictly speaking, is an ex-

tended metric of growth and not an inequality indicator.

Rewriting equation 1.1, one may easily appreciate that the shared prosperity premium represents the change in the total income share of the bottom 40, as follows:

$$g_{shareB40} = g_{40} - g_{mean} = \text{the shared prosperity premium} \qquad (1.2)$$

where $g_{shareB40}$ is the growth in the income share of the bottom 40; g_{40} is the income growth of the bottom 40; and g_{mean} is the growth of the mean.

While the shared prosperity indicator is useful in gauging the progress in achieving the ambition of leaving no one behind, a positive value in the shared prosperity premium ensures an extra focus on the particular progress of those who are most in need. It shows that the relative growth in incomes or consumption among this population segment is larger than that observed among the rest of the distribution.

Poverty, shared prosperity, and the global goals

The World Bank's first goal—reducing the poverty rate to 3.0 percent by 2030—encompasses the world. Yet, not all countries or regions or groups within countries can be expected to reach the goal individually. However, an even more ambitious target, eradicating extreme poverty "for all people everywhere" by 2030, was adopted by the United Nations General Assembly in September 2015 as part of the first Sustainable Development Goal.

This slight difference in targets between the World Bank's goal and the Sustainable Development Goal—3 percent versus zero—is not accidental. As countries have eradicated extreme poverty, the speed at which they have been able to eliminate the last pockets of poverty has varied considerably. Some countries have witnessed a slowdown in poverty reduction in the last stages of the process, such as Australia, Canada, the United Kingdom, and the United States.[12] Moreover, even if most countries significantly reduce poverty by 2030, the persistence of conflicts and disasters means there will likely remain a small, but significant number of people living in extreme poverty. In part for this reason, the World Bank goal of reducing poverty is restricted to narrowing the share of the world population living below the international poverty line to less than 3.0 percent by 2030.

The United Nations has also built on the concept of shared prosperity for Sustainable Development Goal 10, on inequality. This development goal aims to "progressively achieve and sustain income growth of the bottom 40 percent of the population at a rate higher than the national average" by 2030 (target 10.1).[13] The United Nations is using the shared prosperity premium, defined above, to measure progress.

In addition, in 2016, the G20 adopted the shared prosperity premium indicator to monitor the progress of its members in making their economies more inclusive.

The global community, by putting these issues at the forefront of policy making, has an unprecedented opportunity to help push governments and citizens into action to end extreme poverty and promote more inclusive societies.

The importance of data in tracking progress and spurring action

Monitoring progress on the two World Bank goals involves a massive effort in data collection and harmonization. Though not the only essential element, national household surveys are mandatory in estimating the proportion of people who are living in extreme poverty based on the international poverty line and in gauging the extent to which the bottom 40 benefit from economic growth.[14]

While measurement of the shared prosperity goal is not associated with specific additional data requirements relative to the poverty goal, and while it does not rely on the use of PPPs, it does pose specific challenges. Thus, within countries, slight methodological changes in survey questionnaires from round to round or in the composition of the consumption or income indicator

may drive significant changes in the shared prosperity indicator.[15]

Amid such issues, the availability of good-quality household surveys is perhaps the most critical need. Indeed, limited availability or a complete lack of household surveys not only hampers efforts to monitor poverty and shared prosperity, but also the capacity to design policies and interventions that can reach those who need them the most. Household surveys therefore need to be undertaken with regularity, must be comparable from one round to another, and must be of good quality. Meeting any of these requirements is not common practice in many developing countries.

Figure 1.1 illustrates the status of household survey availability among developing countries by reporting the number of national poverty estimates available each year. Household survey data availability has considerably improved over time. However, poverty and welfare estimates are typically not available immediately after a survey has been conducted because processing the data with confidence takes time. This is the cause of the precipitous drop in available poverty estimates in 2014 and 2015: household surveys collected in those years have not yet yielded an official, validated poverty estimate. Global poverty estimates are therefore typically reported with a three-year lag, although ambitious efforts are under way to ensure more frequent household surveys and hopefully allow for more up-to-date reporting in the future.[16]

To monitor the trends in poverty, surveys need to be conducted regularly, at least every three years or even more frequently. Figure 1.2 shows the data availability during all possible 10-year periods between 1990 and 2013. The progress is evident. The number of countries on which there is no poverty estimate over any 10-year period fell from 50 in 1990–99 to 21 in 2004–13. That the progress achieved so far is insufficient is equally evident. In 2004–13, 74 countries still lacked the basic data required to monitor poverty and shared prosperity over two points in time within a 10-year span. Indeed, these countries have no data

FIGURE 1.1 Available Country Poverty Estimates, by Region and Year

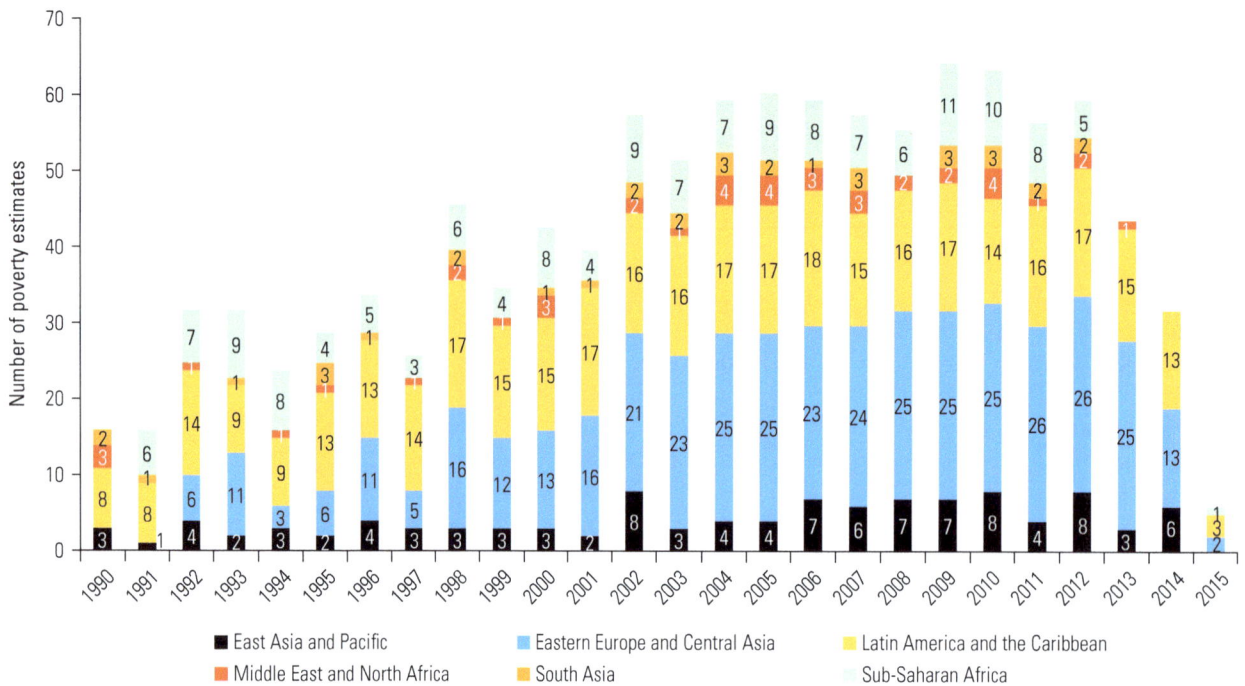

Source: Poverty and Equity Data (database), World Bank, Washington, DC, http://povertydata.worldbank.org/poverty/home/.
Note: The presentation follows the definition of the developing world employed by Serajuddin et al. (2015), which includes 150 countries and territories in the early 1990s and 155 in 2013. High-income countries such as the original members of the Organisation for Economic Co-operation and Development (OECD), where extreme poverty is assumed to be zero, are not considered in this sample.

FIGURE 1.2 Availability of Poverty Data, by All Possible 10-Year Periods, 1990–2013

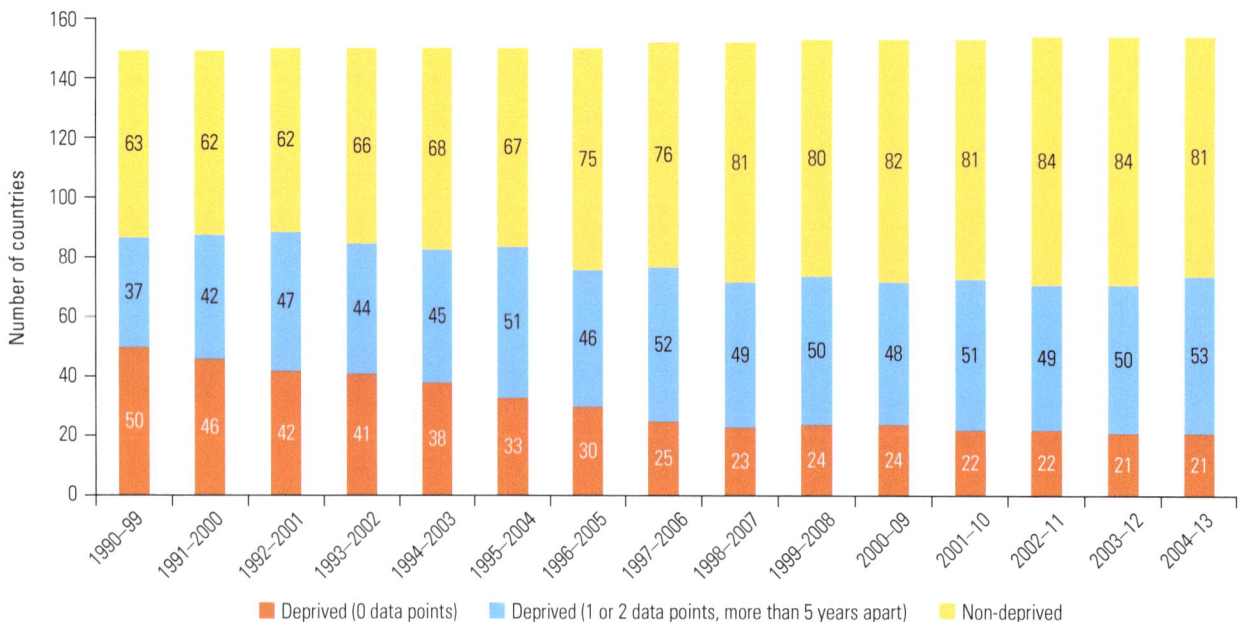

Source: Poverty and Equity Data (database), World Bank, Washington, DC, http://povertydata.worldbank.org/poverty/home/.

points at all, have only one data point each, or have two data points, but more than five years apart. This constitutes the definition of a country that is data deprived, which is the case of these 74 countries today.

It is also worrisome that data deprivation is unequally distributed worldwide. The data gaps within regions vary widely. In Eastern Europe and Central Asia, 28 of 30 countries have at least three data points in the most recent 10-year period, 2004–13. At the other extreme, most Sub-Saharan African countries only have one survey for the entire 10-year span: a total of 35 of 48 countries in Sub-Saharan Africa are data deprived. The Middle East and North Africa region and the East Asia and Pacific region are also severely data deprived. In Latin America and the Caribbean, countries typically either have excellent survey coverage (with a data point for almost every year) or no data points at all (often, in the Caribbean subregion).

Zero data points does not necessarily mean that no survey has been carried out. It may be that surveys are deemed insufficient in quality and comparability or that access to the data is not granted to the World Bank and its partners. The following statistics provide an illustration of the dire effects of one of these issues, comparability. If one discounts the surveys in Sub-Saharan Africa that are not nationally representative, that were not conducted at similar times of the year (to control for seasonality in consumption patterns), and that use different instruments in collection, the typical African country would have conducted only 1.6 comparable surveys in the 22 years between 1990 and 2012.[17]

Multiple challenges drive data deprivation. The funding of surveys is often ad hoc and unpredictable, reflecting lack of commitment, competing priorities, poor coordination, or a combination of all these factors. Weak technical capacity, weak governance in data collection, and a lack of globally accepted methodological standards also pose severe challenges.[18]

The World Bank's commitment to monitoring extreme poverty and shared prosperity therefore represents a critical call to upgrade and expand the availability of appropriate data, particularly where these are needed the most. In 2015, the World Bank committed to supporting the poorest countries in undertaking at least one household survey every three years and is now working closely with governments and partner institutions to broaden and improve data quality and availability in other crucial areas.[19]

A special focus in 2016: taking on inequality

Preceding the launch of the new World Bank goals by several years, *World Development Report 2006: Equity and Development* described the extraordinary inequality of opportunity across the world.[20] Since 2006, substantial progress has been made in reducing poverty, expanding prosperity, combating hunger, enhancing education and health services, and lowering maternal and child mortality. Do the large inequalities of 10 years ago persist today? What can be done to eliminate them?

The World Bank devotes this first flagship report on poverty and shared prosperity to addressing these questions. Although the findings indicate that there has been progress in establishing greater equality across the globe, there is also no room for complacency: we continue to live in a world characterized by intolerable inequality of opportunity, gender disparities, and deprivations, particularly in health, education, safe water and sanitation, nutrition, and consumption.

The issue of the sustainability of prosperity is as relevant today as 10 years ago. People worldwide are paying closer attention and taking and demanding action to tackle a broad range of inequalities more effectively. Today, few stakeholders question that equality of opportunity should be a central concern in the design and implementation of policies to foster development and inclusive growth.

Taking on inequality implies that prosperity must be shared meaningfully within developed and developing countries. The less well off must be at center stage if societies worldwide are to achieve the stability and well-being to which they aspire. Growth alone will not do the job; any type of growth will not suffice. Growth must be sustainable to achieve the maximum possible increase in living standards among the less well-off.

Reducing deprivations among the poorest, increasing their living standards, and leveling the playing field correspond to notions of fairness and justice and resonate across societies on their own merits. Nonetheless, continuing the notable progress in poverty reduction and shared prosperity that took place over the first decade of the 2000s is at risk because of the somewhat lower growth today and the projected global slowdown. In the last few years, economic growth has been sluggish worldwide, a period typically described as the Great Recession. Figure 1.3 illustrates the pattern of slowing growth among the main economic powerhouses, such as Brazil, the Russian Federation, India, China, and South Africa (together known as BRICS), the European Union (EU), and the United States, in which per capita GDP growth rates are exhibiting recurrent ups and downs. These economies

are experiencing double or triple dips in growth. The first dip took place in 2009, when the per capita GDP growth of these economies plummeted to negative values or zero, followed by a strong rebound in 2010. Growth then declined again in these economies, marking a second dip. In the United States, the dip was short-lived because the economy rebounded again in 2012, but slowed once more in 2013 (the third dip). In Europe, the rebound took longer and materialized in 2014. The BRICS economies have been slowing since 2011.

This report finds that the goal of eliminating extreme poverty will not be achieved by 2030 without significant shifts in within-country inequality. Ultimately, poverty reduction can occur through higher average growth, a narrowing in inequality, or a combination of the two. So, if poverty reduction is to be achieved in a context of slow growth, such as the current context, more equitable income or consumption distribution will be required.

Taking on inequality also matters for other reasons. It can bolster economic growth if it is carried out smartly.[21] There is no inevitable trade-off between efficiency and equity.[22] For example, investing in early childhood development (ECD) among underprivileged children can help prevent the emergence of inequalities in cognitive development and health status and, by enabling a more successful accumulation of human capital among individuals who would otherwise lag throughout the rest of the life cycle, improve future earnings and life chances. Trimming down inequalities in opportunity and outcomes among individuals, populations, and regions may also generate additional benefits through political and social stability and social cohesion.

This inaugural flagship report on poverty and shared prosperity documents trends in income inequality, identifies recent country experiences that have been successful in reducing such inequalities, analyzes key lessons drawn from these experiences, and synthesizes the rigorous evidence on public policies that can shift inequality to bolster poverty reduction and shared prosperity. Specifically, the report addresses the following questions:

FIGURE 1.3 **Double and Triple Dips in Growth, Selected Economies, 2006–15**

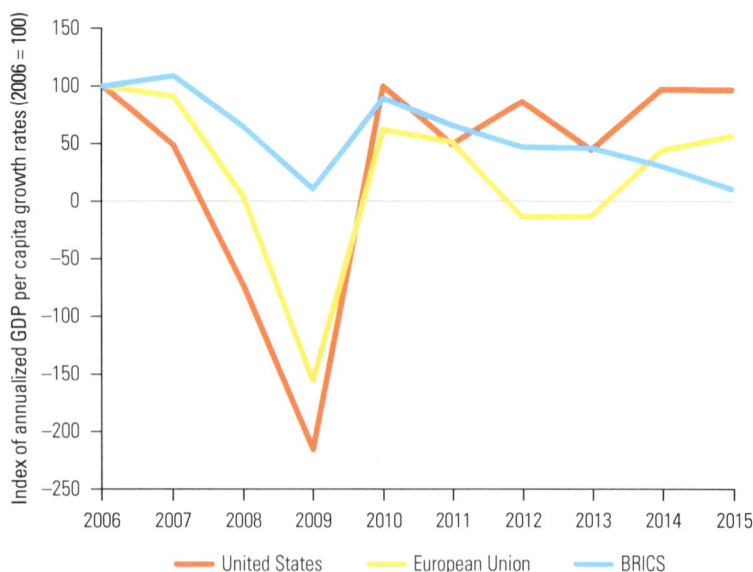

Source: WDI (World Development Indicators) (database), World Bank, Washington, DC, http://data.world bank.org/data-catalog/world-development-indicators.
Note: The data on the European Union and BRICS are population-weighted averages of the respective national per capita GDP growth rates.

- What is the latest evidence on the levels and evolution of global extreme poverty and shared prosperity?
- Which countries and regions have been more successful in terms of progress toward these goals and which are lagging?
- What does the global context of lower economic growth mean for the poorest people and countries?
- How can narrowing inequality contribute to ending extreme poverty and improving the welfare of the least well off?
- What does the evidence show concerning global and between- and within-country inequality trends?
- What does the evidence tell us about how countries and interventions have successfully reduced inequality?

To address these questions, the report is organized in six chapters, including this introduction. Chapter 2 presents the latest numbers on global and regional poverty using the international extreme poverty line of US$1.90 (2011 PPP). The chapter also discusses the geographical concentration of poverty and the composition of global poverty, complementing the global headcount numbers with a profile of global poverty.

Chapter 3 presents the latest shared prosperity data on the largest possible set of countries on which at least two comparable data points are available circa 2008–13, that is, 83 countries covering 75 percent of the world's population. The analysis identifies the best and worst performers in terms of the growth of the bottom 40. The chapter also shows that, in the context of declining global and regional growth rates and an outlook of weaker growth, the continuation of the progress achieved so far toward ending poverty by 2030 is at serious risk. Poverty trajectories to 2030 are simulated under several scenarios of growth and changes in shared prosperity, providing insights on the additional reductions in inequality required to end poverty.

Chapter 4 focuses on income inequality. It presents the most recent trends on global and between- and within-country inequalities and contrasts them with secular long-term trends. The analysis separates fact from fiction and clarifies much of the con-fusion on global trends, which can often be properly explained simply by selecting the appropriate inequality indicator, country, or time period for analysis.

Chapter 5 briefly discusses the drivers that explain recent notable successes in boosting shared prosperity and reducing inequality within countries. What have successful countries done to reduce income inequality, while inequality has been widening in other economies? Among the constellation of policies that have been implemented, this chapter identifies key levers in reducing income inequality and boosting shared prosperity in selected countries. Country cases assess how macroeconomic management, sectoral reforms, the expansion of safety nets, responses to external shocks, and initial conditions or context all contribute to boost shared prosperity. Five countries have been chosen based on their success in sharing prosperity and reducing inequality: Brazil, Cambodia, Mali, Peru, and Tanzania. These countries have also been chosen with the aim of achieving diversity in terms of region, income group, and distinctive contexts.

Chapter 6 explores the drivers of inequality reduction by examining interventions rather than country-specific experiences. It reviews emerging as well as consolidated evidence on how interventions successfully address the roots, drivers, and outcomes of inequality, while supporting economic growth and poverty reduction. The chapter focuses on early childhood development (including breastfeeding), universal health care, quality teaching, conditional cash transfers (CCTs), investments in rural infrastructure (roads and electrification), and taxation. The choice of policy interventions is highly selective and responds to the availability of rigorous evidence that supports reliable lessons and reflects some of the policy areas highlighted by the country narratives in chapter 5. The interventions chosen confirm the multiple pathways through which policies can successfully promote equality. The chapter also provides several general lessons useful in establishing a basic agenda of interventions that overcome equity-efficiency and implementation trade-offs.

Notes

1. Basu (2013).
2. Unless otherwise indicated, income and consumption are henceforth used interchangeably.
3. The methodology was originally applied by Ravallion, Chen, and Sangraula (2008), who established a first set of countries.
4. Ferreira et al. (2016).
5. World Bank (2015a).
6. Chandy and Smith (2014).
7. In this report, shared prosperity is estimated as the growth rate of real survey per capita income or consumption among the bottom 40 over a five-year period that ends three years before the publication of the report. Only countries with surveys meeting the following criteria are included: (a) the latest household survey for the country falls between 2011 and 2015 and (b) the survey for the first year of the period is the nearest survey collected five years before the most recent survey available; thus, only surveys collected between three and seven years before the most recent survey are considered in the inclusion or exclusion of countries.
8. Among the prominent references to the bottom 40, see Kuznets (1955); McNamara (1972).
9. Saavedra-Chanduvi (2013).
10. Lakner, Negre, and Prydz (2014).
11. Where $g_{shareB40}$ denotes the growth rate of the income share of the bottom 40. Equation 1.1 follows from differentiating the following identity: $\mu_{40} = \frac{s_{40}}{0.4} * \mu$, where s_{40} is the income share of the bottom 40, and μ and μ_{40} are the overall mean and the mean of bottom 40, respectively. Equation 1.1 holds in continuous time; as t becomes larger, it becomes an approximation. Also see Dollar, Kleineberg and Kraay (2016); Rosenblatt and McGavock (2013).
12. World Bank (2015a).
13. Sustainable Development Knowledge Platform (database), Department of Economic and Social Affairs, United Nations, New York, https://sustainabledevelopment.un.org/.
14. The following are also essential: censuses, because they make possible the design of the household surveys; price data, to adjust trends in income and consumption over time and ensure geographical comparability; and national accounts and administrative data, which can be used, for example, to adjust for underreported incomes or consumption.
15. Estimates of the growth in income or consumption of the bottom 40 are based on comparisons at two points in time, which may include years that do not correspond to the most recent survey in all countries. The growth rates must therefore be annualized, and, although this makes them more readily comparable, the operation is only performed on rates in those countries on which more than two surveys are available within the period under analysis.
16. United Nations (2014).
17. Beegle et al. (2016).
18. World Bank (2015a).
19. World Bank (2015b).
20. World Bank (2005).
21. Interventions aimed at narrowing inequality can also result in economic distortions, thus affecting efficiency and, ultimately, growth.
22. Interventions that reduce inequality without compromising economic growth are described here generically as equity-enhancing policies. *World Development Report 2006: Equity and Development* (World Bank 2005) calls them efficient redistribution policies. The change in the term in this report aims to avoid any confusion around the notion of redistribution. Redistribution may be strictly understood as removing resources from one individual or group and giving them to another individual or group. However, not all equity-enhancing policies must rely on redistribution in this strict sense. Some may achieve progressive distributional changes simply through legislation. For example, legislation on the minimum wage does not involve any direct government redistribution of resources, but often nonetheless affects the distribution of income. Moreover, the term redistribution is frequently used among pundits to refer to anonymous changes in the distribution regardless of their cause. Efficiency is also subject to alternative interpretations. The arguments presented in this report that tackle inequality draw from an idea of efficiency developed by Kaldor and Hicks in the late 1930s whereby an increase in overall incomes may be desirable even at the cost

of a few losers (Hicks 1939; Kaldor 1939). In contrast, efficiency can also be understood in the Pareto (1906) sense that no one can be made more well off without hurting someone else. The efficient equity-enhancing initiatives discussed in this report are based on the concepts of Kaldor and Hicks.

References

Basu, Kaushik. 2013. "Shared Prosperity and the Mitigation of Poverty: In Practice and Precept." Policy Research Working Paper 6700, World Bank, Washington, DC.

Beegle, Kathleen, Luc Christiaensen, Andrew Dabalen, and Isis Gaddis. 2016. *Poverty in a Rising Africa.* Africa Poverty Report. Washington, DC: World Bank.

Chandy, Laurence, and Cory Smith. 2014. "How Poor are America's Poorest? U.S. $2 a Day Poverty in a Global Context." Policy Paper 2014–03, Global Economy and Development at Brookings, Brookings Institution, Washington, DC.

Dollar, David, Tatjana Kleineberg, and Aart Kraay. 2016. "Growth is Still Good for the Poor." *European Economic Review* 81 (C): 68–85.

Ferreira, Francisco H. G., Shaohua Chen, Andrew Dabalen, Yuri Dikhanov, Nada Hamadeh, Dean Jolliffe, Ambar Narayan, Espen Beer Prydz, Ana Revenga, Prem Sangraula, Umar Serajuddin, and Nobuo Yoshida. 2016. "A Global Count of the Extreme Poor in 2012: Data Issues, Methodology, and Initial Results." *Journal of Economic Inequality* 14 (2): 141–72.

Hicks, John. 1939. "The Foundations of Welfare Economics." *Economic Journal* 49 (196): 696–712.

Kaldor, Nicholas. 1939. "Welfare Propositions in Economics and Interpersonal Comparisons of Utility." *Economic Journal* 49 (195): 549–52.

Kuznets, Simon. 1955. "Economic Growth and Income Inequality." *American Economic Review* 45 (1): 1–28.

Lakner, Christoph, Mario Negre, and Espen B. Prydz. 2014. "Twinning the Goals: How Can Shared Prosperity Help to Reduce Global Poverty?" Policy Research Working Paper 7106, World Bank, Washington, DC.

McNamara, Robert S. 1972. "Annual Address by Robert S. McNamara, President of the Bank and Its Affiliates." *Summary Proceedings, Annual Meetings of the Boards of Governors*, Report 53408, 16–31. Washington, DC: World Bank.

Pareto, Vilfredo. 1906. *Manuale di economia politica: Con una introduzione alla scienza sociale.* Milan: Società editrice libraria.

Ravallion, Martin, Shaohua Chen, and Prem Sangraula. 2008. "Dollar a Day Revisited." Policy Research Working Paper 4620, World Bank, Washington, DC.

Rosenblatt, David, and Tamara J. McGavock. 2013. "A Note on the Simple Algebra of the Shared Prosperity Indicator." Policy Research Working Paper 6645, World Bank, Washington, DC.

Saavedra-Chanduvi, Jaime. 2013. "Why Didn't the World Bank Make Reducing Inequality One of Its Goals?" Let's Talk Development (blog), September 23, https://blogs.world bank.org/developmenttalk/why-didn-t-world -bank-make-reducing-inequality-one-its -goals.

Serajuddin, Umar, Hiroki Uematsu, Christina Wieser, Nobuo Yoshida, and Andrew Dabalen. 2015. "Data Deprivation: Another Deprivation to End." Policy Research Working Paper 7252, World Bank, Washington, DC.

United Nations. 2014. "A World That Counts: Mobilising the Data Revolution for Sustainable Development." November, Independent Expert Advisory Group on a Data Revolution for Sustainable Development, United Nations, New York.

World Bank. 2005. *World Development Report 2006: Equity and Development.* Washington, DC: World Bank; New York: Oxford University Press.

———. 2015a. *A Measured Approach to Ending Poverty and Boosting Shared Prosperity: Concepts, Data, and the Twin Goals.* Policy Research Report. Washington, DC: World Bank.

———. 2015b. "World Bank's New End-Poverty Tool: Surveys in Poorest Countries." Press Release, October 15. http://www.world bank.org/en/news/press-release/2015/10/15 /world-bank-new-end-poverty-tool-surveys -in-poorest-countries.

Global Poverty

Chapter 2 presents the latest data on global and regional poverty using the international extreme poverty line of US$1.90 (2011 purchasing power parity [PPP] U.S. dollars). The chapter discusses the geographical concentration of poverty and complements the global headcount ratio and data by providing a profile of global poverty. It also reflects on recent methodological changes and their consequences on global estimates.

The global poverty estimate for 2013 is 10.7 percent of the world's population, or 767 million people. This confirms the continuation of the rapid downward trend in the poverty headcount ratio since 1990 (an average of 1.1 percentage points per year). The reduction in 2013 is even greater than the average, with a decline in the headcount ratio of 1.7 percentage points. In absolute net terms, this represents 114 million fewer poor people in a single year. Much of the observed reduction was driven by remarkable progress in the East Asia and Pacific region (71 million fewer poor) and South Asia (37 million fewer poor). A significant change in the geography of poverty has meant that Sub-Saharan Africa was hosting more than half the world's poor in 2013. This is despite the fact that the African subcontinent experienced progress in lowering both the headcount ratio (1.6 percentage points) and the number of the poor (4 million in 2012–13). However, these achievements are modest compared with reductions in East Asia and Pacific and in South Asia. Other regions with lower poverty rates and totals—notably, Eastern Europe and Central Asia, as well as Latin America and the Caribbean—saw marginal declines in 2012–13. The profile of the global poor shows they are predominantly rural, young, poorly educated, mostly employed in the agricultural sector, and living in larger households with more children.

Monitoring global poverty

Ever since the first World Development Report, *World Development Report 1990: Poverty*, the share of people living on less than US$1.90 per person per day has been steadily declining.[1] This has occurred at a rapid average pace of 1.1 percentage points a year. Overall, the total number of poor has also decreased steadily and dramatically throughout the period, except for the 1997–99 span of increasing poverty associated with the Asian financial crisis. Signifi-

cant progress in poverty reduction has been accompanied by important improvements in data availability, although substantial gaps remain (see chapter 1). As a result, the global poverty headcount in 2013 incorporated survey-based estimates on 137 countries.[2]

In 2013, an estimated 767 million people were living under the international poverty line of US$1.90 a day (table 2.1). This means that almost 11 people in 100, or 10.7

TABLE 2.1 World and Regional Poverty Estimates, 2013

Region	Headcount ratio (%)	Poverty gap (%)	Squared poverty gap (%)[a]	Poor (millions)
East Asia and Pacific	3.5	0.7	0.2	71.0
Eastern Europe and Central Asia	2.3	0.6	0.3	10.8
Latin America and the Caribbean	5.4	2.6	1.8	33.6
Middle East and North Africa[b]	—	—	—	—
South Asia	15.1	2.8	0.8	256.2
Sub-Saharan Africa	41.0	15.9	8.4	388.7
Total, six regions	12.6	3.8	1.8	766.6
World	10.7	3.2	1.5	766.6

Sources: Annex 2A; most recent estimates, based on 2013 data using PovcalNet (online analysis tool), World Bank, Washington, DC, http://iresearch.worldbank.org/PovcalNet/.
Note: Poverty is measured using the 2011 US$1.90-a-day PPP poverty line. The six-region total includes all developing regions. World includes all developing regions, plus industrialized countries. Definitions of geographical regions are those of PovcalNet. — = not available.

a. The squared poverty gap attaches increasing weights to the poor the further below the poverty line they are. The higher the squared poverty gap, the greater the share of the poor reporting extremely low consumption levels.
b. Estimates on the Middle East and North Africa are omitted because of data coverage and quality problems. The population coverage of available household surveys is too low; the share of the total regional population represented by the available surveys is below 40 percent. There are also issues in the application of the 2011 PPP U.S. dollar to the region. These issues revolve around the quality of the data in several countries experiencing severe political instability, breaks in the consumer price index (CPI) series, and measurement or comparability problems in specific household surveys. These caveats suggest that more methodological analyses and the availability of new household survey data are both needed before reliable and sufficiently precise estimates can be produced.

percent, were poor, 1.7 percentage points lower than the global headcount ratio in 2012. Given the low standard of living implied by the US$1.90-a-day threshold, poverty remains unacceptably high despite the recent progress.

The poverty gap provides a measure of how far below the poverty line the poor in a given country or region fall. This gap is expressed as a share of the poverty line and represents the average distance to the poverty line among all the poor. While the global poverty gap is small (3.2 percent), the poverty gap in Sub-Saharan Africa is almost five times larger (15.9 percent). This indicates that the region not only houses the largest number of the poor of any region in the world, but also that the region's poor are, on average, living much further below the US$1.90-a-day extreme poverty threshold.

Figure 2.1 depicts the steady decline in the share and total number of the poor in the world since 1990. Since 2002, in particular, the global headcount ratio has followed a steady downward trajectory, showing no sign of slowing down even during the global financial crisis (2008–09). Despite the more rapid demographic growth in poorer areas, this strong trend culminated in 114 million people lifting themselves out of extreme poverty in 2013 alone. (See box 2.1 and annex 2A.)[3]

The global number of the poor has fallen dramatically in only slightly more than two

FIGURE 2.1 The Global Poverty Headcount Ratio and the Number of the Extreme Poor, 1990–2013

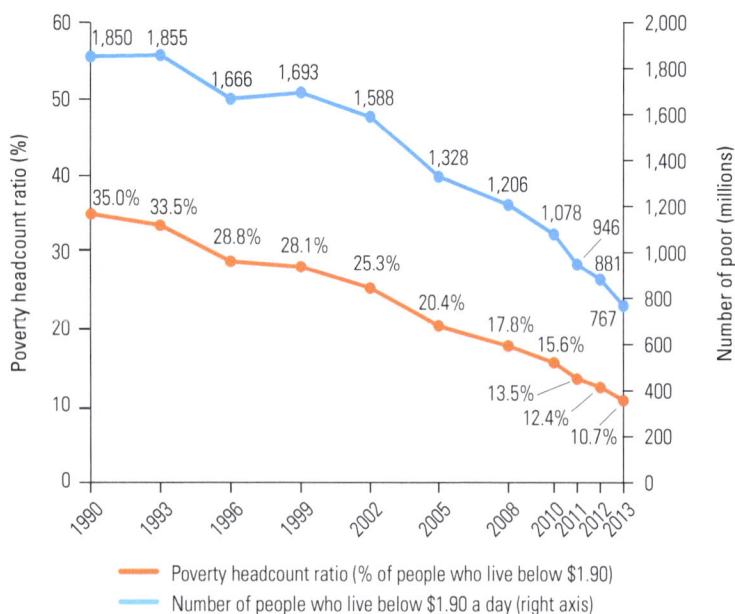

Sources: Annex 2A; most recent estimates, based on 2013 data using PovcalNet (online analysis tool), World Bank, Washington, DC, http://iresearch.worldbank.org/PovcalNet/.
Note: Poverty is measured using the 2011 US$1.90-a-day PPP poverty line.

decades (figure 2.1). There were almost 1.1 billion fewer people living in poverty worldwide in 2013 than in 1990, a period in which the world population grew by almost 1.9 billion. The total number of poor dropped from over 1.8 billion to 767 million during these years. This implies an average of almost 50 million persons escaping poverty every year in net terms, equivalent to the population of Colombia or the Republic of Korea. The progress was even more impressive in 2002–13, when an average of 75 million people, similar to the population of Germany or Turkey, moved out of poverty annually.

As extreme poverty has declined globally, the regional profile of poverty has shifted as a consequence of uneven progress. In 2013, Sub-Saharan Africa accounted for more of the poor—389 million people—than all other regions combined; the share of the region in the global total was 50.7 percent (see figure 2.2). This is a remarkable change in the geography of global poverty during the two decades since 1990, when half of the poor were living in East Asia and Pacific. Indeed, Sub-Saharan Africa first overtook East Asia and Pacific in 2005 and then South Asia in 2011 as the region with the largest number of the poor worldwide. In 2013, one-third of the global poor were living in South Asia. The East Asia and Pacific region was home to 9.3 percent, while the Latin America and Caribbean region and the Eastern Europe and Central Asia region reported global poverty shares of 4.4 percent and 1.4 percent, respectively.

FIGURE 2.2 Where Are the Global Poor Living? The Global Poor, by Region, 2013

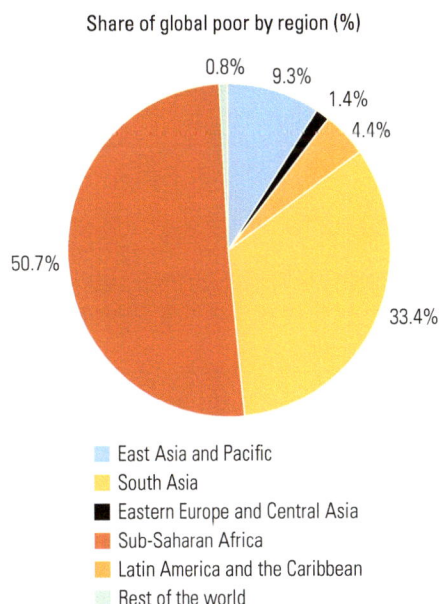

Share of global poor by region (%)

0.8% 9.3% 1.4% 4.4% 50.7% 33.4%

- East Asia and Pacific
- South Asia
- Eastern Europe and Central Asia
- Sub-Saharan Africa
- Latin America and the Caribbean
- Rest of the world

Source: Most recent estimates, based on 2013 data using PovcalNet (online analysis tool), World Bank, Washington, DC, http://iresearch.worldbank.org/PovcalNet/.

FIGURE 2.3 Regional and World Trends, Number of the Extreme Poor, 1990–2013

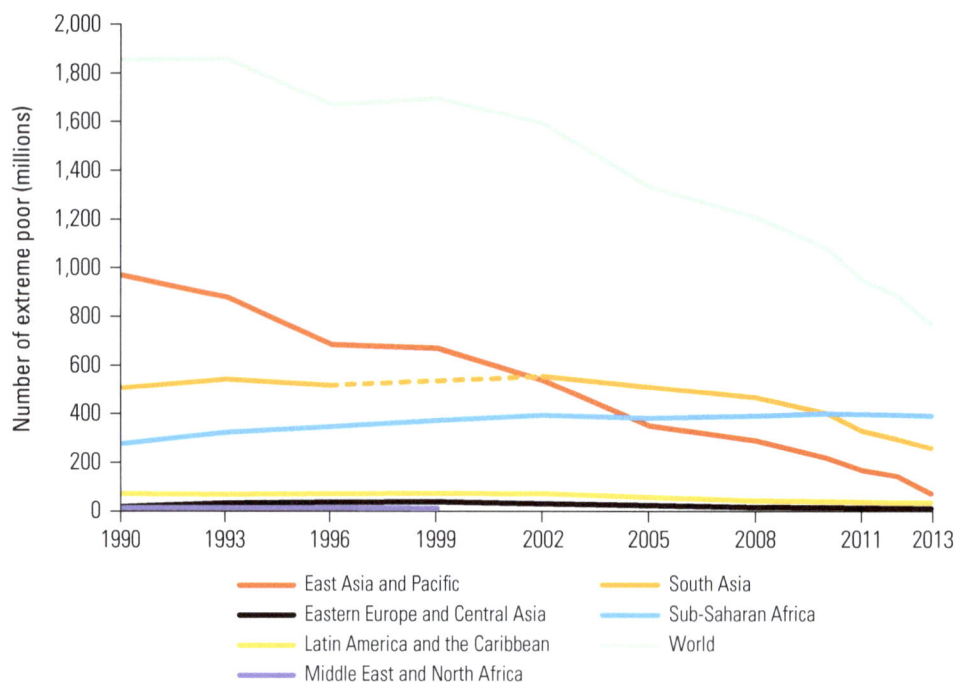

Sources: Annex 2A; most recent estimates, based on 2013 data using PovcalNet (online analysis tool), World Bank, Washington, DC, http://iresearch.worldbank.org/PovcalNet/.
Note: Poverty is measured using the 2011 US$1.90-a-day PPP poverty line. The breaks in the trends shown in the figure arise because of the lack of good-quality data.

Most of the changing geography of global poverty arises from the lagging performance of Sub-Saharan Africa in reducing poverty relative to East Asia and Pacific and to South Asia. The growing number of the poor in Sub-Saharan Africa stands out as an exception (figure 2.3). The increase in Sub-Saharan Africa occurred despite significant reductions in the share of the poor in the regional population and substantial economic growth in the subcontinent (figure 2.4).[4] As a result, the number of people living below the international poverty line in Sub-Saharan Africa has gradually expanded since the early 1990s—with the exception of 2002–05—and peaked in 2010. Thereafter, the total number of the poor in the region appears to have somewhat declined, from 399 million to 389 million by 2013. In absolute terms, the ability of economic progress to reduce poverty in Sub-Saharan Africa has been partly offset by population growth, and in many cases, an unequal distribution of the benefits of the economic growth.[5]

The implication of the current geography of global and regional poverty is that if the goal of ending poverty is to be achieved, most of any future decline will have to come from Sub-Saharan Africa, and to a lesser extent, South Asia. This is so because the future role of East Asia and Pacific in total poverty reduction will narrow following the rapid reductions already attained. In sum, future progress toward the global poverty goal is likely to taper off in coming years if an acceleration in current poverty reduction trends does not take place in Sub-Saharan Africa.

The trends in regional poverty reduction help unpack the global trend in the headcount ratio (see figure 2.4). In this case, the East Asia and Pacific region showed a strong performance. In the 23-year period up to 2013, the region managed to reduce its headcount ratio by a staggering 56.7 percentage points, down to 3.5 percent, close to the World Bank's global target of 3.0 percent by 2030. In the latest 2013 data round, the poverty rate in the Latin Amer-

FIGURE 2.4 Regional and World Trends, Extreme Poverty Headcount Ratio, 1990–2013

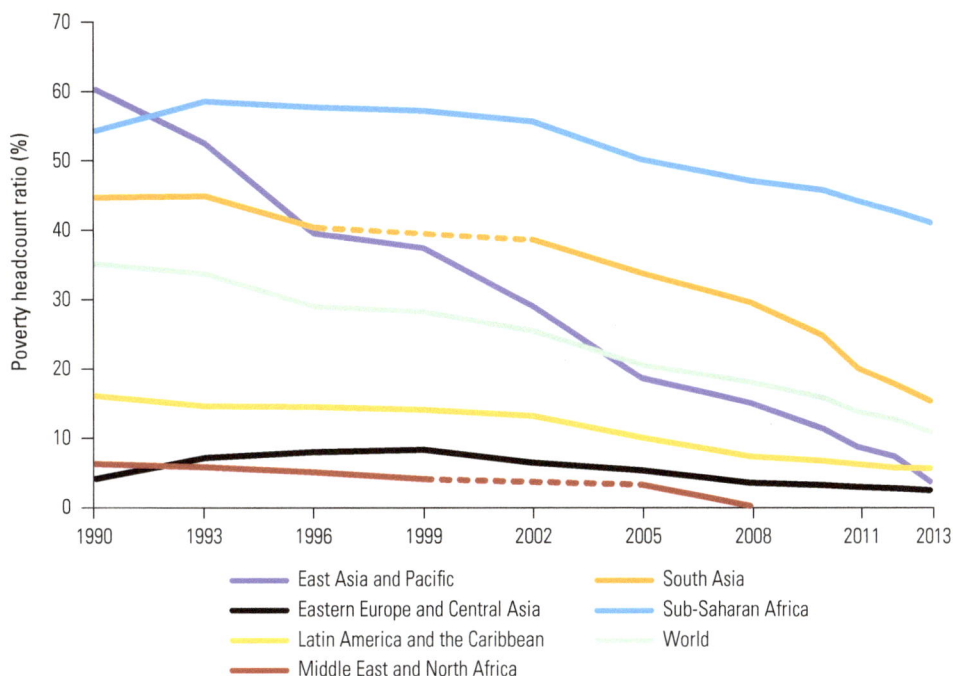

Sources: Annex 2A; most recent estimates, based on 2013 data using PovcalNet (online analysis tool), World Bank, Washington, DC, http://iresearch.worldbank.org/PovcalNet/.
Note: Poverty is measured using the 2011 US$1.90-a-day PPP poverty line. Breaks in the trends shown in the figure arise because of the lack of good-quality data.

ica and Caribbean region (5.4 percent) appeared to taper off in 2008–13, following the significant declines in 2002–08, with annual rates of reduction of 1.0 percentage point in the latter, but only 0.3 in the former. The Eastern Europe and Central Asia region maintained a slow, but steady decline in the headcount ratio, to around 2 percent.[6] The poverty estimates in South Asia indicate substantial progress, particularly in the five years up to 2013, when the annual average reduction reached 2.9 percentage points. Indeed, the region, in which almost one person in two was extremely poor only 25 years ago, reduced the share of poverty dramatically, to 15.1 percent, at an average decline of 1.3 percentage points a year.

In 2012–13, the changes in poverty were remarkable. The world's headcount ratio fell from 12.4 percent to 10.7 percent, and the number of the poor declined by 114 million. This sharp drop is mostly explained by the cuts in the number of the poor in two regions, the East Asia and Pacific re-

gion (71 million) and South Asia (37 million), which represent respective reductions in the headcount of 3.6 and 2.4 percentage points. The former is explained largely by the substantial contraction in the estimates for China and Indonesia, whereas the latter is driven by India's performance. (For a discussion of the methodological changes in these countries, see annex 2B.) Meanwhile, in Sub-Saharan Africa, the number of the poor declined by only 4 million, a 1.6 percentage point change that leaves the average regional headcount ratio at 41.0 percent, which is still high. The share of the poor in Eastern Europe and Central Asia decreased by about a quarter of a percentage point, down to 2.3 percent, while in Latin America and the Caribbean, the share was reduced by 0.2 percentage points, leaving the 2013 headcount ratio at 5.4 percent.

The largest number of the global poor live in lower-middle-income countries (figure 2.5). This is despite the greater average income and lower headcount ratios of these countries relative to low-income coun-

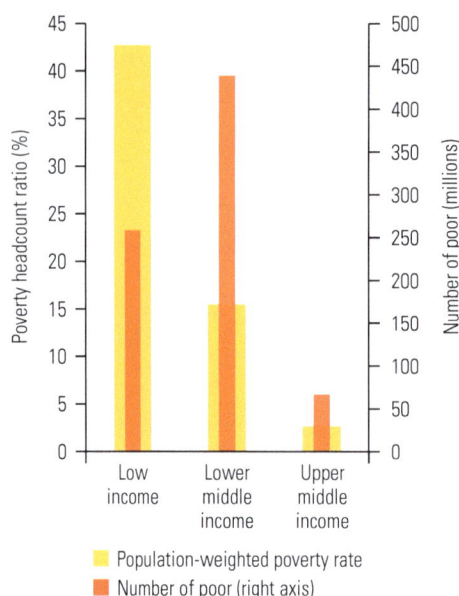

tries. Around 439 million people in lower-middle-income countries live below the international poverty line (the right y-axis in figure 2.5). This is 181 million more than in low-income countries. Driving this result is the fact that some of the most populous countries in the world, with large numbers of poor in absolute terms, are in this lower-middle-income category. More generally, fewer people live in low-income countries, which accounted for 8 percent of the global population in 2013, compared with 40 percent in lower-middle-income countries and 35 percent in upper-middle-income countries.

The countries with the highest poverty headcount ratios and the largest number of the poor are not the same (figures 2.6 and 2.7). All countries in the first category—the highest poverty headcount ratios—are in Sub-Saharan Africa, and only three of them appear in both categories, namely, the Democratic Republic of Congo, Madagas-car, and Mozambique. The red bars super-imposed on the headcount ratios in figure 2.6 show the number of the poor. Among the countries with the highest headcount ratios, at almost 60 percent and above, the Democratic Republic of Congo is the country housing the largest number of poor by far through a combination of an extremely high poverty rate (75.9 percent) and a large population, implying around 55 million poor people. The high rates in Madagascar (78.0 percent) and Mozambique (60.0 percent) result in lower absolute poverty numbers, 17.9 million and 15.9 million, respectively, because of the smaller populations of these countries.

Although over half the world's poor live in Sub-Saharan Africa, four of the top 10 countries by the number of the poor are not in this region, namely, Bangladesh, China, India, and Indonesia (see figure 2.7, where the red bars show the number of the poor). This is because, despite the relatively low headcount ratios, these four countries have large populations. India is by far the country with the largest number of people living under the international US$1.90-a-day poverty line, 224 million, more than 2.5 times as many as the 86 million in Nigeria, which has the second-largest population of the poor worldwide. Thus, Sub-Saharan Africa has one in two of the poor worldwide, while India accounts for one in three (see table 2.1).

Overall, in our sample, 243.5 million people live in countries with poverty headcount ratios above 50 percent, while around 356.0 million live in economies where the ratio ranges from 30 percent to 50 percent. These figures are relevant in so far as a higher share of poverty is often associated with lower average income or consumption among the poor and therefore a wider poverty gap. Thus, in Sub-Saharan Africa, the average consumption of the poor is US$1.16 a day (2011 PPP), which is US$0.74 below the international poverty line.[7] The magnitude of the poverty gap indicates how difficult the eradication of poverty will be in the near future as the World Bank goal of eradicating extreme poverty comes within reach. The gap gives a sense of the urgency and also the effort still required to lift up

FIGURE 2.6 Poverty Headcount Ratios, Top 10 Countries, 2013

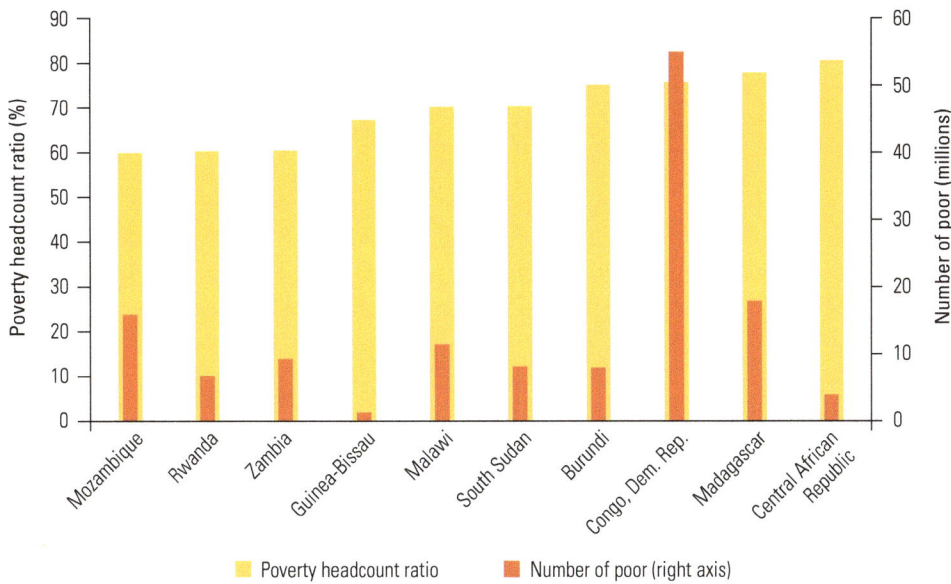

Source: Most recent estimates, based on 2013 data using PovcalNet (online analysis tool), World Bank, Washington, DC, http://iresearch.worldbank.org/PovcalNet/.
Note: Poverty is measured using the 2011 US$1.90-a-day PPP poverty line.

FIGURE 2.7 Number of the Poor, Top 10 Countries, 2013

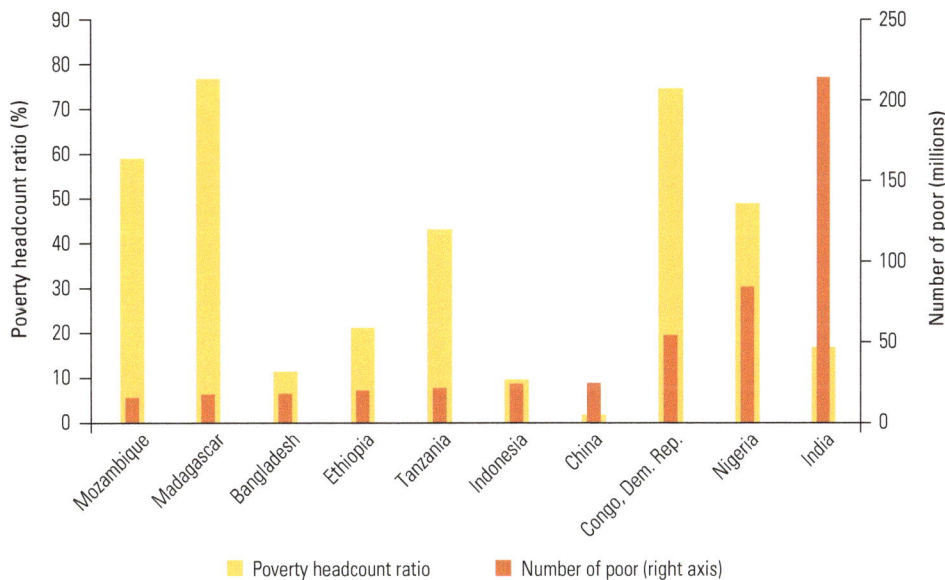

Source: Most recent estimates, based on 2013 data using PovcalNet (online analysis tool), World Bank, Washington, DC, http://iresearch.worldbank.org/PovcalNet/.
Note: Poverty is measured using the 2011 US$1.90-a-day PPP poverty line.

people living below the poverty line, especially those living far below it.

Figure 2.8 shows the downward trends in the global poverty gap and in the headcount ratio over the last two decades. The head-count ratio shows a more rapid decline than the poverty gap. This difference in pace has been particularly marked since 2010. If this difference persists, the downward trend in the headcount ratio may begin to taper off

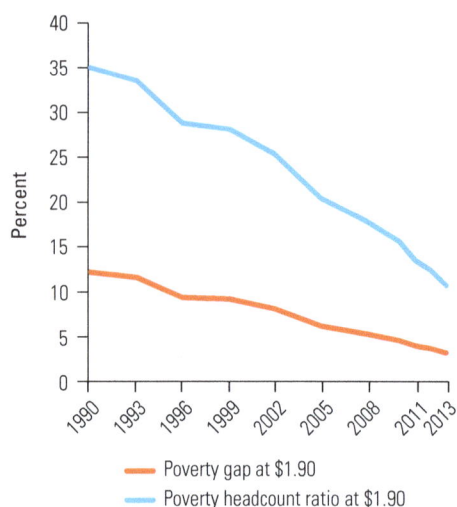

Sources: Annex 2A; most recent estimates, based on 2013 data using PovcalNet (online analysis tool), World Bank, Washington, DC, http://iresearch.worldbank.org/PovcalNet/.

as the poverty gap more slowly narrows. This combination may indicate that it is the relatively less poor that are moving out of poverty. This may have important implication in terms of slower future poverty reductions.

Multiplying the income needed to lift every poor individual out of poverty by the total number of the poor in the world provides a rough indication of the order of magnitude of the cost of ending poverty. This is not meant to be a policy prescription or a judgment on specific current policies but a low-bound approximation of the cost of achieving the poverty goal under stylized and simplifying assumptions, key among them is that the income shortfall to the poverty line is a reasonable initial approximation to the cost of eliminating poverty.[8] While this represented 1.0 percent of the world's GDP in 1990, it would have required less than 0.2 percent in 2013, which is 10.0 percent more than all the official development assistance that year.[9] It is also about 50 percent of the tax revenue estimated to be annually lost through tax avoidance.[10] The income shortfall relative to the poverty line among the worldwide poor is therefore almost negligible in comparison with the global economy. This is a

strong reminder that poverty eradication is well within reach (as also suggested by recent projections; box 2.2) and that a better effort at sharing prosperity would be instrumental in increasing the speed at which the goal is reached. Chapter 3 examines this challenge by providing an assessment of the World Bank's shared prosperity goal based on the most recently available data.

A profile of the poor in the developing world

Exploring the characteristics of the poor is key to a better understanding of the circumstances and contexts surrounding poverty. A large database of household surveys from 89 developing countries provides insights into this issue by facilitating demographic profiles of the poor at the US$1.90 per person per day poverty line and at a higher line of US$3.10 per person.[11] These poverty profiles reveal that the global poor are predominantly rural, young, poorly educated, mostly employed in the agricultural sector, and live in larger households with more children.[12] Figure 2.9 reports the share of the poor who live in rural areas (80 percent of the poor worldwide), work in agriculture (64 percent), are 14 years of age or younger (44 percent), and have no formal education (39 percent). The data also confirm wide regional variations in the distribution of the poor across these characteristics.

Figure 2.10 displays the share of the poor at the US$1.90-a-day and the US$3.10-a-day global poverty lines by urban or rural residence, age category, employment in agriculture or nonagriculture, and educational attainment. Poverty rates are more than three times higher among rural residents than among urban dwellers: 18.2 percent versus 5.5 percent, respectively. Agricultural workers are more than four times more likely to be poor relative to people employed in other sectors of the economy. Educational attainment is inversely correlated with poverty. A small share of primary-school graduates are living in poverty: the share of people who completed primary school but not secondary school and who are living below the US$1.90 poverty line is 8.0 percent. Among those who

In 2015, the World Bank published a projected extreme poverty headcount ratio—9.6 percent of the world's population for that year—using $1.90-a-day poverty line at 2011 PPP. In 2016, the analytical exercise was repeated using the same methodology. The projected global poverty headcount ratio for 2016 is 9.1 percent.

This projection is based on the latest available household survey information on each country and incorporates assumptions that allow past consumption and income to be updated to current levels. Thus, the exercise applied a national accounts–based growth rate to adjust the latest available survey mean income or consumption to 2016. The growth projection of per capita private consumption expenditure was used across the board except for the Sub-Saharan Africa region, where the growth projection of per capita GDP was used instead. Elsewhere, projected GDP growth was used only if growth projections for private consumption expenditure were missing in a given country. In four countries, both GDP and private consumption expenditure were missing; so the average growth rate of per capita GDP during the three most recent years available was used. Empirically, it has been established that, on average, household survey–based growth captures about 87 percent of national accounts based growth.[a] As a consequence, in the application of national accounts–based growth projections to update household survey–based consumption or income means, an adjustment factor of 0.87 was used across the board, except for China and India, where alternative factors reflect the discrepancies between national account– and household survey–based

growth more accurately: 0.72 for China and 0.51 for India. Furthermore, it is assumed that projected growth was distributionally neutral between 2013—the latest year for which poverty is actually estimated, not projected—and 2016. This means that the gains of growth are assumed to have been equally distributed across population groups in each country, for example, among poor and nonpoor households.

This methodological description highlights that poverty projections are associated with additional challenges relative to poverty estimates. This increases the uncertainty around the accuracy of the projections. Producing projections requires that consumption or income data derived from actual observations in every country, for instance, from household surveys, be adjusted to estimate more recent income or consumption. This is so because, in the projected year, 2016 in this case, there is no available household survey from which to draw estimates. Moreover, the growth rates used in this exercise rely on projections rather than observed, revised, and vetted rates for 2016. The further ahead projections look relative to a reference year, the more the assumption that the past is a good measure of the future becomes questionable. Thus, even the growth projections between 2013 and 2016 do not fully capture global and regional shifts, such as the weakening of international commodity prices or the slower growth in Latin America and the Caribbean, in Sub-Saharan Africa, or, more generally, among emerging market economies and low-income economies.[b] For these reasons, poverty projections need to be viewed with extreme caution.

Source: World Bank calculations.
a. Ravallion (2003).
b. World Bank (2016).

have attended university, the share is 1.5 percent.[13] Similar differences are observed if poverty incidence is measured relative to the US$3.10-a-day poverty line.

A complete demographic poverty profile should also include a gender dimension. However, the global poverty database does not contain information on the consump-

FIGURE 2.9 Profile of the Poor, by Characteristics and Region, 2013

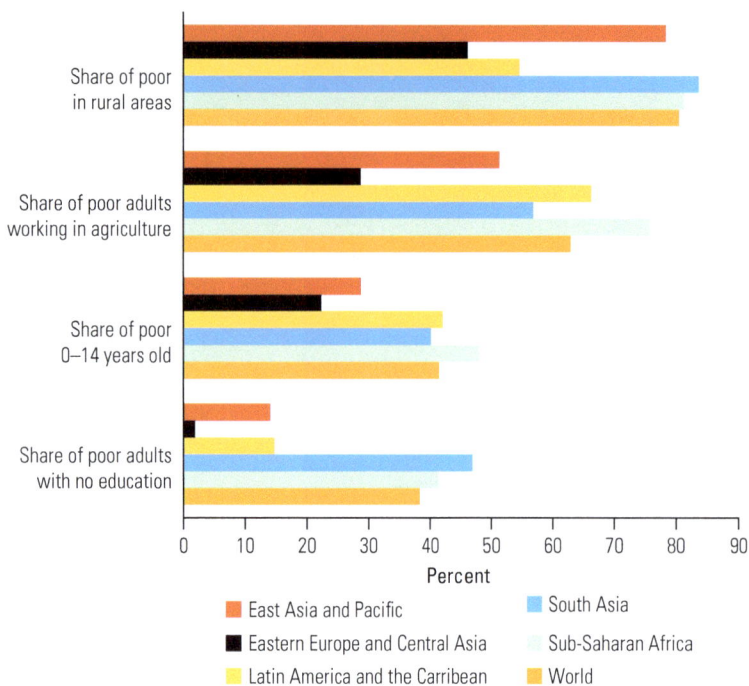

Source: Castañeda et al. 2016.
Note: Poverty is measured using the 2011 US$1.90-a-day PPP poverty line.

FIGURE 2.10 Profile of the Extreme and Moderate Poor, by Selected Characteristics, 2013

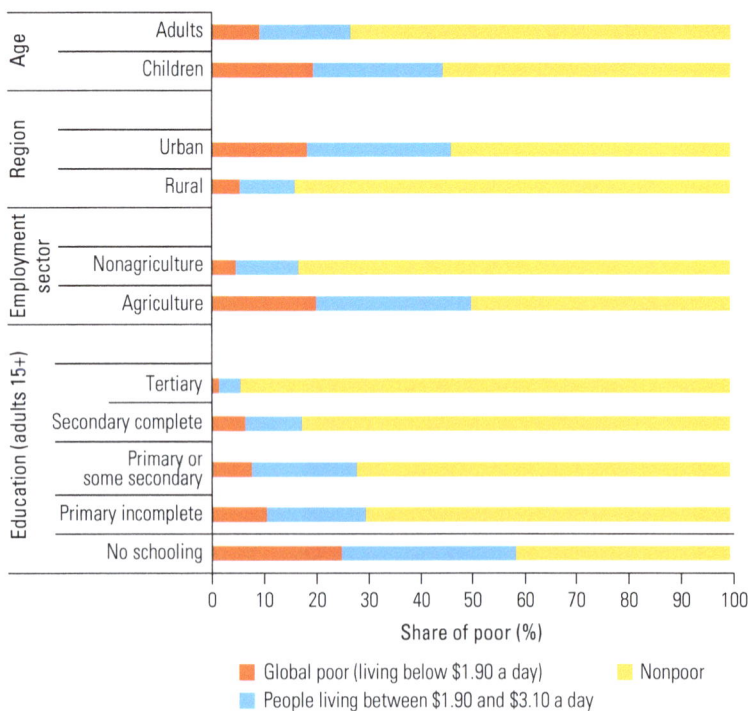

Sources: Castañeda et al. 2016; Newhouse et al. 2016.

tion or incomes of individuals within a household, only on the total and per capita household consumption or income. Without information on the intrahousehold allocation and use of resources, the study of gender poverty trends and profiles must remain limited to differences in poverty rates between woman-headed and man-headed households. Yet, woman-headed households may not be representative of the welfare of many women in developing countries. Women may head a household because they have the means to live independently or because men household members are absent but sending remittances. Women in such households would show lower poverty rates. There are, however, other contexts in which estimates of poverty headcount ratios may be higher in gender terms. For instance, in situations of national or local conflict, households led by widows may be a significant share of all households and present disproportionally high poverty rates. Using the characteristics of household heads does not provide a reliable picture of gender gaps because it overlooks intrahousehold discrimination and uncooperative practices within households in sharing resources evenly and according to each member's needs.[14]

Meanwhile, age profiles confirm that children are more likely to be poor than adults.[15] Children under 18 account for half the global poor in 2013, but less than a third of the sample population (32 percent) (figure 2.11). Younger children contribute especially heavily to the poverty headcount, much more than their share in the world's population.

In Sub-Saharan Africa, children are much more likely than adults to be living on less than US$1.90 a day, and almost half of all the poor on the subcontinent are 14 years of age or younger. The region also contributes the most to global child poverty: 52 percent of the extremely poor children worldwide live in Sub-Saharan Africa. Among countries, the largest contributor is India, where 30 percent of the world's poorest children live.

These estimates of global child poverty are limited. As in the case of poverty among women, they do not account for the intra-

FIGURE 2.11 Age Profile of the Poor, 2013

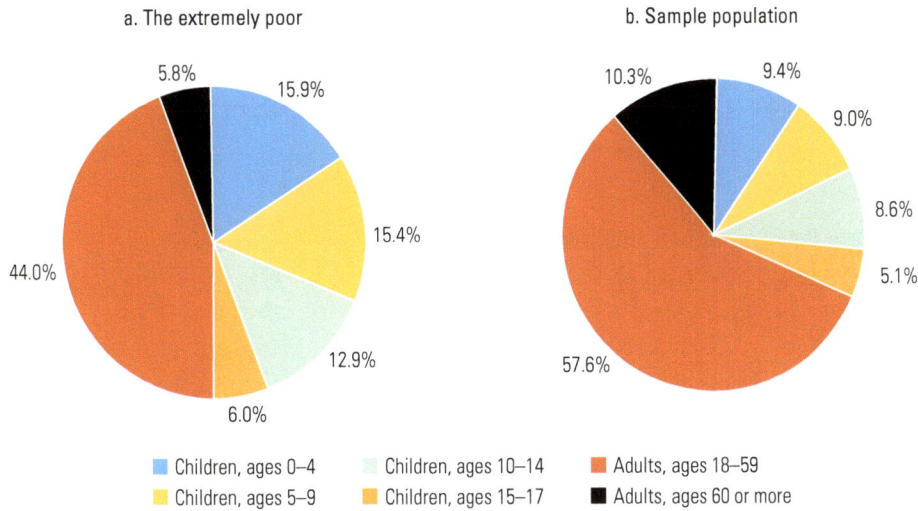

a. The extremely poor

5.8%
15.9%
15.4%
12.9%
6.0%
44.0%

b. Sample population

10.3%
9.4%
9.0%
8.6%
5.1%
57.6%

■ Children, ages 0–4   ■ Children, ages 10–14   ■ Adults, ages 18–59
■ Children, ages 5–9   ■ Children, ages 15–17   ■ Adults, ages 60 or more

Source: Newhouse et al. 2016.

household allocation and use of resources. They also assume identical physical needs across household members of different ages and ignore the scale economies associated with larger households.[16] Strong assumptions are required to address intrahousehold allocation issues with the information currently available through household surveys.[17] Variations in physical need and scale economies, however, are often addressed through the use of equivalence scales. Moreover, the US$1.90-a-day threshold can be adapted to account for the fact that the international per capita poverty standard does not reflect differing individual needs.[18] While there is widespread agreement on the benefit of making such adjustments, there is no agreement on how to do this properly. Nonetheless, recent evidence using alternative equivalence scales, economies of scale, and possible adjustments of the US$1.90 international poverty line confirms beyond a doubt that children exhibit higher poverty rates than adults.[19]

Annex 2A

Historical global and regional poverty estimates

TABLE 2A.1 Historical Trends, World Extreme Poverty Estimates, 1990–2013

Year	Poverty line (PPP US$/day)	Headcount ratio (%)	Poverty gap (%)	Squared poverty gap (%)	Poor (millions)	Population (millions)
1990	1.9	35.0	12.2	5.8	1,850.1	5,283.1
1993	1.9	33.5	11.6	5.5	1,855.4	5,537.8
1996	1.9	28.8	9.4	4.4	1,666.3	5,788.6
1999	1.9	28.1	9.2	4.3	1,692.9	6,034.9
2002	1.9	25.3	8.1	3.8	1,588.1	6,274.7
2005	1.9	20.4	6.2	2.9	1,327.5	6,514.0
2008	1.9	17.8	5.3	2.4	1,205.6	6,758.3
2010	1.9	15.6	4.6	2.1	1,077.5	6,923.7
2011	1.9	13.5	4.0	1.8	946.3	7,006.9
2012	1.9	12.4	3.7	1.7	880.9	7,089.5
2013	1.9	10.7	3.2	1.5	766.6	7,176.1

Source: Most recent estimates, based on 2013 data using PovcalNet (online analysis tool), World Bank, Washington, DC, http://iresearch.worldbank.org/PovcalNet/.

TABLE 2A.2 Historical Trends, Regional Poverty Headcount Ratios, 1990–2013

Percent

Region	1990	1993	1996	1999	2002	2005	2008	2010	2011	2012	2013
East Asia and Pacific	60.2	52.4	39.4	37.2	29.0	18.4	14.9	11.1	8.4	7.1	3.5
Eastern Europe and Central Asia	4.0	6.9	7.8	8.1	6.3	5.1	3.3	3.0	2.7	2.6	2.3
Latin America and the Caribbean	15.8	14.4	14.2	13.9	13.0	9.8	7.1	6.5	6.0	5.6	5.4
Middle East and North Africa	6.0	5.6	4.8			3.0	2.8				
South Asia	44.6	44.8	40.3		38.5	33.6	29.4	24.6	19.9	17.5	15.1
Sub-Saharan Africa	54.3	58.4	57.7	57.1	55.6	50.0	47.0	45.7	44.1	42.6	41.0
World	35.0	33.5	28.8	28.1	25.3	20.4	17.8	15.6	13.5	12.4	10.7

Source: Most recent estimates, based on 2013 data using PovcalNet (online analysis tool), World Bank, Washington, DC, http://iresearch.worldbank.org/PovcalNet/.

TABLE 2A.3 Historical Trends, Number of Extreme Poor, by Region, 1990–2013

Millions

Region	1990	1993	1996	1999	2002	2005	2008	2010	2011	2012	2013
East Asia and Pacific	965.9	876.8	683.8	669.0	535.1	349.2	288.2	218.2	166.9	141.8	71.0
Eastern Europe and Central Asia	18.2	32.2	36.3	37.8	29.3	23.8	15.5	14.2	13.0	12.2	10.8
Latin America and the Caribbean	71.2	68.3	70.7	72.2	70.6	55.6	41.9	38.8	36.4	34.1	33.6
Middle East and North Africa	13.7	13.6	12.4			9.2	6.7				
South Asia	505.0	541.5	517.0		552.4	508.3	464.7	400.3	327.9	293.3	256.2
Sub-Saharan Africa	276.1	323.1	346.1	371.3	391.3	381.5	389.1	399.1	395.7	393.1	388.7
World	1,850.1	1,855.4	1,666.3	1,692.9	1,588.1	1,327.5	1,205.6	1,077.5	946.3	880.9	766.6

Source: Most recent estimates, based on 2013 data using PovcalNet (online analysis tool), World Bank, Washington, DC, http://iresearch.worldbank.org/PovcalNet/.

Annex 2B

Technical note: global poverty measurement using 2013 data

The new 2016 round of global poverty measures based on the most recent available data incorporates the following changes from the 2015 round of poverty measures. This annex explains changes in the PPPs, the household survey data, the consumer price index (CPI), population data, and national accounts. It also defines the regions used throughout the report.

Changes in purchasing power parities

In the new 2016 round, the poverty measures for all countries are based on consumption PPPs from the 2011 round of data collection by the International Comparison Program; see ICP (International Comparison Program) (database), World Bank, Washington, DC, http://siteresources. world bank.org/ICPEXT/Resources/ICP _2011.html. The PPP exchange rates include benchmark countries where actual price surveys were conducted, as well as regression-based PPP estimates where such surveys were not conducted. Details on the regression model for the PPP estimation can be found in World Bank (2015).

Changes in the countries that, in the previous 2015 round, still used 2005 PPPs instead of 2011 PPPs include the following: (1) the 2005 PPPs of Bangladesh, Cabo Verde, Cambodia, and Lao PDR are replaced in this round by 2011 PPPs; (2) for countries in the International Comparison Program region of West Asia, 2011 regression-based consumption PPPs are used in this round.

Changes in household survey data

More than 35 new household surveys have been added to the World Bank's global database, and over 100 other surveys have been updated. See Global Consumption Database, World Bank, Washington, DC, http:// datatopics.worldbank.org/consumption/.

The World Bank's global poverty and shared prosperity monitoring taskforce uses more than 1,200 household surveys from about 150 countries. See, for example, GDSP (Global Database of Shared Prosperity), World Bank, Washington, DC, http://www .worldbank.org/en/topic/poverty/brief/ global-database-of-shared-prosperity.

Changes in the CPI, population data, and national accounts data

The CPI data used for global poverty estimation among 116 countries are taken from the WDI database. See WDI (World Development Indicators) (database), World Bank, Washington, DC, http://data.world bank.org/data-catalog/world-development -indicators.

China and India use rural and urban CPIs (as provided by the national statistics offices). Monthly CPIs are used by 25 countries; most are in the Latin America and the Caribbean region. Another seven countries—Bangladesh, Cambodia, Ghana, Iraq, Lao PDR, Malawi, and Tajikistan—use the implied, that is, the expected CPI.

Population data have been updated as part of the global poverty estimation exercise. Most population data differ from the data of the previous year. Total population changes in 21 countries are significant, that is, they range between 0.5 million and 4.5 million.

National accounts data have also been updated: per capita GDP, private consumption, and expenditure data have all been updated.

Middle East and North Africa region

As part of this new round of global poverty measurement, a detailed reassessment of the 2011 PPPs has been conducted for Egypt, Iraq, Jordan, and the Republic of Yemen. It found that the coverage and quality of the 2011 PPP price data for most of these countries were hindered by the exceptional period of instability they faced at the time of the 2011 exercise of the International Comparison Program. Moreover, the poverty estimates resulting from using alternative regression-based PPPs still seem to underestimate poverty severely in these economies, as well as in Lebanon and the Syrian Arab Republic (but not in West Bank and Gaza).

In the Middle East and North Africa region, the exclusion of Egypt, Iraq, Jordan, and the Republic of Yemen and the lack of recent data on Algeria and Syria imply that the remaining countries account for only a third of the region's population, below the 40 percent threshold of regional population coverage needed to report region-representative estimates.

Adding to this low coverage is the fact that the failure to include data on Egypt, Iraq, and the Republic of Yemen and the lack of recent data on Syria, which are likely to face increasing poverty rates due to instability and civil conflicts, will seriously underestimate regional poverty rates.

As a compromise between precision and coverage, the regional poverty totals and headcount ratios are not reported for the Middle East and North Africa, but an estimate of the number of the poor is included in the global total (based on regression-based PPPs and 2011 PPPs, depending on the country).

Bangladesh's poverty numbers

A detailed assessment of price data in Bangladesh involving the Bangladesh Bureau of Statistics and the Asian Development Bank has recently determined that the price data is of good quality and that the 2011 PPP reflects the purchasing power of the Bangladesh taka relative to the U.S. dollar more accurately than the 2005 PPP does. Therefore, the World Bank has adopted the 2011 US$1.90 a day PPP to measure the extreme poverty index for Bangladesh in the context of global extreme poverty monitoring. According to the new estimates, the proportion of the extreme poor in Bangladesh was 18.5 percent in 2010, the year of the most recent household survey. This represents a significantly lower estimate than the previous one for that year (43.3 percent). Yet, the update of the historical poverty rates in Bangladesh using the US$1.90 poverty line consistently shows the stable and sizable reduction in poverty since 1990 more accurately than the previous series using the 2005 $1.25-a-day PPP poverty line.

China's 2013 survey

A large part of the decline in poverty incidence in East Asia and Pacific in this new round based on 2013 data is attributable to China and Indonesia. The 2013 household survey in China is the first integrated nationwide household survey in that country. This means that it is not comparable with the previous household surveys, in which rural and urban areas were sampled separately. In addition, the most significant change in the 2013 national household survey relative to previous household surveys was the inclusion of imputed rents into income and consumption aggregates for the first time.

In 2012–13, China's poverty rate based on a US$1.90-a-day poverty line (in 2011 PPP) declined by about 4 percentage points, of which half, that is, about 2 percentage points, can be traced to changes in the survey methodology. The actual poverty reduc-

TABLE 2B.1 Poverty Estimates Based on China's Old Survey Methodology, 2013

Coverage	Poverty line, (PPP US$/day)	Headcount ratio (%)	Poverty gap (%)	Squared poverty gap (%)	Poor (millions)
East Asia and Pacific	1.9	5.1	0.66	0.22	102.2
World	1.9	11.1	3.23	1.54	797.8

Sources: Annex 2A; most recent estimates, based on 2013 data using PovcalNet (online analysis tool), World Bank, Washington, DC, http://iresearch.worldbank.org/PovcalNet/.

tion not explained by these methodological changes was therefore 2 percentage points in 2012–13 (table 2.1 in the main text and table 2B.1 above).

The World Bank's poverty estimates on China are based on grouped distributions, which are often not as precise as direct estimates based on the full distribution of household income and consumption aggregates. In 2013, China's poverty headcount ratio under the US$1.90-a-day poverty line was 2.2 percent using individual record data, as confirmed by the National Bureau of Statistics, while it was 1.9 percent based on grouped data.

India's poverty numbers

For this report, as with many other countries, the total poor population in India is based on estimates rather than actual numbers provided through a household survey collected in the year of reference, in this case, 2013. Such estimates are subject to a great deal of uncertainty, which typically arises because of revisions of national accounts in each country. This is also the case in India, on which the estimates for 2013 and the adjusted historical series reflect the government's periodic revisions of the growth in private consumption expenditure and the population. Notwithstanding the revisions, no methodological change underpins the 2013 poverty estimates for India with respect to 2012.

In addition, the poverty estimates for India at the global poverty line are historically based on the Uniform Reference Period consumption aggregate, which involves a 30-day recall among respondents in the recording of all items of consumption. For 2011/2012, this implies a poverty rate of 21.2 percent at the US$1.90 poverty line. Since 2009, however, the Multiple Mixed

Reference Period has also been used in the collection of consumption data. The methodology is closer to best international practice. It relies on recall periods among respondents of 7, 30, and 365 days, depending on the items of consumption. If the consumption estimate derived from the latter methodology had been used to estimate India's poverty rate, the result at the US$1.90 poverty line would have been a substantially lower 12.4 percent in 2011/2012. The application of the methodology is still being tested. Its adoption would eventually lead to a substantial downward revision of the poverty numbers in India.

Definition of geographical regions and industrialized economies

In the past, PovcalNet used the World Bank's income classification back to 1990 to track the Millennium Development Goals. Starting this round, a new regional geographical classification is used. The income-country categories within the six geographical regions are (a) low- and middle-income countries and (b) countries eligible to receive loans from the World Bank (such as Chile) and recently graduated countries (such as Estonia). See "World Bank Country and Lending Groups," World Bank, Washington, DC, https://datahelpdesk.world bank.org/knowledgebase/articles/906519 -world-bank-country-and-lending-groups. See also PovcalNet (online analysis tool), World Bank, Washington, DC, http:// iresearch.worldbank.org/PovcalNet/.

The rest of the high-income economies are listed within the category of industrialized economies, including the following: Andorra; Antigua and Barbuda; Aruba; Australia; Austria; The Bahamas; Bahrain; Barbados; Belgium; Bermuda; British Virgin Islands; Brunei Darussalam; Canada; Cayman Islands; Channel Islands; Curacao; Cyprus; Denmark; Finland; France; French Guiana; French Polynesia; Germany; Gibraltar; Greece; Greenland; Guadeloupe; Guam; Iceland; Ireland; Isle of Man; Israel; Italy; Japan; Korea; Kuwait; Liechtenstein; Luxembourg; Macao SAR, China; Malta; Monaco; Netherlands; New Caledonia; New Zealand; Norway; Oman; Portugal; Qatar; Saint-Martin; Saudi Arabia; Singapore; Sint Maarten; Spain; St. Kitts and Nevis; Sweden; Switzerland; Taiwan, China; Turks and Caicos Islands; United Arab Emirates; United Kingdom; United States; and the U.S. Virgin Islands.

Notes

1. World Bank (1990).
2. The remarkable increase in the availability and use of household surveys has allowed an enhancement in the coverage of global poverty data. During the early stages of global poverty measurement, much depended on imputations based on a few countries. Over two decades later, the World Bank's global poverty and shared prosperity monitoring task relies on more than 1,200 household surveys from about 150 countries.
3. The calculation is in net terms. Of the 114 million reduction in the number of the poor, 31 million correspond to methodological changes implemented in China's 2013 national survey, which, for the first time, incorporated imputed rents and replaces the previously separate rural and urban surveys.
4. This means that the number of the poor was growing more slowly than the total population during this period.
5. Bifurcation is the term sometimes used to describe the fact that half the countries in Sub-Saharan Africa have done relatively well in terms of distributional changes, while the other half have not (Beegle et al. 2016).
6. If the historical experiences of countries that have already eliminated poverty is a good indication of the future, the pace of poverty reduction in some regions should taper off. Some countries that have eliminated poverty experienced poverty rates falling almost linearly to zero, while the rates in other countries declined more slowly. For example, Austria and Japan sustained a linear reduction in both the number and the share of the poor as they neared poverty eradication. If the Latin America and Caribbean region and the Eastern Europe and Central Asia region were to continue their trends in the reduction of the number of the poor in the last decade, they may be close to eradicating extreme poverty soon. This will depend on their success in addressing remaining pockets of poverty.
7. With the exception of the Seychelles, the region's poverty data are based on consumption.
8. The resources needed to help all the poor reach a standard of living at the poverty line through policy interventions would surely be greater than the aggregated income shortfall to the poverty line if realistic assumptions about the administrative costs involved in identifying the poor, targeting, ensuring effectiveness, delivery, coordination, use of country systems, and responding to political economy considerations are taken into account. These costs would certainly render the amount identified in the text insufficient to eradicate poverty even if the allocation was perfect. The analysis here is therefore merely informative about orders of magnitude in relative economic terms.
9. WDI (World Development Indicators) (database), World Bank, Washington, DC, http://data.worldbank.org/data-catalog /world-development-indicators.
10. Zucman (2015).
11. This section draws largely on Castañeda et al. (2016) and Newhouse et al. (2016).
12. Castañeda et al. (2016).
13. Castañeda et al. (2016) analyze the robustness of these results by comparing different lineup methods and different ways to adjust welfare aggregates, weights, and poverty lines. They find only minimal differences. They also check for fixed effects and sensitivity to missing data. The resulting demo-

graphic profile thus paints a robust picture of global poverty.

14. Doss (2013); World Bank (2011).
15. This subsection draws on Newhouse et al. (2016).
16. Lanjouw and Ravallion (1995).
17. Dunbar, Lewbel, and Pendakur (2013).
18. Batana, Bussolo, and Cockburn (2013); Ravallion (2015).
19. Newhouse et al. (2016).

References

Batana, Yélé, Maurizio Bussolo, and John Cockburn. 2013. "Global Extreme Poverty Rates for Children, Adults, and the Elderly." *Economics Letters* 120 (3): 405–07.

Beegle, Kathleen, Luc Christiaensen, Andrew Dabalen, and Isis Gaddis. 2016. *Poverty in a Rising Africa.* Washington, DC: World Bank.

Castañeda, Andres, Dung Doan, David Newhouse, Minh C. Nguyen, Hiroki Uematsu, João Pedro Azevedo, and Data for Goals Group. 2016. "Who Are the Poor in the Developing World?" Policy Research Working Paper 7844, World Bank, Washington DC.

Doss, Cheryl. 2013. "Intrahousehold Bargaining and Resource Allocation in Developing Countries." *World Bank Research Observer* 28 (1): 52–78.

Dunbar, Geoffrey, Arthur Lewbel, and Krishna Pendakur. 2013. "Children's Resources in Collective Households: Identification, Estimation, and an Application to Child Poverty in Malawi." *American Economic Review* 103 (1): 438–71.

Lanjouw, Peter F., and Martin Ravallion. 1995. "Poverty and Household Size." *Economic Journal* 105 (433): 1415–34.

Newhouse, David, Pablo Suarez-Becerra, Martin C. Evans, and Data for Goals Group. 2016. "New Estimates of Extreme Poverty for Children." Policy Research Working Paper 7845, World Bank, Washington, DC.

Ravallion, Martin. 2003. "Measuring Aggregate Welfare in Developing Countries: How Well Do National Accounts and Surveys Agree?" *Review of Economics and Statistics* 85 (3): 645–52.

———. 2015. "On Testing the Scale Sensitivity of Poverty Measures." *Economics Letters* 137 (C): 88–90.

World Bank. 1990. *World Development Report 1990: Poverty.* Washington, DC: World Bank; New York: Oxford University Press.

———. 2011. *World Development Report 2012: Gender Equality and Development.* Washington, DC: World Bank.

———. 2015. *Purchasing Power Parities and the Real Size of World Economies: A Comprehensive Report of the 2011 International Comparison Program.* Washington, DC: World Bank. http://siteresources.worldbank.org/ICPEXT/Resources/ICP-2011-report.pdf.

Zucman, Gabriel, 2015. *The Hidden Wealth of Nations.* Chicago: University of Chicago Press.

Shared Prosperity

This chapter reports on the latest progress achieved in the promotion of shared prosperity worldwide. Shared prosperity is measured as the growth in the income or consumption of the bottom 40 percent of the population in a country (the bottom 40). The larger the growth rate in the incomes of the bottom 40, the more quickly economic progress is shared with the poorer segments of society. Performance on this indicator is examined by country rather than globally.

The latest data suggest that the bottom 40 benefited from income growth in many countries in circa 2008–13 even though the period encompasses the global financial crisis of 2008–09. Overall, the bottom 40 experienced positive income growth in 60 of the 83 countries monitored. This means that 89 percent of the population covered in the dataset resided in countries in which the income or consumption of the bottom 40 grew. A total of 49 countries reported a positive shared prosperity premium: the income growth among the bottom 40 exceeded that of the mean (and therefore, the income growth of the top 60).

Nonetheless, there is no room for complacency. In 23 of the countries, the incomes of the bottom 40 declined, and, in 15 of the countries, the contraction in the income or consumption of the bottom 40 was larger than the corresponding contraction at the mean. In these countries, the living conditions deteriorated more quickly among the bottom 40 than among the rest of the population.

Shared prosperity: where we stand

In 2016, based on data on the most updated spell, circa 2008–13, the World Bank's Global Database of Shared Prosperity reported annualized growth rates among the bottom 40 and the overall mean growth rate for 83 countries.[1] Though the sample covered 75 percent of the world's population in 2013, it included fewer than half the world's countries. The geographical coverage across regions was not uniform. Of the 83 countries, 24 belonged to a single region, Eastern Europe and Central Asia, while East Asia and Pacific, Latin America and the Caribbean, and Sub-Saharan Africa contributed 8, 16, and 9 countries, respectively. In South Asia, 4 countries were covered, and, in the Middle East and North Africa, 2. The population coverage also differed across regions. At the high end, the coverage was 94 percent in the East Asia and Pacific region and somewhat lower in Eastern Europe and Central Asia (89 percent), South Asia (87 percent), and Latin America and the Caribbean (86 percent). The coverage in the Middle East and North Africa was lower, at 32 percent, and the share of the population covered in Sub-Saharan Africa was substantially lower, at 23 percent.[2] The

TABLE 3.1 Shared Prosperity, Circa 2008–13

Region	Countries (number)	Population (millions)	Population (%)	Countries, growth in mean < 0 (number)	Countries, SP > 0 (number)	Country average SP (%)	Countries, SP premium > 0 (number)	Population-weighted average, SP premium (pp)[a]	Countries, Palma premium, > 0 (pp) (number)[b]
East Asia and Pacific	8	2006.2	94	0	8	5.0	7	0.7	7
Eastern Europe and Central Asia	24	479.1	89	10	15	1.5	12	0.3	14
Latin American and the Caribbean	16	622.0	86	3	15	4.1	12	1.4	12
Middle East and North Africa	2	350.1	32	1	2	1.8	1	2.7	1
South Asia	4	1,698.1	87	0	4	3.7	3	−0.4	2
Sub-Saharan Africa	9	948.3	23	1	8	2.7	4	0.6	5
Industrialized countries	20	1,072.4	68	10	8	−1.0	10	0.2	11
World	83	7,176.1	75	25	60	2.0	49	0.4	52

Source: GDSP (Global Database of Shared Prosperity), World Bank, Washington, DC, http://www.worldbank.org/en/topic/poverty/brief/global-database-of-shared-prosperity.
Note: SP = shared prosperity (growth in average income or consumption of bottom 40). pp = percentage point. Population coverage refers to 2013.
a. Population-weighted shared prosperity premiums are relative to the covered population in each region or in the world.
b. The Palma premium (p) is here defined as the difference between the growth in the mean of the bottom 40 and the growth in the mean of the top decile ($p \equiv g_{40} - g_{r10}$).

latter is a stark reminder of the data gaps (see chapter 1).

Though the period encompassed the global financial crisis of 2008–09, the growth in income of the bottom 40 was positive in 60 of the 83 countries, and negative in the other 23 in 2008–13 (table 3.1). Of the world's population, 67 percent (89 percent of the population captured by the Global Database of Shared Prosperity) were living in countries in which the income or the consumption of the bottom 40 grew in 2008–13.[3] This is a substantial proportion, particularly because one-quarter of the world's population is not covered by the dataset and could presumably increase the share.[4] The simple average income or consumption growth among the bottom 40 across all countries monitored was 2.0 percent. If the worldwide estimate is calculated weighing each country's population, the resulting average shared prosperity is more than double the unweighted indicator, reaching an annualized 4.3 percent. The strong performance of highly populated countries such as Brazil, China, India, and Indonesia drive this result.

All regions report positive average income or consumption growth among the bottom 40. East Asia and Pacific, Latin America and the Caribbean, and South Asia showed the best average growth performance among the bottom 40, with annualized rates of 5.0 percent, 4.1 percent, and 3.7 percent, respectively. They are followed by growth rates of 2.7 percent in Sub-Saharan Africa, 1.8 percent in the Middle East and North Africa, and 1.5 percent in Eastern Europe and Central Asia. The bottom 40 in industrialized countries experienced an average contraction of 1.0 percent of income.

Figure 3.1 reports country-specific performance. Countries are ranked by the size of the income growth of the bottom 40 (from largest positive growth to largest contraction) within each region. For each country, the growth in the income or consumption of the bottom 40 is compared with the growth in income or consumption of the mean. The Democratic Republic of Congo showed the largest income growth rate among the bottom 40, an annualized rate of 9.6 percent in circa 2008–13. Five countries saw growth rates of income or consumption of the bottom 40 of 8.0 percent or above, namely, Belarus, China, Democratic Republic of Congo, Mongolia, and Paraguay. A growth rate in the income or consumption of the bottom 40 ranging between 4.0 percent and 8.0 percent was reported in 19 countries: Bhutan, Bolivia, Brazil, Cambodia, Chile, Colombia, Ecuador, Georgia, Kazakhstan, the former Yugoslav Republic of Macedonia, Moldova, Nicaragua, Panama, Peru, the Russian Federation, the Slovak Republic, Thailand, Uruguay, and Vietnam. This ranking suggests that large increases occurred in all regions and among low-, middle-, and high-income countries.

FIGURE 3.1 Shared Prosperity, 83 Countries, 2008–13

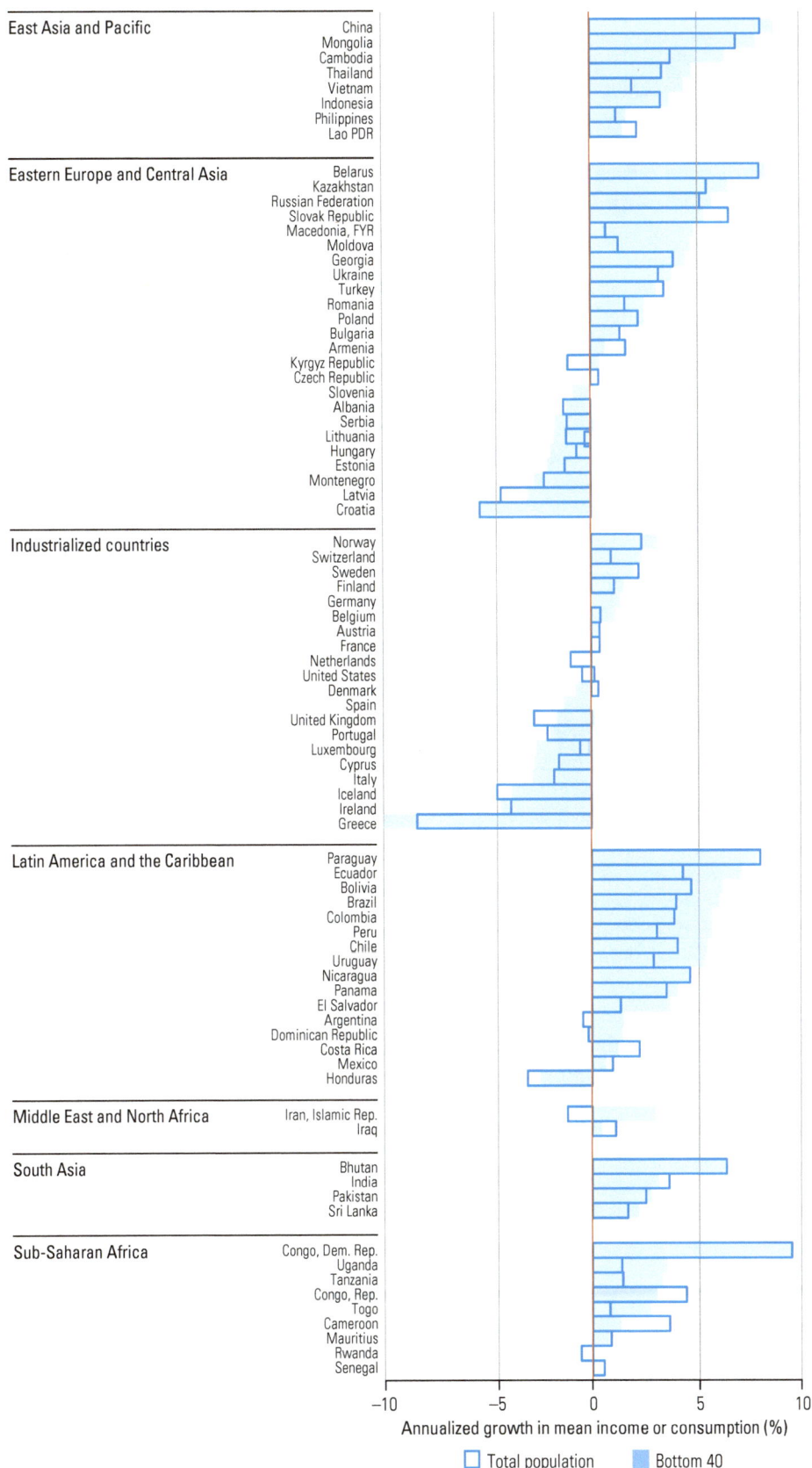

East Asia and Pacific
China
Mongolia
Cambodia
Thailand
Vietnam
Indonesia
Philippines
Lao PDR

Eastern Europe and Central Asia
Belarus
Kazakhstan
Russian Federation
Slovak Republic
Macedonia, FYR
Moldova
Georgia
Ukraine
Turkey
Romania
Poland
Bulgaria
Armenia
Kyrgyz Republic
Czech Republic
Slovenia
Albania
Serbia
Lithuania
Hungary
Estonia
Montenegro
Latvia
Croatia

Industrialized countries
Norway
Switzerland
Sweden
Finland
Germany
Belgium
Austria
France
Netherlands
United States
Denmark
Spain
United Kingdom
Portugal
Luxembourg
Cyprus
Italy
Iceland
Ireland
Greece

Latin America and the Caribbean
Paraguay
Ecuador
Bolivia
Brazil
Colombia
Peru
Chile
Uruguay
Nicaragua
Panama
El Salvador
Argentina
Dominican Republic
Costa Rica
Mexico
Honduras

Middle East and North Africa
Iran, Islamic Rep.
Iraq

South Asia
Bhutan
India
Pakistan
Sri Lanka

Sub-Saharan Africa
Congo, Dem. Rep.
Uganda
Tanzania
Congo, Rep.
Togo
Cameroon
Mauritius
Rwanda
Senegal

Annualized growth in mean income or consumption (%)

☐ Total population   ■ Bottom 40

Source: GDSP (Global Database of Shared Prosperity), World Bank, Washington, DC, http://www.worldbank.org/en/topic/poverty
/brief/global-database-of-shared-prosperity.
Note: The data show the annualized growth in mean household per capita income or consumption. See table 3A.1, annex 3A.

Greece experienced the largest contraction in incomes among the bottom 40, an annualized 10.0 percent decline in 2008–13. Other countries with large contractions in the income or consumption of the bottom 40, at 3.0 percent or more annually, were Croatia, Iceland, Ireland, Italy, and Latvia. The negative performance reflects the problems of a period marked by the 2008–09 global financial crisis and its repercussions, which are still widely felt in Western Europe and in Eastern Europe and Central Asia. In Latin America, Honduras is the only country showing a contraction (2.5 percent annually). In 15 of the 23 countries exhibiting negative growth in the income or consumption of the bottom 40, the contraction was greater than that of the mean (see figure 3.1).

The bottom 40 in relative terms: the shared prosperity premium

The second World Bank goal, enhancing shared prosperity, focuses on growth in the income or consumption of the bottom 40, but a comparison between this and the income or consumption growth of the entire population, that is, the growth of the mean, supplies insights into how the gains of economic growth are shared across society more generally. Such a comparison indicates the extent to which distributional changes favor this group relative to the top 60. The additional growth represents a premium among the bottom 40 relative to the mean, the *shared prosperity premium*. If the premium is positive, the bottom 40 outperforms the average growth rate of total income and of the top 60. If the premium is negative, the overall growth rate and that of the top 60 exceed that of the bottom 40.[5]

Consider the stark comparison between Cambodia and Cameroon, two countries with similar average consumption growth across the population, 3.9 percent and 3.7 percent, respectively, circa 2008–13, but showing different growth values among the bottom 40: high in Cambodia, 6.5 percent, but weak in Cameroon, 1.3 percent. This implies that the growth in consumption of

the top 60 was 2.1 percent a year in Cambodia and 5.3 percent in Cameroon. Such differences produce contrasting effects on inequality trends. While, in Cambodia, the Gini index fell by 4.4 points during the spell, and it rose by 3.7 points in Cameroon.[6]

A comparison of shared prosperity premiums across the countries on which information is available—the monitored sample of 83 countries—describes a generally positive picture. Of the entire sample circa 2008–13, income growth among the bottom 40 was greater than the growth of the mean in 49 countries. In the remaining 34 countries, the bottom 40 fared less well than the rest of the population. Globally, the population-weighted shared prosperity premium is positive, but small, at 0.4 percentage points, similar to the average across countries (0.5 percentage points).

Around 3.5 billion people were living in countries in which the shared prosperity premium was positive in circa 2008–13. This represents 65 percent of the population covered by the sample of countries monitored (5.4 billion people, or 75 percent of the world population). In contrast, almost 1.9 billion people, or 35 percent of the population covered, are living in countries that experienced a negative premium. China and India, which, together, represent 37 percent of the world population and 49 percent of the population covered in the monitored sample, drive much of these aggregate results, with opposed shared prosperity premiums of 0.6 and −0.5 percentage points, respectively.

Regionally, 7 of 8 countries in East Asia and Pacific (almost 100 percent of the regional population) and 12 of 16 countries in Latin America and the Caribbean (74 percent) show positive shared prosperity premiums, while this is true of 3 of 4 countries in South Asia (only 14 percent of the regional population because of India's negative shared prosperity premium). Less encouraging are the results in Eastern Europe and Central Asia, in industrialized countries, and in Sub-Saharan Africa, where positive and negative shared prosperity premiums are observed in similar proportions within each of the three regions. This is also true of the Middle East and North Africa, but this only includes a limited sample of 2 countries.

The average population-weighted shared prosperity premium is positive in all regions, save South Asia, where India's large population and negative premium heavily influences the negative regional average. In the remaining regions, the shared prosperity premiums are positive: under 1 percentage point in East Asia and Pacific (0.7), Eastern Europe and Central Asia (0.3), and Sub-Saharan Africa (0.6) and in excess of 1 percentage point in Latin America and the Caribbean (1.4) and the Middle East and North Africa (2.7). Industrialized countries have a meager shared prosperity premium of only 0.2 percentage points.

The share of countries that experienced a positive shared prosperity premium was practically the same in circa 2008–13 as in 2007–12. Around 60 percent of the countries in the sample reported a positive premium in both rounds. This comparison requires caution, however. Possible changes in the shares of countries with positive premiums respond to changes both in the growth performance of countries and in the composition of the sample of countries, and the impact of the latter can easily dominate that of the former.

Incomes of the bottom 40 and the top 10: the Palma premium

The shared prosperity premium fails to capture much of the variation in incomes that affects the topmost earners. To account for such intragroup differences, especially among the top earners, an indicator comparing income growth among the bottom 40 and the top 10 is used, the *Palma premium*.[7] Similar to the shared prosperity premium, which compares the relative growth in income or consumption among the bottom 40 and the mean, the Palma premium reports the growth rate in income or consumption among the bottom 40, minus the growth rate in the top 10. Even if the top 10 achieves lower income growth than the bottom 40, the income or consumption gain of the average household in the top 10 is typ-

ically larger in absolute terms than the gain of the average household in the bottom 40.

Of the 83 countries in the sample in 2008–13, the income or consumption of the bottom 40 in 52 countries grew more quickly relative to the top 10, while the opposite occurred in the remaining 31 countries. The differences in the growth rates of the bottom 40 and the top 10 are reported in the Palma premium column in table 3.1. The larger number of countries with positive Palma premiums suggests that more countries experienced narrowing income inequality than widening inequality over the period. An examination of the Gini index in a separate dataset—PovcalNet—confirms this (see chapter 4).[8] These encouraging results were driven primarily by three regions, namely, East Asia and Pacific, Latin America and the Caribbean, and South Asia.

Care should be taken in interpreting these results, however, given the well-known shortcomings in household survey data, from which the Palma premium is calculated, namely, the high rates of survey nonresponse at the top; the underreporting of incomes, particularly (but not only) capital incomes; and the use of consumption (instead of incomes) in many countries, thus omitting the greater savings at the top.[9]

Who are the bottom 40?

People in the bottom 40 differ in income or consumption across countries. They also differ in other dimensions of well-being such as the educational performance of children, women's access to health care services, food insecurity and child stunting, access to safe water, and access to the Internet, as recently detailed in the World Bank *Global Monitoring Report 2015/16*.[10]

Moreover, the populations monitored to construct the indicator of the growth in income or consumption among the bottom 40 differ from the global extreme poor. Measured according to the global poverty line of US$1.90 (2011 purchasing power parity [PPP]) per person a day, all the poor in, say, Brazil, China, Honduras, India, or South Africa have similar incomes below the monetary threshold, that is, less than

FIGURE 3.2 The Bottom 40, Brazil, India, and the United States, circa 2013

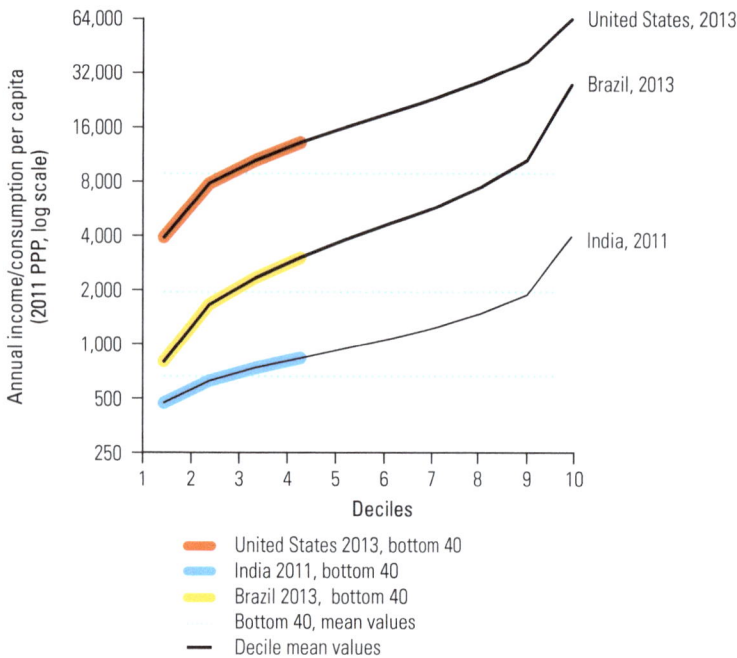

Sources: Updated from Lakner and Milanović 2013; World Bank 2015.

US$1.90 PPP. However, in the case of shared prosperity, income or consumption among the bottom 40 may differ considerably across countries. Figure 3.2 illustrates this by plotting the average income or consumption for each decile of the income distribution in three countries at starkly different levels of development, namely, Brazil, India, and the United States, in around 2013. Clearly, the bottom 40 in these three countries experience different living standards. Thus, the mean incomes of the bottom 40 in Brazil are equivalent to the living standards of the ninth richest decile in India. An analogous comparison holds between the United States and Brazil. Whereas the annual mean income among the bottom 40 in the United States is US$8,861 per person (in 2011 PPP), the bottom 40 earn US$1,819 in Brazil and US$664 in India, about 13 times less than in the United States. Only the top 10 in India earn sufficient average incomes to be part of the bottom 40 in the United States if that is where they had been located.

An immediate consequence of this country heterogeneity in absolute income or consumption across the bottom 40 is that

the group of people on whom the second World Bank goal, the shared prosperity goal, focuses is not the same as the poor globally, on whom the first goal focuses. The most recently updated estimates available show that, while 88.5 percent of the extreme poor in the world are among the bottom 40 in their respective countries, around 11.5 percent of the world's extreme poor are not captured by the national bottom 40 thresholds (box 3.1). This is because the incidence of extreme poverty in the countries in which these people live exceeds 40 percent. Conversely, 76 percent of the people who are among the bottom 40 in their countries are not among the extreme poor according to the US$1.90-a-day global poverty line.

The distinctions between the bottom 40 and the extreme poor are relevant in monitoring poverty and shared prosperity and in policy design. Progress in the extreme poverty goal does not automatically mean progress in shared prosperity and vice versa. The people in the bottom 40 have different incomes across countries (figure 3.3). In some, such as the Democratic Republic of Congo and Togo, all the bottom 40 are also among the extreme poor. In contrast, only a fraction of people in the bottom 40 in Chile, Russia, and Turkey are also living below the international poverty line. A significant share of the bottom 40 in these countries are living on five or more times the equivalent of the global poverty line. Meanwhile, in other countries, the bottom 40 are living on less than five times the global poverty line. This is the case in Armenia, Brazil, Costa Rica, the Kyrgyz Republic, Peru, and Thailand, in which the shares of the extreme poor among the bottom 40 are insignificant. In these countries, monitoring the two World Bank goals separately is necessary to understand with precision the progress in achieving better living conditions among those most in need. In the latter two groups of countries, policy interventions that reduce extreme poverty may or may not be effective in boosting shared prosperity if the two groups—the poor and the bottom 40—are composed of distinct populations. Chapters 5 and 6 examine policy interventions that may boost shared prosperity successfully.

The Bottom 40 versus the Poor

The overlap between the populations in the bottom 40 and the global poor varies across countries. Figure B3.1.1 illustrates how the extreme poor, the bottom 40, and the top 60 were distributed globally in 2013. The full area represents the world population. In 2013, the extreme poor (yellow and red areas) covered about 10.7 percent of the world population. Of the extreme poor, 88.5 percent were within the bottom 40 in their respective countries (red area),

while 11.5 percent were among the top 60 (yellow area). In 2013, the bottom 40 represented 2.9 billion people (red and blue areas). Of this group, 24.0 percent (red area) were among the extreme poor, and 76.0 percent (blue area) were not. This illustrates how the extreme poor are mostly situated within the bottom 40 of their countries of residence. However, it also demonstrates that a large share of the bottom 40 across the world are not among the extreme poor.

FIGURE B3.1.1 **Distribution of the Extreme Poor, the Nonpoor, the Bottom 40, and the Top 60, 2013**

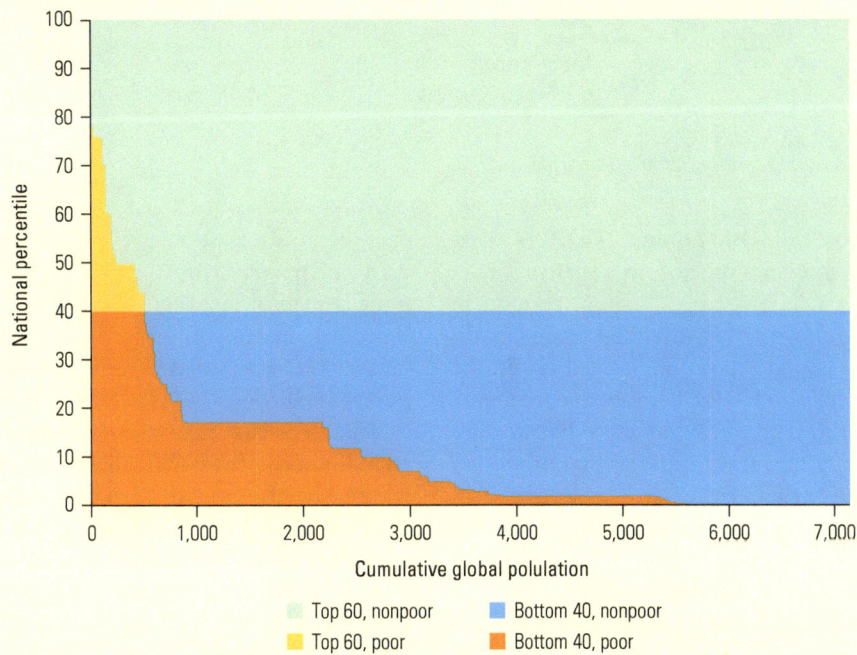

Legend:
- Top 60, nonpoor
- Top 60, poor
- Bottom 40, nonpoor
- Bottom 40, poor

Source: Inspired by Beegle et al. 2014 and updated with 2013 data.
Note: The figure has been constructed from vertical bars representing countries sorted in descending order by extreme poverty headcount ratio (from left to right). The width of each bar reflects the size of the national population. The figure thus illustrates the situation across the total global population.

Is the poverty goal attainable at current levels of growth and shared prosperity?

Economic growth has been sluggish worldwide since the global financial crisis that began in 2008. Figure 1.3 (chapter 1) shows a pattern of slowing growth among the main economic powerhouses, including Brazil, Russia, India, China, and South Africa (together known as the BRICS), the European Union (EU), and the United States. These economies are experiencing double or triple dips in growth. The first dip took place in 2009, when the per capita growth

FIGURE 3.3 Income Group Composition, the Bottom 40, Selected Countries, Circa 2013

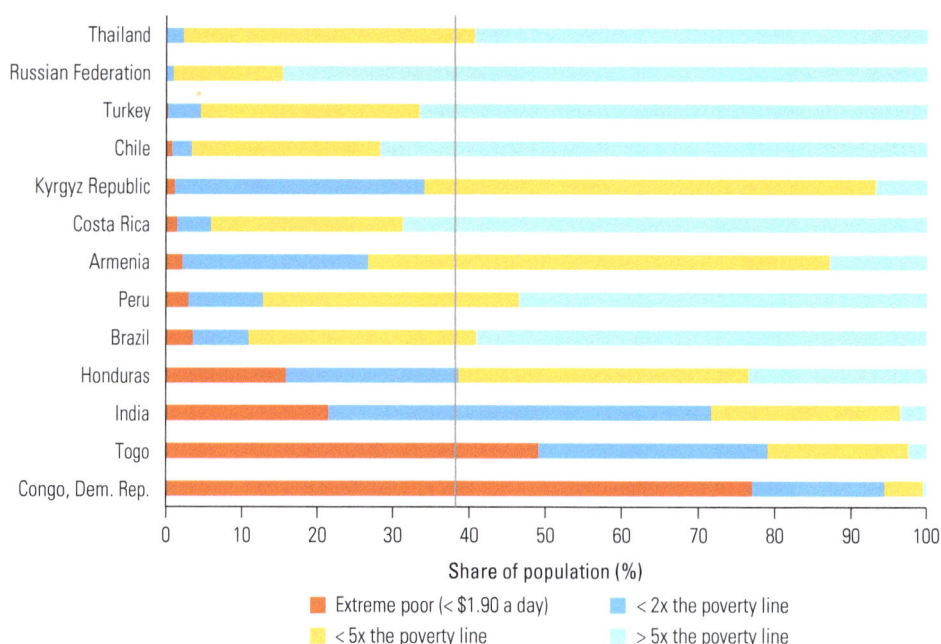

Share of population (%)

- ■ Extreme poor (< $1.90 a day)
- ■ < 5x the poverty line
- ■ < 2x the poverty line
- ■ > 5x the poverty line

Source: Updated from World Bank 2015.
Note: Countries are sorted by increasing poverty headcount ratio.

in gross domestic product (GDP) of these economies plummeted to negative values or zero, followed by a strong rebound in 2010. Growth then declined again, marking a second dip. In the United States, the dip was short-lived because the economy rebounded in 2012, but then dipped once more in 2013 (the third dip). In Europe, the rebound took longer and materialized in 2014. Growth in the BRICS economies has been slowing since 2011.

More recently, the worldwide growth outlook has been revised downward several times, especially among commodity-exporting countries. For example, the World Bank growth update in June 2016 reduced its estimate of global GDP growth for 2017 from 3.1 percent to 2.8 percent relative to the forecast in January 2016 and from 3.2 percent to 2.4 percent for commodity-exporting emerging and developing economies.[11] Longer-term projections also suggest declining growth rates in 2010–30, well below the 2000–10 average rates.[12] These downward revisions of economic growth should not lead to doubts about the ability of growth to reduce poverty and the compelling evidence that growth rather than

changes in distribution has been the main driver of poverty reduction. However, it is a mathematical fact that, in a context of a slowdown in growth, a more equal distribution will be required to achieve the same poverty reduction.

This begs the question of whether the goal of ending poverty is still within reach if such sluggish growth rates and inequality levels were to persist. Simulations have been conducted to address this question (box 3.2). Figure 3.4 shows the results of simulations of the trajectory of the global poverty headcount ratio under various assumptions about the level of growth and changes in the distribution, as measured by the shared prosperity premium (see above). This helps simulate the impact that changes in the shared prosperity premium have on the global headcount ratio over time. Assuming, in these simulations, that every economy continues to grow at the rate of the 10 years leading up to 2013, the poverty goal can only be reached with a positive shared prosperity premium (panel a, figure 3.4). This means that the bottom 40 needs to grow on average more quickly than the mean. The solid line in panel a, figure 3.4,

BOX 3.2 Simulating Poverty Trajectories

The simulations in figure 3.4 begin with the most updated household surveys in 2013.[a] In the simulations up to 2030, country mean income is assumed to grow at a constant country-specific rate based on historic growth rates in the national accounts, adjusted for the observed differences between the national accounts and the growth shown in household surveys. For the historic growth rates, two periods are presented here: the 10 years and 20 years leading up to 2013. For country population, United Nations projections are used.[b] Different distributional changes defined by the shared prosperity premium are incorporated. This premium is defined as the difference between the growth of the bottom 40 and the growth in the mean, and it can be positive (the pro-poor scenario) or negative (the pro-rich scenario). The different headcount trajectories correspond to a single value for the shared prosperity premium imposed on all countries. A linear growth incidence curve is assumed so as to specify the distributional change fully, which, for simplicity, is imposed on all countries regardless of past performance. This is only one of the possible assumptions about the nature of the pro-poor growth that could take place in the future among the infinite ways one might attain a given positive shared prosperity premium consistent with a specific growth rate in the mean. The report website incorporates an interactive online tool that allows users to produce their own simulations independently by choosing a growth rate for the mean across countries and for the shared prosperity premium. The Stata program developed for these simulations is also publicly available on the website. This program can be used with both grouped and microdata and accommodates a range of functional forms of the growth incidence curve.

Source: Lakner, Negre, and Prydz 2014.
a. See Lakner, Negre, and Prydz (2014) for details on the methodology. These household surveys are also used in the estimation of the regional and global poverty headcount ratios reported in this chapter and in chapter 2.
b. Health Nutrition and Population Statistics (database), World Bank, Washington, DC, http://databank.worldbank.org/data/reports.aspx?source=health-nutrition-and-population-statistics.

shows the distribution-neutral scenario, which is the poverty trajectory without any distributional change, that is, if the growth of the bottom 40 and the growth of the mean are equal. Without distributional changes, more than 4 percent of the world's population are projected to be poor in 2030, above the World Bank 3 percent goal.

Under a scenario whereby growth is more inclusive, the global poverty headcount is simulated to reach less than 3 percent in 2030. This would be achieved through a shared prosperity premium of 1 percentage point, that is, a scenario whereby the growth in the income of the bottom 40 exceeds, on average, the growth in the income of the mean by 1 percentage point worldwide. If the premium were 2 percentage points, the goal of a 3 percent global headcount ratio would be achieved by 2025. It is important

to be clear that this is the analytical result from a set of simulations. However, in practice, this does not mean that every country must improve the distribution of incomes to achieve the poverty goal by 2030. The result indicates that, under current average growth trajectories, reductions in inequality will be key to reaching the poverty goal by 2030. This is so under specific assumptions about how economic growth and the related distributive changes will occur up to 2030. For the poverty goal to be accomplished by 2030, improvements in the distribution of incomes need to take place among countries in which there are high numbers of poor, relatively wide inequality levels, and weak economic growth.

These simulations offer a good indication of the challenges ahead. Under a scenario based on the 10-year historic growth

FIGURE 3.4 Boosting Shared Prosperity and Ending Poverty, 2013–30

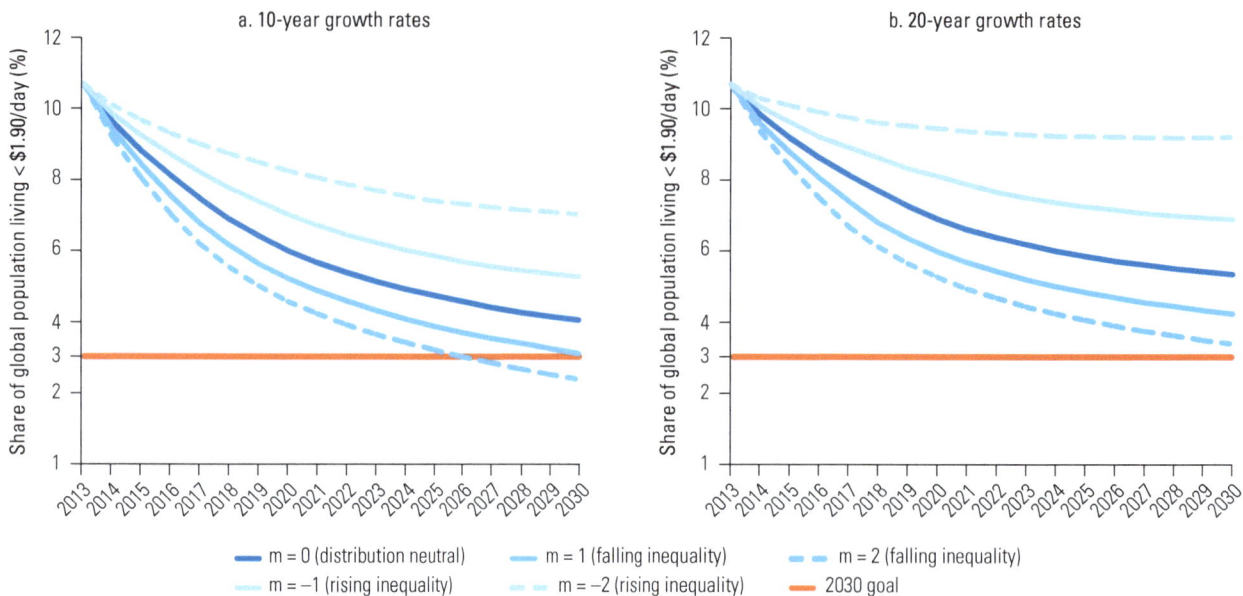

a. 10-year growth rates

b. 20-year growth rates

Legend:
- m = 0 (distribution neutral)
- m = 1 (falling inequality)
- m = 2 (falling inequality)
- m = −1 (rising inequality)
- m = −2 (rising inequality)
- 2030 goal

Source: Updated results based on Lakner, Negre, and Prydz 2014.
Note: m = the assumed shared prosperity premium, that is, the growth in income or consumption among the bottom 40, minus the growth in income or consumption at the mean. For example, m = 2 indicates that the growth in income among the bottom 40 exceeds the growth in income at the mean in each country by 2 percentage points.

rates, a shared prosperity premium of at least 1 percentage point would be needed to achieve the poverty goal by 2030. This is twice the average level of shared prosperity premiums observed between 2008 and 2013 (0.5). This stresses the importance of accelerating the sharing of prosperity especially within countries having large numbers of the extreme poor. Pro-rich scenarios with negative shared prosperity premiums, that is, the income growth of the mean exceeds that of the bottom 40, show that the 3 percent goal in the global headcount ratio would not be reached by 2030.

Panel b in figure 3.4 shows that the simulations based on the country-specific growth rates over the last 20 years before 2013 (which, on average, are lower than the 10-year historic growth rates) require an even greater shared prosperity premium to achieve the poverty goal. For instance, under the distribution-neutral growth path, the projected poverty headcount in 2030 is over 5 percent with the 20-year growth rates, compared with 4 percent with the last 10-year growth rates. Indeed, the average shared prosperity premium of 1 percentage point will not fulfill the World Bank goal by

2030 if the average 20-year growth rates persist until 2030.

Based on these simulations, the goal of eliminating extreme poverty by 2030 cannot be achieved unless prosperity is shared more quickly, growth rates are greater than the 10- and 20-year historical averages used in the simulations, or both. Nonetheless, this is entirely possible, particularly because these findings are simulations, not predictions.[13]

Conclusions: continued progress, but no room for complacency

The diagnosis of shared prosperity in the countries on which data are available circa 2008–13 is fairly favorable in terms of both the headline indicator of growth in income or consumption among the bottom 40 and the shared prosperity premium. In 60 of the 83 countries on which it is possible to construct these indicators, there has been progress toward achieving shared prosperity, and, in 49 countries, the shared prosperity premium has been positive. This means that 89 percent and 65 percent of the population covered in this sample are living in countries showing positive advances in shared prosperity or in the shared prosperity premium, respectively. The Palma premium, which measures the difference between the bottom 40 and the top 10 in average income growth, is positive in 52 of the 83 (or 67 percent of the population covered in the sample).

This suggests that the number of countries experiencing improvements in the living conditions of the bottom 40 and declining relative income inequality is greater than the number of countries experiencing deterioration in living conditions and rising inequality. This is confirmed through an examination of the Gini index from a separate dataset, PovcalNet (see chapter 4).[14] This progress is all the more significant given that it has taken place in a period marked by the global financial crisis of 2008–09, the magnitude of which had not been seen since the Great Depression of the 1930s. There was also a crisis involving spikes in food prices in 2008 and 2010 with profound effects on developing countries.

Nonetheless, it is a source of concern that 40 percent of the population covered in the sample is living in countries where income or consumption is growing more quickly among the top 60 than among the bottom 40, and a 10th of the population covered in the sample is living in countries in which income among the bottom 40 is contracting. This reinforces the need for prudential macroeconomic policies to prevent such large systemic crises, as well as policy interventions that raise income-earning opportunities among the poor, enable their human capital accumulation, and protect them from risks (see chapters 5 and 6).

Another source of concern is the small value of shared prosperity. While the average growth of income and consumption among the bottom 40 worldwide was 2.0 percent circa 2008–13 (4.3 percent if the data are population-weighted), the average shared prosperity premium was only 0.5 percent during the same spell (or 0.4 percent if the data are population-weighted). Is this average in the premium sufficient to support large reductions in inequality and poverty so as to achieve the World Bank's twin goals by 2030? Simulations in this chapter suggest that greater prosperity sharing will be required to end poverty by 2030.

Behind the global aggregates lie large regional differences and large differences within each region. Among high-income countries, Greece has experienced a contraction of 10.0 percent a year in the incomes of the bottom 40, while, in Eastern Europe and Central Asia, Belarus has reported a rise in the incomes of the bottom 40 in excess of an annualized 8.0 percent. In Latin America and the Caribbean, the incomes of the bottom 40 contracted by more than 2.5 percent in Honduras, while, in Paraguay, they expanded by 8.0 percent annually. In Sub-Saharan Africa, the annualized growth in consumption among the bottom 40 averaged 9.6 percent in the Democratic Republic of Congo during 2008–13.

The results reported here are subject to significant caveats on data quality, particularly the accuracy of the income and consumption data on the top of the distribution, which is known to be severely underrepresented in the household surveys used in this monitoring exercise. Information available in the World Wealth and Income Database suggests that accounting for better information on top incomes (typically by accessing income tax data) can change trend conclusions across countries (also see box 4.5, chapter 4).[15] Furthermore, regarding data availability, it is worth stressing that before the results of this monitoring exercise can be truly global, around 25 percent of the world's population will need to be included in the Global Database of Shared Prosperity.[16]

Annex 3A

Shared prosperity estimates based on the latest surveys, by country, circa 2008–13

TABLE 3A.1 Shared Prosperity Estimates, Circa 2008–13

Country	Period[a]	Type[b]	Annualized growth in mean consumption or income per capita (%)[c, d]		Mean consumption or income per capita (US$ a day PPP)[c]			
					Baseline		Most recent year	
			Bottom 40	Total population	Bottom 40	Total population	Bottom 40	Total population
Albania	2008–12	c	−1.22	−1.31	4.28	7.81	4.08	7.41
Argentina[e]	2009–14	i	1.51	−0.43	6.45	19.70	6.95	19.28
Armenia	2009–14	c	0.69	1.64	3.20	5.76	3.31	6.25
Austria	2007–12	i	0.37	0.39	27.78	52.68	28.31	53.73
Belarus	2009–14	c	8.46	8.16	7.54	13.16	11.32	19.48
Belgium	2007–12	i	1.14	0.44	25.79	46.88	27.29	47.92
Bhutan	2007–12	c	6.53	6.47	2.58	5.91	3.54	8.08
Bolivia	2009–14	i	6.32	4.78	3.09	10.83	4.20	13.69
Brazil	2009–14	i	6.14	4.07	3.96	15.18	5.34	18.53
Bulgaria	2007–12	i	1.29	1.37	6.77	14.70	7.22	15.73
Cambodia	2008–12	c	6.52	3.89	2.39	4.60	3.08	5.36
Cameroon	2007–14	c	1.33	3.71	1.56	4.08	1.71	5.27
Chile	2009–13	i	5.57	4.13	6.16	20.14	7.65	23.68
China	2008–12	C	8.87	8.23	—	—	—	—
Colombia	2009–14	i	5.80	3.97	3.00	12.20	3.98	14.82
Congo, Dem. Rep.	2004–12	c	9.58	9.63	0.29	0.76	0.58	1.51
Congo, Rep.	2005–11	c	3.07	4.52	1.00	2.96	1.20	3.86
Costa Rica	2010–14	i	1.23	2.24	6.62	20.34	6.95	22.23
Croatia	2009–12	i	−5.40	−5.35	9.97	20.33	8.44	17.24
Cyprus	2007–12	i	−2.75	−1.58	27.10	50.79	23.57	46.91
Czech Republic	2007–12	i	0.15	0.37	15.70	25.81	15.82	26.30
Denmark	2007–12	i	−0.75	0.32	28.65	48.29	27.58	49.05
Dominican Republic	2009–13	i	1.42	−0.18	4.02	12.48	4.26	12.40
Ecuador	2009–14	i	7.25	4.38	2.98	9.58	4.23	11.88
El Salvador	2009–14	i	3.74	1.35	3.28	9.32	3.94	9.96
Estonia	2007–12	i	−2.10	−1.24	12.84	24.56	11.55	23.07
Finland	2007–12	i	1.55	1.07	26.72	46.79	28.86	49.35
France	2007–12	i	0.19	0.39	26.58	51.51	26.83	52.53
Georgia	2009–14	c	4.58	4.00	2.11	5.41	2.64	6.58
Germany	2006–11	i	1.35	0.14	26.51	52.41	28.35	52.79
Greece	2007–12	i	−10.02	−8.40	16.32	34.68	9.63	22.36
Honduras	2009–14	i	−2.53	−3.13	2.48	9.11	2.18	7.77
Hungary	2007–12	i	−1.93	−0.67	10.89	19.32	9.88	18.69
Iceland	2007–12	i	−3.85	−4.56	33.07	58.69	27.17	46.47
India	2004–11	c	3.20	3.70	1.46	2.81	1.82	3.63
Indonesia	2011–14	c	3.84	3.41	2.11	4.82	2.36	5.33
Iran, Islamic Rep.	2009–13	C	3.05	−1.20	6.57	17.41	7.41	16.59
Iraq	2007–12	c	0.46	1.11	3.97	7.00	4.06	7.41
Ireland	2007–12	i	−4.38	−3.88	26.17	50.03	20.92	41.05
Italy	2007–12	i	−2.86	−1.82	21.24	43.54	18.37	39.72
Kazakhstan	2008–13	c	6.65	5.59	5.17	9.13	7.13	11.99

(Box continues next page)

Country	Period[a]	Type[b]	Annualized growth in mean consumption or income per capita (%)[c, d]		Mean consumption or income per capita (US$ a day PPP)[c]			
					Baseline		Most recent year	
			Bottom 40	Total population	Bottom 40	Total population	Bottom 40	Total population
Kyrgyz Republic	2009–14	c	0.40	−1.09	3.08	5.57	3.14	5.28
Lao PDR	2007–12	c	1.53	2.24	1.90	3.84	2.05	4.29
Latvia	2007–12	i	−3.04	−4.33	9.69	22.38	8.31	17.94
Lithuania	2007–12	i	−1.77	−1.16	10.14	20.99	9.28	19.79
Luxembourg	2007–12	i	−2.67	−0.54	38.29	72.80	33.44	70.85
Macedonia, FYR	2009–13	I	4.98	0.73	3.36	9.46	4.08	9.74
Mauritius	2006–12	c	0.76	0.86	5.31	11.02	5.54	11.56
Mexico	2010–14	i	0.66	0.96	3.42	10.29	3.51	10.69
Moldova	2009–14	c	4.84	1.32	4.33	8.76	5.48	9.35
Mongolia	2010–14	c	8.03	7.05	4.01	8.05	5.46	10.58
Montenegro	2009–14	c	−2.72	−2.27	8.64	16.27	7.53	14.51
Netherlands	2007–12	i	−0.01	−0.99	28.06	51.72	28.05	49.21
Nicaragua	2009–14	i	4.71	4.72	2.62	7.54	3.30	9.50
Norway	2007–12	i	3.17	2.39	33.37	58.45	39.00	65.77
Pakistan	2007–13	c	2.81	2.53	2.07	3.81	2.44	4.42
Panama	2009–14	i	4.14	3.58	4.83	17.38	5.91	20.72
Paraguay	2009–14	i	8.01	8.16	3.80	12.68	5.59	18.77
Peru	2009–14	i	5.78	3.11	3.71	11.96	4.91	13.94
Philippines	2006–12	i	1.71	1.22	2.17	6.42	2.40	6.91
Poland	2007–12	i	2.57	2.26	9.68	19.97	10.98	22.34
Portugal	2007–12	i	−1.99	−2.14	12.89	27.97	11.65	25.11
Romania	2007–12	i	2.59	1.62	3.71	8.80	4.21	9.54
Russian Federation	2007–12	c	5.86	5.27	7.60	19.42	10.10	25.11
Rwanda	2010–13	c	0.04	−0.57	0.92	2.76	0.93	2.71
Senegal	2005–11	c	−0.01	0.54	1.30	3.06	1.29	3.16
Serbia	2008–13	c	−1.73	−1.13	7.60	13.44	6.96	12.70
Slovak Republic	2007–12	i	5.48	6.67	12.46	20.27	16.27	28.00
Slovenia	2007–12	i	−0.84	−0.28	20.64	33.44	19.79	32.97
Spain	2007–12	i	−1.32	0.00	17.14	36.25	16.04	36.25
Sri Lanka	2006–12	c	2.21	1.66	2.96	6.80	3.37	7.51
Sweden	2007–12	i	2.04	2.25	26.22	45.14	29.01	50.46
Switzerland	2007–12	i	2.43	0.93	30.49	63.18	34.38	66.19
Tanzania[f]	2007–11	c	3.36	1.42	1.05	2.49	1.23	2.67
Thailand	2008–13	c	4.89	3.47	5.15	12.45	6.54	14.77
Togo	2011–15	c	2.76	0.82	0.89	2.63	0.99	2.71
Turkey	2008–13	c	3.18	3.54	5.94	14.29	6.94	17.01
Uganda	2009–12	c	3.59	1.37	1.28	3.25	1.42	3.39
Ukraine	2009–14	c	3.93	3.29	6.51	10.74	7.89	12.63
United Kingdom	2007–12	i	−1.67	−2.78	23.89	51.10	21.96	44.38
United States	2007–13	i	−0.16	−0.43	—	—	—	—
Uruguay	2009–14	i	5.48	2.95	7.33	21.72	9.56	25.12
Vietnam	2010–14	c	4.51	2.00	3.29	7.61	3.93	8.24

Source: GDSP (Global Database of Shared Prosperity), World Bank, Washington, DC, http://www.worldbank.org/en/topic/poverty/brief/global-database-of-shared-prosperity.

Note: All estimates are in 2011 PPP U.S. dollars. — = not available.

a. Refers to the years in which the underlying household survey data were collected. In cases in which the data collection period bridged two calendar years, the first year in which data were collected is reported. The range of years refers to two survey collections, the most recent survey within the range and the nearest survey collected five years before the most recent survey. For the final year, the most recent survey available between 2011 and 2015 is used. Only surveys collected between three and seven years before the most recent survey are considered for the earlier survey.

b. Denotes whether the data reported is based on consumption (c) or income (i). Capital letters indicate that grouped data are used.

c. Based on real mean per capita consumption or income measured at 2011 PPP using data in PovcalNet (online analysis tool), World Bank, Washington, DC, http://iresearch.worldbank.org/PovcalNet/. On some countries, the means are not reported because of grouped or confidential data.

d. The annualized growth rate is computed as (Mean in year 2/Mean in year 1)^(1/(Year 2 – Year 1)) – 1.

e. Covers urban areas only.

f. Ex ante evaluation of these surveys suggest that they are not comparable. However, the poverty assessment attempted to create a more comparable series and also applied additional methodological techniques to establish comparability and consistency among welfare aggregates.

Notes

1. GDSP (Global Database of Shared Prosperity), World Bank, Washington, DC, http://www.worldbank.org/en/topic/poverty/brief/global-database-of-shared-prosperity.

2. As a consequence, the results on shared prosperity may be affected by selection bias if countries having poorer survey coverage also perform relatively poorly.

3. GDSP (Global Database of Shared Prosperity), World Bank, Washington, DC, http://www.worldbank.org/en/topic/poverty/brief/global-database-of-shared-prosperity.

4. The sample-based average may even underestimate the true share of the population exhibiting positive growth in the income of the bottom 40 worldwide. This is so because the dataset used for this analysis covers 75 percent of the total population. To the extent that the remaining 25 percent includes countries in which the incomes of the bottom 40 grew, the reported average underestimates the true value.

5. The shared prosperity premium is a relative measure in the sense that it analyzes income gains relative to initial income. For an individual with an initial income of US$1.00, a 10 percent increase in income means an extra US$0.10 in income, whereas, for an individual with an income of US$1,000, a 10 percent increase corresponds to an extra US$100. A positive shared prosperity premium means that the relative income or consumption growth rate among the bottom 40 is larger than the relative growth rate in the rest of society. However, this does not necessarily mean that the bottom 40 gain more income in absolute terms. If the initial inequality is wide, the bottom 40 may show above average growth in incomes, but still gain less in absolute terms than the average individual. Chile exhibited a positive shared prosperity premium in 2009–13. The incomes of the bottom 40 grew an average of 1.4 percentage points a year more quickly than the national average. However, this translated into an income gain per capita of only US$1.49 a day among the bottom 40, whereas the entire population received an average extra income of US$3.54 a day. Growth in Brazil and Russia followed a similar pattern. The shared prosperity premium in Brazil was positive (2009–14), at 2.1 percentage points; yet, the bottom 40 gained only an extra US$1.38 a day, while the population as a whole gained an extra US$3.35 on average. In Russia (2007–12), a small positive shared prosperity premium translated into a gain of US$2.50 among the bottom 40 and a gain of US$5.69 at the national mean. The more unequal a country is initially, the less effective a positive shared prosperity premium becomes in offsetting inequality. A more unequal country is also much more likely to have a positive shared prosperity premium. If the bottom 40 are quite poor, then every extra US$0.01 will make a large difference in the growth rate. Conversely, if the top of the population distribution is quite rich, they will need much more extra income to make a dent in the growth rate in income. A positive shared prosperity premium is a necessary first step in promoting equality, but it is rarely sufficient alone to close the inequality gap.

6. Reported changes refer to 2008–12 in Cambodia and 2007–14 in Cameroon.

7. The premium is named after José Gabriel Palma, a Chilean economist who has long been devoted to the study of inequality. The Palma premium is inspired by the Palma ratio, but they are not identical. The latter is the ratio of the income share of the top 10 to that of the bottom 40, while the premium is defined as the difference in income growth among these groups. See Cobham and Sumner (2016); Palma (2016).

8. PovcalNet (online analysis tool), World Bank, Washington, DC, http://iresearch.worldbank.org/PovcalNet/.

9. The issue of missing top incomes is discussed in more detail in chapter 4, box 4.5. The chapter also discusses evidence based on tax records in selected countries showing that top income shares have increased sharply in recent years. However, this type of evidence is not available in all countries. An increasing income share among the top 1 percent is also not necessarily inconsistent with a positive Palma premium, that is, with more rapid growth in the incomes of the bottom 40 than in the incomes of the top 10.

10. World Bank (2016a).

11. World Bank (2016b).

12. IMF (2015, 2016); OECD (2014); World Bank (2016b).

13. Relative to historic growth rates, the growth rates over the last 10 years have been rather high, especially in developing countries. Furthermore, there are substantial downside risks to any long-run growth projection, for example, because of climate change (Hallegatte et al. 2016).

14. PovcalNet (online analysis tool), World Bank, Washington, DC, http://iresearch .worldbank.org/PovcalNet/.

15 WID (World Wealth and Income Database), Paris School of Economics, Paris, http:// www.parisschoolofeconomics.eu/en/research /the-world-wealth-income-database/. See Alvaredo et al. (2013).

16. GDSP (Global Database of Shared Prosperity), World Bank, Washington, DC, http:// www.worldbank.org/en/topic/poverty/brief /global-database-of-shared-prosperity.

References

Alvaredo, Facundo, Anthony B. Atkinson, Thomas Piketty, and Emmanuel Saez. 2013. "The Top 1 Percent in International and Historical Perspective." *Journal of Economic Perspectives* 27 (3): 3–20.

Beegle, Kathleen, Pedro Olinto, Carlos E. Sobrado, Hiroki Uematsu, and Yeon Soo Kim. 2014. "Ending Extreme Poverty and Promoting Shared Prosperity: Could There Be Trade-Offs between These Two Goals?" *Inequality in Focus* 3 (1): 1–6.

Cobham, Alex, and Andy Sumner. 2016. "Is It All About the Tails? The Palma Measure of Income Inequality." Center for Global Development Working Paper 343, Center for Global Development, Washington, DC.

Hallegatte, Stephane, Mook Bangalore, Laura Bonzanigo, Marianne Fay, Tomaro Kane, Ulf Narloch, Julie Rozenberg, David Treguer, and Adrien Vogt-Schilb. 2016. *Shock Waves: Managing the Impacts of Climate Change on Poverty.* Climate Change and Development Series. Washington, DC: World Bank.

Hoy, Chris, and Emma Samman. 2015. "What If Growth Had Been as Good for the Poor as Everyone Else?" Report (May), Overseas Development Institute, London.

IMF (International Monetary Fund). 2015. *World Economic Outlook, October 2015: Adjusting to Lower Commodity Prices.* World Economic and Financial Surveys Series. Washington, DC: IMF.

———. 2016. "Subdued Demand, Diminished Prospects." World Economic Outlook Update, January 19, IMF, Washington, DC.

Lakner, Christoph, and Branko Milanović. 2013. "Global Income Distribution: From the Fall of the Berlin Wall to the Great Recession." Policy Research Working Paper 6719, World Bank, Washington, DC.

Lakner, Christoph, Mario Negre, and Espen Beer Prydz. 2014. "Twinning the Goals: How Can Shared Prosperity Help to Reduce Global Poverty?" Policy Research Working Paper 7106, World Bank, Washington, DC.

OECD (Organisation for Economic Co-operation and Development). 2014. *OECD Economic Outlook.* Vol. 2014/2 (November). Paris: OECD.

Palma, José Gabriel. 2016. "Measuring Income Inequality: Comments on 'Do Nations Just Get the Inequality They Deserve? The "Palma Ratio" Reexamined.'" In *Regions and Regularities*, vol. 2 of *Inequality and Growth: Patterns and Policy*, edited by Basu Kaushik and Joseph E. Stiglitz, 35–97. International Economic Association Series. London: Palgrave Macmillan.

World Bank. 2015. *A Measured Approach to Ending Poverty and Boosting Shared Prosperity: Concepts, Data, and the Twin Goals.* Policy Research Report. Washington, DC: World Bank.

———. 2016a. *Global Monitoring Report 2015/16: Development Goals in an Era of Demographic Change.* Washington, DC: World Bank.

———. 2016b. *Global Economic Prospects, June 2016: Divergences and Risks.* Washington, DC: World Bank.

Inequality

4

Chapter 4 first explains why inequality of outcomes—specifically, the inequality in income or consumption expenditure—matters both by itself and in the context of reducing poverty. Second, it documents trends in income inequality, distinguishing between global, between-, and within-country inequalities. In doing so, it relies on a recent and comprehensive sample of countries.

Evidence points to several facts, some largely acknowledged, others likely to surprise. Fact number one: global inequality—the inequality among all citizens worldwide, regardless of country of residence—increased from the industrial revolution through the 1980s. Fact number two: an exceptional period of falling global inequality has been observed since the early 1990s, which has been especially marked since 2008. Fact number three: global inequality is wider today than it was in the 1820s, despite the recent reduction. Fact number four: most of the recent reduction in global inequality derives from the convergence of income among countries mostly because of the rapid growth in populous developing countries, notably China and India. Fact number five: the share of income going to the top 1 percent is known to have increased in many countries on which information is available. Fact number six: within-country inequality for the average country, that is, considering the country-specific trends in all countries, only started to narrow in 1998. Fact number seven: for every country showing an increase in the Gini index of more than one Gini point between 2008 and 2013, there are more than two other countries showing a reduction in the Gini by the same amount. And fact number eight: while inequality may certainly widen, it can also narrow. Despite all these facts, inequality remains unacceptably high: the Gini exceeds 50 in several countries, and, in Haiti and South Africa, it even exceeds 60.

Inequality matters

The strong progress in poverty reduction and shared prosperity that took place over the first decade of the 2000s is at risk because of the global slowdown in growth. Indeed, the World Bank goal of eliminating extreme poverty by 2030 cannot be achieved in the current global context without significant shifts in within-country inequalities. Poverty reduction in a country can typically be decomposed into higher average growth, a reduction in inequality, or a combination of the two.[1] So, to achieve the same poverty reduction during a slowdown in growth, a more equal distribution is required.

Inequality is the thematic focus of this year's report. Addressing inequality because it slows down poverty reduction implies an instrumental concern for inequality, that is, addressing inequality is only a means to confront another problem, namely, absolute poverty. This report examines inequality because of this instrumental concern, but also for intrinsic reasons. Individuals express concern with rising inequality, broadly defined. In fact, their perceptions of increasing inequality—even though objective measures of inequality declined—have been argued to be one of the factors contributing to the Arab Spring (see box 4.2). Furthermore, evidence from experimental studies suggests that individuals do not act exclusively in a purely self-interested manner, but often reveal a deep-rooted concern for fairness in outcomes.[2] Leveling the playing field, that is, reducing inequality of opportunity, therefore relates to notions of fairness and justice and resonates across societies on its own merits.[3]

Inequality in outcomes and inequality of opportunity are intimately connected.[4] While reasonable people might disagree over the desirable level of inequality in incomes or consumption expenditures or whether a particular increase should be of concern, an important reason for caring about inequality in outcomes today is that it leads to inequality of opportunity among the next generation.[5] If families have vastly different economic resources, some children in some families will face an unfair start in life, and public policy will have to make a great effort to overcome these differences in initial conditions. At the same time, reducing inequality of opportunity today reduces inequality of outcomes tomorrow (see chapter 6). The focus is therefore not only on preventing the transmission of poverty and income disparities across generations, but also on the transmission of unfair advantages to the next generation.

Furthermore, narrowing inequality—as in the case of reducing poverty—is compatible with boosting economic growth. *World Development Report 2006: Equity and Development* provides a strong empirical underpinning to the claim that interventions that narrow inequality—whether intended or not—can also be good for growth and long-term prosperity.[6] This type of intervention can boost economic efficiency if markets are missing or imperfect, because they fail to provide credit opportunities, insurance against shocks, or access to prop-

erty rights by the poor, and if institutions are inequitable (disproportionally benefiting the wealthy through, for example, regressive subsidies). To the extent that this efficient redistribution breaks off the intergenerational reproduction of inequalities, it both addresses the roots and drivers of inequality and lays out the foundations for long-term growth, which helps end poverty and expand shared prosperity. Otherwise, societies may fall into inequality traps whereby children in disadvantaged families lack the same opportunities to attend good-quality schools, end up earning less in the labor market, or continue to have less voice in the political process, and the cycle of underachievement persists.

Evidence also suggests that there are no inevitable trade-offs between efficiency and equity considerations. Cross-country studies of the effect of inequality on growth have failed to produce evidence that supports the existence of a trade-off in this case. Rather, they point to inconclusive results (box 4.1). In addition to these macrolevel studies, analysts have also used microlevel evidence to examine equity-efficiency trade-offs associated with specific policies, where they may certainly exist. For example, taxation may create disincentives on labor supply or drive economic activity into informality. In Mexico, efficiency costs in the form of lower productivity and lower growth in gross domestic product (GDP), caused by high social security contributions from formal employment and generous noncontributory social safety nets, are estimated to be on the order of 0.9 percent and 1.4 percent of GDP, respectively.[7] Another classic example is consumer subsidies. While these subsidies are typically intended to protect the consumption of the poor, they often end up disproportionally benefiting the rich, who consume more in absolute terms than the poor. For instance, the International Monetary Fund reports that, in a sample of 32 countries in the Middle East and North Africa, Sub-Saharan Africa, and Latin America and the Caribbean, the richest 20 percent of the population captures more than six times as much of the benefit of fuel subsidies as the poorest 20 percent.[8]

BOX 4.1 Cross-Country Studies of the Effect of Inequality on Growth

A large body of literature uses cross-country data to examine whether inequality is bad for subsequent growth. Conceptually, the effect of inequality might go either way: if higher inequality leads to the more rapid accumulation of savings, it may spur growth; if it leads to suboptimal investment in education or in health care, it may have a negative effect on growth.

Recent research by the International Monetary Fund has claimed that lower inequality in disposable income is associated with more rapid and more durable growth for a given level of redistribution.[a] The robustness of the findings has been questioned, however, because of the presence of weak instruments in the econometric technique, a pervasive issue in this field of research.[b] After accounting for weak instruments, the coefficients turn insignificant; so, it is not possible to draw any conclusion about the effect of inequality on growth, whether positive or negative. Furthermore, the analysis relies on a dataset that extensively imputes inequality measures across countries, thus warranting further validation of estimates as more data are collected.[c]

Previous studies have also found inconclusive results using a wider range of econometric techniques and datasets.[d] *World Development Report 2006* found many examples of specific policies that reduce inequality and are also good for growth, but this sort of evidence has not been confirmed with macroeconomic data.[e] The earliest macrolevel papers used data for a single cross-section of countries and found a negative effect of inequality on growth.[f] Later papers, which used panel data, found positive effects of inequality on subsequent growth.[g] Yet other studies argued for a nonlinear relationship, which could explain these unstable results.[h]

Motivated by the ambiguity of the effect of inequality on growth both conceptually and empirically, a recent set of papers decomposes overall inequality into components that may be especially harmful to growth. In particular, it may be expected that inequality of opportunity is harmful for growth, while the effect of inequalities that arise because of differences in effort may act in the opposite direction.[i] There is some evidence that inequality of opportunity may be bad for growth, at least subnationally. Across U.S. states, inequality of opportunity is found to have a negative effect on growth.[j] A similar effect is found across Brazilian municipalities.[k] Across countries in the world, however, there is no robust evidence of a negative effect.[l]

Source: Ferreira et al. 2014.
a. Ostry, Berg, and Tsangarides (2014); also see Dabla-Norris et al. (2015).
b. Kraay (2015) shows that confidence intervals consistent with weak instruments are much wider. In particular, they include a wide range of positive and negative values for the coefficient on inequality in the growth regression. Kraay examines a number of papers using similar econometric techniques and considers alternative instrument specifications. This methodological critique is not unique to Ostry, Berg, and Tsangarides (2014), but applies to many studies using system generalized method of moments estimators. These estimators are frequently used in cross-country growth regressions.
c. The dataset being used is the Standardized World Income Inequality Dataset (Solt 2016). Jenkins (2015) offers a detailed description of the dataset and the conceptual issues with the cross-country imputations.
d. See the summary by Voitchovsky (2009).
e. World Bank (2005).
f. Alesina and Rodrik (1994); Persson and Tabellini (1994).
g. Forbes (2000).
h. Banerjee and Duflo (2003).
i. The decomposition of inequality into components related to opportunities and effort, respectively, has been suggested by Roemer (1998).
j. Marrero and Rodríguez (2013).
k. Teyssier (2015).
l. Using two global datasets, Ferreira et al. (2014) do not find support for the proposition that inequality of opportunity is bad for growth.

This focus on inequality is not meant to question the critical role of economic growth in improving the living conditions of the poor and, particularly, the bottom 40 percent of the income or consumption distribution (the bottom 40).[9] Voluminous evidence confirms that commonly acknowledged good macroeconomic policies—control of inflation, promotion of competition policy to reduce economic concentration, trade openness, and macroeconomic stability—and good governance are the foundations of sustainable growth, which, ultimately, is good for the poor and the bottom 40.[10] Others have highlighted the importance of investing in human development (improving access, but also quality and the institutional delivery of basic services) and insuring against risks (especially among the poor and those without access to contributive forms of insurance) as additional pillars to support the role of economic growth in poverty reduction. Historic evidence confirms that countries following such strategies have been more successful in achieving a rapid pace and wide breadth in poverty reduction.[11] Bangladesh, Brazil, China, Ethiopia, and Vietnam are some examples providing a compelling illustration.[12]

Empirical evidence using cross-country income data—the most recent and comprehensive covering 121 countries between 1967 and 2011—concludes that the average incomes of the bottom 40 within each country tend to grow at the same pace as the average incomes in the respective country.[13] Figure 4.1 illustrates this empirical finding with the most recently available data. Countries in which growth at the mean is large also show the largest growth in the incomes of the bottom 40. Conversely, countries with negative growth rates in the mean also show declines in the incomes of the bottom 40. Consistent with these two findings, evidence suggests that average income growth appears uncorrelated with changes in the share of the incomes of the bottom 40. Between 1967 and 2011, the average income growth in countries was 1.5 percent a year during a typical five-year period, while changes in the share of incomes of the bottom 40 were close to zero. As a result, some estimates suggest that average income growth explains as much as three-quarters of the variation in income growth of the bottom 40.[14] As countries grow more quickly, the growth of the bottom 40 may be expected to increase as well. Thus, growing the economy, boosting shared prosperity, and reducing poverty are three absolutely compatible goals.[15]

Although economic growth is essential in sustaining improvements in living standards at the low end of the income distribution, growth alone typically falls short of delivering the maximum sharing of prosperity. In the empirical evidence cited above, a quarter of the variation in the growth of the incomes of the bottom 40 across countries derives from sources

FIGURE 4.1 Growth of the Bottom 40 versus Growth at the Mean, 2008–13

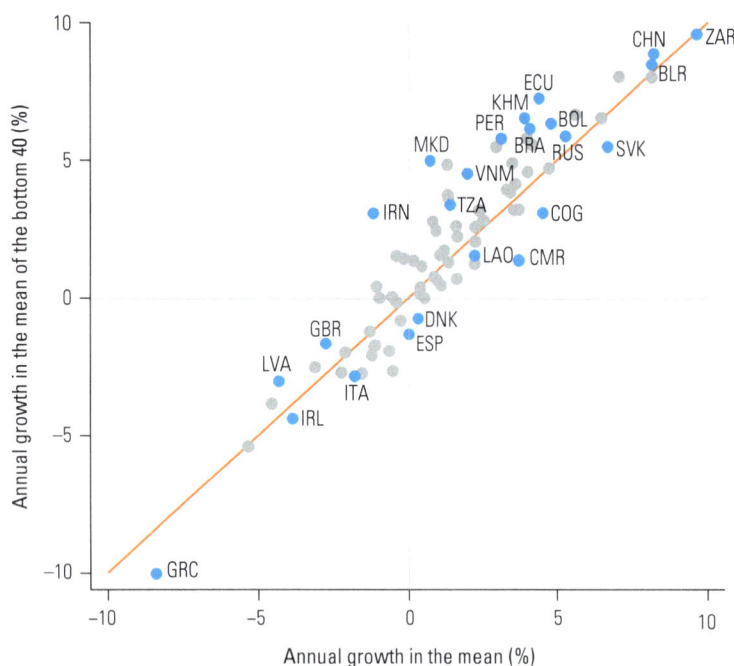

Source: Calculations based on household survey data in GDSP (Global Database of Shared Prosperity), World Bank, Washington, DC, http://www.worldbank.org/en/topic/poverty/brief/global-database-of-shared-prosperity.
Note: The figure shows annualized growth rates in per capita household income or consumption expenditures over circa 2008–13. The red line is a 45-degree line, that is, in economies along this line, the bottom 40 grew at the same rate as the total population. The bottom 40 in economies below the line experienced slower growth relative to the overall population.

other than economic growth. It is also clear in figure 4.1 that, in a substantial number of countries, the growth in the income or consumption of the bottom 40 lies below the growth in the mean. In such countries, the growth of the top 60 exceeds that of the bottom 40, and increasing inequality may emerge from this type of growth. This is the case even in settings characterized by rapid economic growth (and, thus, high growth in mean incomes) and lower-than-average growth in incomes among the bottom 40, such as the Republic of Congo and the Lao People's Democratic Republic. Consequently, regardless of the importance of economic growth in boosting shared prosperity, a premium associated with poverty reduction that arises from narrowing inequality needs to be directly exploited through specific policy interventions. For instance, from 2008 to 2013, Cambodia and Cameroon had similar growth rates in the mean (3.9 and 3.7 percent, respectively), but the average incomes of the bottom 40 grew at 6.5 percent in the former and only 1.3 percent in the latter (see figure 4.1). (The specific choices a few countries have made to boost shared prosperity successfully and the specific policy interventions that are more conducive to narrowing inequality are addressed in chapters 5 and 6.)

Including the less privileged in the process of growth and investing in their human capital may also be good for growth. For example, removing credit constraints on the poorest and the bottom 40 and developing insurance mechanisms for them are expected, respectively, to lead to higher growth through productivity gains and to limit the impacts of natural disasters on economies. Improving the human capital of the poor by promoting early childhood development (ECD) and good-quality education; investing in infrastructure that connects, for example, smallholder farmers with markets; and enhancing the coverage and quality of electricity services have been shown to have positive effects on economic growth, while improving the living conditions of the poor (see chapters 5 and 6). Policy choices and economic growth from now until 2030 will continue to affect the pace of sharing prosperity and ending poverty. If these choices are made smartly, and economic growth is strong and sustainable, the twin goals of the World Bank will be within reach.[16]

There are still other reasons why inequality matters for the twin goals.[17] Reducing inequalities of opportunity and of outcomes among individuals, populations, and regions is conducive to political and social stability as well as social cohesion. Yet, this outcome is not certain, as the recent

---

BOX 4.2 Perceptions of Inequality in the Middle East and North Africa

Inequality is a multifaceted phenomenon; yet, discussions about it are often restricted to income-wealth-consumption metrics.[a] Increasingly, however, evidence from the field on subjective well-being has demonstrated the importance of individual perceptions in the analysis of inequality, for example, on satisfaction with basic services, governance, or economic mobility.

Inequality in the Middle East and North Africa region presents an illustrative case of marked differences between subjective assessments and objective measures. These differences help explain the conditions leading to the Arab Spring in early 2011 that traditional metrics of income or wealth inequality failed to capture.

From 1950 through the 1990s, countries in the region had made

steady progress in the equitable distribution of the gains from economic growth.[b] Low by comparison with other developing regions, the population share of the extreme poor had declined further in almost all countries.[c] In the early 2000s, income inequality was also moderately low in comparison with other developing regions. The region achieved the Millennium Development Goals in

(Box continues next page)

poverty reduction and access to infrastructure services (especially Internet connectivity and drinking water and sanitation), and was also successful in reducing hunger and child and maternal mortality and in raising school enrollments.[d]

Nonetheless, the period was also accompanied by a deterioration in critical factors associated with life satisfaction. These factors include declining trust in the governance of institutions; declining standards in public services and local and national government accountability; an erosion in law and order and the impartiality and independence of the judiciary; a growing shortage of formal sector jobs offering job security and benefits, especially among educated youth; and a growing sense of despondency whereby people believe their opportunities for success are shrinking, economic mobility is becoming divorced from their efforts, and future generations are less likely to enjoy any gains in standards of living.[e]

Average life satisfaction in the region since the early 2000s has been declining.[f] It is below the global average and lower than the average expected for countries at a similar level of development. Part of this effect may be caused by the unhappy growth paradox, whereby rapid economic growth is destabilizing in the short run, particularly in transition economies. According to this paradox, improving macroeconomic conditions and the anticipation of benefits from this growth lead to disappointment when the level of self-reported well-being fails to meet the expectations (figure B4.2.1).[g]

The systematic gap between trends in the actual income

FIGURE B4.2.1 **Actual versus Anticipated Feelings of Well-Being, Middle East and North Africa**

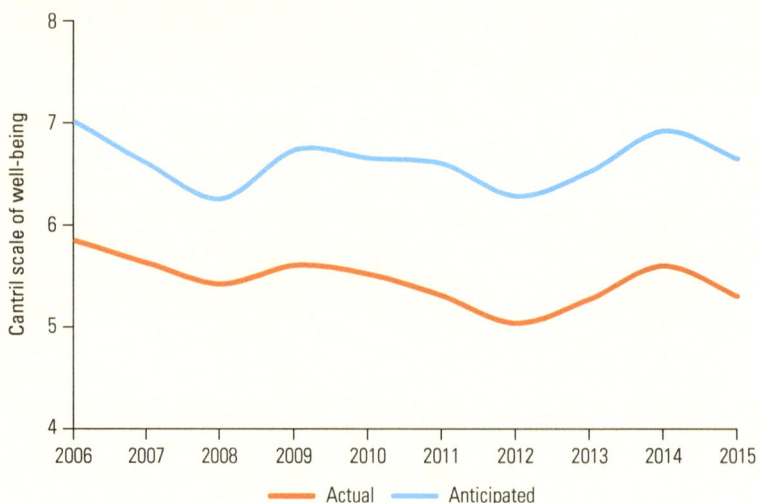

Source: Chattopadhyay and Graham 2015, based on data in Gallup World Poll, Gallup, Washington, DC, http://www.gallup.com/services/170945/world-poll.aspx.
Note: Data refer to Algeria, Bahrain, Egypt, the Islamic Republic of Iran, Iraq, Israel, Jordan, Kuwait, Lebanon, Libya, Morocco, Oman, Qatar, Saudi Arabia, Syria, Tunisia, United Arab Emirates, West Bank and Gaza, and the Republic of Yemen. The estimates are population weighted. The 0–10 Cantril Scale of Well-Being (the Cantril Self-Anchoring Scale), a metric of self-reported individual well-being, is presented to respondents as follows: "Imagine a ladder with steps numbered 0–10. Suppose 10 represents the best possible life for you, and 0 represents the worst possible life for you. On which step of the ladder would you say you personally feel you stand today (current)" and "about five years from now (anticipated)." For additional details, see Gallup (2011a).

distribution and how the distribution is perceived is expanding in the region. Thus, in the Arab Republic of Egypt during the early 2000s, people at lower incomes felt they were more affluent than they actually were, but this perception had reversed by 2008–09, when the same groups thought they were less well off than they actually were.[h] This sense of declining economic fortunes in the lower end of the income distribution was compounded by a rising sense of vulnerability and dissatisfaction among middle groups in the income distribution above the bottom 40.[i]

The rising dissatisfaction and the widening gap between

objective and subjective measures of satisfaction have consequences. The three most important motivations of the unrest behind the Arab Spring cited by more than half of the respondents to recent Arab Barometer surveys are a desire to enhance economic conditions, fight corruption and cronyism, and promote social and economic justice.[j]

Is the experience in the region likely to be replicated elsewhere? Evidence across countries suggests that the association between perceptions of relative inequality and reported life satisfaction is neither linear nor unidirectional. Individuals and

(Box continues next page)

societies differ in who they regard as a reference group, and this leads to differences in subjective evaluation. In addition, people tend to misstate their own income and wealth.[k] Moreover, different societies view the significance of relative inequality differently. Some countries are more tolerant of greater income disparities if they genuinely regard such disparities as the result of fair returns within a meritocratic system, whereas other societies consider the same income disparities as unacceptable.[l] The Arab Spring demonstrates that attitudes toward historical norms can change if a broadening share of a population yearns for a more equitable distribution of prosperity.[m] The combination of shifting attitudes and growing frustration because of long-run unmet expectations may constitute a serious threat to social and political stability, especially if macroeconomic growth is perceived to have no benefits for low- and middle-income population groups.

Sources: Arampatzi et al. 2015; Chattopadhyay and Graham 2015; Gallup 2011b; Gallup World Poll, Gallup, Washington, DC, http://www.gallup.com/services/170945/world-poll.aspx; Graham 2016; Graham and Lora 2009; Hassine 2015; Iqbal and Kiendrebeogo 2014; Khouri and Myers 2015; Ncube and Hausken 2013; Verme et al. 2014; World Bank 2015, 2016a.

a. World Bank (2016a).
b. Hassine (2015); Ncube, Anyanwu, and Hausken (2013).
c. World Bank (2015).
d. Iqbal and Kiendrebeogo (2014).
e. Arampatzi et al. (2015); Chattopadhyay and Graham (2015); Khouri and Myers (2015).
f.   Life satisfaction is often measured using the Cantril ladder of life metric (Cantril 1965).
g. Graham and Lora (2009) coined the phrase "unhappy growth paradox" as a reflection of the declines in life satisfaction during periods of rapid economic growth that also results in drastic upheaval in old social and economic norms, while the new ones that replace them take time to stabilize. This pattern was evident in transition economies of Eastern Europe in the 1990s and, more recently, in China and India.
h. Gallup (2011b).
i.   Gallup (2011b).
j.   Verme et al. (2014), using data in WVS (World Values Survey) (database), King's College, Old Aberdeen, United Kingdom, http://www.worldvaluessurvey.org/wvs.jsp. See also Arab Barometer Public Opinion Survey Series (database), Inter-university Consortium for Political and Social Research, Institute for Social Research, University of Michigan, Ann Arbor, MI, http://www.icpsr.umich.edu/icpsrweb/ICPSR/series/508.
k. van der Weide, Lakner, and Ianchovichina (2016).
l.   Arampatzi et al. (2015); Chattopadhyay and Graham (2015).
m. Arampatzi et al. (2015) using 2012–14 data in Arab Barometer Public Opinion Survey Series (database), Inter-university Consortium for Political and Social Research, Institute for Social Research, University of Michigan, Ann Arbor, MI, http://www.icpsr.umich.edu/icpsrweb/ICPSR/series/508.

experience of Brazil and the Arab Spring indicate (box 4.2). Overall, however, threats to achieving the World Bank goals arising from extremism, political turmoil, and institutional fragility are less likely in more cohesive societies. In contrast, political instability is more likely to emerge and more difficult to eradicate in societies where economic growth and social policies have reduced poverty without addressing interpersonal and regional disparities, whether objectively measured or subjectively perceived. It is worth recalling that the Arab Spring began in Tunisia, a country with a long and strong record of economic growth and poverty reduction, but also with pervasive regional disparities and a history of cronyism and corruption.[18]

Separating fact from myth: what is the evidence on inequality?

Reductions in inequality are important intrinsically and because they are associated with reductions in absolute poverty and greater sharing of prosperity. There are also a lot of misconceptions about recent changes in inequality. Some narratives suggest there has been an unrelenting increase in inequality worldwide. Many will be familiar with the evidence on top incomes rising more quickly than average incomes in a number of countries.[19] Figure 4.2, panel a, shows that the income share of the richest 1 percent in the United States has been rising steeply since the 1970s, after falling in the

FIGURE 4.2 The Top 1 Percent Income Share, Selected Economies

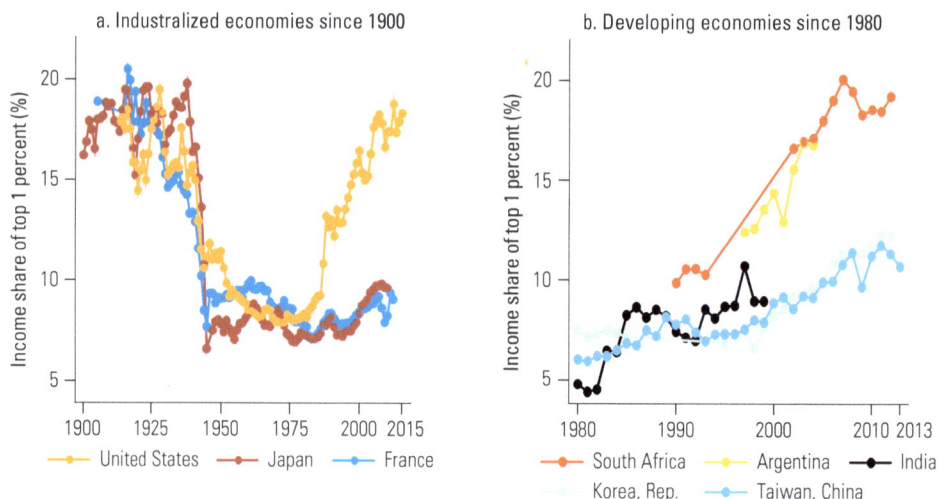

a. Industrialized economies since 1900

b. Developing economies since 1980

Source: Calculations based on data of WID (World Wealth and Income Database), Paris School of Economics, Paris, http://www.parisschoolofeconomics.eu/en/research/the-world-wealth-income-database/.
Note: The figure shows the share of national income (excluding capital gains) going to the richest 1 percent of national populations. These measures are typically derived from tax record data. For South Africa, the figure shows the top 1 percent income share among adults.

first half of the 20th century. In contrast, in France and Japan, not only do the richest control a much smaller share of national income, but their share has also risen much less. This is remarkable because all three countries had similar top income shares at the beginning of the 20th century. The long-run evidence on developing countries is more limited because of the lack of tax record data. Figure 4.2, panel b, shows the upward trends in the income shares of the top 1 percent in selected developing economies since the 1980s. In South Africa, the top income share roughly doubled over a period of 20 years and is comparable to the levels observed in the United States.

Globally, there has been a long-term secular rise in interpersonal inequality. Figure 4.3 shows the global Gini index since 1820, when relevant data first became available. The industrial revolution led to a worldwide divergence in incomes across countries, as today's advanced economies began pulling away from others. However, the figure also shows that, in the late 1980s and early 1990s, the global Gini index began to fall. This coincided with a period of rapid globalization and substantial growth in populous poor countries, such as China and India.

FIGURE 4.3 Global Income Inequality, 1820–2010

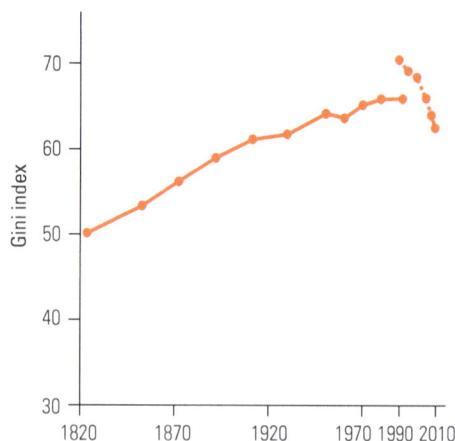

Source: Based on figure 1 (p. 27) of *The Globalization of Inequality* by Francois Bourguignon (Princeton University Press 2015). Used with permission.
Note: The discontinuity in the series represents the change in the base year of the purchasing power parity (PPP) exchange rates from 1990 to 2005. The figure uses GDP per capita in combination with distributional statistics from household surveys. Figure 4.5 uses income (or consumption) per capita directly from household surveys, expressed in 2011 PPP exchange rates.

According to household surveys, national inequality measured by the Gini index also rose steeply in a number of developing countries. Figure 4.4 shows the

FIGURE 4.4 Long-Run Changes in the Gini Index, Selected Developing Countries, 1980–2014

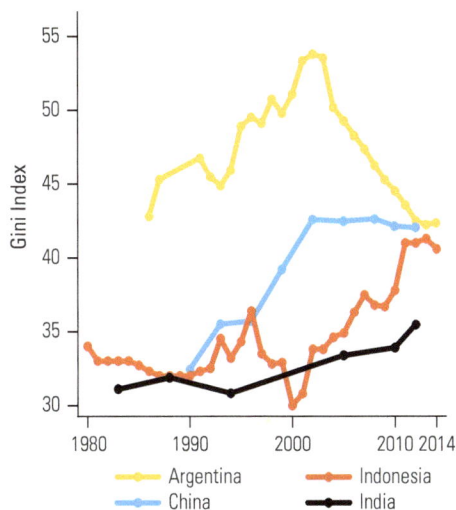

Sources: World Bank 2016b; PovcalNet (online analysis tool), World Bank, Washington, DC, http://iresearch.worldbank.org /PovcalNet/.
Note: The welfare aggregate in Argentina is income; in all other countries it is consumption.

Gini index of Argentina, China, India, and Indonesia, on which longer-run data are available. In Argentina and China, inequality widened appreciably until the early 2000s, while the rise in Indonesia began around the same time. The increase in inequality in India has been more muted and began in the second half of the 2000s. In contrast, during the 2000s, inequality narrowed sharply in Argentina and in some other Latin American countries.[20] The drop was so pronounced that the inequality levels in Argentina and China became comparable.[21] Inequality has been stabilizing in China and, to some extent, in Indonesia in recent years, though at a much higher level than 20 years ago.

Against the context of these long-run developments, the remainder of this chapter analyzes recent changes in inequality more systematically. In this report, inequality in disposable income or consumption expenditure is measured among individuals.[22] Disposable income is defined as net market income (that is, after personal income taxes and social security contributions have been deducted), plus any direct social transfers. Other outcome measures, whether monetary (such as wealth) or nonmonetary (such as health care and education) are ignored as are the inequalities among subgroups (for example, by sex or ethnicity).[23] Income or expenditure is measured at the household level (thus ignoring inequality among household members) and assigned to each individual on a per capita basis (thus avoiding the complication of accounting for economies of scale in larger households). The analysis is conducted in two stages. First, estimates are reported for interpersonal global inequality. Second, the focus shifts to inequality within countries. Only relative measures of inequality, typically the Gini index, are considered.[24]

This is only one perspective on inequality. Other dimensions are no less important and may be trending in different directions. Thus, people's perceptions about inequality may be different from actual trends (see box 4.2). People might care about wealth inequality, inequalities in access to basic services, or the inequality between urban and rural areas or across geographical regions. Furthermore, all the standard inequality measures used here are relative, but people may be concerned with absolute differences (box 4.3). While the results here are compared with alternative datasets, such comparisons are difficult because inequality measures may be different, for example, after the application of equivalence scales or the use of households instead of individuals as the unit of analysis.[25] For instance, in Argentina, the use of equivalence scales— adjusting consumption by size and age— reduces the Gini index from 41.9 to 39.4, compared with the per capita estimates.[26]

There are several reasons for interpreting these results carefully.[27] First, as with any global analysis, the data coverage of countries is incomplete. Despite considerable progress, good-quality data are still missing in various countries. These include many fragile countries, as well as some countries in the Middle East, the African continent, the Caribbean, and the Pacific. Annex 4A describes the countries included in the analysis and their shares in regional populations. For example, in 2013, the data covered about a third of the population in the Middle East and North Africa region and around half the population in Sub-Saharan Africa.

Absolute versus Relative Inequality

Standard measures of inequality, such as the Gini index, are relative. Relative measures of inequality obey the scale invariance axiom, which says that an inequality measure ought to remain unchanged in the face of any transformation that multiplies all incomes by the same constant, such as a simple rescaling from euros to U.S. dollars. This implies that, if all incomes grow at the same rate, the Gini index remains unchanged. This may be associated with quite different absolute gains, however, depending on the dispersion in incomes in the initial distribution.

The red lines in figure B4.3.1 show how average incomes or consumption of deciles have grown in Argentina (panel a) and Uganda (panel b) over the past 10 years. In Argentina, incomes have grown much more quickly among the poor than among the rich. As a result, the Gini index fell from 50.2 to 42.3. In Uganda, consumption among the bottom nine deciles grew at almost the same rate, while the consumption of the top decile grew more slowly. Thus, the Gini index fell from 45.2 to 42.4. The blue lines in the two panels show the absolute annual gains by decile. In absolute terms, the richer deciles gained much more over the period, reversing the conclusions based on relative gains.

FIGURE B4.3.1 **Comparing Absolute and Relative Gains across the Distribution**

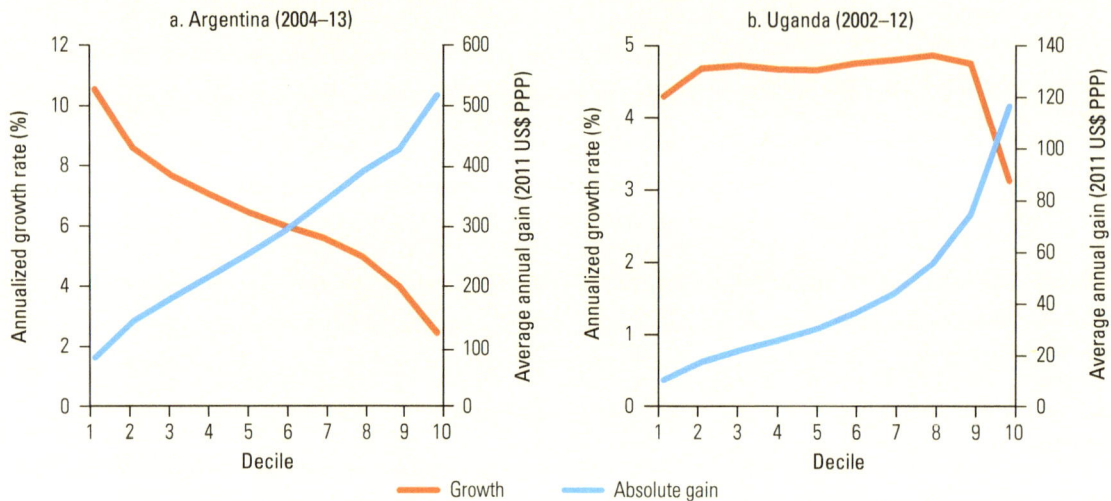

a. Argentina (2004–13)

b. Uganda (2002–12)

— Growth   — Absolute gain

Source: PovcalNet (online analysis tool), World Bank, Washington, DC, http://iresearch.worldbank.org/PovcalNet/.
Note: The welfare aggregate in Argentina is income, while consumption expenditure is used in Uganda. According to Beegle et al. (2016), the spell used for Uganda is based on two comparable surveys. The red line is a variant of the growth incidence curve showing annualized growth rates of average income or consumption by decile group. The blue line shows absolute gains per year in 2011 PPP U.S. dollars.

Relative measures of inequality are conceptually appealing because, for instance, they allow inequality and economic growth to be analyzed separately. However, perceptions about widening income gaps often carry absolute connotations. Thus, in experimental studies, university students in Germany, Israel, the United Kingdom, and the United States are approximately evenly split between caring about relative measures and caring about absolute measures.[a] An analysis of absolute differences can, in any case, provide a complementary perspective.[b]

a. Ravallion (2016).
b. For instance, Atkinson and Brandolini (2010) argue that global inequality analyses in particular need to consider both absolute and relative differences.

Second, for the sake of consistency, the analysis relies on the same welfare aggregate to measure inequality that is used in chapters 2 and 3 to estimate poverty and shared prosperity, respectively. This means that the analysis tends to use consumption expenditure for most developing countries and income for the industrialized countries

Comparison of Levels and Trends in Income and Consumption Inequality

In a number of countries in Eastern Europe and Central Asia, both income- and consumption-based Gini indexes are available for the same years. Figure B4.4.1 plots the income Gini (left axis) against the consumption Gini (right axis) for all the countries where such a comparison is possible for 2013. It is clear that consumption-based Gini indexes are considerably lower than income-based Gini indexes. But rankings remain somewhat similar. For example, Georgia and Turkey are the two most unequal countries in the sample, but Poland moves up from rank 8 to rank 3 if consumption is used instead of income.

Figure B4.4.2 addresses the issue of whether inequality trends are different if consumption is used instead of income. For the set of shared prosperity spells introduced in chapter 3 (from around 2008 to 2013), the figure plots the change in the Gini index for the two welfare aggregates. While there are some large differences (notably, Romania), both welfare aggregates point in the same direction, and one aggregate does not produce a consistently smaller change than the other.

FIGURE B4.4.1 Levels of Income and Consumption, Gini Indexes, 2013

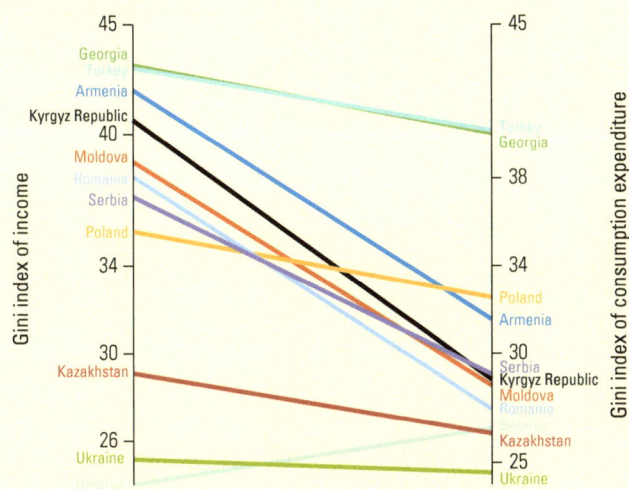

FIGURE B4.4.2 Trends in Income and Consumption, Gini Indexes, Circa 2008–13

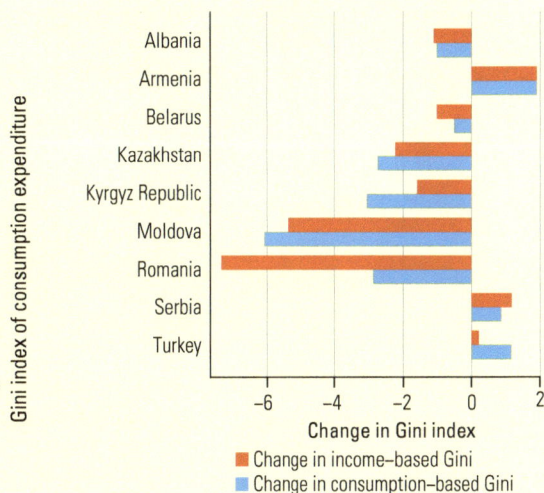

Source: Calculations based on data from the ECAPOV database harmonization as of April 2016, Europe and Central Asia Team for Statistical Development, World Bank, Washington, DC.
Note: In Poland and Romania, the World Bank uses income surveys for poverty monitoring. All other countries in the two figures use consumption expenditure.

and for Latin America.[28] Given that the marginal propensity to consume declines with income, or that savings increase with income, consumption expenditure tends to be more equally distributed than income. Compared with an analysis using income distributions exclusively, the data presented here would therefore systematically understate inequality in some countries. While this is a serious issue, an income distribution cannot be inferred reliably from an expenditure distribution.[29]

Box 4.4 assesses the effects of using income or consumption surveys in Eastern Europe and Central Asia, where it is possible to measure Gini indexes for both welfare aggregates in the same year. The ranking of countries by the Gini index is somewhat robust to whether consumption or income is used, although there are some notable exceptions. However, this only considers the ranking within a region, not across the world, and it is not obvious that this relationship would also hold in other regions. It is important to keep this in mind when comparing inequality levels between, for example, Latin America and the Caribbean (mostly income surveys) and Sub-Saharan

Africa (mostly consumption surveys). Box 4.4 also shows that time trends are similar between the two welfare aggregates.

A third reason for caution is that the coverage of household surveys within countries is also typically incomplete at the top tail. While this is not an issue in measuring poverty, it is important in measuring inequality accurately (see chapter 1), as well as in other areas of public policy such as fiscal policy. Survey enumerators typically face difficulties interviewing the richest households, and, if they do conduct interviews, the rich may understate their incomes. Furthermore, the coverage of the income surveys that are used for some emerging economies is incomplete in terms of entrepreneurial and capital incomes (important income sources at the top).[30] Finally, consumption surveys tend to understate true living standards at the top because consumption declines with income or because expenditure on durables (which are more important at the top) is poorly measured.[31]

Thus, it is likely that the household surveys used in this chapter understate the level of inequality. While the evidence from administrative records remains seriously limited in developing countries, complementary evidence suggests that top incomes might have been rising more quickly. Household surveys may therefore also underestimate the trend in inequality. For example, the labor share has been declining in many countries, while billionaire wealth on rich lists has been growing rapidly.[32] Box 4.5

BOX 4.5 Comparing Trends in Inequality: Household Surveys and Administrative Records

Administrative data on top incomes, typically based on tax records, have become available for a sizable number of rich countries.[a] In developing countries, the availability of these data is more limited, and, where they are available, data quality may be problematic given the absence of broad income taxes in many developing countries and the incomplete taxation of capital incomes.

Figure B4.5.1 compares the income share of the top 1 percent and the Gini index of Brazil between 2006 and 2012. While the Gini index has been falling steadily over this period, by almost 4 Gini points, the top income share has been on an upward trend. Part of this divergence may derive from definitional differences, such as the use of tax units versus households or of gross incomes versus disposable incomes. However, this evidence may also suggest that the Gini index misses important changes in the top tail; particularly that top incomes have grown more quickly than mean incomes.

FIGURE B4.5.1 Comparison of Top Incomes and the Gini Index, Brazil, 2006–12

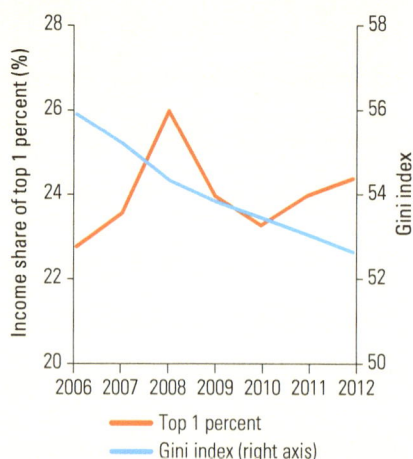

Source: World Bank compilation based on Souza, Medeiros, and Castro 2015; PovcalNet (online analysis tool), World Bank, Washington, DC, http://iresearch.worldbank.org/PovcalNet/.
Note: The red line shows the trend in the income share of the top 1 percent of individuals from tax record data. The two data series rely on different units of analysis (tax units versus households) and different welfare aggregates (disposable versus taxable gross income).

a. Thanks to the pioneering work of Alvaredo et al. (2013). See WID (World Wealth and Income Database), Paris School of Economics, Paris, http://www.parisschoolofeconomics.eu/en/research/the-world-wealth-income-database/.

compares the trends in household survey–based measures of inequality with administrative data on top incomes in Brazil, where such a comparison is possible in recent years. In other developing countries, such as Argentina or South Africa, the movement in the two measures has been rather similar.[33]

Global inequality

However imperfect, this compilation of household surveys remains the only source of distributional statistics on a large set of countries. Global inequality, defined here as the inequality in income among all persons in the world irrespective of their country of residence, is an aspect of inequality that is often overlooked in discussions that focus on country-specific inequality.[34] During a period of rapidly increasing global integration, some of the poorest economies were growing rapidly, thus raising average living standards, but many of the same countries also experienced increasing inequality within their borders. Global inequality captures the overall effect of both forces.

Global inequality has diminished for the first time since the industrial revolution. The global Gini index rose steadily by around 15 Gini points between the 1820s and the early 1990s, but has declined since then (see figure 4.3).[35] While the various methodologies and inequality measures show disagreement over the precise timing and magnitude of the decline, the decline since the middle of the last decade is confirmed across multiple sources and appears robust.[36] The estimates presented in figure 4.5 show a narrowing in global inequality between 1988 and 2013. The Gini index of the global distribution (represented by the blue line) fell from 69.7 in 1988 to 62.5 in 2013, most markedly since 2008 (when the global Gini index was 66.8). Additional exercises confirm that these results are reasonably robust, despite the errors to which the data are typically subject.[37]

Global inequality is at a much higher level than inequality within countries. Few countries have Gini indexes above 60 (see below). This is not surprising given that the global distribution includes everyone from the poorest Congolese to the richest Norwegian. Another way to illustrate this

FIGURE 4.5 Global Inequality, 1988–2013

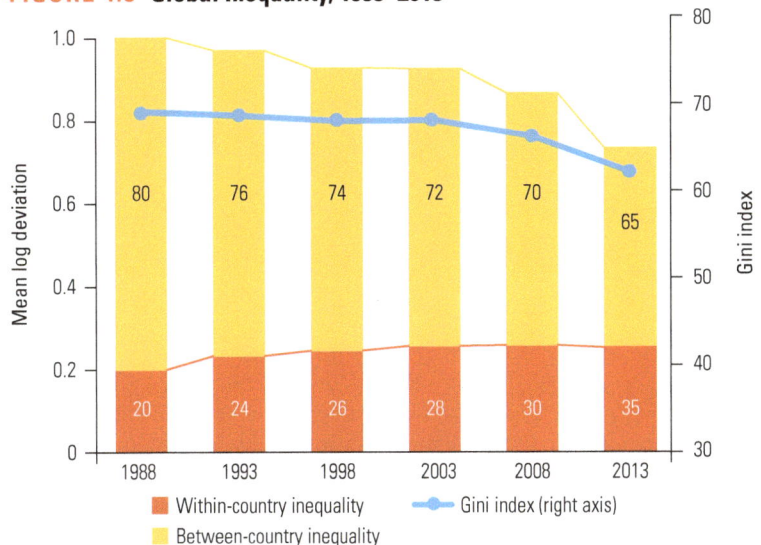

Sources: Lakner and Milanović 2016a; Milanović 2016; calculations based on PovcalNet (online analysis tool), World Bank, Washington, DC, http://iresearch.worldbank.org/PovcalNet/.
Note: For each country, household income or consumption per capita is obtained from household surveys and expressed in 2011 PPP exchange rates. Each country distribution is represented by 10 decile groups. The line (measured on the right axis) shows the level of the global Gini index. The height of the bars indicates the level of global inequality as measured by GE(0) (the mean log deviation). The red bars show the corresponding level of population-weighted inequality within countries. The level of between-country inequality, which captures differences in average income across countries, is shown by the yellow bars. The numbers in the bars refer to the relative contributions (in percent) of these two sources to total global inequality.

is to decompose global inequality into differences within and between countries. This allows an understanding of how much of the change in global inequality is explained by countries reducing the inequality among them (that is, reducing the differences in average incomes across countries) relative to the reduction in inequality within each one of the countries (that is, the differences in incomes within a country). This decomposition is shown by the bars in figure 4.5. The total height of the bars captures global inequality as measured by GE(0) (the mean log deviation), while the red and yellow bars show the within and between contributions, respectively. In contrast to the Gini, GE(0) is a bottom-sensitive inequality measure that can be additively decomposed into within- and between-country components. This decomposability feature makes this indicator appealing for this type of analysis.

Between two-thirds and four-fifths of global inequality stems from differences in average incomes across countries (between-country inequality). The reduction in overall global inequality was mostly driven by a decline in this component, that is, average incomes converged across countries.[38] This reflects the rapid growth in average incomes in populous countries such as China and India. These developments were counteracted to some extent by an increase in within-country inequality, especially in the 1990s. Between 2008 and 2013, within-country inequality stabilized or even declined slightly, which, together with the strong convergence effect, led to a marked decline in global inequality. As a result of these developments, within-country differences explain an increasing share of global inequality, as shown in figure 4.5.

A mixed picture emerges if one examines the separate regional distributions. Inequality increased within most regions, with the notable exception of Latin America and the Caribbean. For instance, inequality among all Sub-Saharan Africans rose between 1993 and 2008, driven by widening between-country inequality, although within-country differences remain the dominant source (around 60 percent).[39] In contrast, growing regional inequality within East Asia and Pacific was driven by rising within-country inequality.[40] This also implies that most of the convergence observed at the global level has been between regions.

Within-country inequality

Most studies of inequality focus on within-country inequality, which remains the level at which most policies operate. Our analysis of within-country inequality, the most comprehensive among recent studies, covers all available countries regardless of region or income level, as compiled in PovcalNet.[41] Described in more detail in the annex to this chapter, the analysis defines six benchmark years (in five-year intervals between 1988 and 2013) to which country-year observations within a two-year window on either side are grouped. This allows a more meaningful comparison across countries over time, because many countries lack data for every year. On average, there are 109 countries per benchmark year (table 4A.2 in the annex). Figure 4.6 offers four ways of summarizing what has hap-

pened to average within-country inequality in the world. Whatever the approach, average inequality within countries increased in the 1990s, but has been falling in recent years according to most specifications.

The population-weighted average Gini (solid blue line in figure 4.6) captures the change in within-country inequality for the average person in the world. Therefore, the individual remains the unit of analysis as in the global inequality analysis (see above).[42] The population-weighted average Gini rose sharply between 1988 and 1998, by some 6 points, from 34 to 40. Over this period, the average person in the world was thus living in a country in which inequality was growing steeply. Since then, inequality has declined slightly, by almost one point, but remains at a higher level than 25 years ago.

Next, the analysis presents unweighted averages. These averages allow us to capture how different countries have fared over time in terms of reducing inequality, thus learning from their successes (see chapter 5 for a discussion of a few selected country cases). Thus, this part of the analysis treats China and Honduras the same in calculating the average, regardless of the fact that the population of China is much larger than the population of Honduras. As shown by the solid red line in figure 4.6, the unweighted average Gini index also increased during the 1990s, but by a smaller amount. The simple average worldwide increased by around 5 points, from 36 in 1988 to 41 ten years later, and declined thereafter, reaching 38 in 2013.[43]

Because not every country conducts a household survey every five years, the country composition changes across these five-year periods. To avoid such compositional shifts, inequality trends are studied for a smaller sample of countries that have household surveys in each of the five-year periods considered. The dashed lines in figure 4.6 repeat the unweighted and weighted averages, but include the same set of 41 countries throughout the period.[44] The average inequality in this set of countries follows a similar trend. Taken together, the analysis suggests that, in the average country, inequality may have peaked in the late 1990s and early half of the 2000s and has declined in the latter half of the 2000s. Inequality in this smaller sample is also wider in 2013 than the levels 25 years previously.

The levels and trends in average inequality are quite different across regions, although the most recent decline is broad-based. Figure 4.7 shows the unweighted average Gini index across seven regions. Within-country inequality tends to be higher in developing countries than in developed countries, the latter grouped in this analysis as industrialized countries (a subset of high-income countries).[45] The highest levels of inequality are observed in Latin America and the Caribbean. Contributing to the intrinsically high levels of inequality, within-country inequality in Latin America and the Caribbean is measured using income-based surveys that are expected to show higher levels of inequality.

Latin America and the Caribbean stands out as a region that has been successful in narrowing inequality in the last 10 to 15 years, also driving the decline in the global average.[46] However, these declines occurred after a prolonged increase during the 1980s (not shown) and 1990s, such that, by 2012, the average Gini in the region had returned to the level of the early 1980s.[47] Hence, the long-run progress in the reduction of inequality in Latin America and the Caribbean has been limited. Furthermore, the downward trend has slowed, and inequality recently stagnated.[48]

The average Gini in Sub-Saharan Africa has declined steadily since the early 1990s, but continues to be the second highest after the Gini in Latin America.[49] In Eastern Europe and Central Asia, average inequality rose sharply after the fall of the Berlin Wall, but has since been on a declining trend (see figure 4.7).[50] Similarly, inequality rose sharply during the transition to a market economy in some East Asian countries. The average industrialized country experienced an increase in the Gini index from 30 in 1988 to 33 in 2008. From 2008 to 2013, average inequality appears to have fallen in all regions except South Asia and the Middle East and North Africa, where data are limited.[51]

Providing a simple explanation for these regional inequality trends is particularly challenging because countries within

FIGURE 4.6 **Average Within-Country Inequality, 1988–2013**

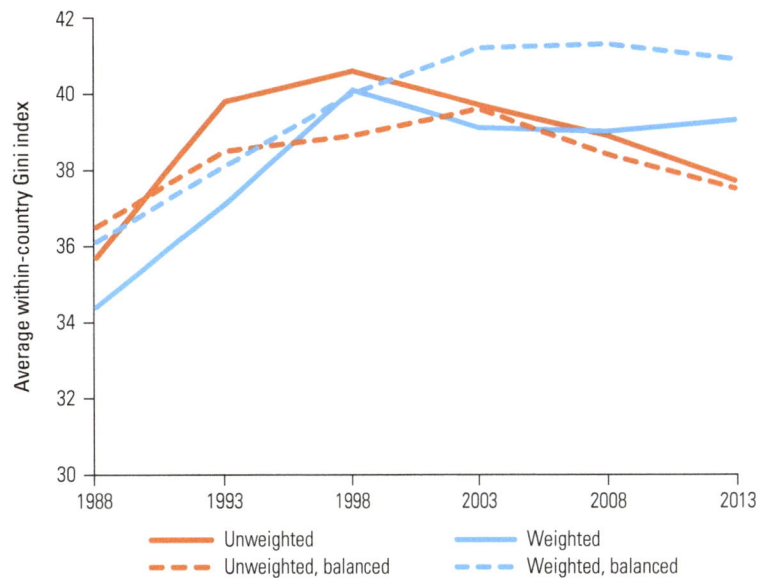

Source: World Bank calculations based on data in Milanović 2014; PovcalNet (online analysis tool), World Bank, Washington, DC, http://iresearch.worldbank.org/PovcalNet/; WDI (World Development Indicators) (database), World Bank, Washington, DC, http://data.worldbank.org/data-catalog/world-development -indicators (see annex 4A).
Note: The solid lines show the trend in the average within-country Gini index with and without population weights in the full sample (an average 109 countries per benchmark year). The dashed lines refer to the balanced sample, that is, using only the set of 41 countries on which data are available in every benchmark year.

FIGURE 4.7 **Trends in the Average Gini, by Region, 1988–2013**

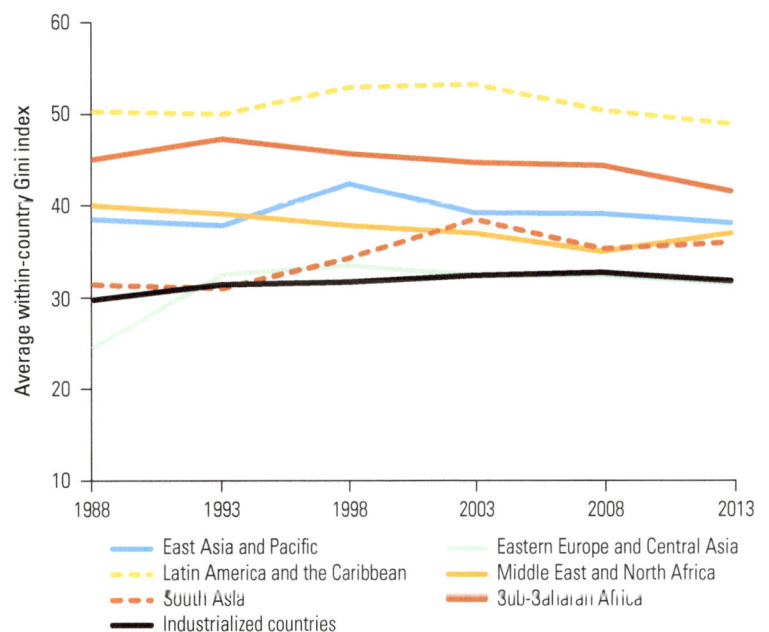

Source: World Bank calculations based on data in Milanović 2014; PovcalNet (online analysis tool), World Bank, Washington, DC, http://iresearch.worldbank.org/PovcalNet/ (see annex 4A).
Note: The lines show the average within-country Gini index by region. It is the simple average in the full sample without weighting countries by population. Industrialized countries is a subset of high-income countries. See chapter 2, annex 2B, for the list of industrialized countries.

FIGURE 4.8 The Gini Index, 101 Countries, 2013

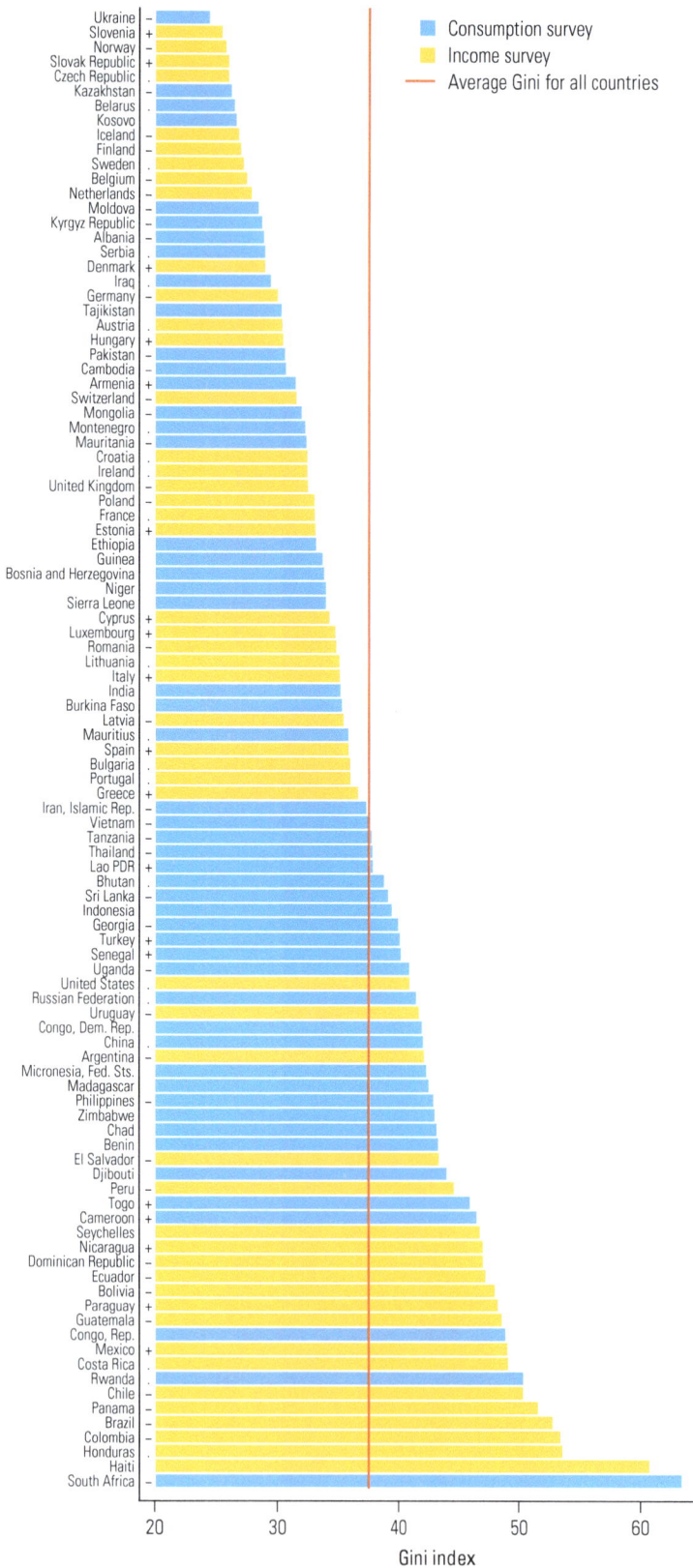

Countries (top to bottom): Ukraine −, Slovenia +, Norway −, Slovak Republic +, Czech Republic −, Kazakhstan −, Belarus ., Kosovo −, Iceland −, Finland −, Sweden −, Belgium −, Netherlands −, Moldova −, Kyrgyz Republic −, Albania −, Serbia −, Denmark +, Iraq ., Germany −, Tajikistan −, Austria ., Hungary +, Pakistan −, Cambodia −, Armenia +, Switzerland −, Mongolia −, Montenegro ., Mauritania −, Croatia ., Ireland ., United Kingdom −, Poland −, France −, Estonia +, Ethiopia ., Guinea ., Bosnia and Herzegovina ., Niger ., Sierra Leone ., Cyprus +, Luxembourg +, Romania −, Lithuania ., Italy +, India ., Burkina Faso ., Latvia −, Mauritius ., Spain +, Bulgaria ., Portugal ., Greece +, Iran, Islamic Rep. −, Vietnam −, Tanzania −, Thailand −, Lao PDR +, Bhutan ., Sri Lanka −, Indonesia ., Georgia −, Turkey +, Senegal +, Uganda −, United States ., Russian Federation ., Uruguay −, Congo, Dem. Rep. ., China ., Argentina −, Micronesia, Fed. Sts. ., Madagascar ., Philippines −, Zimbabwe ., Chad ., Benin ., El Salvador −, Djibouti ., Peru −, Togo +, Cameroon +, Seychelles ., Nicaragua +, Dominican Republic −, Ecuador −, Bolivia −, Paraguay −, Guatemala ., Congo, Rep. ., Mexico +, Costa Rica ., Rwanda ., Chile −, Panama −, Brazil −, Colombia −, Honduras ., Haiti ., South Africa −.

Legend:
- Consumption survey
- Income survey
- Average Gini for all countries

x-axis: Gini index (20, 30, 40, 50, 60)

Source: World Bank calculations based on data in Milanović 2014; PovcalNet (online analysis tool), World Bank, Washington, DC, http://iresearch.worldbank.org/PovcalNet/ (see annex 4A).

Note: Countries are sorted by the Gini index. The red line shows the unweighted average Gini index in 2013. "+" = increase in the Gini > 1 Gini point, 2008–13. "−" = decline in the Gini > 1 Gini point. "." = change in the Gini within 1 Gini point. See the detailed discussion in the text around table 4.1.

---

a region may exhibit distinctive trends and specific drivers behind the trends. Instead of providing a simplistic explanation, it is more useful to look closely at the country variations within regions and to understand how the common drivers of inequality—such as gaps in human capital accumulation, differences in access to jobs and income-generating opportunities, and government interventions to address market-based inequalities such as taxes and transfers—are relevant in each country. The remainder of this chapter looks at the variations in within-country inequality in each region, while chapter 5 focuses on selected countries that have successfully reduced inequality, and chapter 6 centers on specific interventions that have been shown to reduce inequality and poverty without major efficiency and equity trade-offs in several countries around the world.

The bars in figure 4.8 show the level of the Gini index across the 101 countries on which data are available for 2013. The figure highlights whether a country uses income or consumption expenditure, confirming that most of the high-inequality countries use income surveys. The most unequal country in the world is South Africa, followed by Haiti, each of which has a Gini index in excess of 60. Another Sub-Saharan African country (Rwanda) and seven other Latin America and Caribbean countries (Brazil, Chile, Colombia, Costa Rica, Honduras, Mexico, and Panama) make up the top 10 most unequal countries in the world. All the most equal countries are in the group of industrialized countries or in Eastern Europe and Central Asia.

More broadly, all Latin America and Caribbean countries have Gini indexes in excess of 40, and the Gini in a third of those countries is above 50 (figure 4.9). There is almost no overlap between Latin America and the Caribbean and the two other regions that primarily use income surveys, namely, the industrialized countries and Eastern Europe and Central Asia. The other region that exhibits high inequality is Sub-Saharan Africa, especially the southern countries.[52] More than half the African countries in the sample have Gini indexes in excess of 40. The reported measures of inequality in Sub-Saharan Africa use predominantly consumption expenditure; income-based inequality statistics would likely be higher.

Short- and long-run trends in within-country inequality

Results based on an analysis of trends are often sensitive to the beginning and end points. The trends chosen in this chapter begin around 1993 given the limited data availability in the developing world (especially Africa) before that year. This choice might underestimate the rise in inequality. For example, the surge in inequality in many Eastern European countries following the fall of the Berlin Wall had already occurred. During the 1980s, inequality rose steeply in some rich countries, such as the Netherlands, the United Kingdom, and the United States.[53] For these reasons, two sets of country-level spells are analyzed (as discussed in annex 4A). First, the long-run spells include all countries that have an observation around 1993 and 2008, as long as the welfare aggregate (income or consumption) is the same. Second, the sample of short-run trends from 2008 to 2013 is based on the strictly comparable shared prosperity spells used in chapter 3. Comparisons need to be drawn carefully because the regional composition of the two sets of spells is different. Thus, the set of short-run spells includes fewer countries, especially in South Asia and Sub-Saharan Africa. This reflects issues of data comparability and availability, which are discussed in detail in a recent report on Sub-Saharan Africa.[54]

Figure 4.10 plots the final year against initial year Gini indexes for the long-run (panel a) and short-run (panel b) spells. Countries above the line experienced increasing inequality, whereas countries below the line saw a decline. Between 1993 and 2008, large falls are observed. This might indicate successful reductions in inequality, but also some problems with survey comparability, especially in Sub-Saharan Africa. The other major region with declining inequality appears to have been Latin America and the Caribbean. The changes between 2008 and 2013 were smaller for the (also

FIGURE 4.9 Distribution of the Gini Index, 2013

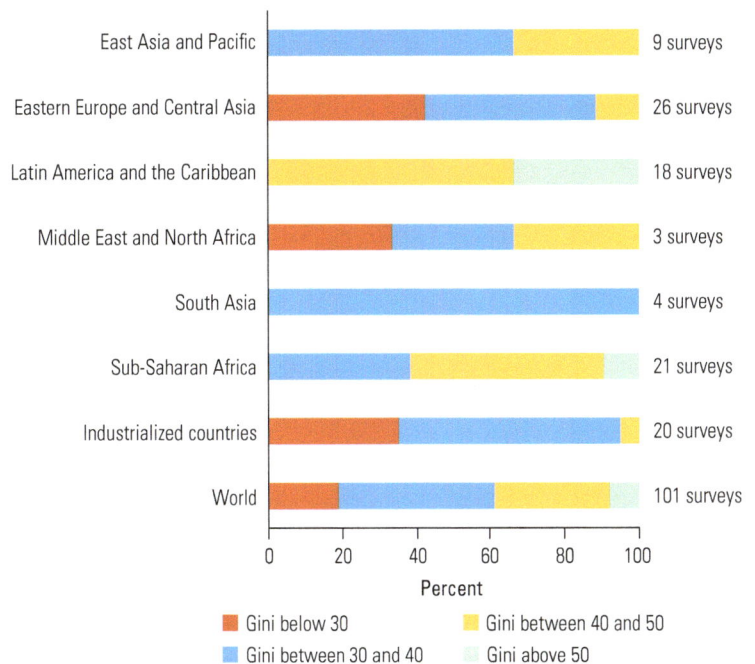

Source: World Bank calculations based on data in Milanović 2014; PovcalNet (online analysis tool), World Bank, Washington, DC, http://iresearch.worldbank.org/PovcalNet/ (see annex 4A).
Note: The figure shows that 2013 data were available on 101 countries. Of these, 8 had a Gini index exceeding 50; 6 were in Latin America and the Caribbean, and 2 in Sub-Saharan Africa. Some 31 had a Gini index between 40 and 50: 12 in Latin America and the Caribbean, 11 in Sub-Saharan Africa, 3 each in East Asia and Pacific and Eastern Europe and Central Asia, and 1 each in the Middle East and North Africa and in the industrialized countries. Some 43 countries had a Gini index between 30 and 40: 12 each in Eastern Europe and Central Asia and in the industrialized countries, 8 in Sub-Saharan Africa, 6 in East Asia and Pacific, 4 in South Asia, and 1 in the Middle East and North Africa. Some 19 countries had a Gini index below 30: 11 in Eastern Europe and Central Asia, 7 in the industrialized countries, and 1 in the Middle East and North Africa.

smaller) sample of countries. The majority of countries appear to fall below the line, that is, they show a declining Gini index, and the decline in Latin America and the Caribbean appears even more pronounced. A few country examples are highlighted in figure 4.10, panel b, indicating that decreases in inequality have been observed across all levels of inequality (high and low), income groups (low- and middle-income categories), and regions.

Table 4.1 summarizes within-country trends in inequality by region more systematically. The sample in the 15 years between 1993 and 2008 includes 91 countries, 42 of which showed increasing inequality; 39 had a declining Gini index; and 10 showed no significant changes, that is, changes below 1 Gini point in either direction.[55] Hence, the number of countries with rising inequality

FIGURE 4.10 Trends in the Within-Country Gini Index, 1993–2013

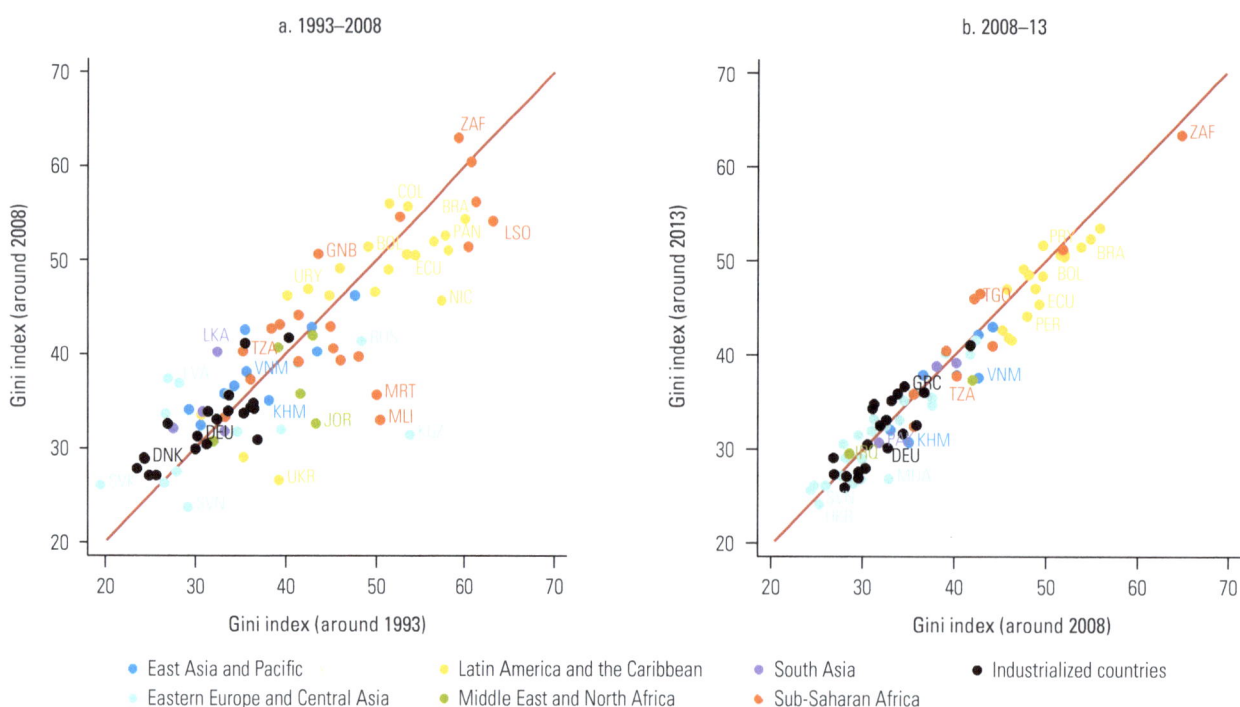

a. 1993–2008

b. 2008–13

- East Asia and Pacific
- Eastern Europe and Central Asia
- Latin America and the Caribbean
- Middle East and North Africa
- South Asia
- Sub-Saharan Africa
- Industrialized countries

Source: Calculations based on data in Milanović 2014; PovcalNet (online analysis tool), World Bank, Washington, DC, http://iresearch.worldbank.org/PovcalNet/ (see annex 4A).
Note: Economies along the red (45-degree) line experienced no change in inequality. In economies below (above) the line, inequality narrowed (widened).

TABLE 4.1 Countries with an Increasing or Decreasing Gini Index and the Average Gini
Number

	Long-run trend (1993–2008)						Short-run trend (2008–13)					
	Number of countries:				Mean Gini		Number of countries:				Mean Gini	
	↑	+/– pp	↓	Total	1993	2008	↑	+/– pp	↓	Total	2008	2013
East Asia and Pacific	5	1	3	9	37.8	39.1	1	1	5	7	39.2	37.3
Eastern Europe and Central Asia	5	2	6	13	33.9	32.5	6	8	9	23	31.9	31.4
Latin America and the Caribbean	8	0	11	19	49.0	47.0	3	2	12	17	49.7	48.0
Middle East and North Africa	1	1	3	5	39.8	36.4	0	1	1	2	35.3	33.4
South Asia	3	0	1	4	31.0	34.5	0	1	2	3	36.7	36.2
Sub-Saharan Africa	8	2	10	20	47.6	45.1	3	2	4	9	44.1	43.8
Industrialized countries	12	4	5	21	31.4	32.6	6	6	8	20	32.0	31.8
World	42	10	39	91	40.1	39.3	19	21	41	81	37.9	37.1

Source: World Bank calculations based on data in Milanović 2014; PovcalNet (online analysis tool), World Bank, Washington, DC, http://iresearch.worldbank.org/PovcalNet/ (see annex 4A).
Note: Increases and decreases refer to changes that are greater than 1 Gini point in absolute value. The unweighted average Gini index is estimated over the sample of 91 countries (left panel) and 81 countries (right panel).

was slightly higher than the number of countries with falling inequality. Yet, the average Gini among these 91 countries actually declined by 0.8 Gini points, from 40.1 to 39.3

(thus, barely significant). This is because, among countries with narrowing inequality, the Gini index fell by a larger amount than it increased in the rising countries. However, inequality widened more rapidly in larger countries. The populous countries where the Gini index increased sharply include Bangladesh (5 points), China (7 points), and Indonesia (5 points).[56]

During the long-term spell, 1993–2008, the Latin America and Caribbean region stands out because of falling Gini indexes: 58 percent of the countries in the region showed a decline, and the average Gini declined by 2 points (3.5 points with population weights). Meanwhile, many East Asia and Pacific countries (56 percent of the countries) and South Asian countries (75 percent) in the sample saw inequality rising. The average Gini in East Asia and Pacific and in South Asia rose by 1.3 points (5.7 with weights) and 3.5 points (2.8 with weights), respectively. In the industrialized countries, the average Gini increased, and inequality increased in over half the countries. The Sub-Saharan African countries are roughly evenly split into increasing and decreasing inequality, with a decline on average.[57] The conclusions for the Middle East and North Africa region need to be interpreted carefully because of limited data availability in the region.

The evidence suggests that there was a shift toward declining inequality between 2008 and 2013. However, the interpretation of the analysis needs to be cautious because the global financial crisis occurred during this period. The number of countries with decreasing inequality in this more recent spell is more than double the number of the countries with rising inequality. The Gini index fell by more than 1 point in 41 of 81 countries (51 percent of the sample of countries). On average, the Gini fell marginally by 0.8 points during this period. Populous countries with falling Gini indexes include Brazil (−2.4 points), Pakistan (−1.2), and Vietnam (−5.1). This development toward narrowing inequality can be observed across all regions. Hence, relative to the earlier period, the change has been most pronounced in East Asia and Pacific and in South Asia, where inequality had increased steeply between 1993 and 2008. Latin America and the Caribbean made the biggest contribution to declining inequality, accounting for almost half the total decline.

Concluding remarks

This chapter has presented empirical evidence on trends in income inequality using the latest available data from household surveys. The number of countries and household surveys analyzed makes this exercise the most current and complete assessment of within-country inequality worldwide. Yet, the analysis has limitations, namely, the changing and incomplete country composition of the sample and the likely underreporting of top incomes in household surveys. These caveats aside, there was a steady reduction in global inequality, defined as inequality among all individuals in the world, between 1988 and 2013. This was driven by the strong convergence in average incomes across countries, that is, by reductions in the inequality between countries. This fall in between-country inequality coincided with a period of rapid globalization and high growth, notably in some populous developing countries, such as China and India. Furthermore, the most marked reduction in global inequality occurred between 2008 and 2013, straddling the period of the global financial crisis and the subsequent slowdown in the global economy.

This reduction in global inequality constitutes a recent shift in an otherwise long-term secular rise in interpersonal inequality that began during the industrial revolution in the 1820s, which is as far back as the data allow, and that lasted through the 1980s. Furthermore, during the recent exceptional period of global inequality reduction, the share of the incomes of the top 1 percent has increased in a number of countries on which information is available. This is true in developed and emerging economies as long-term evidence from Argentina, India, the Republic of Korea, South Africa, and the United States confirms. Clearly, there are no grounds for complacency. In fact, even after the recent decline, global inequality is wider than the within-country inequality observed in most countries in the world.

The average country is more unequal today than 25 years ago. Within-country inequality as a whole—that is, considering together the trends of all countries on which evidence is available—only started to narrow in the last decade, after peaking in the 1990s. Inequality remains unacceptably high in many countries around the world. Developing countries tend to exhibit higher levels of inequality than developed countries. Latin America and the Caribbean, along with Sub-Saharan Africa, stand out as historically high-inequality regions. But it is precisely the Latin American region that has been more successful in reducing inequality than any other region.

Another critical finding of the country analysis is that, for every country in which inequality widened by more than 1 Gini point (19 of 81 countries) in recent years, it narrowed in more than two countries by over 1 point (41 out of 81 countries). More than a third of the population in the sample were living in a country in which the Gini had fallen by more than 1 point.

While this is good news, overoptimism is out of place. There should be no presumption that these favorable and exceptional recent trends will continue. The growth slowdown in developing and emerging economies, if it becomes protracted, is likely to delay further reductions in global inequality. Closely related is the secular decline in commodity prices. (The earlier boom in commodity prices had funded many equity-enhancing public investments within countries.) Climate change is projected to have significant negative distributional as well as poverty effects both globally and within countries. A recent analysis projects a larger decline in the incomes of the bottom 40 than the expected decline in the average incomes of the entire population, a consistent result across several scenarios of climate change projections, economic growth, and adoption of adaptive policy interventions.[58] This is because this group has lower-quality assets, less access to protection mechanisms, and is more vulnerable to the negative effects of climate change on agricultural productivity, weather shocks, food prices, and diseases. Finally, signs of a backlash against the free movement of goods, people, and ideas have emerged in a number of countries. Even though it is entirely speculative, such a backlash could hurt the poor if it were to reverse the inequality reductions observed since 2008 at a global level. While globalization has certainly produced both winners and losers, it is highly unlikely that undoing it will lead to sustaining or increasing the pace of the recent reduction in global inequality into the long run.

Beyond global processes, a country's income inequality is also a choice. Domestic policy choices explain, to a large extent, recent within-country inequality reductions, often combining solid macroeconomic management with coherent sectoral policies. (Chapter 5 examines the policy choices that have led to a reduction in inequality and an expansion in shared prosperity in selected countries. Chapter 6 assesses specific policy interventions that have had a demonstrated effect in reducing inequalities.)

Annex 4A

Data construction

Global inequality database

The estimates of global interpersonal inequality (see figure 4.5) are primarily based on Lakner and Milanović (2016a), who cover the period 1988 to 2008. Here, their data have been converted into 2011 purchasing power parity (PPP) exchange rates, and their estimates have been updated to 2013 using data from PovcalNet and Milanović (2016). The data update is constructed in exactly the same way as the Lakner and Milanović (2016a) dataset: surveys need to be within two years of a benchmark year; consecutive surveys need to be at least three and no more than seven years apart; and the welfare aggregate (income or consumption expenditure) must remain the same for a country over time.[59] Table 4A.1 shows the share of the global or regional population that is covered by the surveys included in the database. The regional definitions in table 4A.1 follow Lakner and Milanović (2016a) and are different from the regions used in this chapter. In 2013, 80 percent of the global population was covered.

The regions with the lowest coverage are the Middle East and North Africa, Sub-Saharan Africa, and Other Asia. This is relevant because changes in the sample composition could have important effects on the level of global inequality. However, the decline in global inequality between 2008 and 2013 is robust to a number of modifications, such as using a balanced sample of countries throughout.

Database of within-country Gini indexes

The primary source of the country-level Gini data is the October 2016 release of PovcalNet.[60] For most countries, PovcalNet computes these statistics directly from microdata.[61] To increase the geographic coverage, data from the All the Ginis database (Milanović 2014) are also used.[62] Because not every country holds a household survey annually, observations are grouped into six benchmark years from 1988 to 2013 in five-year intervals. If data for a benchmark year are not available, the nearest year within a

TABLE 4A.1 Population Coverage of the Data Used in the Global Inequality Estimates

Region	Benchmark year						Mean
	1988	1993	1998	2003	2008	2013	
World	81	92	92	94	94	80	89
(Number of surveys)	(74)	(114)	(119)	(137)	(139)	(103)	(114)
Mature economies	95	99	99	96	98	86	96
China	100	100	100	100	100	100	100
India	100	100	100	100	100	100	100
Other Asia	75	86	89	89	90	69	83
Middle East and North Africa	61	69	64	68	70	19	59
Sub-Saharan Africa	28	73	68	80	86	40	62
Latin America and the Caribbean	89	94	96	97	95	97	95
Russian Federation, Central Asia, Southeastern Europe	22	80	86	100	90	88	78

Sources: Lakner and Milanović 2016a; Milanović 2016; World Bank calculations based on PovcalNet (online analysis tool), World Bank, Washington, DC, http://iresearch.worldbank.org/PovcalNet/

Note: The cells in the table show the share of the global or regional population (in percent) accounted for by the surveys included in the database. The last column is the simple average over the benchmark years from 1988 to 2013. The regions are defined in Lakner and Milanović (2016a).

TABLE 4A.2 Population Coverage of the Data Used in the Analysis

Share of regional population covered by data (%)

	World	East Asia and Pacific	Eastern Europe and Central Asia	Latin America and the Caribbean	Middle East and North Africa	South Asia	Sub-Saharan Africa	Industrialized countries
A. Full sample								
1988 (73 countries)	79	90	93	91	42	96	10	75
1993 (102 countries)	88	95	87	93	76	97	68	77
1998 (106 countries)	71	95	82	95	70	22	71	75
2003 (135 countries)	91	95	99	94	77	98	77	78
2008 (136 countries)	92	96	93	95	72	98	70	95
2013 (101 countries)	80	94	90	92	32	87	52	69
B. Sub-samples								
Balanced[a] (41 countries)	46	88	14	79	22	11	4	66
Long-run trends[a] (91 countries)	84	95	83	87	62	97	53	76
Short-run trends[a] (81 countries)	54	81	87	90	32	12	21	69

Sources: WDI (World Development Indicators) (database), World Bank, Washington, DC, http://data.worldbank.org/data-catalog/world-development-indicators; World Economic Outlook Database, International Monetary Fund, Washington, DC, https://www.imf.org/external/pubs/ft/weo/2016/01/weodata/index.aspx.
Note: The cells in the table show the share of the global or regional population (in percent) accounted for by the surveys included in the database. For the balanced and trend samples, the population coverage refers to the final year.
a. For the balanced and trend samples, the population coverage refers to the final year.

two-year window around the benchmark year is chosen.[63] These estimates do not extrapolate or interpolate, and they mix income and consumption surveys, as discussed in the main text.

Table 4A.2 shows the population coverage of the resulting database by region.[64] The regional definition used throughout this chapter follows the World Bank's geographical classification, except for the industrialized countries category, which is a subcategory of the World Bank's high-income countries group.[65]

In the main sample, as many countries as possible are used in each benchmark year. This implies, however, that the country sample may change from year to year, which could lead to spurious changes arising from such sample attrition. To abstract from such changes, results are also presented for the sample of countries that are present in every benchmark year between 1988 and 2013 (see the balanced sample row in table 4A.2). Countries included in this sample also need to have the same welfare metric (income or consumption) in all years.

Figure 4.10 in the main text compares changes in inequality over two periods: 1993–2008 (long run) and 2008–13 (short run). The population coverage of these samples is shown in the last two rows of table 4A.2. These samples are different from those described above because, if a country is to be included, it needs to be observed in the initial and final year of the period considered.[66] Furthermore, only countries that have the same welfare measure (income or consumption) in both these years are included.[67] The long-run trend sample is thus a subset of the benchmark-year sample. The short-run sample is based on the World Bank Global Database of Shared Prosperity (see chapter 3).[68] This database includes countries with surveys around 2008 and 2013 in which welfare aggregates satisfy a high standard of comparability.[69] The subset of 75 countries for which the initial and final years fit the benchmark years 2008 and 2013 is then selected.[70] In particular, the initial year has to be between 2006 and 2010 and the final year between 2011 and 2015. Where possible, additional countries from last year's version of the shared prosperity database (covering 2007–12 on average) are included, as long as they fit these requirements. This produces the sample of 81 countries' short-run spells.

There exists a large number of alternative sources for data on Gini indexes (or other distributional statistics). As reviewed in detail in a recent special issue of the *Journal of Economic Inequality* (Ferreira, Lustig, and Teles 2015), these databases cover distributional statistics that are calculated directly from microdata, compiled from secondary data, or imputed. PovcalNet is the only database that uses (almost exclusively) microdata and that covers all countries in the world. Other microdata-based sources have a more limited geographical coverage. For instance, Eurostat, the Luxembourg Income Study, and the Organisation for Economic Co-operation and Development (OECD) focus on high-income countries, while the Socio-Economic Database for Latin America and the Caribbean (SEDLAC) covers only countries in Latin America and the Caribbean. The global coverage of Povcal-Net comes at a cost of lower comparability, such as in the use of both income and consumption surveys. PovcalNet is used here because it is based on microdata (as opposed to, for example, the World Income Inequality Database) and because of its global coverage.

In a background paper for this report, the results discussed here are compared with the other microdata-based sources mentioned above. Comparisons need to be done carefully because these sources may use different equivalence scales, welfare aggregates, or surveys.[71] While the within-country trends are quite similar, the levels of inequality can be quite different. However, the ranking of countries by level of inequality is reasonably robust across the data sources.

Notes

1. As discussed in the Overview, this decomposition was formalized by Datt and Raval-lion (1992). This does not imply that every inequality-reducing transfer would reduce the poverty headcount ratio. For instance, a pro-poor transfer among the poor would leave the poverty headcount ratio unchanged.
2. Clark and D'Ambrosio (2015); World Bank (2005).
3. Leveling the playing field aims at removing obstacles to a decent life that individuals may face because of circumstances fixed at birth, such as sex, belonging to a particular ethnic group or race, or family religious environment. These circumstances are, to a large extent, external to the decisions, ef-

forts, or talents of the individual. (Chapter 6 discusses interventions that have been successful in equalizing opportunities.)

4. According to *World Development Report 2006: Equity and Development*, while "outcomes matter, we are concerned with them mainly for their influence on absolute deprivation and their role in shaping opportunities" (World Bank 2005, 3). Brunori, Ferreira, and Peragine (2013) find that, across countries, measures of inequality of opportunity are positively correlated with measures of inequality of outcomes. They also find a negative correlation between inequality of opportunity and inter-generational mobility. Similarly, Corak (2013) shows a negative correlation between inequality of outcomes and mobility.
5. Atkinson (2015).
6. World Bank (2005). Interventions that reduce inequality without compromising economic growth are described here generically as equity-enhancing policies (see chapter 1). *World Development Report 2006: Equity and Development* calls these "efficient redistribution" policies (see World Bank 2005, 74).
7. Levy (2008).
8. Clements et al. (2015).
9. Dollar, Kleineberg, and Kraay (2016) and Dollar and Kraay (2002) document the central importance of growth for a range of social welfare functions, including, for instance, the growth of the bottom 20 and the bottom 40 or the growth of the income share of the bottom 20.
10. The evidence is exhaustively reviewed by the Commission on Growth and Development (2008).
11. For example, see Gill, Revenga, and Zeballos (2016).
12. For example, as discussed in Gill, Revenga, and Zeballos (2016), China's economic growth has been critical to poverty reduction since the onset of China's deep economic transformation in 1978, first based on agricultural productivity gains and then on export orientation. China's levels of human capital were already acceptable at the start of the reforms, and its traditional safety net has been transformed into a modern social assistance system.
13. Dollar, Kleineberg, and Kraay (2015, 2016); World Bank (2016a).

14. Dollar, Kleineberg, and Kraay (2015, 2016); World Bank (2016a).

15. Bourguignon (2004) described this poverty-growth-inequality triangle more than 10 years ago. A sizable literature discusses the relationships among poverty reduction, growth, and inequality. Analogous to the evidence presented here, this literature implies that changes in inequality are, on average, uncorrelated with economic growth, as reviewed by Ferreira (2012).

16. World Bank (2016a).

17. Reducing inequality is not always associated with good outcomes. For example, the reduction of inequality observed in the Middle East and North Africa region coexisted with an increasing sense of frustration and resentment drawing from redistribution without voice, a shortage of quality jobs in the formal sector, poor-quality public services, and a lack of government accountability. A lesson from this experience is that how inequality is reduced matters: a system of generalized subsidies conceived to reduce poverty and inequality did not overcome the rising frustration because of waning opportunities. See World Bank (2015).

18. World Bank (2014).

19. For example, see Atkinson and Piketty (2007, 2010).

20. See, for instance, López-Calva and Lustig (2010).

21. This is remarkable given that the household survey in Argentina uses income, while China uses consumption expenditure. Inequality in income tends to be greater than inequality in consumption.

22. This section uses household surveys from around the world, relying primarily on PovcalNet, an online tool that allows users to access the World Bank's repository of household surveys. It is designed mainly to allow users to replicate World Bank estimates of absolute poverty, but it also provides distributional statistics such as the Gini index. See PovcalNet (online analysis tool), World Bank, Washington, DC, http://iresearch.worldbank.org/PovcalNet/.

23. This chapter concentrates on vertical inequality, that is, comparing the rich and the poor. A horizontal perspective might look at differences among people based on sex, ethnicity, location of residence, or age. These are beyond the scope of this chapter. The World Bank has worked extensively on measuring and monitoring horizontal inequalities, for example, through the calculation of the human opportunity index. This index measures access to basic services and corrects the observed access rate by the degree of intergroup inequality. The relevant roles played by race and ethnicity, gender, age, location, and socioeconomic status of households have been accounted for and compared in Latin America and the Caribbean, Sub-Saharan Africa, and the Middle East and North Africa. See Barros et al. (2009); Dabalen et al. (2015); Krishnan et al. (2016).

24. A relative measure obeys the scale invariance axiom (see box 4.3). Among relative measures, the analysis here does not involve tests for robustness to alternative measures (or Lorenz dominance more generally), but mostly relies on the Gini index.

25. Detailed robustness checks are presented in Lakner and Silwal (2016). See also the special issue of the *Journal of Economic Inequality* that reviews the various inequality databases (Ferreira, Lustig, and Teles 2015).

26. SEDLAC (Socio-Economic Database for Latin America and the Caribbean), Center for Distributive, Labor, and Social Studies, Facultad de Ciencias Económicas, Universidad Nacional de La Plata, La Plata, Argentina; Equity Lab, Team for Statistical Development, World Bank, Washington, DC, http://sedlac.econo.unlp.edu.ar/eng/statistics.php.

27. As summarized by Beegle et al. (2016), other aspects that could make surveys incomparable include changes in survey design (for instance, urban or national coverage), implementation (such as effects of seasonality), or the questionnaires (for example, a recall period for consumption expenditure). Although PovcalNet enforces some degree of comparability across countries, differences might exist in terms of these aspects or the type of spatial price adjustment. In addition to the potential nonresponse at the top tail, surveys might exclude the poorest living in remote regions or poorly measure their incomes; for instance, Meyer et al. (2015) discuss missing transfer incomes in the United States.

28. See the explanation of the twin goals in the Overview and in chapter 1. For ease of expo-

sition, we tend to refer to income and consumption interchangeably in this chapter, unless otherwise indicated.

29. See Anand and Segal (2015). Some authors, such as Alvaredo and Gasparini (2015) in their recent review of inequality trends in developing countries, use an additive or multiplicative adjustment factor to reduce the income-based Gini indexes in Latin America. Regarding definitional differences in general (such as gross versus net income, or equivalence scales), Atkinson and Brandolini (2001) caution against simple across-the-board adjustments. Furthermore, any such adjustment would be inconsistent with the World Bank approach to measuring poverty and shared prosperity.

30. Alvaredo and Gasparini (2015).

31. Aguiar and Bils (2015).

32. Karabarbounis and Neiman (2014).

33. Alvaredo and Gasparini (2015).

34. The perspective of global inequality adopted here corresponds to Concept 3 in the Milanović (2005) taxonomy.

35. Bourguignon (2015).

36. As reviewed by Anand and Segal (2015), the main methodological differences concern (1) the use of GDP per capita or average household survey income, (2) the adjustment for differences between income and consumption surveys, and (3) different PPP exchange rates. The methodology used in figure 4.5, which is described in more detail in Lakner and Milanović (2016a), is consistent with the approach to global poverty measurement (see chapter 2). It uses household survey income or consumption expressed in 2011 PPP U.S. dollars without adjusting for differences between income and consumption surveys. Given the data limitations in the early years, each country distribution is approximated by 10 deciles. This tends to underestimate within-country (and thus global) inequality, but the difference is small (Anand and Segal 2015). In a slightly different version of the global distribution, the shift from percentiles to deciles reduces the global Gini by around 0.5 points.

37. These errors refer to both sampling- and nonsampling-related sources, which analysts can do little to correct once the surveys are collected. However, while no estimates of sampling uncertainty are available, the decline between 1988 and 2013 is robust to a number of robustness checks (Lakner and Milanović 2016b). First, there exists Lorenz dominance; so, the assessment is robust to alternative measures of inequality (Atkinson 1970). Second, the decline is similar if the same set of countries is used throughout, instead of the largest possible sample in every year. This is important because the population coverage declines in 2013, especially in Sub-Saharan Africa (see annex 4A). Furthermore, as shown by Lakner and Milanović (2016a), the fall between 2003 and 2008 is even more dramatic if an adjustment for the underreporting of top incomes is included.

38. This convergence effect is greater if GDP per capita is used instead of the means from household surveys. As a result, studies that adjust to GDP per capita, such as Bourguignon (2015), find a decline in global inequality that is more rapid than the results presented here.

39. Jirasavetakul and Lakner (2016).

40. China's growth has pushed down between-country inequality in the region, while the increase in inequality in China has pushed up the within-country component.

41. These are not the first results on average within-country inequality. For instance, World Bank (2005) and Ferreira and Ravallion (2009) follow a similar structure of discussing the context of global inequality before focusing on within-country inequality. What sets our analysis apart from the recent literature is that it covers all available countries regardless of region or income level. In contrast, Alvaredo and Gasparini (2015), who also use PovcalNet data, only cover developing countries and adjust for differences in inequality levels between income and consumption surveys. Morelli, Smeeding, and Thompson (2015) are also closely related, but they cover only rich and (some) middle-income countries. See PovcalNet (online analysis tool), World Bank, Washington, DC, http://iresearch.worldbank.org /PovcalNet/.

42. In fact, this estimate can be directly compared with the within-country inequality part of the global decomposition (figure 4.5), although there exist small differences. However, these differences are unlikely to be significant. Furthermore, they may arise

from multiple sources, such as differences in the inequality measure (mean log deviation vs. Gini index), the country coverage, and the use of decile groups vs. the full microdata.

43. Owing to the equal treatment of countries in the unweighted analysis, the impact on the worldwide trend of the rapid increase in inequality in large countries, notably, China, is less than the impact on the weighted estimates of average within-country inequality.

44. In addition, for a country to be included in the balanced sample, it needs to have the same welfare measure (income or consumption) throughout, as explained in more detail in annex 4A.

45. See chapter 2, annex 2B, for the list of industrialized countries.

46. The decline in inequality in the region is supported by the expansion in real hourly earnings among the bottom of the wage distribution and, to a lesser extent, the middle part of the earnings distribution. The decline in wage inequality in Latin America has been closely associated with a reversal in the college/primary education premium and in the urban-rural earnings gap, coupled with a steady drop (which accelerated markedly beginning in the first decade of the 2000s) in the high school/primary education premium as well as a decline in the experience premium across all age-groups. See Rodríguez-Castelán et al. (2016).

47. Székely and Mendoza (2015).

48. Cord et al. (2016); Gasparini, Cruces, and Tornarolli (2016).

49. Regional averages can mask substantial variability across countries. This is also notable in the case of Sub-Saharan Africa, where countries are almost evenly split across rising and falling inequality in recent years (see Beegle et al. 2016; Cornia 2014).

50. Milanović and Ersado (2010).

51. One reason the trends in regional averages need to be interpreted carefully is the change in country composition from one benchmark year to the next, especially in regions with many countries that do not have surveys every five years. This explains some of the large changes in East Asia and South Asia illustrated in figure 4.7.

52. This has been noted by Ferreira and Ravallion (2009). Africa's wide inequality has also been discussed by Beegle et al. (2016) and Cornia (2014). Milanović (2003) argues that African inequality is too high given the relatively widely shared land ownership.

53. Morelli, Smeeding, and Thompson (2015) report trends in the Gini index of equivalent household income drawn from data of the Organisation for Economic Co-operation and Development (OECD) and national statistical offices.

54. See Beegle et al. (2016).

55. As a rough adjustment for sampling errors, we ignore changes within 1 point. With a lack of confidence intervals, any such cutoff value is essentially arbitrary. We follow Alvaredo and Gasparini (2015), who use 1 point, which, they argue, is typically significant in the SEDLAC surveys (also see Statistics Canada, referenced by Atkinson 2003). Atkinson, Rainwater, and Smeeding (1995) refer to a change in the Gini index between 1 and 2 points as a modest increase. Other authors have used +/− 1 percent or +/− 2 percent (Burniaux et al. 1998; Smeeding 2000), which would correspond to 0.4 Gini points and 0.8 points, respectively, evaluated at the average within-country Gini of 40 in our sample. This suggests that our cutoff value is relatively conservative. However, even if such changes may be statistically significant, they are not necessarily economically significant, for which Atkinson (2003) proposes a 3 point cutoff (in his sample of OECD countries). Without any adjustment for sampling errors, inequality increases (falls) in 46 (45) countries in the long-run spells, and in 30 (51) countries in the short-run spells.

56. As a result, the population-weighted average Gini in this sample increased by 2.1 points, from 37.1 to 39.2, between 1993 and 2008.

57. However, there might be issues with survey comparability. Cornia (2014) also documented this bifurcation of inequality trends in Sub-Saharan Africa. Recently, Beegle et al. (2016) find that a set of African countries with at least two strictly comparable and recent surveys is split evenly into rising and falling inequality. Their surveys are drawn from the 2000s and, so, concern a slightly different period relative to the trends in this chapter.

58. Hallegatte et al. (2016).

59. Lakner and Milanović (2016a) explain the data construction in more detail. In the 2013 benchmark year, one exception has been made to achieve sufficient population coverage: the 2009/10 and 2011/12 surveys in India are only two years apart.

60. These data are publicly available from PovcalNet (online analysis tool), World Bank, Washington, DC, http://iresearch.worldbank.org/PovcalNet/. They are supplemented with data from the earlier releases of PovcalNet where possible.

61. For a small number of countries on which microdata are not available (for example, China), PovcalNet continues to use grouped data, in combination with a parametric Lorenz curve.

62. In the final database of benchmark years, about 9 percent of observations are drawn from the All the Ginis database, especially during the earlier years. While the All the Ginis database includes a mix of primary and secondary sources, it is used here only for the observations that are based on the Luxembourg Income Study. These observations are calculated directly from microdata using per capita household disposable income among individuals (Milanović 2014), which is consistent with PovcalNet. For the database, see All the Ginis (dataset), World Bank, Washington, DC, http://go.worldbank.org/9VCQW66LA0.

63. Among surveys that are equidistant to the benchmark year, the more recent survey is preferred. For a few countries, the years that were used for a particular benchmark year were changed so that the countries have the same welfare aggregate throughout and can thus be included in the balanced subsample.

64. Population data are obtained from World Development Indicators, supplemented with data in World Economic Outlook for any missing countries. See World Economic Outlook Database, International Monetary Fund, Washington, DC, https://www.imf.org/external/pubs/ft/weo/2016/01/weodata/index.aspx; WDI (World Development Indicators) (database), World Bank, Washington, DC, http://data.worldbank.org/data-catalog/world-development-indicators.

65. The World Bank geographical classification is available at "World Bank Country and Lending Groups," World Bank, Washington, DC, https://datahelpdesk.worldbank.org/knowledgebase/articles/906519-world-bank-country-and-lending-groups. See chapter 2, annex 2B, for the list of industrialized countries.

66. This is also different from the balanced sample, in which countries need to be present in all years in between.

67. For countries for which the welfare measure changes, the initial and final years (within the two-year window defined by the benchmark years) are changed where possible. For these countries, some of the observations included in the trend sample are thus slightly different from the ones included in the original cross-sectional benchmark-year sample. For instance, this applies to Bulgaria, Kazakhstan, and Ukraine.

68. For the data and documentation, see GDSP (Global Database of Shared Prosperity), World Bank, Washington, DC, http://www.worldbank.org/en/topic/poverty/brief/global-database-of-shared-prosperity.

69. These comparability standards are stricter than for the long-run sample, for which it is only required that the welfare aggregate be either income or consumption. Beegle et al. (2016) discuss the issues around comparing consumption aggregates over time.

70. Another requirement is that an estimate of the Gini index be available in PovcalNet for the same year and welfare aggregate. The World Bank Global Database of Shared Prosperity reports estimates of shared prosperity, but no Gini indexes.

71. See Lakner and Silwal (2016). For example, the Luxembourg Income Study and OECD use the square root of household size, while, in Eurostat's scale, the weight varies with the age of the household member.

References

Aguiar, Mark, and Mark Bils. 2015. "Has Consumption Inequality Mirrored Income Inequality." *American Economic Review* 105 (9): 2725–56.

Alesina, Alberto, and Dani Rodrik. 1994, "Distributive Politics and Economic Growth." *Quarterly Journal of Economics* 109 (2): 465–90.

Alvaredo, Facundo, Anthony B. Atkinson, Thomas Piketty, and Emmanuel Saez. 2013. "The Top 1 Percent in International and Historical Perspective." *Journal of Economic Perspectives* 27 (3): 3–20.

Alvaredo, Facundo, and Leonardo Gasparini. 2015. "Recent Trends in Inequality and Poverty in Developing Countries." In *Handbook of Income Distribution*, vol. 2A, edited by Anthony B. Atkinson and François Bourguignon, 697–805. Handbooks in Economics. Amsterdam: North-Holland.

Anand, Sudhir, and Paul Segal. 2015. "The Global Distribution of Income." In *Handbook of Income Distribution*, vol. 2A, edited by Anthony B. Atkinson and François Bourguignon, 937–79. Handbooks in Economics. Amsterdam: North-Holland.

Arampatzi, Efstratia, Martijn Burger, Elena Ianchovichina, Tina Röhricht, and Ruut Veenhoven. 2015. "Unhappy Development: Dissatisfaction with Life in the Wake of the Arab Spring." Policy Research Working Paper 7488, World Bank, Washington, DC.

Atkinson, Anthony B. 1970. "On the Measurement of Inequality." *Journal of Economic Theory* 2 (3): 244–63.

———. 2003. "Income Inequality in OECD Countries: Data and Explanations." *CESifo Economic Studies* 49 (4): 479–513.

———. 2015. *Inequality: What Can Be Done?* Cambridge, MA: Harvard University Press.

Atkinson, Anthony B., and Andrea Brandolini. 2001. "Promise and Pitfalls in the Use of 'Secondary' Data-Sets: Income Inequality in OECD Countries as a Case Study." *Journal of Economic Literature* 39 (3): 771–99.

———. 2010. "On Analyzing the World Distribution of Income." *World Bank Economic Review* 24 (1): 1–37.

Atkinson, Anthony B., and Thomas Piketty, eds. 2007. *Top Incomes over the Twentieth Century: A Contrast between Continental European and English-Speaking Countries.* New York: Oxford University Press.

———, eds. 2010. *Top Incomes: A Global Perspective.* New York: Oxford University Press.

Atkinson, Anthony B., Lee Rainwater, and Timothy M. Smeeding. 1995. "Income Distribution in Advanced Economies: Evidence from the Luxembourg Income Study (LIS)." Luxembourg Income Study Working Paper 120, LIS Cross-National Data Center, Luxembourg.

Banerjee, Abhijit, and Esther Duflo. 2003. "Inequality and Growth: What Can the Data Say?" *Journal of Economic Growth* 8 (3): 267–99.

Barros, Ricardo Paes de, Francisco H. G. Ferreira, José R. Molinas Vega, and Jaime Saavedra-Chanduvi. 2009. *Measuring Inequality of Opportunities in Latin America and Caribbean.* With Mirela de Carvalho, Samuel Franco, Samuel Freije-Rodríguez, and Jérémie Gignoux. Latin American Development Forum Series. Washington, DC: World Bank; New York: Palgrave Macmillan.

Beegle, Kathleen, Luc Christiaensen, Andrew Dabalen, and Isis Gaddis. 2016. *Poverty in a Rising Africa.* Washington, DC: World Bank.

Bourguignon, François. 2004. "The Poverty-Growth-Inequality Triangle." Working Paper 125, Indian Council for Research on International Economic Relations, New Delhi.

———. 2015. *The Globalization of Inequality.* Translated by Thomas Scott-Railton. Princeton, NJ: Princeton University Press.

Brunori, Paolo, Francisco H. G. Ferreira, and Vito Peragine. 2013. "Inequality of Opportunity, Income Inequality, and Economic Mobility: Some International Comparisons." Policy Research Working Paper 6304, World Bank, Washington, DC.

Burniaux, Jean-Marc, Thai-Thanh Dang, Douglas Fore, Michael F. Förster, Marco Mira d'Ercole, and Howard Oxley. 1998. "Income Distribution and Poverty in Selected OECD Countries." OECD Economics Department Working Paper 189 (March), Organisation for Economic Co-operation and Development, Paris.

Cantril, Hadley. 1965. *The Pattern of Human Concerns.* New Brunswick, NJ: Rutgers University Press.

Chattopadhyay, Soumya, and Carol L. Graham. 2015. "From Arab Spring to Fall: Some Insights from the Economics of Well-Being." Brookings Institution, Washington, DC.

Clark, Andrew E., and Conchita D'Ambrosio. 2015. "Attitudes to Income Inequality: Experimental and Survey Evidence." In *Handbook of Income Distribution*, vol. 2A, edited by Anthony B. Atkinson and François Bourguignon, 1127–1208. Handbooks in Economics. Amsterdam: North-Holland.

Clements, Benedict, Ruud de Mooij, Sanjeev Gupta, and Michael Keen, eds. 2015. *Inequality and Fiscal Policy.* Washington, DC: International Monetary Fund.

Commission on Growth and Development. 2008. *The Growth Report: Strategies for Sustained Growth and Inclusive Development.* Washington, DC: World Bank. https://openknowledge .worldbank.org/handle/10986/6507.

Corak, Miles. 2013. "Income Inequality, Equality of Opportunity, and Intergenerational Mobility. *Journal of Economic Perspectives* 27 (3): 79–102.

Cord, Louise, Oscar Barriga Cabanillas, Leonardo Lucchetti, Carlos Rodríguez-Castelán, Liliana D. Sousa, and Daniel Valderrama, 2016. "Inequality Stagnation in Latin America in the Aftermath of the Global Financial Crisis." *Review of Development Economics* May 19.

Cornia, Giovanni Andrea. 2014. "Income Inequality Levels, Trends, and Determinants in Sub-Saharan Africa: An Overview of the Main Changes." Università degli Studi di Firenze, Florence.

Dabalen, Andrew, Ambar Narayan, Jaime Saavedra-Chanduvi, and Alejandro Hoyos Suarez. 2015. *Do African Children Have an Equal Chance? A Human Opportunity Report for Sub-Saharan Africa.* With Ana Abras and Sailesh Tiwari. Directions in Development: Poverty Series. Washington, DC: World Bank.

Dabla-Norris, Era, Kalpana Kochhar, Frantisek Ricka, Nujin Suphaphiphat, and Evridiki Tsounta. 2015. "Causes and Consequences of Income Inequality: A Global Perspective." IMF Staff Discussion Note SDN/15/13 (June), International Monetary Fund, Washington, DC.

Datt, Gaurav, and Martin Ravallion. 1992. "Growth and Redistribution Components of Changes in Poverty Measures: A Decomposition with Applications to Brazil and India in the 1980s." *Journal of Development Economics* 38 (2): 275–95.

Dollar, David, Tatjana Kleineberg, and Aart Kraay. 2015. "Growth, Inequality, and Social Welfare: Cross-Country Evidence." *Economic Policy* 30 (82): 335–77.

———. 2016. "Growth is Still Good for the Poor." *European Economic Review* 81: 68–85.

Dollar, David, and Aart Kraay. 2002. "Growth Is Good for the Poor." *Journal of Economic Growth* 7 (3): 195–225.

Ferreira, Francisco H. G. 2012. "Distributions in Motion: Economic Growth, Inequality, and Poverty Dynamics." In *The Oxford Handbook of the Economics of Poverty*, edited by Philip N. Jefferson, 427–62. New York: Oxford University Press.

Ferreira, Francisco H. G., Christoph Lakner, María Ana Lugo, and Berk Özler. 2014. "Inequality of Opportunity and Economic Growth: A Cross-Country Analysis." Policy Research Working Paper 6915, World Bank, Washington, DC.

Ferreira, Francisco H. G., Nora Lustig, and Daniel C. Teles. 2015. "Appraising Cross-National Income Inequality Databases: An Introduction." *Journal of Economic Inequality* 13 (4): 497–526.

Ferreira, Francisco H. G., and Martin Ravallion, 2009. "Poverty and Inequality: The Global Context." In *The Oxford Handbook of Economic Inequality*, edited by Wiemer Salverda, Brian Nolan, and Timothy M. Smeeding, 599–638. New York: Oxford University Press.

Forbes, Kristin. 2000. "A Reassessment of the Relationship between Inequality and Growth." *American Economic Review* 90 (4): 869–87.

Gallup. 2011a. "Understanding How Gallup Uses the Cantril Scale." *Latest News.* Gallup, Washington, DC. http://www.gallup.com/poll /122453/understanding-gallup-uses-cantril -scale.aspx.

———. 2011b. "Egypt from Tahrir to Transition." *Latest News.* Abu Dhabi Gallup Center, United Arab Emirates. http://www.gallup.com /poll/157046/egypt-tahrir-transition.aspx.

Gasparini, Leonardo, Guillermo Cruces, and Leopoldo Tornarolli. 2016. "Chronicle of a Deceleration Foretold: Income inequality in Latin America in the 2010s." Documento de Trabajo 198 (May), Center for Distributive, Labor, and Social Studies, Facultad de Ciencias Económicas, Universidad Nacional de La Plata, La Plata, Argentina.

Gill, Indermit, Ana Revenga, and Christian Zeballos. 2016. *Grow, Invest, Insure: A Game Plan to End Poverty.* Washington, DC: World Bank.

Graham, Carol L. 2016. *Happiness for All? Unequal Lives and Unequal Hopes in the Land of the Dream.* Princeton, NJ: Princeton University Press.

Graham, Carol L., and Eduardo Lora. 2009. *Paradox and Perceptions: Quality of Life in Latin America.* Washington, DC: Brookings Institution Press.

Hallegatte, Stephane, Mook Bangalore, Laura Bonzanigo, Marianne Fay, Tomaro Kane,

Ulf Narloch, Julie Rozenberg, David Treguer, and Adrien Vogt-Schilb. 2016. *Shock Waves: Managing the Impacts of Climate Change on Poverty*. Climate Change and Development Series. Washington, DC: World Bank.

Hassine, Nadia Belhaj. 2015. "Economic Inequality in the Arab Region." *World Development* 66: 532-56.

Iqbal, Farrukh, and Youssouf Kiendrebeogo. 2014. "The Reduction of Child Mortality in the Middle East and North Africa: A Success Story." Policy Research Working Paper 7023, World Bank, Washington, DC.

Jenkins, Stephen P. 2015. "World Income Inequality Databases: An Assessment of WIID and SWIID." *Journal of Economic Inequality* 13 (4): 629–71.

Jirasavetakul, La-Bhus Fah, and Christoph Lakner. 2016. "The Distribution of Consumption Expenditure in Sub-Saharan Africa: The Inequality among All Africans." Policy Research Working Paper 7557, World Bank, Washington, DC.

Karabarbounis, Loukas, and Brent Neiman. 2014. "The Global Decline of the Labor Share." *Quarterly Journal of Economics* 129 (1): 61–103.

Khouri, Rami, and Joanne J. Myers. 2015. "Perspectives from Inside a Tumultuous Middle East: Syria-Iraq-ISIS-Russia and Iran." Public Affairs, Global Ethics Forum TV Series (November 18), Carnegie Council for Ethics in International Affairs, New York. http://www.carnegiecouncil.org/studio/multimedia/20151118/index.html.

Kraay, Aart. 2015. "Weak Instruments in Growth Regressions: Implications for Recent Cross-Country Evidence on Inequality and Growth." Policy Research Working Paper 7494, World Bank, Washington, DC.

Krishnan, Nandini, Gabriel Lara Ibarra, Ambar Narayan, Sailesh Tiwari, and Tara Vishwanath. 2016. *Uneven Odds, Unequal Outcomes: Inequality of Opportunity in the Middle East and North Africa*. Directions in Development: Poverty Series. Washington, DC: World Bank.

Lakner, Christoph, and Branko Milanović. 2016a. "Global Income Distribution: From the Fall of the Berlin Wall to the Great Recession." *World Bank Economic Review* 30 (2): 203–32.

———. 2016b. "Global Inequality after the Great Recession." World Bank, Washington, DC.

Lakner, Christoph, and Ani Rudra Silwal. 2016. "Inequality Increasing Everywhere? Conflicting Evidence from an Updated Global Database of Household Surveys." World Bank, Washington, DC.

Levy, Santiago. 2008. *Good Intentions, Bad Outcomes: Social Policy, Informality, and Economic Growth in Mexico*. Washington, DC: Brookings Institution Press.

López-Calva, Luis F., and Nora Lustig, eds. 2010. *Declining Inequality in Latin America: A Decade of Progress?* New York: United Nations Development Programme; Washington, DC: Brookings Institution.

Marrero, Gustavo A., and Juan Gabriel Rodríguez. 2013. "Inequality of Opportunity and Growth." *Journal of Development Economics* 104: 107–22.

Meyer, Bruce D., Wallace K. C. Mok, and James X. Sullivan. 2015. "Household Surveys in Crisis." *Journal of Economic Perspectives* 29 (4): 199–226.

Milanović, Branko. 2003, "Is Inequality in Africa Really Different?" Policy Research Working Paper 3169, World Bank, Washington, DC.

———. 2005. *Worlds Apart: Measuring International and Global Inequality*. Princeton, NJ: Princeton University Press.

———. 2014. "All the Ginis, 1950–2012 (updated in Autumn 2014)." November, World Bank, Washington, DC. http://go.worldbank.org/9VCQW66LA0.

———. 2016. *Global Inequality: A New Approach for the Age of Globalization*. Cambridge, MA: Harvard University Press.

Milanović, Branko, and Ersado, Lire, 2010. "Reform and Inequality during the Transition: An Analysis Using Panel Household Survey Data, 1990–2006." Working Paper 2010–62, World Institute for Development Economics Research, Helsinki.

Morelli, Salvatore, Timothy Smeeding, and Jeffrey Thompson. 2015. "Post-1970 Trends in within-Country Inequality and Poverty: Rich and Middle-Income Countries." In *Handbook of Income Distribution*, vol. 2A, edited by Anthony B. Atkinson and François Bourguignon, 593–696. Handbooks in Economics. Amsterdam: North-Holland.

Ncube, Mthuli, John Anyanwu, and Kjell Hausken. 2013. "Inequality, Economic Growth, and Poverty in the Middle East and North Africa (MENA)." Working Paper 193

(December), African Development Bank, Tunis, Tunisia.

Ostry, Jonathan, Andrew Berg, and Charalambos Tsangarides. 2014. "Redistribution, Inequality, and Growth." IMF Staff Discussion Note SDN/14/02 (April), International Monetary Fund, Washington, DC.

Persson, Torsten, and Guido Tabellini. 1994. "Is Inequality Harmful for Growth?" *American Economic Review* 84 (3): 600–21.

Ravallion, Martin. 2016. *The Economics of Poverty: History, Measurement, and Policy.* New York: Oxford University Press.

Rodríguez-Castelán, Carlos, Luis F. López-Calva, Nora Lustig, and Daniel Valderrama. 2016. "Understanding the Dynamics of Labor Income Inequality in Latin America." Policy Research Working Paper 7795, World Bank, Washington, DC.

Roemer, John E. 1998. *Equality of Opportunity.* Cambridge, MA: Harvard University Press.

SEDLAC (Socio-Economic Database for Latin America and the Caribbean), Center for Distributive, Labor, and Social Studies, Universidad de La Plata, La Plata, Argentina; World Bank, Washington, DC (accessed June 14), http://sedlac.econo.unlp.edu.ar/eng/index .php.

Smeeding, Timothy M., 2000 "Changing Income Inequality in OECD Countries: Updated Results from the Luxembourg Income Study (LIS)." In *The Personal Distribution of Income in an International Perspective*, edited by Richard Hauser and Irene Becker, 205–24. Berlin: Springer-Verlag.

Solt, Frederick. 2016. "Standardizing the World Income Inequality Database." *Social Science Quarterly* 90 (2): 231–42.

Souza, Pedro H. G. Ferreira de, Marcelo Medeiros, and Fabio A. Castro. 2015. "'Top Incomes in Brazil: Preliminary Results." *Economics Bulletin* 35 (2): 998–1004.

Székely, Miguel, and Pamela Mendoza. 2015. "Is the Decline in Inequality in Latin America Here to Stay?" *Journal of Human Development and Capabilities* 16 (3): 397–419.

Teyssier, Geoffrey. 2015. "Inequality of Opportunity and Growth: An Empirical Investigation in Brazil." Paper presented at the sixth meeting of the Society for the Study of Economic Inequality, Université du Luxembourg, Campus Kirchberg, Luxembourg, July 13–15.

van der Weide, Roy, Christoph Lakner, and Elena Ianchovichina. 2016. "Is Inequality Underestimated in Egypt? Evidence from House Prices." Policy Research Working Paper 7727, World Bank, Washington, DC.

Verme, Paolo, Branko Milanović, Sherine Al-Shawarby, Sahar El Tawila, May Gadallah, and Enas Ali A. El-Majeed. 2014. *Inside Inequality in the Arab Republic of Egypt: Facts and Perceptions across People, Time, and Space.* World Bank Study Series. Washington, DC: World Bank.

Voitchovsky, Sarah. 2009. "Inequality and Economic Growth." In *The Oxford Handbook of Economic Inequality*, edited by Wiemer Salverda, Brian Nolan, and Timothy M. Smeeding, 549–74. New York: Oxford University Press.

World Bank. 2005. *World Development Report 2006: Equity and Development.* Washington, DC: World Bank; New York: Oxford University Press.

———. 2014. *The Unfinished Revolution: Bringing Opportunity, Good Jobs, and Greater Wealth to All Tunisians.* Development Policy Review (May). Washington, DC: World Bank.

———. 2015. "Inequality, Uprisings, and Conflict in the Arab World." *MENA Economic Monitor* (October), World Bank, Washington, DC.

———. 2016a. *Global Monitoring Report 2015/16: Development Goals in an Era of Demographic Change.* Washington, DC: World Bank.

———. 2016b. *Indonesia's Rising Divide: Why Inequality Is Rising, Why It Matters, and What Can Be Done.* Jakarta: World Bank.

Reductions in Inequality: A Country Perspective

5

This chapter describes the key drivers behind the remarkable progress achieved by selected countries in boosting shared prosperity, narrowing inequality, and reducing poverty. These countries—Brazil, Cambodia, Mali, Peru, and Tanzania—are diverse in terms of geographical location, income status, development trajectory, and historical background. The heterogeneity of their experiences facilitates an examination of how environment, macroeconomic policies, sectoral strategies, and the management of external shocks interact to produce successful outcomes.

The countries all exercised cautious macroeconomic management, appropriately dealt with external shocks, and implemented extensive and orderly economic and social sector reforms. They also benefited from a global context that was particularly favorable, with abundant and cheap credit in international markets, booming trade, and high commodity prices. These steps and the context allowed rapid, sustainable, and inclusive growth. They also highlight the importance of labor markets in translating economic growth into an expansion in opportunities by creating jobs and increasing earnings, promoting the integration of individuals otherwise excluded from economic and social advancement, and reducing gaps among workers owing to gender, residence, or sector. Country-specific choices also play a role in rolling back inequalities. Thus, the minimum wage and safety nets have played a substantial role in Brazil, while the shift from agriculture toward light manufacturing and services in Cambodia opened up employment for the poor.

The examples confirm that good macroeconomic policies are essential to fostering shared prosperity. Rapid, sustained economic growth and a favorable context render the effort to establish equality easier. Coherent domestic policies, fiscal space, and improvement in the functioning of labor markets help undermine inequality. While the specific drivers are likely to diverge across countries, sustaining inequality reduction into the future may require some of the same elements: regular investments in human capital accumulation, enhanced productivity, economic diversification, spending on infrastructure to link lagging regions, and the framing of adequate safety nets. These country experiences also demonstrate that success in narrowing inequality does not necessarily translate into success on other economic, political, and social fronts. For example, conflict has recently resurged in Mali after two decades of relative stability. Despite some diversification in the economy, the absence of growth and competition continue to characterize the private sector in Tanzania. And recent decisions regarding the control of fiscal balances and inflation in Brazil have contributed to the recession in that economy as the global context has become less favorable.

Introduction

Since the early 1990s, income inequality has been declining globally. There are, however, large regional differences. The Latin America and Caribbean region, which has shown historically high levels of income inequality, has witnessed more progress. Overall, country experiences confirm that inequality can widen as well as narrow. This begs a fundamental question: what have successful countries done to cut into income inequality that other economies have not done? Among the constellation of policies that have been implemented, this chapter identifies the key levers in a few selected countries. It also stresses the importance of the favorable global context during much of the period analyzed: low interest rates, high international commodity prices, and booming international trade. Some countries also experienced favorable shocks that were external to any policy decisions by governments, such as good weather spells and the redirection of trade flows in Mali from neighboring countries affected by conflict.

This chapter assesses how good macroeconomic management, sectoral reform, the strengthening of safety nets, responses to external shocks, and initial conditions all contribute to the effort to trim away at inequality and support shared prosperity. The countries have been chosen with a view to extracting relevant lessons across a wide variety of successful experiences. They are therefore among the top performers in promoting shared prosperity, lessening inequality, and combating extreme poverty during the periods analyzed. To reflect the diversity of experiences, the selection also highlights regional differences; covers low- and middle-income-countries; includes countries at distinct stages of development, for example, agrarian and modern economies; and is sensitive to special historical contexts, such as conflict or high and pervasive levels of inequality.

The countries selected are Brazil, Cambodia, Mali, Peru, and Tanzania. These countries have had great success in sharing prosperity. The rates of income growth among the bottom 40 percent of the income distribution (the bottom 40) have been well in excess of the average growth across the population in each country. According to the latest available information, the growth in the bottom 40 exceeds that of the mean, ranging from about 2 percentage points in Tanzania to almost 5 percentage points in Mali (one of the few countries in the world with negative average growth at the mean), while incomes among the bottom 40 expanded at robust, positive rates. These achievements place these five countries among the top performers in boosting shared prosperity (see chapter 3). As expected from the links between shared prosperity and distributional changes, most of the countries that have achieved large premiums in shared prosperity also exhibit a narrowing in income inequality as measured by the Gini index.

Rather than an exhaustive and detailed causal analysis, the country case studies provide a modest and focused review of the ways in which the nature of growth, policy, and context influence the reduction in inequality and the growth among the bottom 40. The case studies benefit from existing academic research, international and local analytical work, and the evidence of project and operational assessments. Evidence is provided by both partial and economy-wide general equilibrium analyses. It is from multiple sources, such as the wealth of country reports on poverty and social impact analysis that examine the distributive effects of policy reform; systematic country diagnostic reports that establish the key priorities of countries in the effort to achieve the twin World Bank goals of ending poverty and boosting shared prosperity; the Commitment to Equity Initiative, which offers a thorough assessment of the contribution to equality of markets, taxation, and social spending; and decomposition analyses of trends in poverty and inequality reduction.[1]

While the five countries cannot fully represent a global scale, they portray wide-ranging diversity. They are in three regions: Asia, Latin America and the Caribbean, and Sub-Saharan Africa. They are low- or middle-income-countries. Two, Brazil and Peru, are predominantly urban societies, while the populations of the other three countries are largely concentrated in rural areas. In terms of economic growth, the experiences are wide-ranging as well. Most of the countries showed solid annual per capita growth in gross domestic product (GDP) during the period of study: Brazil, 2004–14; Cambodia, 2007–13; Mali, 2001–10; Peru, 2004–14; and Tanzania, 2007–12. However, while robust, per capita GDP growth has been more modest in Brazil and Mali, with annual rates of 2.3 percent in Brazil and 1.2 percent in Mali. Annual per capita GDP growth in the other three countries exceeds these rates: 4.7 percent in Peru, 3.4 percent in Cambodia, and 3.0 percent in Tanzania during their respective spells.

The experience of these countries in reducing poverty and inequality is remarkable. Poverty reductions have been substantial in all five countries, but especially in Brazil, Cambodia, and Peru. The reduction in income inequality has also been considerable in Brazil, Cambodia, Mali, and Peru, though more modest in Tanzania (table 5.1). Hence, in these countries, large poverty declines have typically been coupled with substantive inequality reductions. Notwithstanding these favorable trends, the countries differ in the levels of poverty and inequality. The two Latin American countries showed low poverty and wide inequality; Cambodia had low poverty and narrow inequality; and the two African countries experienced high poverty and wide inequality (table 5.2).

The selected country cases also provide a relevant lesson: success in reducing inequality does not automatically translate into a similar success on other economic, political, or social fronts. For example, the deterioration of governance in Mali that brewed for two decades culminated in conflict in 2012, thus putting a brake on the reductions achieved during the previous decade. In fact, inequality reductions can be short-lived. While achieving substantive reductions in inequality is an accomplishment, sustaining these reductions is a superior feat.

The assessment of country experiences does not seek to provide precise equalizing policy prescriptions. The small number of countries reviewed is a sound argument against any attempt at deriving sweeping

TABLE 5.1 Annualized per Capita GDP Growth and Reductions in Inequality, Selected Countries

Country	Years	Per capita GDP growth, annualized, %	Gini reduction, points
Brazil	2004–14	2.4	5.5
Cambodia	2007–13	3.4	11.0
Mali	2001–10	1.5	6.9
Peru	2004–14	4.8	7.1
Tanzania	2007–12	3.0	2.7

Sources: Tabulations of Equity Lab, Team for Statistical Development, World Bank, Washington, DC, based on data in SEDLAC (Socio-Economic Database for Latin America and the Caribbean); "Measuring Inequality," World Bank, Washington, DC, http://go.worldbank.org/3SLYUTVY00; WDI (World Development Indicators) (database), World Bank, Washington, DC, http://data.worldbank.org/data-catalog /world-development-indicators; PovcalNet (online analysis tool), World Bank, Washington, DC, http:// iresearch.worldbank.org/PovcalNet/.

TABLE 5.2 Typology of Poverty and Inequality Levels, Selected Countries, Circa 2013

Level of inequality	Low to moderate poverty, < 10%	High poverty, > 10%
Low to moderate, Gini < 30	Cambodia	
High, Gini > 30	Brazil Peru	Tanzania Mali

Note: Poverty is defined at the international extreme poverty line of US$1.90 a day in 2011 purchasing power parity (PPP) U.S. dollars. Brazil and Peru's poverty and inequality measures are based on income, while the remaining countries use consumption-based measures. Income inequality is considered high if the Gini index exceeds 30, while poverty is considered high if the incidence is 10 percent or greater.

generalizations. Instead, these country assessments provide succinct narratives on the extent to which shared factors, distinct features, and specific contexts determine recent successes in boosting shared prosperity and reducing inequality in selected countries.

Brazil: multiple policies aligned to redress record inequality

Inequality reduction

Brazil is historically known for its high and pervasive inequality in incomes, in access to basic services, such as education and health care, and in other measures of well-being. In 1989, Brazil's Gini index was 63 and ranked second highest in the world.[2] However, beginning in the mid-1990s, these stubborn levels of inequality started to cede. Mirroring the regional trend in Latin America and the Caribbean, the Gini reached 51 in 2014, 19 percent lower than in 1989 (figure 5.1).

FIGURE 5.1 Trends in the Gini Index, Brazil, 1981–2014

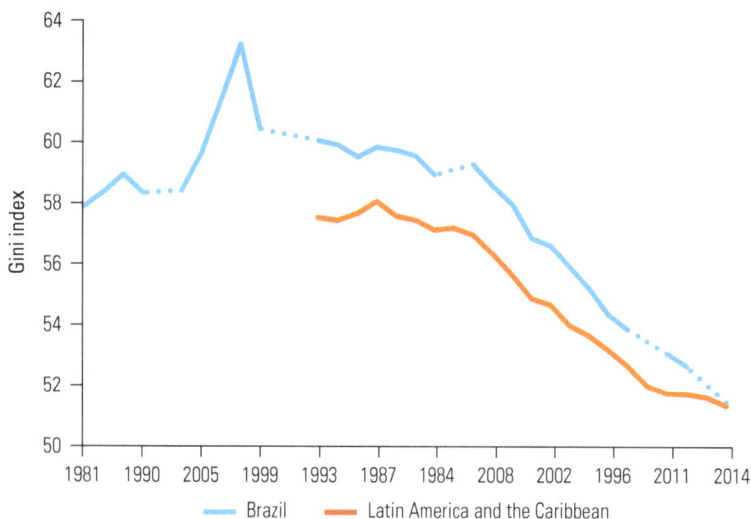

Sources: Tabulations of Equity Lab, Team for Statistical Development, World Bank, Washington, DC, based on data in the SEDLAC database; WDI (World Development Indicators) (database), World Bank, Washington, DC, http://data.worldbank.org/data-catalog/world-development-indicators; PovcalNet (online analysis tool), World Bank, Washington, DC, http://iresearch.worldbank.org/PovcalNet/.
Note: The data are based on a regional data harmonization effort that increases cross-country comparability and may differ from official statistics reported by governments and national statistical offices. The welfare indicator used to compute the Gini is household per capita income. The Gini ranges from 0 (perfect equality) to 100 (perfect inequality). The Latin America and Caribbean aggregate is based on 17 countries in the region on which microdata are available. The Gini index of the Latin America and Caribbean region is computed based on pooled country-specific data previously collapsed into 8,000 percentiles. In cases where data are unavailable for a given country in a given year, values have been interpolated by projecting incomes for that year based on GDP growth and assuming no changes in the distribution of incomes in the interpolated year. Dotted lines cover years in which data are not available or present quality issues.

FIGURE 5.2 Growth Incidence Curve, Brazil, 2004–14

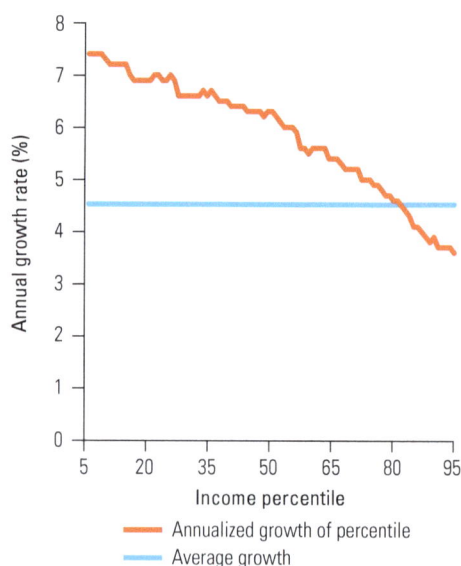

Source: Tabulations of Equity Lab, Team for Statistical Development, World Bank, Washington, DC, based on data in the SEDLAC database.

The incomes of the less well off surged between 2004 and 2014 amid rapid economic growth. Figure 5.2 shows that the average annual growth in the incomes of the bottom 10 doubles that of the top 10. The World Bank's indicator of shared prosperity—the growth rate of household income per capita of the bottom 40—highlights how Brazil's growth in the recent past has disproportionally benefited the poorest households. Between 2004 and 2014, the income growth among the bottom 40 averaged 6.8 percent a year, compared with 4.5 percent for the average Brazilian. Over the same period, incomes among the bottom 40 in Brazil rose at the second fastest rate in the region, only surpassed by Bolivia. This suggests that most of the decline in overall inequality occurred because of a reduction in inequality at the bottom of the income distribution. Alternative evidence drawing on tax records, which are more effective than household surveys at capturing the

individual incomes of top earners, confirms the decline in the Gini, but at a more modest pace.[3]

The marked drop in income inequality helped translate economic growth into large poverty reductions. Between 2004 and 2014, 26.5 million Brazilians exited poverty.[4] While 22 in every 100 people were living on an income of less than R$140 a month in 2004, this was only true of 7 in 100 Brazilians 10 years later.[5] The share of the population living on less than US$1.90 a day (in 2011 purchasing power parity [PPP] U.S. dollars) fell from 11.0 percent to 3.7 percent during the period. Decomposition exercises conclude that about 60 percent of this reduction was caused by the average increase in incomes among Brazilian households (the growth effect), while the remaining 40 percent can be attributed to improvements in income distribution among Brazilians (figure 5.3).

Despite these achievements, the country is still highly unequal. In 2014, the bottom 40 held approximately 12 percent of total income, while the top 20 held 56 percent.[6] That year, Brazil's Gini index of 51, while notably lower than 10 years previously, was

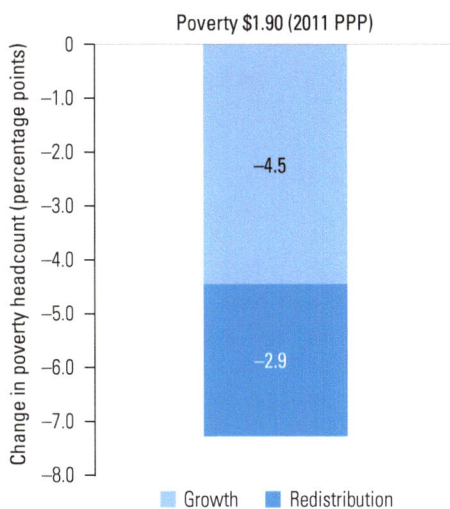

Poverty $1.90 (2011 PPP)

Source: Tabulations of Equity Lab, Team for Statistical Development, World Bank, Washington, DC, based on data in the SEDLAC database.

Note: The data have been calculated using a Shapley approach (Shorrocks 2013) that decomposes the change in the US$1.90-a-day poverty rate (2011 PPP U.S. dollars) into two components: the growth in household per capita income keeping distribution constant (the growth effect) and the change in the distribution of income keeping average income constant (the redistribution effect) as developed by Datt and Ravallion (1992).

the third highest in the region, and Brazil was still the 15th most unequal country in the world.

What drives the reductions in inequality?

The 1988 Constitution, which was adopted following the reinstatement of democracy in 1985, aimed to address the country's historical inequalities by guaranteeing basic social rights, such as free public education, free universal health care, pensions, and social assistance. Policies launched in the 1990s laid the foundations for the inequality declines observed years later. For instance, the creation of the unified health system (*Sistema Único de Saúde*) allowed substantial progress in the level and equity of health outcomes. In addition, education reforms were fundamental in closing education gaps and producing a more highly skilled labor force. In 1996, the government introduced the first broad legal framework

for basic education (*Lei e Diretrizes de Bases*) and national curriculum guidelines. Subsequent education policies were aimed at decentralizing the school system, reducing the costs of education for poor children, and measuring and monitoring results.[7]

A new macro framework in the 1990s created an enabling environment for inequality reduction. First, the introduction of the Real Plan in 1994 allowed the high levels of inflation to be cut that had been an important contributor to increasing inequality in previous years.[8] In the late 1990s, the adoption of inflation targets, floating exchange rates, and a more prudent fiscal policy supported by the Fiscal Responsibility Law in 2000 created a context of macroeconomic stability that prevailed during the next decade.

During the 2000s, the boom in commodity prices generated positive terms of trade to the advantage of Brazil as a major commodity exporter. The resulting macroeconomic stability, combined with the favorable external context, propelled Brazil's economic growth during the 2000s, which accelerated the decline in inequality. The dynamics of the labor market and the expansion of social policies boosted the incomes of the poor.[9] According to World Bank estimates, these two factors accounted for the bulk of the decline in inequality, approximately 80 percent, between 2003 and 2013. Of the decline in the Gini index between these two years, 41 percent was accounted for by labor incomes, and 39 percent by nonlabor income sources such as government transfers.[10]

In terms of the labor market, a fall in the wage gap between skilled and unskilled workers explains a great deal of the decrease in labor income inequality. Various factors drove the narrowing in the wage gap. The large expansion in access to education led to a significant increase in the relative supply of skilled workers. Between 1995 and 2010, the average years of schooling among adults above 25 years of age rose 56 percent, to 7.2 years. More than 4 in 10 workers in 2010 had 11 or more years of formal education, twice the share in the mid-1990s.[11] In addition, positive external conditions fostered an expansion in domestic consumption, favoring activities, especially in non-tradable sectors, such as construction and services, that employed relatively less well skilled workers. Furthermore, there was an increase in formal sector jobs, accompanied by rises in the minimum wage.[12] Though the situation might change under more somber economic conditions and a less favorable external context in the future, increases in the minimum wage during the first decade of the 2000s did not create large distortions in the labor market. Indeed, there were substantial reductions in the wage gaps across urban and rural areas, across regions, between men and women, and between whites and nonwhites with similar educational attainment and experience. A recent study estimates that the fall in gender, race, and spatial wage inequality and the growth in formal sector employment explain about 60 percent of Brazil's drop in labor income inequality between 1995 and 2012.[13]

Moreover, during the first decade of the 2000s, sufficient fiscal space was created for the government to finance large expansions in access to basic services and in social expenditures. For example, access to electricity was almost universal by 2014 in large part because of the rural electrification program *Luz para Todos* (light for all) that provided coverage to 15.2 million people beginning in 2004. Though still low, the share of households among the bottom 40 with a toilet connected to the sewerage network rose from 33 percent to 43 percent between 2004 and 2013. Primary-school enrollment was also close to universal.[14] Nonetheless, the quality of services and uneven service coverage constitute a growing challenge. Children's access to quality services still depends on the economic and social circumstances into which children are born, which indicates that educational opportunities are not equal in Brazil. For instance, parental educational attainment, incomes, and occupation explained about 80 percent of the inequality in children's mathematics test scores in 2012; these tests measure a basic ability to use mathematics in real-world situations.[15]

Targeted government transfers also contributed to the improvement in the living conditions of the poorest. The expansion of *Bolsa Família* (family grant), Brazil's flagship conditional cash transfer (CCT) program, has had a considerable equalizing impact. Between 2004 and 2014, the number of beneficiaries rose from 16 million to 56 million, reaching about a quarter of the country's population. Bolsa Família alone explains between 10 percent and 15 percent of the reduction in income inequality observed in the 2000s.[16] Other targeted transfers, indexed to a growing minimum wage, such as the *Benefício de Prestacao Continuada* (continuous cash benefit), a transfer to the elderly and disabled, were equalizing as well.

According to recent estimates, direct taxes and transfers have reduced the Gini index of market incomes by approximately 6 percent.[17] This is a large reduction by Latin American standards, but a paltry contribution compared with the capacity of the fiscal systems of member countries of the Organisation for Economic Co-operation and Development (OECD) to reduce market income inequalities by up to 33 percent.[18] The in-kind benefits provided through free public education and health care systems are progressive, except for tertiary education, while contributory pensions are clearly regressive.[19] Considering the size of the fiscal system in Brazil, the impact of the system on inequality is small. About three-quarters of the direct transfer benefits (including contributory pensions and unemployment benefits) go to the nonpoor, and the heavy reliance on indirect taxes acts against the inequality reduction derived from direct taxes. In addition, because important government transfers are indexed to it, increases in the minimum wage are associated with a large fiscal cost. Estimates suggest that public expenditures rise by R$350 million on a yearly basis for every R$1 increase in the minimum wage.[20] Thus, despite the contribution of the fiscal system to reducing inequality, there is still significant room for improving the system's impact and efficiency.

In sum, building from important early reforms, macroeconomic stability, economic growth, ample fiscal resources, and favorable external conditions, Brazil has been able to change course toward a more equitable society. The progress in the last decade in terms of poverty and inequality is undeniable. However, the shift in the global economy, the end of the commodity price boom, and a number of policy choices (including, notably, the weakening of fiscal discipline) currently threaten Brazil's past success in reducing income inequality. Reigniting sustainable growth by increasing investment and productivity—including nontradable services produced by low-skilled workers—will be an important precondition for sustaining job creation and boosting the earnings of the poor and vulnerable. Otherwise, the decline in income inequality in Brazil—associated with decisions on minimum wages, social transfers, and shifts in labor demand—runs the risk of being short-lived in the absence of more rapid productivity growth and favorable external conditions.[21] Furthermore, in a context of much tighter fiscal resources, there is a growing need to improve the progressivity and efficiency of taxes and transfers. Expanding the access to basic services—thereby closing the remaining gaps—and improving the quality of these services constitute an immediate priority in the effort to maintain previous successes.

Cambodia: new earning opportunities emerging from impressive growth

Inequality reduction

Cambodia has made significant progress in countering inequality over much of the first decade of the 2000s. This is the result of large segments of Cambodian society, including rural populations, benefiting from the country's impressive economic growth. Annual economic growth averaged 7.8 percent between 2004 and 2014, ranking among the top 15 most rapidly growing economies in the world. GDP per capita increased fourfold, from US$253 in 1993 to around US$1,090 in 2014, and Cambodia is projected to become a lower-middle-income country by 2017.[22] Poor Cambodians have harnessed the opportunities being made available to them by economic growth. As a result, the Gini index fell appreciably, from 37 in 2007 to 26 in 2013, the latest year for which data are available (figure 5.4). This

FIGURE 5.4 Trends in the Gini Index, Cambodia, 2007–13

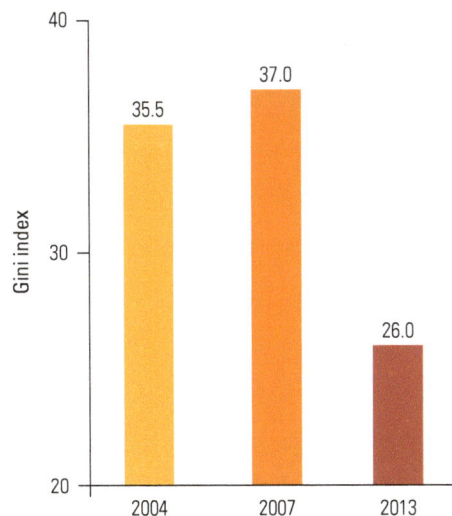

Source: Calculations based on data in "Measuring Inequality," World Bank, Washington, DC, http://go.worldbank.org /3SLYUTVY00; PovcalNet (online analysis tool), World Bank, Washington, DC, http://iresearch.worldbank.org/PovcalNet/. *Note:* The numbers presented here are based on a regional data harmonization effort that increases cross-country comparability and may differ from official statistics reported by governments and national statistical offices. The welfare indicator used to compute the Gini is total household per capita consumption. The Gini ranges from 0 (perfect equality) to 100 (perfect inequality).

reduction in inequality was evident in both urban and rural settings, although at a different pace: more rapid in urban areas other than Phnom Penh and in rural areas and slower in Phnom Penh.[23]

Consumption has grown more rapidly among less well off Cambodians than among the more well off. Annual consumption growth among the bottom 40 averaged 6.3 percent between 2008 and 2013, well above the 3.7 percent average consumption growth across the population and twice the rate among the top 60. During the last two years on which data are available, that is, 2012 and 2013, the growth of consumption among the poorest households surpassed that of richer households significantly (figure 5.5). Indeed, consumption growth among the richest households—the top 33 percent—was below average during these two years. This was so everywhere except in Phnom Penh, where the growth of the poorest 20 percent was negative.[24]

FIGURE 5.5 Growth Incidence Curve, Cambodia, 2012–13

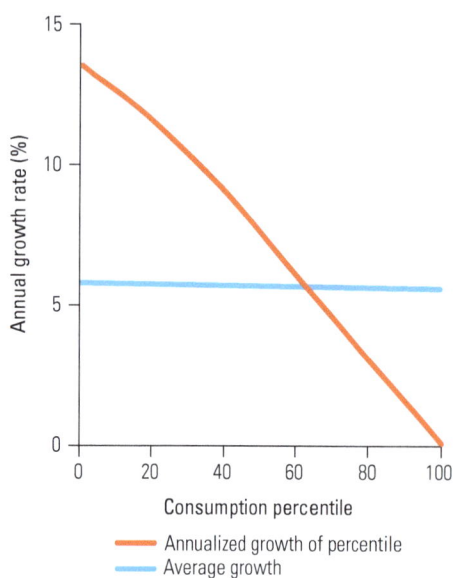

Source: "Measuring Inequality," World Bank, Washington, DC, http://go.worldbank.org/3SLYUTVY00; PovcalNet (online analysis tool), World Bank, Washington, DC, http://iresearch .worldbank.org/PovcalNet/.

FIGURE 5.6 Contributions of Growth and Redistribution Effects to Poverty Reduction, Cambodia, 2008–12

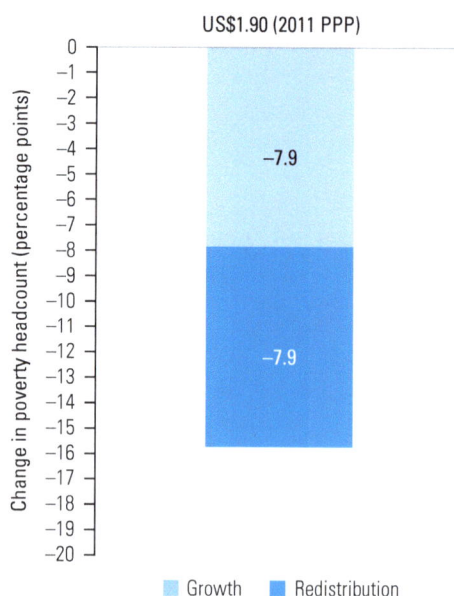

Source: World Bank calculations.
Note: The data have been calculated using a Shapley approach (Shorrocks 2013) that decomposes the change in the US$1.90-a-day poverty rate (2011 PPP U.S. dollars) into two components: the growth in household per capita income, keeping distribution constant (the growth effect), and the change in the distribution of income, keeping average income constant (the redistribution effect), as developed by Datt and Ravallion (1992).

Poverty reduction likewise followed an impressive path during the last decade, an achievement few could have foreseen upon the country's emergence in the 1990s from a past of conflict. The proportion of the population living below the global poverty line declined significantly, from 21 percent to 5 percent, between 2008 and 2012.[25] The rural poverty rate dropped precipitously, coming close to the rates in the capital and other urban areas. According to World Bank estimates, the average growth in consumption across households is responsible for about half the poverty reduction (the growth effect) that took place in Cambodia between 2008 and 2012 (figure 5.6). The other half is explained by the unequal increase in consumption across households, that is, by a consumption growth pattern that favored the less well off (the redistribution effect).

What is behind the reductions in inequality?

In Cambodia, stable domestic macroeconomic conditions, supported by prudent policy making, have generally gone hand in hand with a favorable regional and global environment. In the recent past, the government has maintained the credibility of the macroeconomic policy making that it had built up prior to the global financial crisis and recession in 2008–09. It has adopted a series of countercyclical measures meant to offset the negative effects of downturns. Also, it has gradually moved to restrain fiscal deficits by mobilizing additional revenue and limiting current and capital expenditures. After peaking at 25 percent in 2008, inflation was modest and even fell to roughly 2 percent throughout 2014 and 2015 as a result of low food and oil prices. In addition, official development assistance to finance major infrastructure projects has helped keep the debt under control that might otherwise have soared.[26]

The country's brisk growth since the middle years of the first decade of the 2000s has been largely driven by garment and apparel exports, tourism, real estate, and construction amid a transition away from agriculture.[27] A proliferation of employment opportunities, particularly in salaried or wage positions, has followed the expansion of these sectors. Paid employees constituted 41 percent of the workforce in 2013, up from 22.6 percent in 2004, in large part because of the availability of more of these jobs in the capital.[28] The garment and apparel industry contributed to this observed increase in employment, especially among the poor. Now accounting for fully 80 percent of Cambodia's total exports, garments and related apparel employ the bulk of the country's manufacturing labor force. Because production in the sector is heavily oriented toward exports and because of the prevalence of foreign direct investment in the sector, wages are higher and more stable in garment jobs relative to other jobs. New research indicates that garment jobs improve the well-being of the bottom 40 insofar as these households are more inclined to experience consumption gains from participating in this sector, suffer less from food insufficiency, and report higher school enrollment rates. There have also been increased agricultural investments by rural households that are receiving remittances from nonresident members working in the garment industry. This is a reflection of the fact that this sector predominantly employs young women migrants from rural areas.[29] Furthermore, the garment sector is characterized by a much lower gender wage gap than other sectors and is an important reason why Cambodia has been able to incorporate women into the productive economy. The services sector—encompassing communication, hospitality, trade, and transport—has also improved the employment prospects of the poor.

Although its aggregate economic importance has been declining, agriculture has also contributed to the narrowing in inequality in rural areas over the last several years. The fall in inequality and poverty in the midst of the global financial crisis is partly explained by the agricultural sector's vitality at that time. Farm incomes from agricultural crops, mainly paddy rice, more than doubled between 2004 and 2009, in large part because of rising prices and, to a lesser extent, because of expanding productivity in the smaller agricultural labor force. The government has supported the sector by, for instance, increasing investments in rural roads and working to improve seed distribution, strengthen oversight on the quality and price of imported fertilizers, and support the operation and maintenance of irrigation schemes.[30] The abandonment of commodity price controls and related tax levies arguably had a larger role in helping the poor.[31]

Increasing nonfarm self-employment and rising wages have also been key features of the strides in reducing rural inequality. The trend among the rural poor to diversify household incomes away from agriculture has been rising recently. More well paid employment supported the well-being of rural households with little or no landholdings during the recent agricultural commodity price boom.[32] Average per capita incomes from daily wage labor among rural residents rose 9.5 percent annually in 2004–09, and, as of 2013, wages and salaries represented 43 percent of total rural household income.[33]

Notwithstanding the positive effects of the nonagricultural sectors of the economy on employment and labor incomes, job growth in these sectors has been insufficient to absorb new labor market entrants, reflecting in part the country's young demographic. The seemingly sagging competitiveness of the garment industry since 2012, reflected in the greater real wage growth relative to productivity growth, is also grounds for concern.[34] Several long-standing barriers constraining productivity and investments in agriculture are particularly detrimental to smallholder farmers. These revolve around problems in land tenure, bottlenecks in fertilizer and seed markets, inadequate extension services and irrigation systems, and, among farmers, the lack of savings and access to credit.[35] As a result, smallholders are generally vulnerable to swings in the international prices for rice.

Upgraded infrastructure and social protection are urgent in light of the constraints. Enhanced capacity in electricity generation and distribution, transport (especially rural roads), irrigation, and information and communication technology are often cited as areas of infrastructure in need of expansion or upgrading. In social protection, the government has strived to extend coverage beyond formal employment–based schemes by scaling up the national household targeting system and strengthening relevant governance arrangements in an attempt to safeguard the well-being of the informally employed. Chief among those efforts is the launching of a health equity fund to extend the coverage of health care (see chapter 6). As of 2013, the funds covered more than 2.5 million people in 51 of Cambodia's 81 districts. More recently, the country is undertaking a pilot cash transfer project focused on mother and child health and nutrition. However, there are major problems in coverage and the size of benefits in social assistance programs. Only 2 percent of the poorest 20 percent of Cambodians receive any form of assistance through social safety nets, and the transfers they receive only total 2 percent of poverty-threshold expenditures per intended beneficiary.[36] This adds to the insufficient levels of public spending on health care and education, which, though rising recently, are rather low by international comparison, at approximately 4 percent of GDP combined.[37]

In sum, inequality in Cambodia has declined steadily in the midst of sustained and rapid economic growth and the expanding dynamism of sectors that employ large numbers of relatively less well skilled workers, of which the country has an abundance. Women in the bottom 40 have leveraged their occupations in the production of garments, Cambodia's primary export, to improve the well-being of their households. The service sector, the growth of which is linked to increasing internal demand and tourism, has also facilitated the integration of greater numbers of Cambodians into the labor market. In rural areas, higher agricultural wages, growing off-farm employment, and earnings from rice farming have all had an appreciable impact on inequality. Indeed, rural areas have largely driven the overall trends in inequality and poverty reduction. Even so, obstacles to additional

narrowing in inequality and reductions of poverty are evident in the slowing pace of job creation, which is troublesome, especially given Cambodia's young demographic and the structural constraints that weigh on leading sectors. Scaling up policy efforts and investments in infrastructure and rural development, together with social protection, would help eliminate bottlenecks and sustain the success already achieved.

Mali: a vulnerable economy favored by the vagaries of agriculture

Inequality reduction

In 2014, Mali's gross national income per person was US$650, placing the country among the 15 poorest countries in the world.[38] According to the human development index, which embodies life expectancy, education, and income indicators, the country ranks 179th among 188 countries.[39] About half the population is living in extreme poverty according to the US$1.90 per person per day line; two-thirds of the adult population is illiterate; and life expectancy at birth is 58 years.[40] The economy is undiversified, and the population largely depends on rainfed agriculture. The country is thus highly vulnerable to changes in international prices and weather-related shocks. The conflict and security crisis that originated in the country's northern region in 2012 has added to the current challenges involved in reducing poverty and boosting shared prosperity.

The resurgence of conflict put an end to two decades of political stability. Both the stability and its later demise are attributable to an unsustainable practice of the constant redistribution of positions and resources among a small elite, tendencies to co-opt any potential opposition through payoffs, corruption, nepotism, and impunity. The approach, known as the politics of consensus, has undermined the creation of a professional bureaucracy, independent oversight institutions, and a proper judiciary and weakened the army.[41] Therefore, the reduction of inequality took place during a period of protracted flawed gov-

FIGURE 5.7 Trends in the Gini Index, Mali, 2001–10

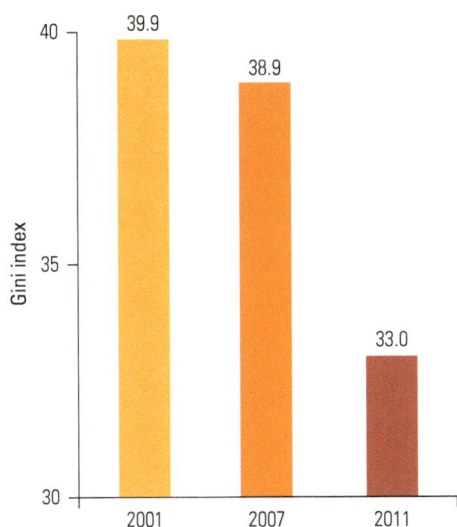

Source: PovcalNet (online analysis tool), World Bank, Washington, DC, http://iresearch.worldbank.org/PovcalNet/.
Note: The numbers presented here are based on a regional data harmonization effort that increases cross-country comparability and may differ from official statistics reported by governments and national statistical offices. The welfare indicator used to compute the Gini is total household per capita consumption. The Gini ranges from 0 (perfect equality) to 100 (perfect inequality).

ernance, which may have affected the pace of inequality reduction, but did not prevent it. Meanwhile, the narrowing of inequality during the past decade was not sufficient to avert conflict.

Before the outbreak of conflict, Mali had made important strides in reducing poverty and improving well-being. Between 2001 and 2010, GDP growth averaged 5.7 percent a year, while GDP per capita growth averaged 1.5 percent.[42] During the period, the growth in the economy was largely inclusive and translated into substantial poverty and inequality declines. Thus, the reduction in inequality was sizable, underscored by a 7 point decrease in the Gini index between 2001 and 2010 (figure 5.7).[43] The share of Malians living on less than US$1.90 a day fell from 57.9 percent to 49.3 percent, although the decline was not sufficient to reduce the number of the poor, which increased to about 360,000 because of the country's high population growth. The improvements in monetary well-being were also accompanied by gains in other import-

ant dimensions such as nutrition and asset ownership. For instance, the prevalence of stunting among under-5-year-olds declined from 43 percent in 2001 to 28 percent in 2010. In addition, mobile phone ownership surged from nearly zero to 67 percent; household ownership of refrigerators doubled, from 5 percent to 11 percent, while television ownership almost tripled, to 37 percent, in the same period.[44]

The progress in reducing poverty and inequality reflects the more rapid consumption growth of the poorest households relative to the consumption growth of richer households (figure 5.8, panel a). The poorest 10 percent showed the largest increases in consumption growth during the period, and households in the top 25 percent actually reduced their consumption between 2001 and 2010. Decomposition exercises that estimate the contribution of growth and redistribution effects to the change in poverty indicate that about 82 percent of the poverty decline observed between 2001 and 2010 originated in changes in the distribution of consumption across households (the redistribution effect), while the remaining 18 percent arose because of the effect of growth, that is, the average increase in consumption experienced by Malian households.[45]

Behind this equalizing pattern, there were important differences across the first decade of the 2000s. During the first part of the decade, the gains in per capita consumption were lower in magnitude, but more widespread across households (figure 5.8, panel b). This allowed more households to exit poverty during this period with respect to the second half: indeed, about 85 percent of the poverty decline that occurred during the decade took place in the first five years. Consumption growth among the poor and nonpoor was similar during the period, which meant that, paradoxically, despite the manifest poverty reduction, there was not a substantive narrowing in inequality. In contrast, during the second part of the decade, the poorest households saw, for reasons explained below, their consumption grow more quickly than the consumption of richer households, which, in fact, declined during the period (figure 5.8, panel c). Because of

FIGURE 5.8 Growth Incidence Curve, Mali, 2001–10

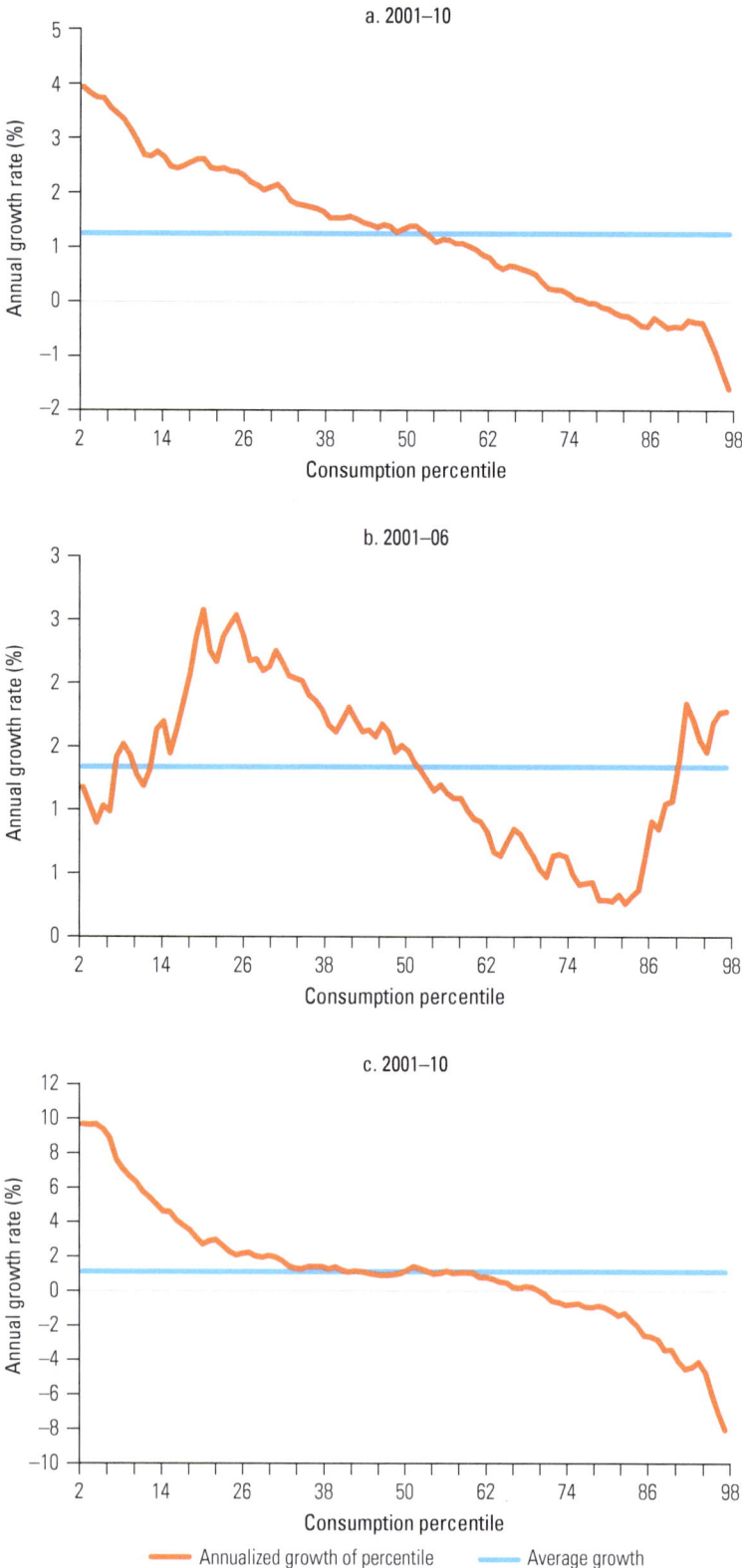

a. 2001–10

b. 2001–06

c. 2001–10

— Annualized growth of percentile   — Average growth

Source: Tabulations based on SSAPOV database harmonization, Sub-Saharan Africa Team for Statistical Development, World Bank, Washington, DC.

FIGURE 5.9 Contributions of Growth and Redistribution Effects to Poverty Reduction, Mali, 2006–09

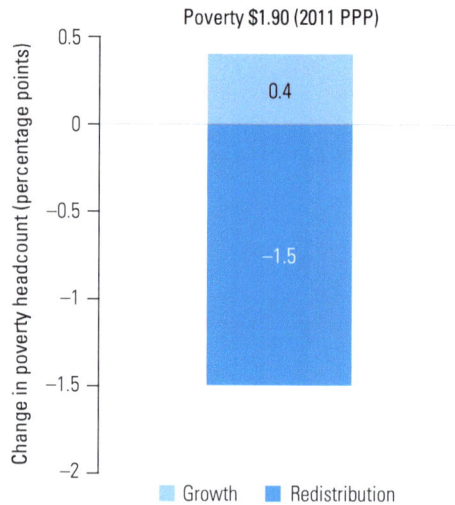

Poverty $1.90 (2011 PPP)

☐ Growth   ■ Redistribution

Source: World Bank calculations.
Note: The data have been calculated using a Shapley approach (Shorrocks 2013) that decomposes the change in the US$1.90-a-day poverty rate (2011 PPP U.S. dollars) into two components: the growth in household per capita income, keeping distribution constant (the growth effect), and the change in the distribution of income, keeping average income constant (the redistribution effect), as developed by Datt and Ravallion (1992).

these distinctive changes in consumption across households, inequality declined (a 5.9 point reduction in the Gini index), while the poverty reduction in the second half of the decade was meager. Indeed, a decomposition of the changes in poverty in 2006–09 reveals that the paltry reduction of poverty in this period is linked to large distributional changes (the redistribution effect) that were partially offset by a growth effect in the opposite direction (figure 5.9).

What is behind the reductions in inequality?

During the 1980s and 1990s, the government of Mali implemented a series of structural reforms aimed at shifting from a state-controlled economy toward a market-oriented system. The reforms included price and trade liberalization, tax reform, and legal and regulatory reforms. In addition, the transition to democracy that had started in the 1990s was followed by two decades of relative political stability that allowed the expansion of access to basic services and improvements in development outcomes.

Relative to previous decades, the 2000s benefited from less volatility in GDP growth. One contributor to the reduced fluctuations was the expansion in cereal production, explained by the liberalization of producer prices, more open cereal markets, and persistently good weather in the second half of the decade. Improvements in cereal production were also supported by water management and irrigation policies and by sustained input subsidies. Subsidies helped expand access and predictability in the supply of fertilizers, and this contributed to the expansion of maize and rice production over the decade.

Because of a surge in its growth, agriculture has been a key driver behind the improvement in living conditions among poor Malians. Approximately 73 percent of Malians and 90 percent of the poor live in rural areas. Most of the poor are net buyers of food. Among those involved in farming activities, own-account production does not permit self-sufficiency, and income has to be supplemented with casual labor and private transfers. The increased production in cereals benefited the labor income of the poor by raising both farm production and off-farm labor income through a higher demand for wage labor by commercial cereal producers. The increased supply of cereals also helped lower local cereal prices and enhance the purchasing power of the poor. Gains in household consumption during the last decade were visible in regions that grow rice (the most important cash crop) and maize and sorghum (two of the main consumption crops).

Another contributor to the higher off-farm incomes of the poor was the expansion in artisanal gold mining in some regions of the country. In addition, the region bordering Senegal benefited from the redirection of trade following the 2002 crisis in Côte d'Ivoire and the improved infrastructure connecting Bamako, the Malian capital, and Senegal. Another contributing factor was remittances. Between 2001 and 2010, there was a threefold rise in per capita remittances among households in border areas with

Mauritania that depended on income from relatives working abroad, mainly in France.[46]

The distinct patterns of inequality and poverty reduction in each half of the first decade of the 2000s described above depend on the changing role of nonagricultural sectors as contributors to growth. In 2001–06, the industry and service sectors and the agricultural sector grew at a similar pace. Hence, the growth of household consumption was fairly widespread so that a vast majority of Malians benefited from growth. In contrast, during 2006–10, manufacturing contracted, while agricultural production, favored by good weather, boomed. The dynamics of the expansion of the agricultural sector did not translate into economy-wide gains, but helped raise the consumption of the poorest households, which were mostly working in agriculture. The boom in agriculture thus improved the well-being of the extreme poor relative to the rest of the population, thereby narrowing inequality.[47]

Public spending has been aligned with the government's poverty reduction strategy and focused on agriculture and education. During the decade, there were important achievements in education and in access to basic services. For instance, between 2001 and 2011, the gross enrollment ratio in primary education rose by about 28 percentage points, reaching about 80 percent. Electricity coverage expanded from 8 percent to 34 percent in these same years. In addition, access to clean drinking water increased from 69 percent to 81 percent. Yet, the coverage and quality of basic services still lagged significantly in rural areas. Public spending in Mali is sensitive to economic shocks as might be expected in an economy highly exposed to weather shocks. This is compounded by the fact that infrastructure investments in health care and education largely depend on donor funding. Targeting remains a challenge. Electricity and fuel subsidies mostly benefit the urban nonpoor, while fertilizer subsidies support the more well off farmers. In 2010, only 3 percent of households in the poorest consumption quintile had access to electricity, compared with 62 percent of the households in the richest quintile. It is also estimated that the top 20 benefited from about three-quarters of the resources allocated through the public education system.[48]

The redistributive role of social transfers has been limited. Most of the country's safety nets are concentrated on food support through subsidized prices and price stabilization. Cash transfers are implemented at a limited scale, and labor-intensive public works programs have been introduced in response to crises. In 2009, around 0.5 percent of GDP was spent on social safety nets, a low amount considering that about one person in two is counted among the extreme poor, and one person in four is food insecure.[49]

Overall, the progress in reducing inequality and poverty in Mali in recent years has been remarkable. In part, this is the result of deliberate policies and political stability and, in part, to good luck in the form of favorable weather and positive external events that have offset negative shocks. However, there are signs of a recent stall in rainfall trends and a progressive increase in temperatures (by 0.8° Celsius since 1975) as a consequence of global warming that will keep the economy highly exposed to climate hazards.[50] Moreover, since 2012, the conflict in the north of the country has put the brakes on the progress of the previous decade. The crisis has disrupted education and health care services in the north, and displaced populations are exerting pressure on service delivery in the south. Restoring security and the realization of the peace agreement are necessary steps to supporting economic growth and sustaining the improvement of living conditions, particularly among those affected by the conflict. Coupled with this priority, enhanced service delivery is still a challenge in sharing prosperity and reducing poverty.

Peru: equalizing investment despite informality and low human capital

Inequality reduction

Between 2001 and 2014, Peru's unprecedented growth led to an increase in real per capita income by a factor of almost two. The economy expanded during the period at an average rate of 5.5 percent a year, among the 15 highest rates in the world. High international mineral prices; rising incomes, mainly in labor-intensive services, commerce, and agriculture; increasing public transfers; and prudent fiscal policies all contributed to improving the distribution of incomes, especially at the bottom of the distribution. Poverty reduction has been remarkable, from poverty rates of 59 percent in 2004 to 23 percent in 2014 (measured using the national poverty line). Extreme poverty also fell by a significant margin, some 12 percentage points, to 4.3 percent in 2014. This implies that about 9 million Peruvians—30 percent of the population—exited from poverty, while 3.2 million escaped extreme poverty (all in net terms). The share of the population living on less than US$1.90 a day (2011 PPP) fell from 12 percent to 3 percent during the period.

The Gini index fell from 51 in 2004 to 44 in 2014, more impressive than the reduction observed in the Latin America and Caribbean region as a whole (figure 5.10). However, income inequality has not narrowed at the same pace in urban and rural areas, with more limited declines in rural settings. Inequality in rural areas, traditionally at lower levels than in urban areas, surpassed urban income inequality in 2008 and has remained wider ever since.[51] Illustrative is the fact that the incidence of stunting among under-5-year-olds was 20 percentage points higher in rural areas than in urban areas despite substantial reductions in stunting overall.

The bottom 40 experienced substantially larger income growth than the top 60. Between 2004 and 2014, the growth rate of real income per capita among the bottom 40 was 6.5 percent, compared to 4.1 percent among the overall population.[52] The growth incidence curve shows that the largest income growth between 2004 and 2014 took place among the poorest households. It also shows that the annual income growth rates were highest among the poorest 25 percent of households and declined among more well off households. Households in the bottom 25 experienced annualized growth rates of about 7 percent between 2004 and 2013, while households in the top 10 saw increases of 3 percent or less (figure 5.11).

FIGURE 5.10 Trends in the Gini Index, Peru, 2004–14

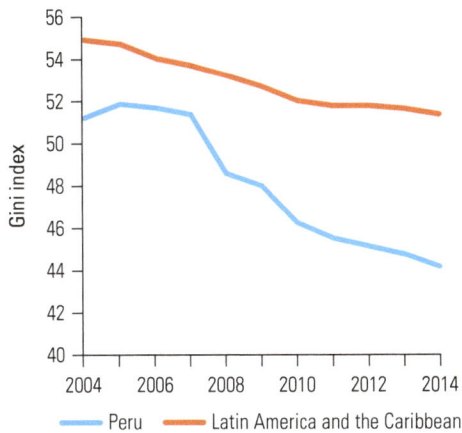

Source: Tabulations of Equity Lab, Team for Statistical Development, World Bank, Washington, DC, based on data in the SEDLAC database.
Note: The numbers presented here are based on a regional data harmonization effort that increases cross-country comparability and may differ from official statistics reported by governments and national statistical offices. The welfare indicator used to compute the Gini is total household per capita income. The Gini ranges from 0 (perfect equality) to 100 (perfect inequality). The aggregate for Latin America and the Caribbean is based on 17 countries in the region on which microdata are available. The Gini index of the Latin American and Caribbean region is computed based on pooled country-specific data that have been collapsed into 8,000 percentiles. In cases where data are unavailable for a given country in a given year, values have been interpolated by projecting incomes for that year based on GDP growth and assuming no changes in the distribution of incomes in the interpolated year.

FIGURE 5.11 Growth Incidence Curve, Peru, 2004–14

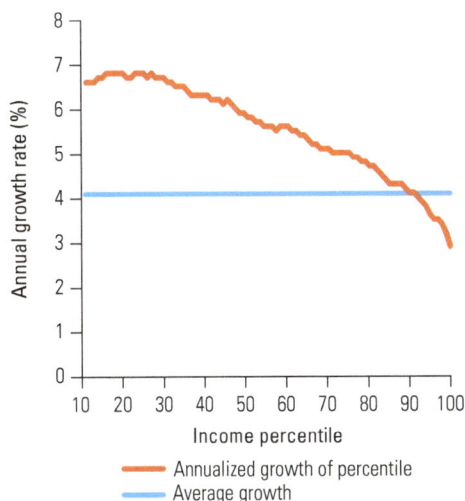

Source: Tabulations of Equity Lab, Team for Statistical Development, World Bank, Washington, DC, based on data in the SEDLAC database.

FIGURE 5.12 Contributions of Growth and Redistribution Effects to Poverty Reduction, Peru, 2004–14

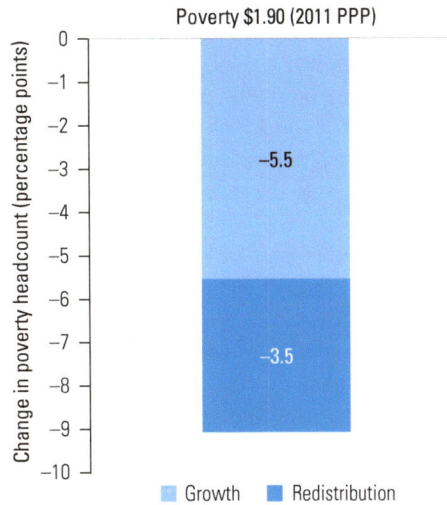

Source: World Bank calculations.
Note: The data have been calculated using a Shapley approach (Shorrocks 2013) that decomposes the change in the US$1.90-a-day poverty rate (2011 PPP U.S. dollars) into two components: the growth in household per capita income, keeping distribution constant (the growth effect), and the change in the distribution of income, keeping average income constant (the redistribution effect), as developed by Datt and Ravallion (1992).

The contributions of the growth of the economy and improvements in the distribution differ considerably. The World Bank's decomposition of the drivers of poverty reduction suggests that the growth effect explains about 61 percent of the reduction in poverty, while the remaining 39 percent is explained by the improvements in the distribution of income across households (figure 5.12).

What is behind the reduction in inequality?

The remarkable improvement in the living conditions of the poor and the bottom 40 results from the outstanding growth of the economy in a context of macroeconomic stability, favorable external conditions, and important structural reforms. The structural reforms implemented in the 1990s laid the foundations for the economic recovery observed since the early 2000s. These reforms included trade and financial liberalization, a more flexible exchange rate regime, and the privatization of state-owned enterprises. The Central Bank was granted more autonomy to strengthen monetary policy, while the National Customs and Tax Administration Superintendence was created to support fiscal policies.

In the early 2000s, prudent macroeconomic policies and high commodity prices brought foreign direct investment into Peru, particularly into the mining sector, boosting private investment. This capital accumulation reached 26 percent of GDP in 2014, up from 18 percent in 2000, and was the main driver of growth, accounting for more than two-thirds of total growth since 2001.[53] The economic growth and high urbanization rates also boosted the demand for services (such as commerce, hotels and restaurants, and transport), thereby expanding employment in the urban informal sector. In rural areas, agricultural productivity rose because of the better connectivity in the sierra region (highlands) following roadbuilding, the introduction of mobile phones, and the expanding industrial production of agro-exports in the costa (coastal) region. Nontraditional agricultural exports have experienced substantial growth in the last 15 years. They include asparagus, grapes, mangoes, paprika, and quinoa. The expansion of employment in urban informal services and higher agricultural productivity have improved labor incomes, which have fueled growth by raising domestic consumption.[54]

The labor market was the main contributor to the reduction in poverty and inequality in the last decade, explaining about three-quarters of the reduction in extreme poverty and 80 percent of the reduction in the Gini.[55] The expansion in the educational attainment of the labor force, which resulted in the more equal distribution of educational attainment, contributed to the decline in labor income inequality.[56] Moreover, the labor market was characterized by high participation rates and low unemployment rates. There was a large narrowing in the wage gap between formal and informal workers, leading to reduced wage inequality. The median monthly wage among informal workers doubled, while formal sector wages grew by 55 percent between 2004 and 2014. The share of the employed in the formal

sector doubled during the period.[57] Yet, restrictive labor regulations, particularly those related to dismissals and nonwage labor costs, contributed to the persistently high rates in informality, at around 70 percent, one of the highest rates in Latin America.

This evidence for Peru confirms that a unique factor cannot explain the trends in labor income inequality. Recent analyses in Peru and elsewhere in the region compellingly show that other factors drive wage inequality, although the evidence on the effects is not always conclusive. These drivers refer, for example, to the following: the quality of education, shifts in the returns to experience, the obsolescence of skills, within-industry wage gaps reflecting the heterogeneity of firms, and the degree of compliance with the minimum wage. These are some of the many aspects underpinning labor inequality trends.[58]

Social spending played a limited role in addressing inequality and poverty during the decade. Recent estimates suggest that public transfers are responsible for less than 10 percent of the poverty reduction during the last decade.[59] One important reason for this limited role is the low level of spending. In 2013, social protection spending was US$375 per person, approximately a third of Mexico's spending and half of Colombia's. Indeed, in Latin America, the level of social spending in Peru exceeded only the social protection spending in Bolivia and Paraguay.[60] Social spending was generally progressive. The introduction of the country's flagship CCT, *Juntos* (together), in 2005, the adoption of results-based budgeting beginning in 2007, and the creation of the Ministry of Social Inclusion in 2011 have all contributed to rendering social protection more well targeted and effective.

Analysts question the quality of public spending in Peru.[61] One manifest case is education. Despite significant gains in preprimary and secondary enrollments, Peru lags comparator countries in scores on the Program for International Student Assessment of the OECD. In 2013, 75 percent of students at level 5 in mathematics in Peru did not possess the standard expected basic mathematics skills of a level-2 student.[62] Public education spending increased during the decade, but education expenditures—2.6 percent of GDP—are still low by international standards. Aiming to improve the quality of secondary education, the government has been implementing a merit-based system for all tenured teachers since 2012.

The quality of human capital is crucial because the favorable conditions that have underpinned growth in Peru have recently started to recede. The external environment is shifting after a sharp decline in commodity prices over the past few years. This spotlights the need to boost the aggregate productivity of the economy to expand the demand for well-paid formal sector jobs.

In sum, the reduction in poverty and inequality in Peru in the last decade took place because of more favorable external conditions, increased internal demand, improved educational attainment, advances in rural connectivity, and the performance of labor-intensive sectors, leading to higher, more equal labor incomes. Educational upgrading was equalizing, though large challenges remain in terms of quality. To a much lesser extent, safety nets contributed to the shrinking in inequality. Maintaining these impressive gains in a much less favorable environment will require that the Peruvian economy sustain policy reforms addressing the main structural weaknesses, the limited productivity resulting from the low quality of human capital, and the high rates of informality.

Tanzania: sharing prosperity in the midst of diversification

Inequality reduction

Tanzania maintained robust and stable economic growth between 2004 and 2014, averaging 6.5 percent a year. After a long period of stagnation, the poverty headcount declined from 34.4 percent in 2007 to 28.2 percent in 2012, while extreme poverty fell from 11.7 percent to 9.7 percent.[63] The reduction in poverty appears more substantial if one uses the international poverty line of US$1.90 per person per day. Based on this measure, the headcount ratio dropped from 59.9 percent to 48.8 percent between 2007 and 2012.

The favorable performance in economic growth and poverty reduction was accompanied by narrowing inequality, although the levels in Tanzania are low relative to the Sub-Saharan African region and much lower than in Latin America and the Caribbean, the world's most unequal region.[64] The Gini index declined from around 39 to 36 between 2007 and 2012 (figure 5.13).[65] Evidence on the shared prosperity indicator suggests that inequality reductions were mainly driven by a larger increase in the consumption accruing to the bottom quintiles. The annual consumption growth among the bottom 40, at 3.4 percent, was well above three times the growth among the top 60, at 1.0 percent. The growth incidence curve between 2007 and 2012 shows that the largest relative increase in consumption took place among the poorest 20 percent, while growth was more moderate among other middle-income groups and negative among the top 15 (figure 5.14). However, because this growth took place from a low base, the absolute gains were modest: it translated

FIGURE 5.13 **Trends in the Gini Index, Tanzania, 2001–12**

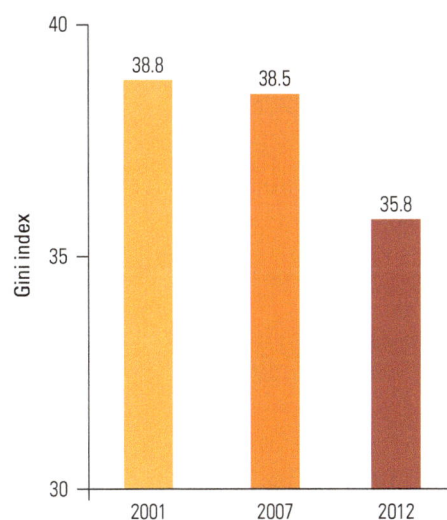

Source: PovcalNet (online analysis tool), World Bank, Washington, DC, http://iresearch.worldbank.org/PovcalNet/.
Note: The numbers presented here are based on a regional data harmonization effort that increases cross-country comparability and may differ from official statistics reported by governments and national statistical offices. The welfare indicator used to compute the Gini is total household per capita consumption. The Gini ranges from 0 (perfect equality) to 100 (perfect inequality).

FIGURE 5.14 Growth Incidence Curve, Tanzania, 2007–12

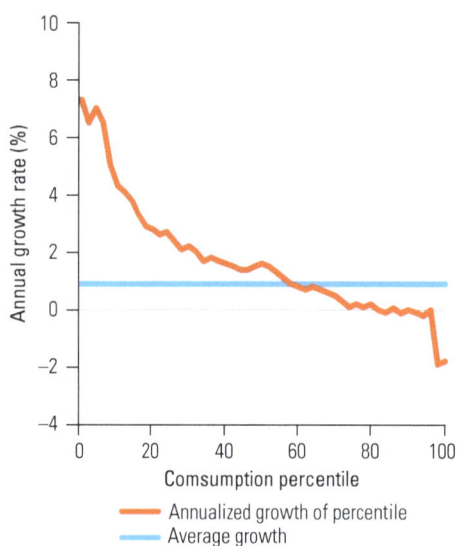

Source: World Bank 2015c based on data of the 2007 and 2011/12 household budget surveys.

FIGURE 5.15 Contributions of Growth and Redistribution Effects to Poverty Reduction, Tanzania, 2007–12

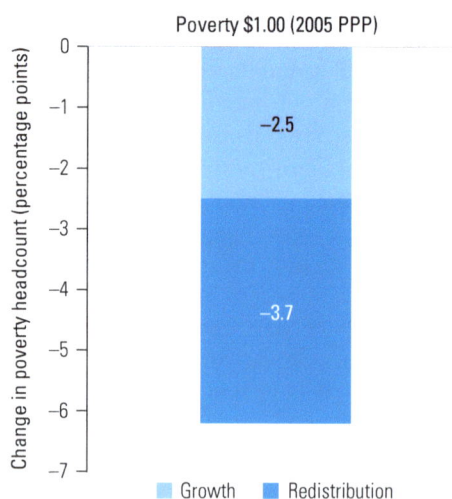

Source: World Bank 2015c using the 2007 and 2011/12 household budget surveys.
Note: The data have been calculated using a Shapley approach (Shorrocks 2013) that decomposes the change in the poverty rate using a national poverty line of T Sh 36,482 per adult per month, equivalent to a US$1.00-a-day poverty rate (2005 PPP U.S. dollars), into two components: the growth in household per capita income, keeping distribution constant (the growth effect), and the change in the distribution of income, keeping average income constant (the redistribution effect), as developed by Datt and Ravallion (1992).

to an additional consumption value of only T Sh 4,300 per adult per month among the poorest quintile, equivalent to approximately 10 percent of the cost of basic consumption needs (less than US$3.00).

A decomposition of the reduction in poverty at the national level between an increase in mean household consumption (the growth effect) and changes in the distribution of household consumption (the redistribution effect) between 2007 and 2012 suggests that distributional changes are more important than growth changes in explaining the reduction.[66] Household consumption growth contributed around 40 percent (or 2.5 percentage points) of Tanzania's poverty reduction, while the narrowing in inequality contributed 60 percent (3.7 percentage points) (figure 5.15).

What is behind the reductions in inequality?

Since independence in 1962, the government of Tanzania has undertaken a gradual and partial transition from a state-led development strategy to a market-based economy. Following the debt crisis in 1986, it undertook structural reforms that opened up the economy to foreign investors and

accelerated economic growth, benefits that continued into the 2000s.[67] The surge in growth in the early 2000s is partly attributable to the pursuit of reforms through the 1990s that sought to increase exports, use scarce foreign exchange more efficiently, reduce the involvement of the public sector in commercial activities, and liberalize the market for goods and services.[68] Steady economic growth was also based on prudent macroeconomic policies to control inflation and restore stability in exchange rates: achievements that were nonetheless challenged by, for example, a high inflation episode in 2011–12. In addition, the transition from a socialist to a market-based economy gave a further, significant boost to domestic production. However, this transition to a market-based economy is not fully completed: the private sector is still characterized by high levels of market concentration and informality and low levels of productivity, mainly because of weak market institutions and a weak business environment. The country is still facing persistent state control over the market, particularly in agriculture.[69]

The economic expansion has been driven since the early 2000s primarily by rapidly growing sectors, particularly communication, financial services, and construction. However, growth in these sectors did not translate into substantive improvements in the living conditions of the poor, the less well educated, or rural residents relative to the more highly skilled residing in urban areas, notably, Dar es Salaam. This explains, in part, a more limited ability of economic growth to reduce poverty during the early years of the first decade of the 2000s. Thus, in 2001–07, consumption growth was greater among the top 60 than the bottom 40, and growth rates were negative among the poorest 10 percent of the population. Since 2007, there has been a surge in basic metal industries, such as construction materials, and in retail trade and manufacturing, particularly agroprocessing in food, beverage, and tobacco products. The expansion of these sectors has allowed greater inclusion in the economy among low-skilled workers, thereby boosting the incomes of the poorer segments of the population.

Despite the increasing importance of manufacturing and services and despite the plans for the future, the economy has historically depended heavily on agriculture, which accounts for around 33 percent of GDP, provides approximately 47 percent of exports, and employs about 70 percent of the workforce. Over two-thirds of the population lives in rural areas, and an estimated 98 percent of rural households engage in agricultural activities. The sector thus plays a key role in supplying food and generating incomes among the rural population. It has also proven highly strategic in the industrialization process through the inputs that it generates for the industrial sector (65 percent) and the food it produces for the urban and industrial labor force.[70] Agriculture has also been subject to greater diversification toward higher-value cash crops (cotton, cashews, tea, and coffee), along with an increase in land productivity, in part because poor households have been shifting from agriculture toward wage employment opportunities amid a process of urbanization within the country.

In addition, advances in the ownership of land and livestock, more-intensive activity among agricultural enterprises, and rising nonfarm employment have contributed to the better living conditions among the poorest. From 2007 to 2012, the enhancements in household endowments were more significant among the bottom 40. The same is true of human development outcomes in the prevalence of malnutrition, infant and maternal mortality, the female literacy rate, secondary-school enrollments, and access to clean drinking water. Nonetheless, much more needs to be done to reduce regional disparities and to expand the access to basic services; coverage rates are still especially low in the supply of electricity and in improved sanitation services.

Although rigorous evaluations have not yet been conducted to confirm the impact, the explicit commitment of the government to adopt policies unambiguously aimed at reducing poverty is consistent with rendering the distribution of income more equitable. This commitment has been realized through two programs: (1) MKUKUTA II, a national strategy for growth and poverty reduction designed to boost the access of the poor to basic services, including health care, primary education, and water and sanitation, and to mobilize financial resources, and (2) the Tanzania Social Action Fund, which encompasses a CCT program, public works, and a community savings component. Although expected to be rolled out among up to 275,000 households, Tanzania's nascent CCT program is reportedly aimed at targeting the poor effectively.[71] The poorest households use resources from this program to increase savings and invest in livestock, an indication that the program helps households reduce risk and improve livelihoods rather than merely raise consumption.[72]

From a fiscal point of view, Tanzania tends to redistribute more than anticipated based on its relatively low income level. Nonetheless, the fiscal system contributes little to reducing inequality. This is largely because several components of the fiscal system impact the distribution of incomes in different directions. Direct taxes, in-kind benefits in education (except in tertiary education), and cash transfers are progressive. Some favorable features among otherwise regressive fiscal tools also contribute to improving the equalizing capacity of the fiscal system. For example, indirect taxes are more progressive in Tanzania than in many Sub-Saharan African countries; beverage and communication excise taxes are progressive; and fertilizer subsidies are close to neutral.[73] Yet, electricity subsidies and tertiary education are regressive, and other programs that are progressive in many countries, such as health care and food assistance, are only neutral in Tanzania.

In sum, Tanzania has achieved a significant improvement in the reduction of income inequality and enhancement in the living conditions of the bottom quintiles of the population despite low income levels. The increasing diversification of the economy into labor-intensive manufacturing and commerce and greater agricultural productivity help explain part of this success. The diversification is being realized within a framework of macroeconomic stability and decades of liberalization, although the private sector remains unproductive and uncompetitive. The new Five Year Development Plan 2016–21 is designed to accelerate structural transformation to turn Tanzania into a semi-industrialized economy, increasingly urbanized, with room for further rural diversification and secondary town development to promote the reduction of regional disparities within the country. Strategic investments in infrastructure and basic services such as electricity and improved sanitation are also expected to promote economic growth and shared prosperity.

Concluding remarks: learning from country experiences

A handful of country experiences cannot be representative at a global scale or sufficient to provide policy prescriptions valid around the world. They are, however, illustrative of the practices and conditions behind significant reductions in inequality under particular circumstances. Despite the small number of experiences reviewed in this chapter, there is no dearth of countries that have recently narrowed income inequality. The bottom 40 enjoyed income or consumption growth rates exceeding the income growth of the mean between 2008 and 2013 in 49 countries. In recent years, reducing inequality is thus not a rare feat even in challenging contexts marked by international crises, local instability and conflict, and unfavorable initial conditions such as substantial poverty and inequality.

The countries reviewed, without exception, have made serious commitments to establishing a stable macroeconomic environment and reducing inflation. They have also benefitted from favorable global conditions in terms of low interest rates, high commodity prices, and booming international trade. In some cases, good macroeconomic policy has been associated with the appropriate management of an external commodity boom, as in Brazil and Peru. In other cases, as in Mali and Tanzania, transformations away from an outdated economic model have been implemented before prudent macroeconomic management emerged. That sound macroeconomic policy is good for equality is hardly surprising given the comprehensive evidence linking such policy with poverty reduction.[74] Our small but diverse sample of countries supports this conclusion across different specific contexts and challenges.

The contribution of economic growth to shared prosperity and inequality reduction is critical. All country cases report vigorous and, in some cases, such as Cambodia, Peru, and Tanzania, impressive average growth rates during the period of analysis. The evidence in each of these countries confirms that rising average income or consumption explains a great deal of the improvement in the living conditions of the poor. More than 60 percent of the decline in poverty in Brazil and Peru has been attributed to a growth effect, that is, a rise in average household incomes, while a more moderate 20 percent contribution is found in Mali (although growth there is found to contribute to raising poverty).

The functioning labor markets have been instrumental in all the countries under analysis in helping translate economic growth and sound macroeconomic policies into a narrowing in inequality and an increase in shared prosperity. The experiences of these countries show that labor markets can help reduce inequalities by expanding job opportunities across emerging markets, as in Cambodia, or traditional sectors, as in Mali and Tanzania; sharing earning opportunities with individuals previously excluded from growth, such as the low-skilled and women in Tanzania and Cambodia; and narrowing earnings gaps across workers, such as between men and women in Cambodia, between economic sectors in Mali, between formal and informal jobs in Brazil and Peru, and between urban and rural residents in Peru.

These five successful cases also highlight the importance of aligning macroeconomic and fiscal policies with sound sector-specific interventions and public investments. Thus, improving the coverage and quality of education, expanding the coverage of public health care, enhancing market connectivity, and establishing or scaling up safety nets to protect vulnerable populations recur in the country narratives. Although not all such interventions took place simultaneously in each country, the lesson is that the coherence of policy choices in macroeconomic and sectoral dimensions is critical to enabling steady reductions in inequality. Thus, appropriate policies and investments were identified and implemented in low-income Cambodia, Mali, and Tanzania during periods of economic diversification and in Brazil and Peru during periods of booming commodity prices.

This does not mean every policy decision in these countries was appropriate. In fact, these country experiences show that good luck—in the form of favorable external events unexpectedly benefiting a country—cannot be a substitute for policy coherence. Positive external shocks may magnify local efforts to reduce inequality. The surge in commodity prices favored the economies of Brazil and Peru, while the rise in the international rice prices clearly helped to raise the inclusive capacity of the Cambodian economy. The economic gains generated by the sudden reorientation of trade flows following conflict in a neighboring country largely fell outside the responsibility of Malian policy makers. However, strengthening the country's fiscal position, preventing a climb in inflation, promoting productive investments and economic diversification, weaving together more effective safety nets, combating corruption and elite capture following such lucky gains do fall under the direct responsibility of policy makers. Countries more willing to undertake such policy choices are also those more likely to sustain inequality reductions. Those that do not make these choices will experience short-lived and fragile reductions in inequality. Thus, the marked differences in the most recent policy choices between Brazil and Peru on fiscal consolidation, the control of inflation, and investments largely explain the stark differences in the most recent growth patterns in these countries (gradual recovery in Peru, recession in Brazil), and the outlook for poverty and inequality (positive in Peru, pessimistic in Brazil).[75]

Beyond the constants of good macroeconomic policy, strong growth, functioning labor markets, and coherent policies, the levers of inequality reduction may also vary considerably across countries. In Brazil, several policies combined led to narrowing inequality, including reforms in health care and education, raising the minimum wage and creating formal jobs, and a remarkable expansion in safety nets. The role of safety nets has been more marked in Brazil than in any other country. In contrast, impressive economic growth in Cambodia has been linked to the emergence of garment manufacturing, tourism, and construction. These sectors opened employment opportunities among the less highly skilled, thus diversifying the incomes of the poor away from subsistence agriculture. In Mali, which is an agrarian economy, the expansion in cereal production has been key to reductions in inequality, along with increased remittances and new trading opportunities with neighboring countries. In Tanzania, diversification in agriculture (toward cash crops) and in the rest of the economy (toward manufactures and retail commerce) explains a good deal of the success. In Peru, rising domestic demand owing to substantial foreign investment in mining has expanded the employment opportunities in the urban informal sector, while a dynamic agriculture has diversified into new exports. Earnings gaps narrowed between formal and informal workers following economic growth, as in the case of Brazil and Cambodia.

While the experiences reviewed in this chapter suggest that reducing inequality can be achieved in many different ways if appropriate building blocks are put in place, sustaining this success may require decisions that are similar to those outlined here. Thus, the five country cases suggest that there are still common policy interventions likely to sustain inequality reduction in developing countries. For example, the situation in countries such as Cambodia, Mali, and Tanzania underscores the need to expand safety nets, which are currently not large enough to protect the poorest. The Brazilian experience, a renowned example of safety net expansion, shows that the entire fiscal system can be designed to have a greater impact in reducing inequality. This is also the case in Tanzania. Improving competition and productivity in the private sector is also a priority in that country. Infrastructure is reportedly a huge obstacle in Cambodia, while, in Mali, dependence on external factors, from donor flows to the vagaries of weather, threaten sustained improvement. In Peru, the quality of education is below regional standards and would represent an obstacle to maintaining or improving economic productivity should more favorable external conditions disappear. The accumulation of quality human capital, diversification in income-earning opportunities among the poor, safety nets that are sufficiently large to protect the poorest, and improved infrastructure to connect lagging regions to economic growth opportunities are all desirable strategies to sustain success in boosting shared prosperity and narrowing inequality.

However, caution needs to be exerted to turn these findings into prescriptions with international validity. This is not only because of the small number of cases analyzed, but also because of the large differences in the contexts and challenges in each country. While Brazil is marked by historically record inequalities, conflict has affected Cambodia and, recently, Mali. Indeed, Mali shows that, although inequality can be reduced during periods of weak governance, such achievements may not be sustained or long-lived. Rapid population growth is also a dominant feature in Mali, which, along with Tanzania, is a low-income country. In Peru, the extent of informality in the economy is among the largest in the region. This chapter thus provides suggestive insights on policy interventions that, among a myriad of alternatives, have worked in specific contexts.

Notes

1. See Azevedo, Inchauste, and Sanfelice (2013); Azevedo, Sanfelice, and Nguyen (2012); Barros et al. (2006); Datt and Ravallion (1992); Inchauste et al. (2014); Lustig (2015) for methodological discussions of the Commitment to Equity Initiative and the decompositions.
2. Ferreira, Leite, and Litchfield (2008).
3. Using data from the national household surveys and tax records to construct a full individual income distribution, Souza, Medeiros, and Castro (2015) show that the Gini index fell by about 1 point between 2006 and 2012, compared with a fall of around 3 points if only household per capita income from the survey is used.
4. The estimate is based on a national poverty line. However, Brazil does not have an official poverty line. The R$140 per capita per month moderate poverty line is derived from the administrative poverty lines defined for the Bolsa Família Program and the *Brasil Sem Miséria* Program.
5. World Bank (2016a).
6. Tabulations of Equity Lab, Team for Statistical Development, World Bank, Washington, DC, based on household survey data, data in the SEDLAC database, and data derived through PovcalNet (online analysis tool), World Bank, Washington, DC, http://iresearch.worldbank.org/PovcalNet/. The information has been updated as of April 2016.
7. López-Calva and Rocha (2012); World Bank (2016a).
8. Ferreira, Leite, and Litchfield (2008).

9. Azevedo et al. (2013); Barros et al. (2010); Ferreira, Firpo, and Messina (2014); Lustig, López-Calva, and Ortiz-Juárez (2013).

10. World Bank (2016a).

11. López-Calva and Rocha (2012).

12. The widening in formality was supported by institutional policies aiming to enforce labor legislation (Ferreira, Firpo, and Messina 2014). In particular, the government expanded the role of the Brazilian Public Prosecutor's Office (Ministério Público) and the Ministry of Labor and Employment. In addition, reforms to improve the efficiency of labor inspections were implemented in 1995. Corseuil, Almeida, and Carneiro (2012) provide evidence from 1996–2006 that establishes a causal relationship between the reforms and increases in formal employment.

13. Ferreira, Firpo, and Messina (2014).

14. World Bank (2016a).

15. Equity Lab tabulations based on household survey data and data in the SEDLAC database.

16. Barros et al. (2010); Osorio and Souza (2012).

17. This means that the income inequality generated by the functioning of the markets—estimated at a Gini index of 55 in 2009—was reduced by 6 percent, or 3.3 percentage points, after direct taxes and transfers are taken into account. Higgins and Pereira (2014); Higgins et al. (2013).

18. Clements et al. (2015); Immervoll et al. (2006). The 33 percent reduction is equivalent to a reduction of about 14 percentage points in the average market income Gini in the OECD.

19. Higgins and Pereira (2014); Higgins et al. (2013).

20. Carneiro (2006).

21. Recent analyses also include other factors in the discussion of trends in labor inequality in Brazil, such as degradation of tertiary education, obsolescence of skills, the heterogeneity of firms within industries, skill-biased technological change, and the role of unions. The interplay of all factors in final wage inequality is complex, and there does not seem to exist a strong consensus on the contribution of these factors. See Silva and Messina (2016).

22. World Bank (2016b).

23. Other urban and rural areas experienced the greatest declines in the Gini index, by 35 percent and 27 percent, respectively, while, in Phnom Penh, the index fell by 19 percent between 2007 and 2013.

24. World Bank (2016b).

25. The proportion of the population living below the national poverty line declined by nearly half, to 23.9 percent, from 2007 to 2009 alone and continued to decline thereafter, although more moderately. In rural areas, poverty was reduced by half between 2007 and 2011, from 51.8 percent to 23.7 percent. World Bank (2014a).

26. IMF (2015).

27. Agriculture's share in GDP was eclipsed by industry's share for the first time in 2007, which was also the year that investment first surpassed the flows of official development assistance to Cambodia.

28. ADB (2014a).

29. Mejia-Mantilla and Woldemichael (2016).

30. In addition, in 2010, the government unveiled an official rice policy that set out to increase annual milled rice exports to a million tons by 2015, a target that went unfulfilled (World Bank 2009).

31. World Bank (2014a).

32. ADB (2014b). Average per capita income from nonfarm self-employment jumped 63 percent between 2004 and 2009, and daily rural wages more than doubled between 2007 and 2012.

33. World Bank (2014a, 2016b).

34. IMF (2015).

35. Recent agricultural productivity gains from an expansion in the arable land under cultivation are not sustainable indefinitely and are thus unable to offset these problems.

36. ADB (2014b); ASPIRE (Atlas of Social Protection Indicators of Resilience and Equity) (database), World Bank, Washington, DC, http://datatopics.worldbank.org/aspire/.

37. Kanbur, Rhee, and Zhuang (2014).

38. Using the Atlas method, in current U.S. dollars; see WDI (World Development Indicators) (database), World Bank, Washington, DC, http://data.worldbank.org/data-catalog/world-development-indicators.

39. UNDP (2014).

40. Data for 2014, WDI (World Development Indicators) (database), World Bank, Washington, DC, http://data.worldbank.org/data-catalog/world-development-indicators.

41. World Bank (2015a).

42. World Bank (2015b, 100).

43. Beegle et al. (2016) have questioned the comparability of surveys in Mali. However, after a careful analysis of the robustness of welfare estimates using the same household surveys, the World Bank (2013) has concluded that the results are robust to alternative choices of poverty lines accounting for comparability issues.

44. World Bank (2015a).

45. World Bank (2015b).

46. World Bank (2015a, 2015b).

47. Josz (2013).

48. World Bank (2015a, 2015b).

49. Cherrier, del Ninno, and Razmara (2011).

50. World Bank (2015a).

51. Vakis, Rigolini, and Lucchetti (2015).

52. World Bank (2016c).

53. WDI (World Development Indicators (database), World Bank, Washington, DC, http://data.worldbank.org/data-catalog/world-development-indicators.

54. World Bank (2016c).

55. Genoni and Salazar (2015).

56. Jaramillo and Saavedra-Chanduvi (2011).

57. World Bank (2016c).

58. Rodríguez-Castelán et al (2016); Silva and Messina (2016).

59. Inchauste et al. (2014).

60. World Bank (2016c).

61. Jaramillo (2013); Lustig et al. (2012).

62. Genoni and Salazar (2015).

63. The poverty figures are for Tanzania mainland only and come from 2007 and 2011/12 Household Budget Survey data. They are estimated using, respectively, the national basic needs poverty line of T Sh 36,482 per adult per month and the national food poverty line of T Sh 26,085 per adult per month. See World Bank (2016d).

64. Tanzania's Gini index in 2012 (35.8) was lower than the 45.1 Sub-Saharan African average and, among East African countries, it was below that of Burundi (46.0), Kenya (47.7), Uganda (44.3), and Rwanda (50.8). It was only slightly higher than the index of Ethiopia (33.6). It was on par with levels of inequality in South Asia and East Asia, which were grouped around 38.4, and significantly lower relative to indexes in Latin America, such as Bolivia, Brazil, and Mexico, where the levels of inequality ranged from 47.0 to 55.2 (World Bank 2015c).

65. There are also issues of comparability among surveys in Tanzania stemming from changes in the survey design and methodological improvements implemented during the 2011/12 household budget survey. The World Bank (2015c) addresses these issues using different methods, including the re-evaluation of the consumption aggregates for the 2007 household budget survey using the same approach as in 2011/12, as well as nonparametric and parametric imputation procedures. The various adjustment methods support the main results presented here.

66. World Bank (2016d).

67. Edwards (2012).

68. Robinson, Gaertner, and Papageorgiou (2011).

69. World Bank (2016d).

70. World Bank (2015c).

71. World Bank (2016e). The estimate includes beneficiaries of public works programs and the expansion of cash transfers.

72. World Bank (2015c).

73. Younger, Myamba, and Mdadila (2016).

74. Commission on Growth and Development (2008).

75. World Bank (2016f).

References

ADB (Asian Development Bank). 2014a. *Cambodia: Diversifying beyond Garments and Tourism, Country Diagnostic Study.* November. Manila: Economics and Research Department, ADB.

———. 2014b. "Cambodia: Country Poverty Analysis 2014." ADB, Manila.

Azevedo, João Pedro, María Eugenia Dávalos, Carolina Díaz-Bonilla, Bernardo Atuesta, and Raul Andres Castañeda. 2013. "Fifteen Years of Inequality in Latin America: How Have Labor Markets Helped?" Policy Research Working Paper 6384, World Bank, Washington, DC.

Azevedo, João Pedro, Gabriela Inchauste, and Viviane Sanfelice. 2013. "Growth without Reductions in Inequality." Background paper, Poverty and Gender Unit, World Bank, Washington, DC.

Azevedo, João Pedro, Viviane Sanfelice, and Minh Cong Nguyen. 2012. "Shapley Decomposition by Components of a Welfare Measure." Unpublished working paper, World Bank, Washington, DC.

Barros, Ricardo Paes de, Mirela De Carvalho, Samuel Franco, and Rosane Mendonça. 2006. "Uma Análise das Principais Causas da Queda Recente na Desigualdade de Renda Brasileira." *Revista Econômica* 8 (1): 117–47.

———. 2010. "Markets, the State, and the Dynamics of Inequality in Brazil." In *Declining Inequality in Latin America: A Decade of Progress?*, edited by Luis F. López-Calva and Nora Lustig, 134–74. New York: United Nations Development Programme; Baltimore: Brookings Institution Press.

Beegle, Kathleen, Luc Christiaensen, Andrew Dabalen, and Isis Gaddis. 2016. *Poverty in a Rising Africa*. Africa Poverty Report. Washington, DC: World Bank.

Carneiro, Francisco Galrão. 2006. "The Effects of the Minimum Wage on the Brazilian Labor Market." In *The Third Dimension of Labor Markets: Demand, Supply, and Institutions in Brazil*, edited by Francisco Galrão Carneiro, Indermit S. Gill, and Ricardo Paes de Barros, 113–44. New York: Nova Science Publishers.

Cherrier, Cécile, Carlo del Ninno, and Setareh Razmara. 2011. "Mali Social Safety Nets." Social Protection and Labor Discussion Paper 1412, World Bank, Washington, DC.

Clements, Benedict, Ruud de Mooij, Sanjeev Gupta, and Michael Keen, eds. 2015. *Inequality and Fiscal Policy*. Washington, DC: International Monetary Fund.

Corseuil, Carlos Henrique L., Rita Almeida, and Pedro Carneiro. 2012. "Inspeção do trabalho e evolução do emprego formal no Brasil." Texto para Discussão TD 1688, Institute for Applied Economic Research, Brasilia.

Commission on Growth and Development. 2008. *The Growth Report: Strategies for Sustained Growth and Inclusive Development*. Washington, DC: World Bank. https://openknowledge.worldbank.org/handle/10986/6507.

Datt, Gaurav, and Martin Ravallion. 1992. "Growth and Redistribution Components of Changes in Poverty Measures: A Decomposition with Applications to Brazil and India in the 1980s." *Journal of Development Economics* 38 (2): 275–95.

Edwards, Sebastian. 2012. "Is Tanzania a Success Story? A Long Term Analysis." NBER Working Paper 17764 (January), National Bureau of Economic Research, Cambridge, MA.

Ferreira, Francisco H. G., Phillippe George Leite, and Julie A. Litchfield. 2008. "The Rise and Fall of Brazilian Inequality: 1981–2004." *Macroeconomic Dynamics* 12 (S2): 199–230.

Ferreira, Francisco H. G., Sergio P. Firpo, and Julian Messina. 2014. "A More Level Playing Field? Explaining the Decline in Earnings Inequality in Brazil, 1995–2012." IRIBA Working Paper 12 (September), International Research Initiative on Brazil and Africa, School of Environment, Education, and Development, University of Manchester, Manchester, United Kingdom.

Genoni, María Eugenia, and Mateo Salazar. 2015. "Steering toward Shared Prosperity in Peru." In *Shared Prosperity and Poverty Eradication in Latin America and the Caribbean*, edited by Louise Cord, María Eugenia Genoni, and Carlos Rodríguez-Castelán, 269–302. Washington, DC: World Bank.

Higgins, Sean, Nora Lustig, Whitney Ruble, and Timothy M. Smeeding. 2013. "Comparing the Incidence of Taxes and Social Spending in Brazil and the United States." CEQ Working Paper 16, Commitment to Equity, Inter-American Dialogue, Washington, DC; Center for Inter-American Policy and Research and Department of Economics, Tulane University, New Orleans.

Higgins, Sean, and Claudiney Pereira. 2014. "The Effects of Brazil's Taxation and Social Spending on the Distribution of Household Income." In "Analyzing the Redistributive Impact of Taxes and Transfers in Latin America," edited by Nora Lustig, Carola Pessino, and John Scott, special issue, *Public Finance Review* 42 (3): 346–67.

IMF (International Monetary Fund). 2015. "Cambodia: Staff Report for the 2015 Article IV Consultation." IMF Country Report 15/307 (October 1), IMF, Washington, DC.

Immervoll, Herwig, Horacio Levy, José Ricardo Nogueira, Cathal O'Donoghue, and Rozane Bezerra de Siqueira. 2009. "The Impact of Brazil's Tax-Benefit System on Inequality and Poverty." In *Poverty, Inequality, and Policy in Latin America*, edited by Stephan Klasen and Felicitas Nowak-Lehmann, 271–301. CESifo Seminar Series. Cambridge, MA: MIT Press.

Inchauste, Gabriela, João Pedro Azevedo, B. Essama-Nssah, Sergio Olivieri, Trang Van Nguyen, Jaime Saavedra-Chanduvi, and Hernan Winkler. 2014. *Understanding Changes in Poverty*. Directions in Development: Poverty Series. Washington, DC: World Bank.

Jaramillo, Miguel. 2013. "The Incidence of Social Spending and Taxes in Peru." CEQ Working Paper 9 (January), Commitment to Equity, Inter-American Dialogue, Washington, DC; Center for Inter-American Policy and Research and Department of Economics, Tulane University, New Orleans.

Jaramillo, Miguel, and Jaime Saavedra-Chanduvi. 2011. "Menos desiguales: la distribución del ingreso luego de las reformas estructurales." Documento de investigación 59, Grupo de Analisis para el Desarrollo, Lima, Peru.

Josz, Christian. 2013. "Mali: Achieving Strong and Inclusive Growth with Macroeconomic Stability." African Development 13/08, International Monetary Fund, Washington, DC.

Kanbur, Ravi, Changyong Rhee, and Juzhong Zhuang, eds. 2014. *Inequality in Asia and the Pacific: Trends, Drivers, and Policy Implications.* Manila: Asian Development Bank; New York: Routledge.

López-Calva, Luis F., and Sonia Rocha. 2012. "Exiting Belindia? Lesson from the Recent Decline in Income Inequality in Brazil." Report 70155, Poverty, Gender, and Equity Unit, Latin America and Caribbean Region, World Bank, Washington, DC.

Lustig, Nora. 2015. "Inequality and Fiscal Redistribution in Middle Income Countries: Brazil, Chile, Colombia, Indonesia, Mexico, Peru and South Africa." CEQ Working Paper 31 (July), Commitment to Equity, Inter-American Dialogue, Washington, DC; Center for Inter-American Policy and Research and Department of Economics, Tulane University, New Orleans.

Lustig, Nora, Luis F. López-Calva, and Eduardo Ortiz-Juárez. 2013. "Declining Inequality in Latin America in the 2000s: The Cases of Argentina, Brazil, and Mexico." *World Development* 44 (C): 129–41.

Lustig, Nora, George Gray Molina, Sean Higgins, Miguel Jaramillo, Wilson Jiménez, Veronica Paz, Claudiney Pereira, Carola Pessino, John Scott, and Ernesto Yañez. 2012. "The Impact of Taxes and Social Spending on Inequality and Poverty in Argentina, Bolivia, Brazil, Mexico and Peru: A Synthesis of Results." CEQ Working Paper 3, Commitment to Equity, Inter-American Dialogue, Washington, DC; Center for Inter-American Policy and Research and Department of Economics, Tulane University, New Orleans.

Mejia-Mantilla, Carolina, and Martha Tesfaye Woldemichael. 2016. "To Sew or Not to Sew? Assessing the Welfare Effects of the Garment Industry in Cambodia." World Bank, Washington, DC.

Osorio, Rafael Guerreiro, and Pedro H. G. Ferreira de Souza. 2012. "O Bolsa Família depois do Brasil Carinhoso: uma análise do potencial de redução da pobreza extrema." Institute for Applied Economic Research, Brasília.

Robinson, David O., Matthew Gaertner, and Chris Papageorgiou. 2011. "Tanzania: Growth Acceleration and Increased Public Spending with Macroeconomic Stability." In *Yes Africa Can: Success Stories from a Dynamic Continent*, edited by Punam Chuhan-Pole and Manka Angwafo, 21–50. Washington, DC: World Bank.

Rodríguez-Castelán, Carlos, Luis F. López-Calva, Nora Lustig, and Daniel Valderrama. 2016. "Understanding the Dynamics of Labor Income Inequality in Latin America." Policy Research Working Paper 7795, World Bank, Washington, DC.

SEDLAC (Socio-Economic Database for Latin America and the Caribbean), Center for Distributive, Labor, and Social Studies, Universidad de La Plata, La Plata, Argentina; World Bank, Washington, DC, http://sedlac.econo .unlp.edu.ar/eng/index.php.

Shorrocks, Anthony. 2013. "Decomposition Procedures for Distributional Analysis: A Unified Framework Based on the Shapley Value." *Journal of Income Inequality* 11 (1): 99–126.

Silva, Joana, and Julián Messina. 2016. "Wage Inequality in Latin America: Trends and Puzzles." Unpublished regional study, Office of the Chief Economist, Latin America and Caribbean Region, World Bank, Washington, DC.

Souza, Pedro H. G. Ferreira de, Marcelo Medeiros, and Fabio Avila de Castro. 2015. "'Top Incomes in Brazil: Preliminary Results." *Economics Bulletin* 35 (2): 998–1004.

UNDP (United Nations Development Programme). 2014. *Human Development Report 2014; Sustaining Human Progress: Reducing Vulnerabilities and Building Resilience.* New York: UNDP.

Vakis, Renos, Jamele Rigolini, and Leonardo Lucchetti. 2015. "Overview; Left Behind: Chronic Poverty in Latin America and the Caribbean." World Bank: Washington, DC.

World Bank. 2009. "International Development Association Program Document, Kingdom of Cambodia: Proposed Smallholder Agriculture and Social Protection Support Operation." Report 48083-KH (June 19), World Bank, Washington, DC.

———. 2013. "Mali: Poverty and Gender Notes." Report 77752-ML (May 31), World Bank, Washington, DC.

———. 2014a. "Where Have All the Poor Gone? Cambodia Poverty Assessment 2013." Report ACS4545, World Bank, Washington, DC.

———. 2014b. "Social Gains in the Balance: A Fiscal Policy Challenge for Latin America and the Caribbean." LAC Poverty and Labor Brief, Report 85162 rev (February), Latin America and Caribbean Region, World Bank, Washington, DC.

———. 2015a. "Republic of Mali, Priorities for Ending Poverty and Boosting Shared Prosperity: Systematic Country Diagnostic (SCD)." Report 94191-ML (June 22), World Bank, Washington, DC.

———. 2015b. "The Geography of Poverty in Mali." Report 88880-ML (April 23), World Bank, Washington, DC.

———. 2015c. "Tanzania Mainland: Poverty Assessment." Report AUS6819 v2, World Bank, Washington, DC.

———. 2016a. *Brazil Systematic Country Diagnostic: Retaking the Path to Inclusion, Growth, and Sustainability*. Report 101431-BR, Washington, DC: World Bank.

———. 2016b. "Cambodia: Poverty Reduction and Equity in 2013." World Bank, Washington, DC

———. 2016c. "Peru Systematic Country Diagnostic: Concept Note." World Bank, Washington, DC.

———. 2016d. "Tanzania Systematic Country Diagnostic: Concept Note." World Bank, Washington, DC.

———. 2016e. "International Development Association Project Paper, United Republic of Tanzania: Productive Social Safety Net (PSSN)." Report PAD1500 (May 20), World Bank, Washington, DC.

———. 2016f. "Macro and Poverty Outlook: Spring Meetings Edition, 2016." World Bank, Washington, DC.

Younger, Stephen D., Flora Myamba, and Kenneth Mdadila. 2016. "Fiscal Incidence in Tanzania." CEQ Working Paper 36, Commitment to Equity, Inter-American Dialogue, Washington, DC; Center for Inter-American Policy and Research and Department of Economics, Tulane University, New Orleans.

Reductions in Inequality: A Policy Perspective

6

This chapter discusses what we know about key domestic policy interventions that are effective in reducing inequality, the benefits they generate, the choices that need to be made concerning their design and implementation, and the trade-offs with which they are associated. The chapter does not provide an exhaustive or comprehensive review of every intervention that could reduce inequality, nor does it supply universal prescriptions. Instead, it focuses on a few policy areas on which there is a sufficient body of rigorous evidence to draw out useful lessons with confidence: early childhood development (ECD), including breastfeeding; universal health care; good-quality education; conditional cash transfers (CCTs); investments in rural infrastructure; and taxation. The several lessons that are revealed through the examination are supported by consolidated and emerging evidence and appear to be generally valid.

Despite progress, disparities persist today that are affecting well-being, the access to basic services, and current and future economic opportunities among the poor. Pathways to reduce inequality are many, from narrowing gaps in income generation opportunities to reducing the potential for inequalities in human capital development before they emerge; smoothing consumption among the most deprived, especially during shocks; and redistributing in favor of the poor.

Although many interventions do not have equalizing objectives, they are associated with equalizing outcomes. Improved competition and economic efficiency are compatible with reducing inequality. The fine points of policy design absolutely matter in determining the extent to which policy interventions lead to reductions in inequality without compromising efficiency. Therefore, in the design of equalizing policies, implementation trade-offs should not be overlooked because of too much attention to efficiency and equity trade-offs.

Nonetheless, universal prescriptions and unique models are problematic. Evidence indicates the value of general principles and the analysis of lessons learned. Integrated, simple, and flexible interventions are more likely to succeed than individual interventions, and the composition of interventions dictates the extent of success. Equalizing interventions are not a luxury exclusive to middle- and high-income countries, nor an option only during periods of prosperity. Good interventions are possible in all settings and at all times, including among low-income countries and during crises, and they may disproportionally favor the poorest households. To achieve this, the most deprived and the most vulnerable must be involved in the interventions. Knowledge about appropriate policies and interventions has increased significantly in recent decades, but more microeconomic data and better analysis of these data are needed.

Introduction

Countries can reduce inequality. This is true of low- and middle-income countries as well as high-income countries. Successful country experiences confirm that good macroeconomic management, solid and steady growth, functioning labor markets, and coherent space for the play of domestic policy lead to reductions in inequality (see chapter 5).

Chapter 6 focuses on what is known about domestic policy interventions that are effective in reducing inequality, the benefits they create, the choices that are necessary in designing and implementing them, and the trade-offs that tend to emerge. The trade-offs involve choices between more equity and more economic efficiency, but also along many other dimensions, for example, deciding who might benefit from an intervention and who may not, who should pay, and whether to promote greater generosity or lower costs.

The focus is on a narrow group of interventions within the coherent space of domestic policies identified in chapter 5 that can successfully reduce inequality without compromising efficiency. There is no attempt to be exhaustive or to offer a comprehensive review of every policy that may narrow inequality or enhance the scope for equality of opportunity. Voluminous reviews of sectoral interventions already exist that provide relevant in-depth assessments. There is much less analysis available on the capacity of certain policies to reduce inequality and the pathways through which this may be accomplished.

The policy areas examined in this chapter are those the evaluation in chapter 5 shows to be relevant in the effort to reduce inequality, alongside macroeconomic management, steady growth, and functioning labor markets. These policy areas are human capital accumulation, investments in infrastructure, and progressive fiscal policies. Within these policy domains, this chapter tightens the focus to selected interventions on which a body of rigorous evidence has been accumulated, including evaluation evidence, thereby allowing lessons to be drawn out with confidence. The specific interventions discussed are ECD, including breastfeeding; universal health care coverage; good-quality education; cash transfers, mostly conditional transfers; investments in rural infrastructure, specifically, rural roads and electrification; and income and consumption taxes.

The selection means that other policy interventions with potential effects on inequality are not included in the assessment. This is not intended to deny the potential equalizing effects of these other interventions; the evidence of the equalizing effects is merely less compelling, is currently being collected, or a general consensus is absent on how to frame the policies to reduce inequality while reaching other objectives. This is the reason interventions revolving around land redistribution or financial inclusion, measures to adapt to climate change, or steps to promote technology and innovation are not included, for example.[1]

Even the highly selective choice of interventions demonstrates that inequality can be successfully confronted from multiple angles. Pathways to reduce inequality are many, from narrowing gaps in income generation opportunities to reducing the potential for inequalities in human capital development to emerge; smoothing consumption among the most deprived, especially during shocks; and redistributing in favor of the poor. The interventions selected in this chapter cover each of these pathways.

One approach to analyzing the evidence consists of following the effects of interventions during an individual's life cycle, which helps determine the short- and long-term equalizing impacts of interventions. Thus, breastfeeding during the first year of life and ECD interventions during the first 1,000 days of life set the foundations for greater opportunities later by preventing nutritional and cognitive development gaps among the poorest children. They are predistribution interventions, that is, they address potential inequalities early on, before the inequalities emerge. By preventing or reducing nutritional and cognitive development gaps, which have long-run consequences on health, education, and future earnings, the interventions also level the playing field and help equalize opportunities throughout the life of an individual. Universal health care coverage and good-quality education increase the human capital of children, youth, and adults. Given the daunting inequalities in health care and education prevailing today, achieving universal health care coverage and good-quality education for all requires that those who are currently excluded from health care and quality education benefit from interventions. Raising the human capital of the excluded also helps level the future playing field. In contrast, CCTs and taxation have short-term effects on income distribution if they, respectively, smooth consumption among the most deprived and redistribute income from the rich to the poor. The construction or improvement of rural roads likewise has immediate effects on the generation of income opportunities by expanding the market connectivity of, for instance, isolated smallholder farmers. In so far as these investments allow the poorest communities to increase and diversify incomes, the strategy should also have an impact on inequality.

Another approach through which one may analyze how policy interventions affect inequality is by way of the functions of the policies. To end poverty, policies can grow the incomes of the poorest; boost their human capital, thereby reducing the gaps between them and other population groups; and protect them from unequalizing shocks, that is, shocks having disproportionate consequences on the poorest relative to less vulnerable population groups.[2] For example, investment in rural infrastructure supports economic growth and other physical investments; ECD, universal health care coverage, and good-quality education constitute investments in human capital; and cash transfers allow individuals to be protected against various consumption shocks and other risks. Policy choices in taxation may affect economic growth as well as the availability of household resources to invest in human capital and access other protection mechanisms.

Organizing the policy discussion around such analytical frameworks allows the following sections to briefly describe the existing evidence on the benefits, impacts, pathways, and implementation issues most relevant to each of these interventions. The assessment offers analysis of multiple evidence-based lessons on successful equalizing interventions across low- and middle-income countries, regions, and contexts.

Early childhood development and nutrition

ECD promotes physical, socioemotional, language, and cognitive development during a child's early years. Breastfeeding and complementary feeding are often integrated in ECD interventions. Investing in such interventions shapes an individual's educational attainment, health, social behavior, and earnings in adulthood.[3] The first 1,000 days of life are especially important: nutritional deficiencies and cognitive underdevelopment during this period are associated with later cognitive delays and lower academic achievement. Reducing inequality through ECD therefore reduces inequalities in ability, educational achievement, health status, and expected adult earnings, gains that are carried over throughout an individual's life.

The current inequalities in ECD are stark. Thus, worldwide, poor children enjoy far less access to ECD programs than their richer peers. Data show that, in 21 of 27 low- or middle-income countries, preschool enrollment rates among the poorest quintile are less than a third of the rates among the richest quintile.[4] These disadvantages are compounded by the fact that poor children also have less access to adequate nutrition, health care services, basic water and sanitation infrastructure, and childcare, which make them more prone to inadequate development. As a result, nearly one under-5-year-old in four worldwide still suffers from stunting (low height for age), a sign of chronic malnutrition and abbreviated child development.[5]

Unlike some policy interventions, ECD programs are not associated with equity-efficiency trade-offs.[6] Investments in ECD interventions typically have economic benefits among individuals as well as society. For example, earnings at ages 28–40 among participants in the HighScope Perry Preschool

Study in the 1960s in the United States (detailed below) were 28 percent higher than the earnings among the control group.[7] Such individual benefits represent about a third to a half of the total payoffs from such interventions, once social benefits—the reduced public spending required to address grade repetition, social assistance transfers, and crime—are taken into account.[8] On breastfeeding, a recent meta-analysis estimates the economic impact of exclusive breastfeeding during a prolonged period (until age 12 months or later) at US$302 billion, or 0.5 percent of the world's gross income.[9]

Given the broad nature of ECD interventions, those interventions reported to have the largest benefits and associated with the most compelling supporting evidence of such benefits are examined here: parenting skills, preschool, breastfeeding, and nutrition.[10]

Parenting skills

Because of the preeminent role the home environment plays in the early development of children, many ECD programs concentrate on parenting skills to promote greater cognitive stimulation among children and higher-quality parent-child interactions. These programs generally involve one or more of three initiatives: home visits, group sessions, and clinic appointments. Research suggests all these programs are largely effective.

The most well known program of this kind in the developing world is a Jamaican intervention that began in 1986 and lasted two years. The Jamaican study targeted toddlers ages 9–24 months who suffered from stunting. The intervention consisted of weekly visits by community health workers to teach parenting skills aimed at fostering cognitive and socioemotional development.[11] It also provided nutrition supplements and psychosocial stimulation. The sample was divided into four groups: one group received stimulation only; one received nutrition only; one received both; and one received neither. Undersized children benefiting from psychosocial stimulation and nutrition interventions caught up with normally sized children 18 months after the start of the program, developing at

FIGURE 6.1 The Mental Development of Stunted Children, Jamaica, 1986–87

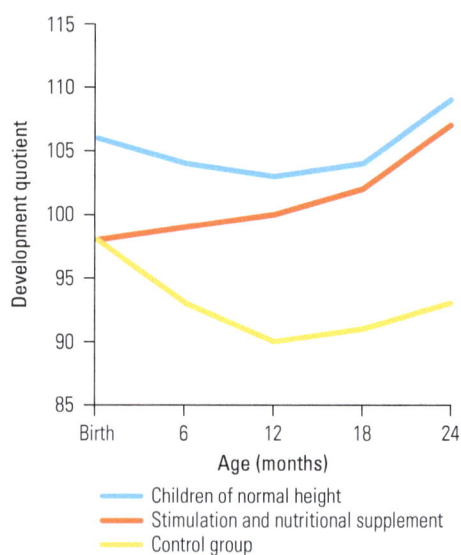

Source: Grantham-McGregor et al. 1991.
Note: Development quotient = age of the group into which test scores place the child, divided by the child's chronological age and multiplied by 100.

a more rapid rate than undersized children who were not participating (figure 6.1).[12] Researchers followed up among the participants 20 years after the intervention and found that the groups receiving stimulation (with or without the nutrition supplement) had 25 percent higher earnings than the control group. This increase in earnings had allowed those in the stimulation program to catch up completely with the nonstunted comparison group, effectively reducing the inequality of incomes across the groups. Meanwhile, the nutrition-only group showed no statistically significant difference with the control group.[13]

Building on the Jamaican success, other countries have adapted the program to local conditions. The results have been widely positive. For instance, a recent randomized controlled trial involving 1,400 children in Colombia that enlisted local mothers to make home visits found substantial benefits in children's cognitive and language development.[14] The program achieved the most success among children with higher baseline levels of development and among children whose mothers had higher levels of schooling. In Bangladesh, another randomized controlled trial involved weekly group meetings, coupled with home visits.[15] The program led to significant benefits in mental development, and children in the program were happier, more cooperative, more vocal, and more responsive. A program in Ecuador found significant improvements in language, memory, and fine motor skills, while a quasi-experiment in Brazil found significant benefits in mental and psycho-motor development in a project involving group workshops among mothers, along with 10 home visits promoting play.[16] A randomized evaluation in Antigua, Jamaica, and St. Lucia studied the impact of a combination of home visits and a package of instructional videos and materials shown to mothers while they waited to see nurses in clinics. The study found substantial benefits to child cognitive development and the parenting knowledge of mothers.[17]

Preschool

A growing body of evidence demonstrates that cognitive and socioemotional gaps become apparent even before children enter primary school. By the age of 4, children in poorer households typically show lower levels of cognitive and language development with respect to their peers.[18] The most well known programs addressing such early cognitive and emotional delays through preschool education are two studies in the United States that followed participants for decades and demonstrated the benefits of preschool.[19] Initiated in 1962, the HighScope Perry Preschool Study randomly assigned 3- and 4-year-olds in low-income households to preschool or no preschool groups, with follow-ups at ages 19, 27, and 40. By age 40, adults who had been in the preschool group had higher earnings, were more likely to be employed and to have graduated from high school, and were less likely to have been arrested, spent time in jail, or used drugs.[20] The other well-known intervention was launched in the early 1980s at the Chicago Child-Parent Center. By age 24, the program participants showed higher high school completion rates, higher rates of four-year college attendance, lower rates of incarceration, and a lower incidence of de-

pression. The estimated premium in lifetime net benefits per program participant relative to the control group was US$78,000.[21] Other preschool programs evaluated in the United States, including the Abecedarian Project and state programs, suggest that the average benefit-to-cost ratio was 6:1–7:1, that is, US$6.00–US$7.00 per US$1.00 invested in preschool.[22]

While no longitudinal study has been conducted in the developing world over such a long period, a number of studies have investigated short-term impacts. In Mozambique, a Save the Children pilot program begun in 2008 in 30 villages in rural Gaza Province has shown positive results, all for an investment of less than US$3 per child per month. A rigorous evaluation shows that the program improves outcomes among children in cognitive, socioemotional, and fine-motor development; increases the chances that children will be in primary school and at their age-appropriate grade; and improves self-reported parental behavior in early stimulation and discipline.[23] A program in Argentina also demonstrates the positive effects of preschool. Between 1993 and 1999, the government built classrooms so an additional 175,000 children could attend preschool. A study in 2006 found that children attending one year of these preschools had higher test scores and better school behavior, including greater attention, effort, and class participation and better discipline.[24]

Improving preschool quality is another avenue to enhancing outcomes among the most disadvantaged children. Quality refers to several aspects of learning, from teacher-student interaction, curriculum selection, professional development, and staff accreditation to classroom size and learning materials. In general, higher quality leads to better learning outcomes, as demonstrated, for example, in Bangladesh and several countries in East Africa.[25] Evidence on preschools as well as primary and secondary education (see the next section) points to the experience and incentives of teachers rather than teacher training as the most effective drivers of improved learning.[26] For example, in Uruguay, among children of mothers with low educational attainment, those who attended preschool were 27 percentage points more likely to remain in school at age 15 than a control group of children who did not participate in preschool. Among children of more well educated mothers, the corresponding effect of preschool was only 8 percentage points.[27]

Richer households are more likely to send their children to preschool, but the children of poor households enjoy bigger benefits if they attend preschool. A survey of 52 countries in the early 2000s found a strong correlation between preschool attendance and wealth and an even stronger correlation with mother's education.[28] Longitudinal studies in the United States and some nonexperimental studies in the developing world show that children with low socioeconomic status or whose mothers have low educational attainment enjoy greater benefits from preschool than more affluent students.[29] In Nepal, Nicaragua, and Uruguay, preschool benefits poor children more than their wealthier counterparts.[30]

Breastfeeding and nutrition

The World Health Organization recommends that mothers start breastfeeding within an hour of birth and exclusively breastfeed for the first six months of life.[31] Exclusive breastfeeding is correlated with lower child mortality; increasing the rate of exclusive breastfeeding to 90 percent worldwide would prevent up to 13 percent of child deaths.[32] Nonbreastfed infants face eight times more risk of death than infants benefiting from exclusive breastfeeding in the first 12 months of life. These risks are larger among girls than boys.[33] A meta-analysis of breastfeeding in low- and middle-income countries estimates that breastfeeding avoids about half of all cases of diarrhea and a third of respiratory infections among infants.[34] Prolonged, exclusive breastfeeding also improves children's cognitive development. A study in Brazil reports the substantial effects of breastfeeding on intelligence, educational attainment, and adult earnings. After 30 years, participants who were breastfed for 12 months or more showed higher intelligence quotients (IQs) (about 4 points higher), more years of ed-

ucation (0.9 years), and higher monthly incomes (R$341, about a third of the current minimum wage) relative to people who had been breastfed for less than a month during a corresponding period in the past.[35] A large randomized trial in Belarus estimated a systematic higher mean of about 6 IQ points among treated children age 6 who had been breastfed throughout the first 12 months of life relative to a control group of nonbreastfed children.[36]

Furthermore, breastfeeding is one of the few positive health behaviors that is more prevalent among poor women than among rich women in low- and middle-income countries. This suggests that promoting breastfeeding can reduce cognitive, health, and future income gaps between rich and poor children. For example, the program evaluated in Belarus randomly assigned maternity hospitals to encourage breastfeeding using the World Health Organization– United Nations Children's Fund guidelines, while similar hospitals served as the control. The intervention led to much higher breastfeeding rates and lower diarrhea rates among infants.[37] Alive and Thrive, a breastfeeding program launched in Bangladesh, Ethiopia, and Vietnam, combines advocacy, community mobilization, and mass media to encourage exclusive breastfeeding. Since 2010, the share of infants under 6 months of age who are exclusively breastfed has increased from 49 percent to 86 percent in places that received the comprehensive communication intervention package. Thus, in Vietnam, exclusive breastfeeding tripled in areas where interpersonal counseling services in health facilities supported mass media campaigns.

However, many women in the developing world do not visit health facilities for prenatal care or to give birth, especially among the poorest quintiles, raising the need for community- or home-based interventions.[38] Evidence from such interventions in Bangladesh, Burkina Faso, India, Mexico, South Africa, and Uganda shows success in initiating and extending the duration of breastfeeding.[39] For example, Bangladesh's large-scale community-based nutrition program, Shouhardo II, reportedly reduced the prevalence of stunting among under-5-year-olds from 62 percent at the time of the project's inception to 49 percent only four years later. Other countries, Brazil chief among them, have engaged for decades in large-scale multidimensional strategies of behavioral change (in Brazil, as part of the National Program for the Promotion of Breastfeeding) with the same sort of positive results described above.[40]

Some programs also deliver complementary feeding. For example, a protein supplement program in Guatemala found that, four decades after the intervention, individuals who were not stunted at age 3 went on to enjoy levels of consumption 66 percent higher relative to individuals who were stunted. Beneficiaries also completed more schooling, had higher cognitive skills, earned higher wages, and were more likely to be employed in higher-paying skilled labor and white-collar jobs. Women in the sample had fewer pregnancies and faced less risk of miscarriages and stillbirths.[41]

Despite this evidence on successful nutrition-only programs, nutrition programs that include stimulation are generally more effective.[42] Similar to the results in the Jamaican home visit study mentioned above, a program in rural Vietnam shows that infants who receive stimulation and nutrition do better than children who only receive stimulation.[43] The stimulation had a greater impact on stunted children, suggesting that the most disadvantaged children may benefit most from integrated approaches. Nutrition programs that include components other than stimulation have also been found to be successful. In Burkina Faso, the Enhanced Homestead Food Production program combined nutrition interventions during the first 1,000 days of life with home gardening, small animal production, and behavioral change communication components over two years. An impact evaluation of the program reports a significant reduction in anemia (14.6 percent) and diarrhea (15.9 percent) among children ages 3–12 months, a reduction in wasting (8.8 percent) in such children, and increases in dietary diversity and the intake of nutrient-rich foods among all age beneficiaries.[44] The success of the Shouhardo community-based program in Bangladesh,

reported above, has been attributed to the combination of nutrition-specific maternal and child interventions with other interventions designed to empower women, promote livelihoods, and improve the health environment of households.

Health care and education

Achieving universal health care

The world has seen significant and sustained improvements in health care access and health outcomes, but inequalities in access and outcomes associated with wealth, sex, and location are still pervasive. From 1990 to 2011, the annual number of deaths among under-5-year-olds fell from 12.0 million to 6.9 million worldwide. The annual global number of maternal deaths and the maternal mortality ratio fell by nearly 50 percent, short of the two-thirds reduction at which the Millennium Development Goals aimed. Over the second half of the 20th century, life expectancy rates increased twice as quickly in middle-income countries such as China and Mexico as in high-income countries.[45] The prevalence of stunting has fallen in 65 percent of countries worldwide, while antenatal care coverage has increased in an even higher share of countries, 78 percent.[46] During the last 25 years, the rate of decline in adult mortality across low-income countries has been more rapid among women than men.[47]

Inequalities in health care are still stark. Poor people face higher risks of malnutrition and death in childhood and lower odds of receiving key health care interventions. In low- and middle-income countries, only 23 percent of households in the poorest quintile have access to improved sanitation, compared with 71 percent in the richest quintile (figure 6.2).[48] Antenatal care coverage declines steeply in poorer populations; the median coverage is less than 50 percent among the poorest quintile of households, compared with a median of 83 percent in the richest quintile. Skilled attendance at birth, an important indicator of the robustness of health service delivery, presents a similar pattern. Immunization coverage and access to improved drinking water

FIGURE 6.2 Median Coverage, Selected Health Care Interventions, by Wealth Quintile, Low- and Middle-Income Countries, Circa 2005–13

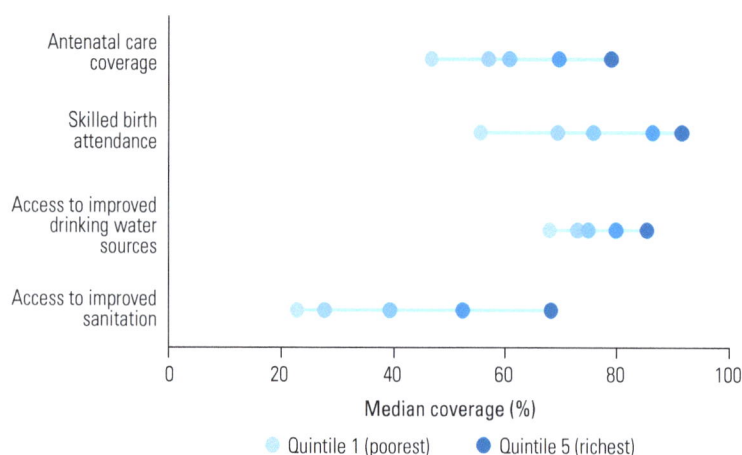

Source: "The World Health Organization's Infant Feeding Recommendation," World Health Organization, Geneva (accessed June 2016), http://www.who.int/nutrition/topics/infantfeeding_recommendation/en/.
Note: Results based on a sample of 83 countries using 2005–13 data or data on the closest available year in STATcompiler (DHS Program STATcompiler) (database), ICF International, Rockville, MD, http://www.statcompiler.com/; MICS (Multiple Indicator Cluster Surveys) (database), United Nations Children's Fund, New York, http://mics.unicef.org/.

show narrower disparities. Rural areas have lower median health care access than urban areas across low- and middle-income countries.[49] Health care inequalities also have a regional dimension: one-third of the countries worldwide that are not making progress in reducing under-5 mortality and expanding immunization are in Sub-Saharan Africa and South Asia.[50]

Reducing such health inequalities is not only fair, it also promotes improvement in the well-being of the poorest, enables their accumulation of human capital, increases their future earnings opportunities, and, as seen in the case of ECD, reduces income gaps with respect to the more well off. Indeed, poor health among the less well off has important economic and distributional impacts besides the obvious implications for health status. Disparities in health outcomes affect the accumulation of human capital among poor children and adults.

Improved health raises income through multiple channels.[51] Thus, better health raises individual productivity because healthier workers are more productive and exhibit lower rates of absenteeism. Studies have found strong causal relationships between levels of nutrition and worker productivity

across different contexts, from farm workers in Indonesia to factory workers in China.[52] For example, in an experimental study in Indonesia, nonanemic workers were found to be 20 percent more productive as measured by kilograms of latex collected per day. A different experimental study in Indonesia found that the income gap between men beneficiaries of iron supplements and nonbeneficiaries had increased by about 20 percent after four months of the intervention (only 6 percent in favor of women beneficiaries). In China, a randomized controlled trial of women cotton mill workers found a 17 percent rise in productivity among women who received 12 weeks of iron supplementation relative to a control group.[53]

Better health improves educational performance among children, because healthier children are more likely to attend school and have greater cognitive capacity for learning. For example, child-deworming interventions in Kenya significantly reduce sickness and improve school attendance among school-age children.[54] Among girls younger than 13 and all boys, school participation rose by 9.3 percent in the first year after deworming relative to the comparison group. The Kenya study estimated the long-run increase in adult incomes deriving from mass deworming at 17 percent, similar to average estimates elsewhere in Africa that deworming could boost income by 24 percent.[55]

The 2013 Lancet Commission estimated the costs and benefits of scaling up core health interventions in 34 low-income countries and 48 lower-middle-income countries.[56] Feasible scenarios involving the narrowing of disparities affecting the poor, rural, and ethnic minority populations would prevent about 10 million deaths by 2035, relative to a scenario of stagnant investments in these countries.[57] Other estimates suggest that expanding the coverage of key existing interventions would cut the preventable deaths associated with pneumonia and diarrhea by two-thirds, at a total cost of US$6.7 billion.[58] Similarly, expanding access through 10 proven interventions, ranging from the treatment of acute malnutrition to vitamin A and zinc supplementation, would avert 900,000 deaths among under-5-year-olds in the 34 countries with the highest under-5 mortality rates, at a cost of US$9.6 billion.[59]

Because of such vast benefits in terms of the lives saved, progress toward universal health care constitutes the most promising and fair strategy to reduce health inequalities, raise the human capital of the poor, and contribute to increasing future earnings and narrowing income gaps simultaneously. Achieving universal health care requires the delivery of timely health services to those who need them, but who are currently outside any form of health care because of their inability to pay, geographical distance to care providers, cultural and gender norms, or citizenship status. Universal health care also implies financial protection against catastrophic or impoverishing expenditures among those who receive health services. Reaching underserved populations inevitably requires narrowing existing coverage gaps and supplying affordable services. In practice, to reach universal coverage, health coverage among the poorest 20 percent of a population must expand much more quickly than the coverage among the more well off.[60]

There are multiple examples of substantial progress toward universal health care among low- and middle-income countries. Thailand's Universal Coverage Scheme enhances equity by bringing a large uninsured population under the umbrella of a national program, greatly reducing catastrophic health payments among the poor, and improving access to essential health services.[61] Within a year of its launch, the scheme was covering 75 percent of the population, including 18 million previously uninsured people.[62]

In Cambodia, efforts to achieve more comprehensive access to health services are articulated through health equity funds. The funds are multistakeholder initiatives in which nongovernmental organizations reimburse public health facilities for treating poor patients, largely eliminating prohibitive fees and improving the quality of care by supplying cash incentives for staff and fa-

cilities to serve patients.[63] As of 2013, health funds covered more than 2.5 million people in 51 of Cambodia's 81 districts, supporting more than a million health center consultations. Between 2000 and 2015, the under-5 mortality rate in Cambodia fell from 108 to 29 deaths per 1,000 live births, one of the most rapid rates of decline in the world.[64]

In Kwara State, one of the poorest states in Nigeria, a community-based health insurance pilot scheme that was conducted in partnership with the national health insurance system and private providers is reported to have increased the use of health care by 90 percent among beneficiaries of the program. It raised their use of modern health care providers and facilities, cut health expenditures by half among beneficiaries, and increased their awareness of the importance of health status. Services were financed by contributions from the state government, the national health insurance system, and payments from community insurance programs. Beneficiaries incurred meager copremiums of US$0.14 per person per year without having to make other out-of-pocket payments.[65]

In Rwanda, the national health insurance program, Mutuelle de Santé, currently covers about 90 percent of the population and provides free coverage for the extreme poor.[66] Out-of-pocket spending fell from 28 percent to 12 percent of total health expenditures during the program's first decade.

These and many other experiences confirm that there is no unique model of success in universal health care.[67] For example, direct public provision networks in China, Colombia, Mexico, and Thailand effectively cover everyone not covered by existing social health insurance mechanisms. Brazil and Costa Rica have unified government-run health insurance and the public provision network into a single health system aimed at covering everyone.[68] Most of these countries have defined an explicit benefit package, legally mandated in some cases, as in Colombia and Thailand, while others simply guarantee a minimum package of services, as in Chile. Other countries have expanded coverage to specific population groups or specific types of interventions as a way of reducing coverage gaps. Thus, Indonesia, Tunisia, Turkey, and Vietnam have expanded programs to poor populations, while programs in Argentina, Ethiopia, India, Kenya, and Peru have focused exclusively on maternal and child health among the poor. Another Indian program focuses on inpatient care for the poor, while Jamaica has focused on the affordable provision of medicines for all.[69]

Successful experiences must typically overcome some trade-offs before universal health care is effectively achieved. Chief among these is the trade-off between service coverage and financial protection. For example, despite substantive progress, Ethiopia has achieved a high level of financial protection, but a low level of service coverage. Brazil and Colombia perform well in service coverage, but do worse in financial protection than Mexico and South Africa. Peru and Vietnam are at similar levels of universal coverage, but Peru dominates in the coverage of prevention services, while Vietnam dominates in treatment. In addressing such trade-offs, countries choose different interventions depending on various factors such as the access to and availability of financing resources, political economy considerations among opposing interest groups, a government's willingness or lack of willingness to launch universal health care–inspired reforms, local technical capacity, and the evidence available to set appropriate priorities in the coverage, beneficiaries, and benefits targeted by universal health care strategies.[70]

Shifting the focus from rising enrollments to achieving education for all

Enrollments of children and adolescents in education systems have grown globally, but universal access to education remains an elusive goal, and progress toward good-quality education is uneven. In 2000, United Nations Educational, Scientific, and Cultural Organization (UNESCO) member countries adopted the target of achieving Education for All by 2015.[71] The effort consisted in reaching measurable goals in promoting gender parity and education quality within each stage of education. Countries made definite progress toward these goals. For example, worldwide, there was a 64 percent rise in enrollment in pre-primary education, and 80 million more children are now enrolled in school relative to a few years ago. Yet, only a third of countries met all the goals by 2015. Indeed, UNESCO data show that 58 million children of primary-school age and 63 million children of lower-secondary-school age are currently not in school.[72] At least 250 million children of primary-school age either fail to advance to grade 4 or do not achieve the minimum learning targets in a given year. In India, 47 percent of children in grade 5 were unable to read a second-grade text; in Peru, half of grade 2 pupils could not read at all.[73]

Poor-quality education has a strong socioeconomic dimension. The poorest children are four times less likely than the richest children to receive primary education. Among the estimated 780 million illiterate adults worldwide, nearly two-thirds are women. (In Sub-Saharan Africa, half of all women are reportedly illiterate.) Within countries, certain population groups—the poor, women, rural residents—face greater hurdles in gaining access to quality education. Large differences in learning outcomes measured through test scores among children are correlated with household incomes across the developing world. Children in the poorest households systematically score below children in the richest households in developing countries; the gap exceeds 50 percentage points in countries such as Gabon, Peru, and South Africa (figure 6.3).

For example, there is no reason poor children in Gabon or India should perform, on average, three or four times less well in mathematics than their richer peers. Allowing such educational disparities to prevail is unjust and inefficient. The disparities exacerbate existing inequalities in knowledge, skills, employability, and future economic prospects. Disparities in the access to and quality of education are a major driver of income inequality within countries worldwide.[74] Such disparities are known to result in persistent, intergenerational poverty gaps because the lack of education among segments of a society feed into economic and political inequalities, driving differences in life chances and opportunities.[75] For example, higher scores on international assessments of reading and mathematics among students are associated with appreciably higher annual per capita growth rates in gross domestic product (GDP).[76] Cross-country comparisons of educational achievement and aggregate growth rates show that an increase of one standard deviation in student reading and mathematics scores—roughly equivalent to improving a country's performance from the median to the top 15 percent—is associated with an increase of 2 percentage points in annual GDP per capita growth.[77] In India, farmers who exhibit a higher level of skills are able to adapt more effectively to new technologies, including the use of mobile phones to make more well informed decisions, and regions characterized by better rates of schooling also show higher rates in the adoption of newer farming techniques and technologies.[78] Schooling has likewise been linked to more productive nonfarm activities in China, Ghana, and Pakistan.[79] More well educated parents also enjoy better health and greater ability to cope with economic downturns.[80] Consequently, developing countries characterized by relatively poor and unequal levels of access to schooling and inadequate quality in education suffer a persistent handicap in growth prospects.

Among the wide-ranging interventions that have sought to address the failings of existing education systems, those attempting to improve the quality of education by focusing on learning, knowledge, and marketable skill development merit special attention. Recent assessments in developed and developing countries highlight successful experiences with improving teaching quality, a critical contributor to increases in learning achievement as measured by test scores. For example, estimates for the United States indicate that, during an academic year, pupils taught by teachers who are at the 90th percentile in effectiveness, are able to learn 1.5 years' worth of material, whereas those taught by teachers at the 10th percentile learn only a half-year's

FIGURE 6.3 **Mathematics Scores, by Household Income Level, Selected Countries, Circa 2007–11**

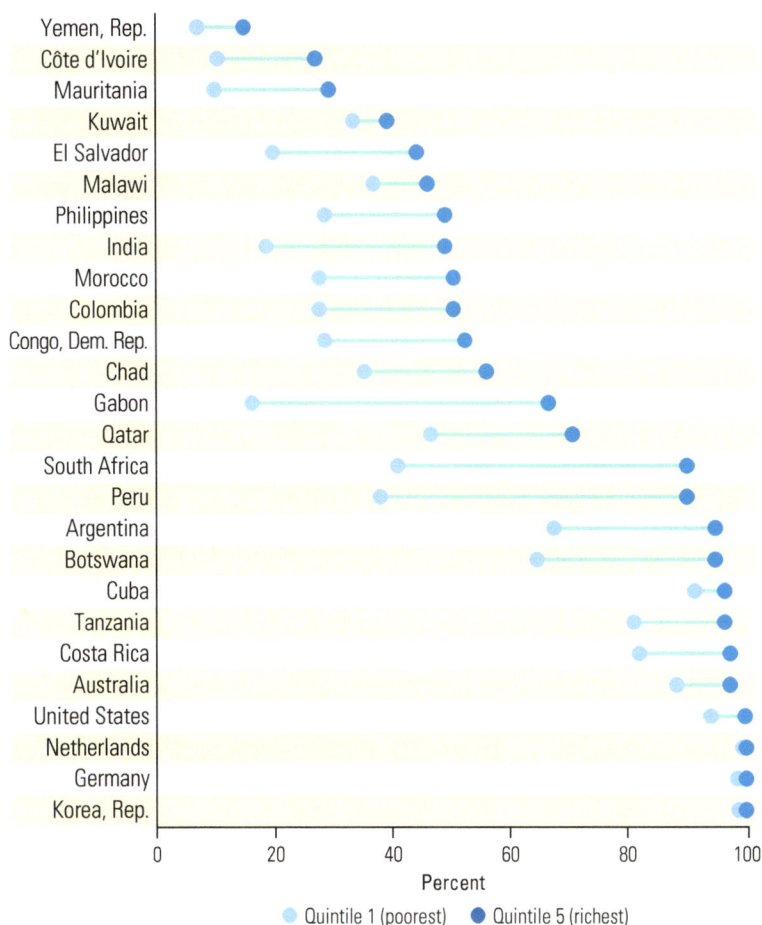

Source: World Bank calculations based on data in WIDE (World Inequality Database on Education), United Nations Educational, Scientific, and Cultural Organization, Paris, http://www.education-inequalities.org/.
Note: The figure indicates the share of primary-school students who satisfy international test standards in mathematics and who are in households in the bottom wealth quintile or in the top wealth quintile. Countries are sorted according to the maximum test score in mathematics reported for any quintile.

worth.[81] Quality teaching also helps instill in children skills and behaviors that—in addition to enabling learning—are rewarded by labor markets.[82] These include attentiveness, memory, self-control, and the ability to shift attention among competing tasks, all developed early in life and proven to be affected by teaching quality.[83] There is also evidence on the impact of teachers on long-term outcomes, such as the probability of college attendance, teenage pregnancies, and future earnings. This evidence, coming from Ecuador and the United States, strongly suggests that the way children are taught affects their future earning trajectories, as well as overall income gaps.[84]

An effective way to improve teacher quality is through financial incentives rewarding teacher attendance and better pedagogy. Quality teaching depends on interactions with children in areas such as emotional support, classroom organization, and instruction.[85] A program for teachers in rural Kenya involving scholarships and teacher incentives improved student test scores, although these benefits were only temporary. In an intervention in rural India, salary incentives among teachers helped improve student test scores, but the impact was greater if the incentives went to individual teachers rather than collectively. There is also evidence in rural India that student attendance increases if incentives are introduced to reduce teacher absenteeism and foster the monitoring of teacher attendance.[86]

In Ecuador, children assigned to rookie teachers—less than three years of experience—learned less than children taught by experienced teachers (after controlling for teacher and classroom characteristics). The same study notes that teacher IQs and personality do not have any significant influence on the differences in learning among students. Instead, the quality of interactions was found to positively correlate with higher test scores and children's attention, self-control, and memory skills.[87] This is consistent with evidence from the United Kingdom gathered by the Education Endowment Foundation.[88] The evidence suggests that strategies aimed at raising teaching quality by promoting greater engagement with pupils and a more open intellectual environment able to foster collaborative peer learning are more effective than additional formal teacher training. In settings as distinctive as India, Kenya, and the United States, teacher certification, tenure, and the type of contract do not seem to make a difference in children's learning.[89]

Evaluations (typically involving randomized controlled trials) confirm that numerous interventions besides teacher quality are correlated with improvements in test scores. The gains have been achieved across diverse educational levels, class sizes, income groups, and settings, including urban and rural locations in different world regions. For example, interventions that focus on improvements in physical facilities, books, other teaching materials, and school management, such as the *Programa para Abatir el Rezago Educativo* in the poorest rural regions of Mexico, or the supplementary classes and library initiatives among children in the Pratham Shishuvachan Program in the slums of urban Mumbai, improved the test scores of poor, chronically disadvantaged urban and rural students.[90] Similarly, increasing the duration of the school day had a positive effect on scholastic achievement and graduation levels in some Latin American countries, particularly among the deprived sections of the society. Evidence indicates that expanding compulsory schooling has had a substantial effect on educational outcomes in Norway, the United Kingdom, and the United States.[91] Furthermore, financial incentives to enroll and remain in school such as CCTs, subsidies, and scholarships have been shown to produce greater gains in scholastic achievements among poorer and disadvantaged students (see below).

All such interventions show great promise to realize education for all and reduce learning gaps among the poorest children. The same is true of emphasizing the measurement of educational achievement based on learning, and not merely coverage, even in countries with a chronic shortage of physical inputs. This calls for greater use of robust and consistent data across countries and across time using sources such as the Trends in International Mathematics and Science Study and the Programme for International Student Assessment for aggregate comparisons and survey-based randomized controlled trials for rigorous microevaluations. Current outstanding efforts to benchmark and monitor progress in learning achievement and socioeconomic correlates include the World Bank's Systems Approach for Better Education Results and UNESCO's Global Education Monitoring Report and World Inequality Database on Education.[92]

Conditional cash transfers

CCTs serve multiple purposes. The first among them is providing the severely deprived with the incomes necessary to meet basic needs. CCTs also protect the poor against the impacts of income shocks associated with seasonal income variations, loss of family breadwinners, famines, or adverse economic shocks.[93] CCTs smooth the consumption of the poor in the face of such shocks. Finally, CCTs enable households to take up investments that they would not otherwise take up, from their children's education to the purchase of livestock or other productive assets.[94] As a result of their multiple functions, CCTs can reduce poverty considerably. Even though it is not an explicit objective of CCTs, by targeting additional incomes on most needy households and preventing household consumption to fall appreciably during periods of stress, CCTs may have equalizing effects in the short run. When they enable investments in ECD and nutrition, education, health care, or productive assets, CCTs contribute to leveling the playing field through greater access to basic services today and increasing income opportunities tomorrow.[95] World Bank simulations using the ASPIRE database suggest reductions in the Gini index by between 0.2 and 2.3 points across the five largest CCT programs worldwide (figure 6.4).

CCTs have been designed and implemented with specific and focused policy objectives, such as *Bolsa Escola* in Brazil, which targets education. Others, such as the *Prospera* Program in Mexico (the rebranded *Oportunidades* Program) and *Bolsa Família* in Brazil, have broad impacts spanning multiple dimensions, such as children's education and health and household consumption expenditures.

CCTs have generally shown positive results at improving child development and nutritional outcomes. In Bangladesh, the Shombob Pilot Program—conditional on mandated regular growth monitoring of children and the participation of mothers in monthly nutrition-related sessions—significantly reduced the incidence of wasting among 10- to 22-month-old infants by 40 percent.[96] Mexico's Prospera Program has increased child growth at the equivalent of 16 percent in mean growth rate per year (corresponding to 1 centimeter) among infants who received treatment between ages 12 and

FIGURE 6.4 Simulated Gini Point Reduction in the Gini Index Attributable to CCTs, Circa 2013

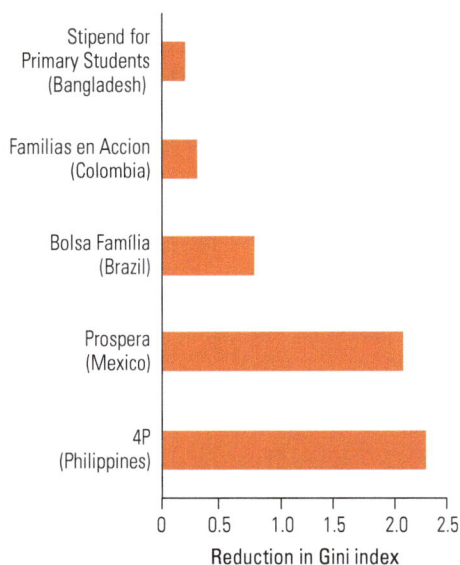

Source: Estimates based on data in ASPIRE (Atlas of Social Protection Indicators of Resilience and Equity) (database), World Bank, Washington, DC, http://datatopics.worldbank.org/aspire/. *Note:* The Gini index of income distribution is measured assuming the absence of transfer programs (pretransfer welfare distribution). Specifically, the Gini inequality reduction is computed as follows: inequality pretransfer, less inequality post-transfer, divided by inequality pretransfer assuming no change in behavior.

36 months. The program also reduced the probability of child stunting—by about a sixth among that age-group—and led to a 12 percent reduction in the incidence of illness among participants ages 0 to 5 years.[97] Nicaragua's Red de Protección Social Program also increased children's height, by 5.5 percentage points among stunted children, 1.7 times more quickly than the rate of annual improvement nationally between 1998 and 2001.[98] In Lesotho, an unconditional cash transfer scheme has been associated with a 16 percentage point drop in the risk of malnourishment among beneficiary children relative to similar children not receiving the transfers.[99] In Ecuador, cash transfers reportedly increased the height of preschool children in the poorest households.[100]

CCTs have been used to promote the adoption of health care services by helping to defray the cost to households otherwise unable to bear the expenses and by encouraging healthy lifestyle habits that would not emerge without behavioral conditioning. These CCTs focus on the demand side of health care services, that is, patients, by seeking to increase their use of preventive health care through regular checkups and vaccinations.[101] Evidence on such CCTs suggests multiple benefits. They can be quite effective at increasing antenatal visits, childbirths with skilled health care professionals in attendance, delivery at health facilities, and the incidence of tetanus toxoid vaccinations among mothers.[102] For example, Mexico's Prospera Program has helped reduce infant mortality and maternal mortality by as much as 11 percent.[103] The benefits are not restricted to children: adult beneficiaries (ages 18–50) had 17 percent fewer sick days and 22 percent fewer days in bed because of illness.[104] Women benefiting from Peru's Juntos cash transfer are 91 percent more likely to be attended by a doctor at childbirth compared with women who are not in the program.[105] Antenatal and postnatal care have been shown to improve, along with facility-based deliveries, in Indonesia and the Philippines.[106] Evidence on the Program Keluarga Harapan, the first household-based CCT in Indonesia, which was implemented in 2007, shows greater usage of primary health care services among all eligible households in areas covered by the program. Antenatal visits by pregnant women rose by over 7 percentage points, the share of assisted deliveries (by midwives, nurses, or doctors, or at medical facilities) increased by approximately 5 percentage points.[107] In India, an impact evaluation of the Janani Suraksha Yojana CCT estimates that the expansion in the use of health facilities attributed to the program resulted in 4.1 fewer perinatal deaths per 1,000 pregnancies, 2.4 fewer neonatal deaths per 1,000 live births, and an increase of 9.1 percentage points in the proportion of fully vaccinated children.[108]

CCTs are also policy instruments affecting the access to and quality of education. The most common forms of demand-side interventions involve transfers that financially incentivize poor households to enroll their children and keep them in school. Also, CCTs provide conditional stipends based on school performance, continued attendance, and graduation that seek to improve performance at school and grade completion. The results indicate substantive overall benefits accruing from the programs. CCTs have successfully raised school enrollments among recipient children worldwide. For example, the Nahouri Pilot Project—a two-year cash transfer program in Burkina Faso that had both conditional and unconditional components—is credited with raising primary and secondary enrollment rates by 22 percent among boys.[109] Similarly, Chile Solidario boosted preschool enrollments by 4–5 percentage points and increased the probability among all children ages 6–14 of enrollment in school by 7 percentage points.[110] In Cambodia, CCTs have raised secondary-school attendance by 26 percentage points, while, in Malawi, the Philippines, and Zimbabwe, the effects on secondary-school attendance are—albeit more modest—still significant, between 5 and 10 percentage points. Evidence on the effects of CCTs where eligibility is limited to only girls, such as in Bangladesh and Pakistan, also demonstrates large rises in enrollments in the range of 11–13 percentage points. Evidence from Mexico's Prospera indicates that such interventions have helped improve enrollment rates mostly by reducing the incidence of dropping out in the critical transition between the primary and lower-secondary levels and between the lower-secondary and higher-secondary levels.[111]

A few studies have also found gains in cognitive ability among children who have been beneficiaries of CCTs in Ecuador and Nicaragua, reporting significant increases in language skills and personal-behavioral skills even after only brief exposure to the programs. Evidence also points to greater benefits among such children in poorer households.[112] In Malawi, enrollments, test scores in English, and the probability of remaining in school among girls in grades 5–8 are reportedly larger—relative to enrolled girls—among recent dropouts rejoining school, who were, on average, poorer and had lower baseline cognitive skills.[113] In Ecuador, on account of Bono de Desarrollo Humano, significant improvement in cognitive skills was reported among children from the poorest quartile of the household income distribution compared with more well off children as a result of the intervention. In Nicaragua, the Atención a Crisis Program resulted in cognitive skill improvements similar to those in Ecuador.

Regarding the unintended effects of CCTs, recent evaluations of programs in Brazil, Chile, Honduras, Mexico, Nicaragua, and the Philippines fail to demonstrate reductions in the labor market participation of beneficiaries relative to nonbeneficiaries or increases in the consumption of alcohol or tobacco or in gambling.[114] In the Philippines, a steep decline in the consumption of alcohol of 39 percentage points has been documented among beneficiary households relative to control groups.[115] The evidence is beginning to show that these programs may also have positive effects in reducing interpersonal violence and street crime in Ecuador and Brazil, respectively.[116] Regarding fertility, evidence suggests that these programs have little or no impact. For example, no effects were found on the total fertility rate among beneficiaries of Prospera in Mexico, and only a slight rise in the fertility rate of 2–4 percentage points was revealed among eligible households in Honduras.[117]

Trade-offs in design and implementation

CCT programs frequently identify eligible recipients geographically and through means testing based on qualifying criteria to rationalize the use of scarce resources and improve program targeting efficiency. Typically, CCT programs incur low administrative costs. The largest five CCT programs in the world spend between 0.09 percent and 0.44 percent of GDP.[118] However, the low costs mask a fundamental trade-off between the size of the benefits and coverage. Most recent data indicate that only about a third of households in the poorest quintile are covered by CCTs worldwide.[119] The average benefit is also small in most countries, especially in low-income countries. The average transfer in the five largest CCT programs worldwide is about 15 percent of the average household consumption of the poorest quintile.[120]

Part of this trade-off is explained by fragmentation in program interventions and poor targeting. Fragmentation occurs if a collection of typically small, unconnected programs target the same demographic groups, regions, and vulnerabilities without coordination or cost-benefit considerations. Multiple ministries often have responsibility for the implementation of the programs, making coordination cumbersome and requiring an institutional vitality that is rare in many low-income countries. However, this does not need to be the case. A recent encouraging example of an effort to tackle fragmentation is Vietnam's commitment to broaden coverage, expand the profile of new beneficiaries, and integrate the multiple objectives of its several cash transfers programs targeted on poor rural regions that, until recently, were not covered by active labor market programs.[121]

Poor targeting occurs if CCT programs fail to reach part of the target population. Poor targeting is often a reflection of weak governance and limited administrative capacity. Context also plays a critical role. The functioning of markets, seasonality, household preferences, and community dynamics all affect the capacity of the programs to deliver benefits effectively to priority beneficiaries.[122] For example, cash transfers are often preferred over in-kind transfers in locations with well-functioning food markets, where recipients can exercise their expanded budgetary options. In contrast, in-kind transfers are preferred in contexts where the market prices for food are volatile and public distribution systems are reliable. Another example is the frequent preference of women for in-kind transfers in social and household contexts where they have less control over the cash.

Numerous design factors also determine the success of CCT programs, such as the size of the transfer, the nature of the conditionality, or the characteristics of the target population. Increasing the size of the transfer often raises the impact of the program. For example, one study concludes that doubling the amount of the transfer in Brazil's Bolsa Escola program would halve the percentage of children in poor households who do not attend school.[123] In Cambodia, an analysis of a program that delivers transfers to students based on poverty status shows that the impacts are not linearly correlated with the size of the transfers. Thus, the differences in student enrollment associated with no stipend relative to a stipend of US$45 were large, but there was no observable difference in outcomes between a stipend of US$45 and a stipend of US$60.[124] In Malawi, the variation in the size of the transfer to the parents of adolescent girls in grades 5–8 did not cause differences in enrollment rates or literacy test scores. However the proportion of cash given directly to schoolgirls was associated with significantly improved school attendance and progress if conditional on school attendance.[125]

There is broad evidence that conditionality determines the impact of a program. Analyses have found that school enrollment was significantly lower among those households in Ecuador and Mexico that believed their cash transfers were unconditional, although the benefits were conditional on school attendance.[126] Simulations in Brazil conclude that CCTs would not have had any impact on school enrollment if they had been delivered as unconditional transfers, while in Mexico, the simulated impact of unconditional transfers on educational attainment would have been only 20 percent of that of conditional transfers.[127] However, this does not imply that conditionality inevitably has an impact. The Malawi program evaluation shows that, relative to the control group of girls, the significant impacts of the transfers on school enrollment and test scores, the probability of early marriage, and pregnancy did not vary between the beneficiaries of the conditional and unconditional transfers associated with the program.

The focus on CCTs is not intended to indicate that unconditional cash transfers exert insignificant impacts on inequality or the living conditions of the poorest. Under some circumstances, such as frail service delivery or onerous targeting, they may be superior to CCTs. Evidence on unconditional cash transfers in Burkina Faso, Kenya, Lesotho, and Zambia shows remarkable impacts on educational attainment, food security, agricultural production, and stimulus to local economies. Indeed, 40 of 48 countries in Sub-Saharan Africa apply these sorts of transfers.[128]

Several general lessons on implementation may be drawn from recent CCT programs. First, transfer programs of all types benefit from the adoption of technological innovations. Technology aids in improving targeting. This was the case of the biometric smart cards used in the Targeted Public Distribution System in Andhra Pradesh, India. Electronic cash disbursements based on smart cards and mobile banking platforms have resulted in lower transaction costs and reduced opportunities for corruption and other losses. For example, the electronic payment of a social transfer in Niger cuts the overall travel time required to collect cash transfers by three-quarters.[129] In South Africa, the cost of disbursing social grants using smart cards is a third of the cost involved in cash disbursements.[130] In Argentina, electronic payments for *Plan Jefes*, a large national antipoverty program, virtually eliminated the reporting of kickbacks, which stood at 4 percent of the payments when these were made in cash. The ease of accessing program benefits and the improved targeting have boosted the adoption of transfer programs even in low-income countries.[131]

Second, CCT programs are enhanced by constant monitoring, evaluation, and adjustment.[132] This is particularly the case in the identification of beneficiaries. Eligibility requirements must be governed by transparent rules, frequently fine-tuned, and flexible, especially if the portfolio of transfers is rich or integrated with other interventions or CCTs as part of crisis response strategies. Increasingly, rigorous evaluations, comprising randomized controlled trials, are being used to assess the direct and spillover effects of interventions integrated within broader safety nets. This is the case of a recent experimental evaluation of multiple interventions involving cash transfers, transfers of productive assets, technical skills training, nutrition and hygiene programs, and access to bank accounts in Ethiopia, Ghana, Honduras, India, Pakistan, and Peru.[133] Successful CCT programs are associated not only with efficient beneficiary identification and targeting, but also precise evaluations of transfer effectiveness. This is the case of programs in Brazil, Chile, Mexico, and, more recently, Ethiopia and the Philippines. Part of the success of emerging CCT programs integrated within other safety net interventions is flexibility. Thus, the ability of safety nets in Ethiopia (the Productive Safety Net Program) and the Philippines (the Pantawid Pamiliya Pilipino Program) to reach thousands of new beneficiaries (millions in the case of Ethiopia) after catastrophic events indicates that the coordination of cash transfers, emergency response, and postdisaster reconstruction is possible and effective in protecting the poor from natural disasters. This was the case of the 4P program in the Philippines, which, in a situation of national calamity, was effective after the conditionality was voided temporarily, and the CCTs were delivered without compliance verification requirements for the duration of the emergency.[134]

Rural infrastructure

Investing in rural roads

New or improved rural roads reduce transportation costs, facilitate the relocation of labor, foster the diversification of livelihoods, enhance access to markets and services, and promote human capital investments. Indeed, good transportation infrastructure has been widely acknowledged to facilitate growth, poverty reduction, and income equality.[135] Empirical estimates across the globe suggest that, along with communication and power infrastructure, the quantity and quality of transportation infrastructure are positively correlated with growth and negatively correlated with income inequality.[136] While the links between infrastructure, growth, and equality are generally recognized across various types of infrastructure, one type—roads—is particularly relevant in rural areas. Of the world's rural population, about a third—one billion people—still live in settlements that are each more than 2 kilometers from the nearest paved road.[137]

New or improved all-weather roads reduce transportation costs and the time needed to reach markets. This enhanced access to markets allows farmers in poor and remote rural areas to obtain higher prices for their outputs and pay lower prices for inputs and consumer goods. Improved rural roads also eliminate or reduce barriers to the reallocation of labor away from agriculture and contribute to the development of new local markets.[138] Roads may lessen credit constraints by helping increase the value of land and, therefore, its collateral price, thus reinforcing the positive effects that cheaper transportation also has on the adoption of fertilizers and new technology. The incentive to invest in physical and human capital has reportedly increased as new off-farm income-generating opportunities emerge because of new or improved rural roads. These fresh opportunities may affect the perceived returns to education, including the returns to the education of women and girls. Women also benefit directly if they are able to participate in construction, rehabilitation, and maintenance activities, typically within a context of public works programs aimed at rural roads.

Although the vast majority of these programs do not aim directly to reduce inequality, but to promote connectivity and improve the living conditions of the poor, they become equalizing because they disproportionally benefit the poorest. This occurs when, for instance, roads benefit rural residents with the least agricultural wealth, such as smallholding farmers and landless workers; when they help diversify earning activities among those who would otherwise spend their time in low-productivity activities or household chores, such as women; or when they contribute to reducing discrimination by, for example, allowing low caste villagers to abandon agriculture and search for more well paid activities.[139] A Bangladesh study suggests that the benefits of the two rural roads programs discussed below are greater among the poorest quartile and are insignificant among the well off in the affected villages.[140] In Georgia, the poor benefited more from an expansion in off-farm employment among women, while the nonpoor benefited more from increased nonagricultural employment and greater access to medical services.[141]

The US$37 billion Pradhan Mantri Gram Sadak Yojana (the prime minister's rural roads scheme), a large rural road construction program in India, has provided paved roads for more than 110 million people, or half the unconnected rural population in the country at the onset of the program in 2001. According to a quasi-experimental analysis, the benefits in newly connected districts include reduction in the levels and dispersion of food prices.[142] Food security improved through diet diversification. Households began spending more on processed and perishable foods and consuming more nonperishable staples. The cultivated area treated with fertilizers expanded by 3 percent, mostly for food rather than cash crops, while 10 percent fewer households reported agriculture as the main source of income. Household earnings rose an average of 8 percent entirely because of wage labor. Enrollment rates among children ages 5–14 increased among both boys and girls, although enrollments among the 14–20 age-group declined. This suggests that rural roads boosted education returns among younger children and employment opportunities among young people.

In Vietnam, the Rural Transport Project I improved 5,000 kilometers of rural roads. The benefits—typically observed two years after the completion of the program—included a 10 percent rise in the share of communes participating in new markets relative to a control group of communes that were not part of the project, a 20 percent growth in private businesses involved in services, such as tailoring and hairdressing, and a 15 percent rise in primary-school completion rates.[143]

In Bangladesh, the Rural Development Program and the Rural Roads and Markets Improvement and Maintenance Program have boosted employment and wages in agricultural and nonagricultural activities, as well as aggregate harvest outputs. Per capita annual spending across households in the projected program areas has risen by about 10 percent.[144]

In Georgia, the share of villages hosting small nonagricultural enterprises increased in project villages more than in control villages; employment and wages among women in off-farm activities also rose in

project villages, while declining in control villages; and waiting times for the arrival of ambulance services were reduced.[145]

Competition is a critical factor in ensuring that benefits reach the poorest. Investments in roads lead to higher transport volumes and lower transport fees only if there is competition among providers. If competition does not exist or is not promoted, more transport opportunities and falling travel times may still emerge, but the poor are less likely to benefit from the improved connectivity because they cannot afford to change their travel patterns (for example, traveling to other villages in search of economic opportunities) or because service quality is not enhanced. Evidence from case studies in Asia confirms that the promotion of competition following the expansion of rural roads disproportionally benefits the poorest.[146] A study among villages in Indonesia, the Philippines, and Sri Lanka finds that, relative to control villages, villagers who benefited from the expansion or rehabilitation of rural roads and the promotion of competition in transportation traveled more frequently to buy provisions, for employment and business, and to obtain documents, and they also required travel times that were shorter by about two-thirds.[147]

Evidence from community-based projects in Georgia, including the rehabilitation of schools, roads, and water supply systems illustrate that the equalizing impacts of investments in roads in poor, isolated, and less densely populated rural settlements are multiplied if the investments are coupled with expansions in schools, medical facilities, banks, agricultural extension services, water and sanitation, and electrification. Interventions must also avoid unintended negative effects on the poor such as an increase in child labor or trading in contraband.[148] Thus, rural road improvements that are accompanied by good maintenance plans help encourage poor households to invest in alternative livelihoods, which they might not undertake if they believe the new all-weather roads will not be maintained. Women-inclusive practices in the rehabilitation and maintenance of roads, the inclusion of girls in new schooling opportunities, and the recognition of equal property rights for women that promote increases in the prices for land need be part of rural road improvement plans.

Electrification

Several studies find that access to electricity boosts household incomes by expanding labor supply and fostering a shift from farm labor to formal employment. Thus, electrification in rural communities in Guatemala and South Africa has led to a 9 percentage point rise in women's employment that cannot be attributed to greater demand because there has been no comparable increase in men's employment.[149] In India, household electrification has been found to raise labor supply by about 16 days a year among men and 6 days a year among women. The increase in labor among men is attributable to a shift from casual wage work and leisure activities, while, among women, it is attributable to an expansion in casual work.[150]

Electrification can also generate additional household income by making small home-based businesses economically viable or more productive. Small enterprises and informal sector businesses often suffer most from the erratic supply of electricity by public utilities, because they cannot afford generators to produce their own electricity and insulate themselves from power outages. Stable supplies of electricity often make business activities, including access to export markets, more productive and economically viable. Indeed, evidence from rural Vietnam shows that households connected to the electricity grid are nine times more likely to be involved in home production than households without such a connection.[151] Incomes from nonfarm activities among the former rose an estimated 29 percent as a result of electrification.

The availability of electric lighting also provides additional opportunities to study and is associated with greater school attendance and school completion rates, especially among girls. The study in Vietnam reports that school enrollment rates among children in households on the electric-ity grid were 9.0 percentage points higher among girls and 6.3 percentage points higher among boys.[152] Electrification was also associated with more average years of schooling by almost a year among girls and 0.13 years among boys.

Rural electrification can have positive community effects. For example, street lighting improves security; clinics with access to electricity can stay open longer and provide cold chains for vaccines; and access to electricity can help reduce absenteeism among health workers and teachers. In Pakistan, absenteeism among teachers in public schools that have electricity is half the rate in other schools. This is particularly relevant for the women teachers required for the education of girls.[153] Moreover, electrification programs can have large and immediate health benefits by decreasing indoor air pollution in poor households, typically by allowing kerosene and firewood to be replaced as energy sources for lighting or cooking. This leads to large reductions in respiratory infections among under-5-year-olds and can potentially lessen the risk of lung cancer among household members. Two years after the baseline in a recent electrification program in northern El Salvador, particle pollution concentration was an average 67 percent lower among households that had been randomly encouraged to electrify relative to those that had not.[154] The change is driven by less kerosene use. These various factors contribute to improving human capital formation among the poorest and therefore have the potential to level the playing field and reduce future inequality.

Electrification can also promote gender equality by freeing up women's time from household chores, such as the collection of firewood, and raising women's employment. There is also evidence that access to electricity increases the income controlled by women through formal employment and the creation of small woman-run enterprises. In South Africa, a rural electricity project led to a large expansion in the use of electric lighting and cooking and steady reductions in wood-fueled cooking, as well as a 9.5 percentage point rise in women's employment.[155] One of the most important uses of electricity after lighting is for television, which can potentially improve health education, reduce fertility, and challenge entrenched perceptions of gender roles.[156] In rural India, access to cable television may result in less tolerance for spousal abuse, less preference for sons rather than daughters, and a greater likelihood young girls will attend school.[157] Similarly, access in rural areas to *telenovelas* (television soap operas) resulted in higher divorce and lower fertility rates in Brazil, which may be related to the empowerment of women through the imitation of role models of emancipated women and the presentation of smaller families.[158]

The potential benefits of electrification are enormous. The International Energy Agency estimates that there were 1.2 billion people without access to electricity in 2013, or 17 percent of the global population. Many more have access only to an insufficient or unreliable supply. Worldwide, approximately 80 percent of people without electricity live in rural areas, and more than 95 percent live in Asia and Sub-Saharan Africa. However, efforts to expand electrification in rural areas often face a trade-off between keeping electrification financially viable by defraying the costs and reaching people who are least able to pay. Households are often required to pay at least part of the connection cost, which can be prohibitively high for the poorest. Yet, there are several ways affordability can be ensured. Bangladesh and Brazil have progressive pricing schemes that offer lower prices to households that consume only small amounts of electricity. South Africa offers a poverty tariff that provides poor households with 50 kilowatt hours of electricity per month at no cost.

Taxation

Choices in the composition and progressivity of taxes determine the capacity of a government to finance interventions that help redistribute income. Moreover, taxes can be designed to ensure that inequality narrows, while keeping efficiency costs low. Programs that foster childhood development and adequate nutrition, improve the access to and quality of education, or ensure broadbased or universal health care

services need to be financed. Taxes therefore constitute an essential component of any successful strategy for guaranteeing equal opportunity. Taxes also raise the revenues needed to finance interventions such as noncontributory pensions or housing subsidies that have deliberate distributional objectives. Some historical examples of tax and benefit reforms aimed at sharing the gains of economic growth and enhancing equity are the 1990 tax reform in Chile immediately after the country's return to democracy and the 1994–99 tax reform of the Katz Commission in postapartheid South Africa. More recently, European Union (EU) countries have embarked on comprehensive fiscal consolidations based on clear equity considerations in response to the 2008–09 financial crisis.[159]

Taxes also have a redistributive role on their own, whether deliberate or unintended. Taxes redistribute income in two ways. They address the income inequality emerging from labor and capital markets by establishing different tax rates to balance the relative contributions of individuals, households, and firms in total revenue collection. This is done in multiple ways, including imposing a tax rate that rises with earned incomes, offering tax credits based on age or household composition for individuals earning similar labor incomes, or exempting some consumption goods from the value added tax (VAT), while raising this tax on others to reflect, for example, the differences in the consumers of basic goods and luxury goods.

Taxes also affect the generation of incomes in labor and capital markets. They influence the labor, savings, and investment decisions of individuals and firms, thus exerting an impact on the market incomes of these individuals and firms. For instance, introducing high tax rates on labor and capital earnings may discourage labor effort among individuals and reduce the extent to which individuals and firms save and invest. High social insurance contributions and payroll taxes make formal work less attractive in highly informal economies with generous noncontributory pension benefits such as Colombia and Mexico. To the extent that taxes introduce distortions, they restrict economic growth and revenue collection. In the case of Mexico, the efficiency costs of taxation have been estimated at 0.9 to 1.4 percentage points of GDP owing to lower labor productivity and GDP growth deriving from the fragmented social security system.[160] Redistribution can thus entail high efficiency costs.

But this does not have to be. There are many ways the efficiency costs of taxes—such as administrative and compliance costs—can be kept to a minimum even if they are difficult to avoid. Taxes can be designed to encourage risk-taking behavior that, ultimately, may boost the returns on investment, or credit constraints can be relaxed so poor households can invest on health care and education. Likewise, there are many ways to achieve effective redistribution, including broadening the tax base. Personal income tax deductions can be carefully designed to avoid those that unduly benefit the more well off and do not generate significant revenue gains, such as deductions for mortgage interest or charitable donations. Earned income tax credits can be used instead of tax allowances to favor labor force participation and engagement in the formal sector because, to earn the credits, taxpayers must be working in the formal sector. Corporate income tax rates can be harmonized with personal income tax rates to prevent distortions in savings and investment decisions relative to hiring. Reduced VAT rates and exemptions can be limited because more well off households benefit the most from their greater consumption, and these reductions and exemptions erode the revenue base and, ultimately, lower the financing available for social spending. Other measures that increase the progressivity of the tax system while raising revenues include property and inheritance taxes, which can also help limit intergenerational inequality. In developing countries, property taxes are underutilized, representing about 0.5 percent of GDP, and declining at a time when the concentration and accumulation of wealth are on the rise worldwide.[161] All these measures boost revenue collection in an equalizing manner, while keeping disincentives to a minimum.

The impact of taxes on inequality depends on the degree of progressivity of each tax, but also on the composition of taxes that support the fiscal system. Conventional wisdom suggests that the more tax systems rely on indirect rather than direct taxes, the less these systems are able to narrow inequalities.[162] This is because indirect taxes are typically more regressive than direct taxes.[163] However, such generalizations are sometimes deceptive.[164] For example, while indirect taxes widen inequality in many middle-income countries, this is not true in Mexico and Peru, where indirect taxes alone reduce market income inequalities, or in Ghana, South Africa, and Sri Lanka, where indirect taxes are mostly neutral. In eight Sub-Saharan African countries, the VAT is reportedly less unequally distributed than market incomes.[165]

Specific country experiences help clarify how composition influences the redistributive capacity of tax systems. Box 6.1 compares how the choice of taxes and the amount of progressivity in two recent tax reforms with similar objectives affect redistributive outcomes. It also describes how the design of fiscal consolidation measures during periods of crisis may have particular redistributive effects.

The redistributive role of taxes is potentially great. In some cases, along with large, well-targeted benefits, taxes can redress market income inequalities dramatically. For example, together, taxes and transfers redistribute important shares of market incomes in the EU, reducing the Gini index of the market income inequalities of the 27 member states by an average of 20 points.[166] But this is not always the case, especially in developing countries. Indeed, the redistributive role of taxes and fiscal systems more generally is often rather limited. A recent comprehensive study comparing the tax and benefit systems of 150 countries concludes that tax systems have had a limited, but inequality-increasing impact since 1990.[167]

There are multiple reasons for the limited redistributive effects of tax systems. The administrative systems of countries, especially low-income countries, are often inadequately funded and staffed, and lack the autonomy, transparency, accountability, and technology to operate in the face of challenges such as a large informal sector

BOX 6.1 Tax Reform and Fiscal Consolidation

Equity-enhancing tax reforms in Chile and Mexico

The recent tax reforms in Chile and Mexico in 2014 and 2010, respectively, confirm the importance of design and composition in determining the redistributive effects of taxes. With similar reform goals, the choices were different, and so were the impacts. Both sets of reforms aimed at reducing fiscal deficits, raising revenue to finance social spending, and enhancing tax equity, that is, ensuring that the tax reforms were progressive. Mexico relied on a combination of increases in the VAT and special taxes on alcohol and tobacco, as well as lottery tickets and telecommunication services. Additionally, Mexico raised the three top rates in the personal income tax schedule. In Chile, the reform focused mainly on corporate taxes. It also increased special indirect taxes, but, in contrast with Mexico, these taxes were not intended to boost revenues, but to reduce the consumption of alcohol, tobacco, and beverages containing sugar.

The two reforms were generally progressive, that is, the more well off bore a higher share of the burden of the reform. However, there were substantive differences in the impacts. In Chile, the top 3 percent of the income distribution bore the burden of the income tax reform. In Mexico, the effects of the changes in income tax rates affected the top 40 percent of the distribution.

The effects of the special consumption taxes were opposite in the two countries: the impacts were progressive in Mexico, but regressive in Chile. In Mexico, the richer deciles ended up paying more in absolute and relative terms than the poor. In Chile, the bottom 40 percent of the income distribution (the bottom 40) paid a higher share of their expenditures than the more well off (though a smaller absolute bill). This is because the share

of expenditures for these goods in Chile was greater among the poor than among other socioeconomic groups. The two countries converge in that the reduction in the expenditures on health-damaging goods was fairly limited, less than 0.5 percent of total household expenditures.

The distributional effects of fiscal consolidation

Reinforcing efficiency and equity considerations becomes more important during periods of crises or protracted fiscal consolidation when the pressures to cut spending and raise revenues grow along with the need to protect the most vulnerable from the consequences of a crisis. However, tax decisions in response to crises also have distributive consequences. In the short run, fiscal consolidation may lead to declines in output, employment, and wages that compound the initial effects of a crisis. These effects tend to widen inequalities because unskilled workers constitute a larger share of wage earners, and unemployment hits already vulnerable youth and women the hardest. Fiscal adjustment affects the level of taxes and spending and often their composition. If, for example, these adjustments rely on raising VAT rates, imposing pension freezes, or cutting the benefits to families with children, they widen inequality, especially in a context of high unemployment and recession.

Nonetheless, it is possible to design fiscal responses to a crisis that are progressive and prevent further widening in inequality. For example, in a sample of 27 episodes of fiscal adjustment in 19 middle-income countries between 1971 and 2001, the Gini index either remained virtually unchanged after the adjustment or rose slightly if the adjustment coincided with a period of economic contraction.[a] In a context of falling oil and natural gas prices, Algeria and Morocco recently reduced the scope of their poorly targeted energy subsidies. Some progressive features of Greece's

(Box continues next page)

or conflict. This weak capacity prevents authorities from raising significant revenues, launching progressive schedules, avoiding evasion, and ensuring compliance.[168]

A limited redistributive role is sometimes the result of the small size of the pie, which does not allow significant redistribution. Even if poor countries were politically and administratively able to shift large shares of income from the rich to the poor, they would need prohibitive marginal income tax rates to end poverty and substantially narrow inequality.[169] However, a recent analysis shows that much of global poverty as defined by the US$1.90 per capita per day poverty line could be eliminated in developing countries by reallocating regressive fossil-fuel energy subsidies and excessive military spending to cash transfers.[170]

Limited redistribution is not exclusively related to low-income countries or, more generally, to a country's level of development. Indeed, certain tax choices limit the redistributive capacity of tax systems in middle- and high-income countries. Thus, Brazil's heavy reliance on consumption taxes that include basic foodstuffs, which represent a disproportionally large share of the poor's consumption budget, reduces the redistributive impact of the fiscal system (chapter 5). For administrative and effi-

ciency reasons, Eastern European countries impose flat-rate income taxes, which render personal income taxes less redistributive than progressive personal income taxes at the same level of revenue collection.

While some analysts believe that more-unequal countries redistribute more, this belief is called into question by the large differences in the level of redistribution across countries at similar levels of inequality.[171] For example, Chile and Colombia share similarly high levels of market inequality, but Chile redistributes income significantly more than Colombia. Mexico and Peru also have similar levels of inequality, but only Mexico redistributes income substantially. Indonesia and the Russian Federation also show comparable, though much lower levels of inequality, but only Russia appears to redistribute significantly.[172] Redistribution is also limited in Ethiopia and Sri Lanka; in South Africa, it is more appreciable.[173] The norm is that the size of the tax benefit system is closely correlated with the redistributive effect. This is important because countries with large tax systems also tend to provide large benefit transfers, which, ultimately, show more redistributive impacts.[174] This explains how Russia and South Africa achieve greater redistribution through the fiscal system than Indonesia and Sri Lanka. Regardless of the inherent ability of taxes to reduce inequality, choices about progressivity, composition, and size thus largely determine the equity effects.[175]

Concluding remarks

The progress documented in this chapter suggests that policy interventions can be designed to narrow inequality and improve the living conditions of the poor in a variety of settings. Yet, the long road ahead argues against any complacency and against the fallacy of sweeping prescriptions that promise success regardless of the diverse challenges, contexts, and uncertainties. Meaningful lessons nonetheless emerge from the evidence of the policy interventions examined in this chapter.

Despite progress, intolerable disparities in well-being still exist that concrete policy interventions could confront directly. In many low- and middle-income countries, preschool enrollment rates among the poorest quintile are less than a third the rates among the richest quintile. Mothers in the bottom 40 across developing countries are 50 percent less likely to receive antenatal care. The poorest children are four times less likely than the richest children to be enrolled in primary education. These children systematically record lower tests scores than children in the richest households, and this gap exceeds 50 percentage points in some developing countries. Among the estimated 780 million illiterate adults worldwide, nearly two-thirds are women. Only one-quarter of the poorest quintile are covered by safety nets, and the share is even smaller in Sub-Saharan Africa and South Asia.

The equalizing effect of interventions must be judged by the impacts they achieve, not those originally (un)intended. Most interventions register impacts on inequality whether unintended or deliberate. These effects can be large or small or short term or lifelong, and they can widen or narrow disparities in incomes, well-being, and opportunity. They occur over multiple pathways. For example, taxes have direct and deliberate redistributive effects, reaching up to 20 points of the Gini index of market incomes in some EU countries. However, there are many other methods for addressing inequality. Thus, investments in rural roads and electrification influence income generation opportunities, employment, and even perceptions of gender roles. Expanding ECD, health care coverage, and good-quality education can reduce cognitive, nutritional, and health status gaps, thereby narrowing inequalities in human capital development and future income opportunities. By smoothing consumption among the most deprived, especially during shocks, CCTs help prevent the widening of inequalities.

Improved competition and economic efficiency are compatible with reducing inequalities. The example of investments in new roads highlights the importance of improving competition in programs aimed at benefiting the poorest. Investments in roads help expand transport volume and lower fares only if there is competition among transport providers. Otherwise, the benefits among the poor are seriously compromised. The resources offered by CCTs can offset numerous economic inefficiencies that, for instance, impede the acquisition of productive assets among poor farmers (such as obstacles in the access to credit markets) and hamper investments in education and health care. Examples of successful efforts to achieve universal health care include initiatives that incentivize health providers to offer more competitive services to people who are excluded.

Trade-offs in implementation should not be overlooked because of excessive attention to efficiency and equity trade-offs. There are numerous examples of equalizing policies that do not compromise economic growth. Given the current gaps in access, investments in ECD, universal health care, and good-quality education have both equity and efficiency benefits. Connecting poor farmers to urban markets can affect the incomes of farm households as well as income gaps among a population. Indeed, in the effort to reduce inequality, policy choices are less often restricted by an imbalance in the equity-efficiency trade-off than by an imbalance in the trade-off between expanding the coverage of an intervention and increasing the benefits; in the trade-off between enhancing the quality of services and increasing access to services through the construction of facilities such as schools or clinics; in the trade-off between expanding the coverage of electrification in rural areas and ensuring program financial viability; in the trade-off between cash or in-kind resource transfers; and in the tradeoff between conditionality and the lack of conditionality. Economic growth and good macroeconomic management contribute to circumventing such implementation policy trade-offs by providing resources, stability, and opportunities to adopt appropriate policies.

The fine points of policy design absolutely matter in ensuring that interventions are equalizing but do not compromise efficiency. Different choices in Chile and Mexico in tax reforms with the same objectives led to different impacts. The ultrarich bore the brunt of the income tax component of the reform in Chile, while, in Mexico, the middle class also largely shared the cost of the reform. ECD programs are most effective if they are aimed at the first 1,000 days of the lives of children, continue during childhood, and integrate psychosocial stimulation, parenting, and nutrition components. In many contexts, incentivizing higher quality in teaching, while making social transfers conditional on school completion may have a greater impact than simply constructing a new school. Defining the package of services that are provided, the level of user contributions in the financing of interventions, and the composition of the target population are all critical to successful reforms aimed at achieving universal health care coverage.

Avoid unexamined reliance on universal prescriptions and unique models of success. Evidence strongly suggests that the implementation of such prescriptions and models do not automatically ensure a reduction in inequality. Nonetheless, some initiatives are more likely than others to generate inequality reductions and improvements in the well-being of the poorest.

Integrated interventions are more likely to succeed than isolated, monolithic interventions, but composition influences the degree of success. If CCTs are combined with other safety net interventions such as transfers of productive assets, skills training, and access to credit and finance, they have

been shown to generate wide-ranging benefits. Investments in rural roads that attract additional investments in public services such as electrification, agricultural extension services, and enhanced water and sanitation services improve not only the connectivity of people to opportunities to meet basic needs, but also security, productivity, and quality of services. Yet, composition is also important if various interventions are combined. For example, at a given level of revenue, fiscal systems in Eastern European countries that depend on flat-rate income taxes sacrifice the redistributive power of progressive personal income taxes, while yielding the same level of revenue collection.

Simplicity and flexibility often drive success. Thus, the ability of the safety net system in the Philippines to scale up to reach hundreds of thousands of beneficiaries after catastrophic events is in part related to the flexibility of the system in the face of emergency situations. CCTs are delivered unconditionally, thereby allowing quick delivery and the scaling-up of the benefits. Exclusive and prolonged breastfeeding is another example of a simple and extraordinarily cost-efficient intervention to improve ECD.

Equalizing interventions are not a luxury reserved for middle- and high-income countries, nor an option only available during periods of prosperity. This chapter provides numerous examples of the implementation of successful interventions in ECD, universal health care coverage, good-quality teaching, CCTs, investment in rural infrastructure, and redistributive tax schemes across low-income countries that should dispel the notion that only middle-income countries can afford equalizing policies. Of course, context always matters: weak capacity, lack of political will, restricted fiscal space, vulnerability to external crises or climate change, internal conflict, and challenging geography are among the obstacles to the reduction of inequality worldwide. They are not insurmountable, however. This is also the case during periods of crises. Examples of CCTs integrated in safety nets that effectively protect the most vulnerable against natural disasters, choices in the way fiscal consolidation occurred in Europe during the 2008–09 financial crisis, and the reform of energy subsidies in some North African countries demonstrate that crisis is not an excuse for failure, but an incentive for the adoption of equalizing interventions.

The poor must be able to participate in and benefit from interventions: good policy choices benefit the poorest. Evidence from ECD programs, initiatives to promote universal health care coverage, and efforts to foster good-quality teaching shows that the most underprivileged children often benefit the most. Yet, this outcome should not be taken for granted. Thus, the more well off households among the targeted population, that is, households with children with higher baseline levels of development and more well educated mothers, are typically more likely to send their children to preschool or to take part in parenting programs. Many rural electrification initiatives are associated with high connection costs to keep electrification campaigns financially feasible, but this often means the poorest households must opt out. Likewise, the immediate winners in new or rehabilitated rural road programs in South Asia are reportedly people who already operate transport vehicles or who can afford to invest in small motorized vehicles. Policy design needs to take such outcomes into account up front and explicitly.

More knowledge! Despite the growing evidence on the impacts of policy interventions, improving the evidence base on initiatives that successfully narrow inequality requires more investment in filling data gaps and enhancing the understanding of the specific pathways through which programs affect inequality (whether intended or unintended). For example, rigorous evaluations have played a critical role in fine-tuning the design of CCTs and advocacy for the desirability of CCTs. Monitoring ECD programs for decades has made the quantification of the long-term effects of such programs possible. The widespread use of randomized controlled trials in new policy areas facilitates the more precise measurement of causal effects of interventions. The formulation of new indicators on, for example, learning or socioemotional development has expanded our knowledge of the impacts of programs to promote women's empowerment and address criminal behavior, risky sexual behavior, and adolescent pregnancy beyond the effects on incomes, employment, and service use that are normally analyzed. Yet, the road ahead is still long and steep. Especially important is the generation of more microeconomic household data, long-term evaluations and panel data, more compelling evidence on the benefits of the integration of multiple interventions, and more information on the potential distributional effects of policy interventions aimed at addressing long-term challenges such as climate change.

Notes

1. On each one of these policy areas, the World Bank has recently published comprehensive reviews, identified sectoral strategies, or conducted evaluations.
2. The approach borrows from the framework of Gill, Revenga, and Zeballos (2016).
3. Duncan et al. (2007); Georgieff (2007); Glewwe, Jacoby, and King (2001); Grantham-McGregor et al. (2007); Hanushek and Woessmann (2008); Heckman, Pinto, and Savelyev (2013); Naudeau et al. (2011a, 2011b); Vegas and Santibáñez (2010); Walker et al. 2007; World Bank (2009).
4. These results refer to data on around 2005 (Alderman 2011).
5. Other forms of undernutrition among children—wasting (low weight for height) and underweight—are more prevalent among the poor by a wide margin worldwide. See UNICEF (2016); World Bank (2015a).
6. Alderman (2011).
7. These estimated income benefits refer to men participants. Among women, the earnings were 22 percent higher than the earnings among the control group. See Heckman et al. (2010).
8. Barnett and Masse (2007); Heckman et al. (2010); Temple, Reynolds, and White (2007).
9. Gillespie et al. (2016).
10. Other common ECD interventions include pregnancy- and birth-related programs, which are discussed in the section on health care from the perspective of mothers.
11. Gertler et al. (2014).
12. Grantham-McGregor et al. (1991).

13. Gertler et al. (2014).
14. Attanasio et al. (2014).
15. Hamadani et al. (2006), cited in Alderman (2011).
16. Berlinksi and Schady (2015); Eickmann et al. (2003); Rosero and Oosterbeek (2011).
17. Berlinksi and Schady (2015); Chang et al. (2015).
18. Berlinksi and Schady (2015); Naudeau et al. (2011a).
19. Murphy at al. (2015).
20. Alderman (2011); Reynolds et al. (2007).
21. Reynolds et al. (2007).
22. Reynolds et al. (2007).
23. Martinez, Naudeau, and Pereira (2012).
24. Berlinski, Galiani, and Gertler (2006).
25. Naudeau et al. (2011a).
26. Araujo et al. (2016); Britto, Yoshikawa, and Boller (2011); Chetty, Friedman, and Rockoff (2014); Engle et al. (2011).
27. Berlinski, Galiani, and Manacorda (2008).
28. Alderman (2011).
29. Nadeau et al. (2011a).
30. Berlinksi and Schady (2015).
31. WHO and UNICEF (2003).
32. Naudeau et al. (2011a); Papp (2014); "The World Health Organization's Infant Feeding Recommendation," World Health Organization, Geneva (accessed June 2016), http://www.who.int/nutrition/topics/infantfeeding_recommendation/en/.
33. The results refer to Bangladesh, Brazil, The Gambia, Ghana, Guinea-Bissau, India, Pakistan, Peru, the Philippines, and Senegal (Sankar et al. 2015). The results disaggregated by boys and girls refer only to Brazil, The Gambia, Ghana, Pakistan, the Philippines, and Senegal. See WHO (2000).
34. Horta and Victora (2013).
35. Victora et al. (2015).
36. Kramer et al. (2008).
37. Der, Batty, and Deary (2008); Kramer et al. (2001, 2002, 2008); Oster (2015).
38. Berlinksi and Schady (2015).
39. Bhandari et al. (2003); Haider et al. (2000); Morrow et al. (1999); Tylleskär et al. (2011).
40. Berlinksi and Schady (2015); Pérez-Escamilla et al. (2012).
41. Hoddinott et al. (2011).
42. Black et al. (2008), cited in World Bank (2009).
43. Naudeau et al. (2011a).
44. Gillespie et al. (2016).
45. Jamison et al. (2013).
46. Wagstaff, Bredenkamp, and Buisman (2014).
47. For example, in India and the Islamic Republic of Iran, the annual rate of decline in adult mortality has been more than 1.0 and 3.5 percentage points higher, respectively, among women than men. See Jamison et al. (2013).
48. "The World Health Organization's Infant Feeding Recommendation," World Health Organization, Geneva (accessed June 2016), http://www.who.int/nutrition/topics/infantfeeding_recommendation/en/.
49. "The World Health Organization's Infant Feeding Recommendation," World Health Organization, Geneva (accessed June 2016), http://www.who.int/nutrition/topics/infantfeeding_recommendation/en/.
50. Wagstaff, Bredenkamp, and Buisman (2014).
51. Bloom and Fisk (2013); Jamison et al. (2013).
52. The studies use iron deficiency, caloric intake, or height as proxies for nutrition. See Alleyne and Cohen (2002).
53. Basta et al. (1979); Li et al. (1994); Thomas et al. (2006).
54. Baird et al. (2015); Miguel and Kremer (2004).
55. See Bleakley (2007). In addition, attempts to quantify the aggregate benefits from improved health care suggest that there are substantive gains in economic growth. Thus, Jamison et al. (2013) report that reductions in adult mortality might have accounted for as much as 11 percent of the overall economic growth seen in low- and middle-income countries in 1970–2000. These trends echo findings on developed countries. For example, improvements in health and nutrition are estimated to account for up to 30 percent of growth in gross domestic product (GDP) in the United Kingdom between 1780 and 1979.
56. See Jamison et al. (2013). The interventions spanned reproductive, maternal, newborn, and child health care; pregnancy-related interventions (antenatal care, treatment of complications associated with pregnancy, delivery interventions, and postpartum care); abortion and associated complications; family planning; diarrhea management; pneumonia treatment; im-

munization; nutrition (breastfeeding and supplementation); HIV prevention activities (community mobilization and work with specific groups such as intravenous drug users and men who have sex with men); the management of opportunistic infections, care, and treatment; collaborative tuberculosis–HIV treatment; malaria (treatment with appropriate drugs for adults, children, pregnant women, and those with severe malaria; indoor residual spraying; long-lasting insecticide-treated mosquito nets; intermittent presumptive treatment in pregnancy); tuberculosis (diagnosis, care, and treatment of drug-sensitive tuberculosis; diagnosis, care, and treatment of multidrug-resistant tuberculosis); neglected tropical diseases; and community-directed interventions to control lymphatic filariasis, onchocerciasis, schistosomiasis, trachoma, and soil-transmitted helminths.

57. See Jamison et al. (2013). Most of the incremental investment costs would be associated with improving health care systems, accounting for 70 percent of all costs in the first 10 years and 60 percent in the second 10 years. Such investments would lead to functional health care systems that can tackle long-term health challenges, not merely temporary improvements in infectious disease or mortality rates.

58. UNICEF (2016).
59. UNICEF (2016).
60. UNICEF (2016).
61. UNICEF (2016).
62. UNICEF (2016).
63. UNICEF (2016).
64. UNICEF (2016).
65. Gustafsson-Wright and Schellekens (2013).
66. UNICEF (2016).
67. Reviewed in Wagstaff et al. (2016).
68. Wagstaff et al. (2016).
69. Wagstaff et al. (2016).
70. Wagstaff et al. (2016).
71. UNESCO (2000).
72. World Bank (2016a).
73. See ASER Center (2011); Crouch (2006); Das, Pandey, and Zajonc (2006).
74. World Bank (2016a).
75. World Bank (2005).
76. See Becker (1962); Becker, Murphy, and Tamura (1990); Hanushek and Woessmann

(2008, 2010); Lucas (1988); Rebelo (1991); Romer (1990) ; Schultz (1961).
77. Hanushek and Woessmann. (2010); World Bank (2011a).
78. Mittal and Tripathi (2009); Rosenzweig and Foster (2010).
79. See Yang (1997) on China; Jolliffe (1998) on Ghana; Fafchamps and Quisumbing (1999) on Pakistan.
80. See Gakidou et al. (2010) on the association between education and good health; Frankensberg, Smith, and Thomas (2003) and Corbacho, Garcia-Escribano, and Inchauste (2007) on the resilience to economic shocks.
81. Effectiveness in teaching is often measured by the value added, that is, student test scores. See Araujo et al. (2016).
82. Araujo et al. (2016).
83. Heckman and Kautz (2012).
84. Araujo et al. (2016); Bau and Das (2016); Chetty, Friedman, and Rockoff (2014).
85. Araujo et al. (2016).
86. See Bau and Das (2016). Some evidence gathered in schools in the United States suggests there is no causal link between teacher incentives and student outcomes. See Fryer (2013); Springer et al. (2012).
87. Teacher behavior is measured by Classroom Assessment Scoring System scores, a protocol that measures teacher behavior in three domains: emotional support, classroom organization, and instruction support. Each domain captures different dimensions, such as positive or negative classroom atmosphere, teacher sensitivity, and regard for the student perspective. Each dimension is given a score of 1–6, from which a total score is obtained. (See Araujo et al. 2016.) The attention, self-control, and memory effects are distinct from the effects of classroom atmosphere and parental influence.
88. Higgins et al. (2015). See also Teaching and Learning Toolkit (database), Education Endowment Foundation, London, https://educationendowmentfoundation.org.uk/evidence/teaching-learning-toolkit/.
89. Dobbie and Fryer (2013); Duflo, Dupas, and Kremer (2011); Kane and Staiger (2008); Muralidharan and Sundararaman (2011).

90. See He, Linden, and MacLeod (2009); Lopez-Acevedo (1999). The findings on the program in Mexico also suggest that doubling the resources allocated per student could overcome a 30 percent deficit in test scores among rural students. However, a meta-study of 30 primary-school interventions associated with physical infrastructure (textbooks, improved buildings) in developing countries finds that only one-third had a significant impact on test scores. See Kremer, Brannen, and Glennerster (2013).

91. Angrist and Krueger (1991); Black, Devereux, and Salvanes (2008); Oreopoulos (2006a, 2006b).

92. See Global Education Monitoring Report (database), United Nations Educational, Scientific, and Cultural Organization, Paris, http://en.unesco.org/gem-report/; SABER (Systems Approach for Better Education Results) (database), World Bank, Washington, DC, http://saber.worldbank.org/index.cfm; WIDE (World Inequality Database on Education), United Nations Educational, Scientific, and Cultural Organization, Paris, http://www.education-inequalities.org/.

93. Gill, Revenga, and Zeballos (2016).

94. Gill, Revenga, and Zeballos (2016).

95. World Bank (2016b).

96. Ferré and Sharif (2014).

97. Behrman and Hoddinott (2005); Gertler (2004).

98. Maluccio and Flores (2005).

99. Pellerano et al. (2014).

100. According to Paxson and Schady (2010), physical outcomes that include improved hemoglobin, height, and fine motor control were 16 percent more likely among children in the bottom income quintile of households who were beneficiaries of the program. In contrast, the program had no statistically significant impact on children in higher-income household quintiles that also received CCTs.

101. Ahmed and Morgan (2011).

102. Glassman et al. (2013); Lagarde, Haines, and Palmer (2009).

103. Fiszbein and Schady (2009), citing Hernández et al. (2005).

104. Gertler and Boyce (2001).

105. Perova and Vakis (2012).

106. Orbeta et al. (2014).

107. World Bank (2011b).

108. Carvalho et al. (2015); Lim et al. (2010).

109. Akresh, de Walque, and Kazianga. (2013).

110. Galasso (2006).

111. Fiszbein and Schady (2009), citing evidence from Schady and Araujo (2008).

112. See Schady and Araujo (2008) for an evaluation of the Bono de Desarrollo in Ecuador; Macours, Schady, and Vakis (2008) on Atención a Crisis and Maluccio and Flores (2005) on Red de Protección Social (the latter two in Nicaragua). The benefits of the programs are limited to enrollments and additional years of schooling, with no gains in the quality of learning, but some in cognitive abilities. The lack of quality gains is also supported by the small increase in wages among students who have benefited from CCT-aided school enrollments. Behrman, Parker, and Todd (2009) find that children exposed to the Prospera Program (the rebranded Oportunidades Program) for two more years earn wages that are about 2 percent higher than the wages earned by other children.

113. See Baird, McIntosh, and Özler (2009). If evaluations fail to find significant impacts on test scores, it is often argued that this might be the result of programs that bring students with less ability back to school. See Filmer and Schady (2009).

114. Evans and Popova (2014).

115. Chaudhury, Friedman, and Onishi (2014).

116. Chioda, de Mello, and Soares (2012); Hidrobo et al. (2012); Walker et al. (2011).

117. Stecklov et al. (2007).

118. Brazil: 0.44 percent of GDP (2011); Mexico: 0.22 percent (2010); the Philippines: 0.40 percent (2013); Colombia: 0.35 percent (2010); Bangladesh 0.09 percent (2009) (World Bank 2015b).

119. This represents the unweighted average of 17 countries on which incidence analysis is available and in which the CCTs are not delivered through pilot programs. Bolivia and Uruguay, where CCTs cover about two-thirds of the poorest quintile, are exceptions. See World Bank (2015b).

120. The value of the average benefit relative to the average income of the poorest households varies widely, from 2.8 percent in

Bangladesh to 22.5 percent in Mexico. See World Bank (2015b).

121. Robalino, Rawlings, and Walker (2012).
122. See Gentilini (2014) for a detailed discussion.
123. See Bourguignon, Ferreira, and Leite (2003). Todd and Wolpin (2006) estimate that incremental increases in the size of transfers in Mexico would have diminishing effects on educational attainment.
124. Filmer and Schady (2009).
125. Baird, McIntosh, and Özler (2009).
126. de Brauw and Hoddinott (2008); Schady and Araujo (2008).
127. Bourguignon, Ferreira, and Leite (2003); Todd and Wolpin (2006).
128. World Bank (2015b). These impacts refer to Burkina Faso's Cash Transfers to Orphans and Vulnerable Children Program, Lesotho's Child Grant Program, Kenya's GiveDirect, and Zambia's Child Grant Program.
129. Aker et al. (2013).
130. CGAP (2011).
131. Aker et al. (2013); Muralidharan, Niehaus, and Sukhtankar (2014); Omamo, Gentilini, and Sandström (2010); Vincent and Cull (2011).
132. Berlinksi and Schady (2015).
133. Banerjee et al. (2015).
134. Hallegatte et al. (2016).
135. Calderón and Chong (2004); Calderón and Servén (2004, 2008); Estache, Foster, and Wodon (2002); Ndulu (2006); Seneviratne and Sun (2013); World Bank (2005).
136. Based on a sample of 100 countries, Calderón and Servén (2008) attribute to infrastructure in, respectively, South Asia and Sub-Saharan Africa 2.7 percentage points and 0.7 percentage points of annual GDP growth in 2001–05 and 6 points and 2 points of the reduction in the regional Gini.
137. World Bank (2015c).
138. These benefits are not automatic, however. Asher and Novosad (2016) describe a successful case of labor reallocation out of agriculture in India, while Banerjee, Duflo, and Qian (2012) present a less successful case of resource reallocation following rural road construction in China, and Bryan, Chowdhury, and Mobarak (2014) do the same in Bangladesh.

139. Asher and Novosad (2016) referring to evidence in India.
140. Khandker, Bakht, and Koolwal (2009).
141. Lokshin and Yemtsov (2005).
142. Aggarwal (2015); Asher and Novosad (2016).
143. Mu and van de Walle (2011).
144. Khandker, Bakht, and Koolwal (2009).
145. Lokshin and Yemtsov (2009).
146. See Hettige (2006). In other cases, safeguards are needed to ensure the more well off in rural communities do not benefit disproportionately from new roads. In case studies in Indonesia, the Philippines, and Sri Lanka, the direct winners of new or improved rural roads were people who already operated transport vehicles or who were able to afford to invest in smaller motorized three-wheelers. The more well educated, the more well informed, and people owning bicycles were able to obtain better wage opportunities because of the improved infrastructure. Relative to the extreme poor, the more well off were twice as likely to start or expand small businesses following the improvements.
147. See Hettige (2006).
148. Hettige (2006).
149. Dinkelman (2011); Grogan and Sadanand (2013).
150. van de Walle et al. (2013).
151. Khandker, Barnes, and Samad (2013).
152. Khandker, Barnes, and Samad (2013).
153. Ghuman and Llloyd (2007).
154. See Barron and Torero (2015). Particle pollution is measured according to the amount of $PM_{2.5}$—or fine inhalable particles with diameters generally 2.5 micrometers or smaller—that is found in the air (definition of the U.S. Environmental Protection Agency).
155. Dinkelman (2011).
156. Clark (2008); Dinkelman (2011); Lipscomb, Mobarak, and Barham (2013); Moser and Holland (1997); World Bank (2011a, 2011c).
157. Jensen and Oster (2009).
158. LaFerrara, Chong, and Duryea (2012).
159. De Agostini, Paulus, and Tasseva (2015); Manuel (2002); Mideplan (1999); Vivian (2006).
160. See Levy (2008). Cuesta and Oliveira (2014) find similar effects in Colombia.

161. Some countries, such as Colombia, Namibia, the Russian Federation, South Africa, and Uruguay, collect more than 1 percent of GDP as recurrent property taxes (Broadway, Chamberlain, and Emmerson 2010; de Ferranti et al. 2004; IMF 2014; Martinez-Vasquez 2008; World Bank 2005).

162. Lustig (2015).

163. Direct taxes cause the more well off to bear the brunt, while indirect taxes cause the poor to bear a larger relative share of the burden, given that the poor spend a higher share of their incomes on consumption.

164. Bird and Zolt (2003).

165. Sahn and Younger (2000).

166. Yet, large country variations are observed across the EU. Reductions in market inequalities are large in Western Europe, but much more limited in the Baltic States (Avram, Levy, and Sutherland 2014; De Agostini, Palaus, and Tasseva 2015).

167. See Martinez-Vasquez, Vulovic, and Moreno-Dodson (2014). Taxes are responsible for an average increase of 1.5 percent in the Gini index of market incomes in the country sample since 1990.

168. Bird and Zolt (2003, 2008).

169. According to the definition of Ravallion (2009), poor countries show consumption per capita under US$2,000 a year (2005 purchasing power parity [PPP] U.S. dollars). However, the more well off developing countries—countries with consumption per capita at US$4,000 per year—would require little additional taxation on the rich to eliminate extreme poverty. (Additional marginal tax rates between 1 percent and 6 percent would be required.) In each country, a rich household is a household that, in the United States, would be categorized as nonpoor. No economic distortions, behavioral changes, or political economy or administrative considerations are taken into account in the analysis, which includes 90 countries on which there are data for around the late 2000s.

170. Hoy and Sumner (2016).

171. Ostry, Berg, and Tsangarides (2014).

172. Inchauste and Lustig (forthcoming); Lustig (2015).

173. Redistributive effects range from less than 1 point to over 4 points (in Brazil) of the Gini for market incomes. South Africa with a reduction of over 7 points in the market income Gini, is an exception among moderate redistributive effects. Redistribution is associated with a reduction in the market income Gini of about 1–3 points in Ethiopia, Jordan, and Sri Lanka; the reductions are larger in Georgia and Russia. See Inchauste and Lustig (forthcoming); Lustig (2015); Younger, Osei-Assibey, and Oppong (2015).

174. See IMF (2014). For example, personal income taxation in developing countries raises an average 1–3 percent of GDP, compared with 9–11 percent of GDP among advanced countries.

175. Country-by-country comparative results need to viewed with caution, however. They are derived based on different methodologies (incidence analysis versus ex ante simulations), the indicator analyzed (income or consumption), conventions (the treatment of pension income), and the categories included (health care and education spending). This implies that the analyses cover different (but always incomplete) segments of the fiscal system. See Inchauste and Lustig (forthcoming).

References

Abramovsky, Laura, Orazio Attanasio, Kai Barron, Pedro Carneiro, and George Stoye. 2014. "Challenges to Promoting Social Inclusion of the Extreme Poor: Evidence from a Large Scale Experiment in Colombia." IFS Working Paper W14/33, Institute for Fiscal Studies, London.

Aggarwal, Shilpa. 2015. "Do Rural Roads Create Pathways out of Poverty? Evidence from India." Working paper, Indian School of Business, Hyderabad, India.

Ahmed, Shakil, and Chris Morgan. 2011. "Demand-Side Financing for Maternal Health Care: The Current State of Knowledge on Design and Impact." Issues Brief 1 (September), Nossal Institute for Global Health, University of Melbourne, Melbourne.

Aker, Jenny, Rachid Boumnijel, Amanda McClelland, and Niall Tierney. 2013. "How Do Electronic Transfers Compare? Evidence from a Mobile Money Cash Transfer Experiment in Niger." Technical Report, Tufts University, Medford, MA.

Akresh, Richard, Damien de Walque, Harounan Kazianga. 2013. "Cash Transfers and Child Schooling: Evidence from a Randomized Evaluation of the Role of Conditionality." Policy Research Working Paper 6340, World Bank, Washington, DC.

Alderman, Harold, ed. 2011. *No Small Matter: The Impact of Poverty, Shocks, and Human Capital Investments in Early Childhood Development.* Human Development Perspectives Series. Washington, DC: World Bank.

Alleyne, George A. O., and Daniel Cohen. 2002. "Health, Economic Growth, and Poverty Reduction: The Report of Working Group 1 of the Commission on Macroeconomics and Health." World Health Organization, Geneva. http://whqlibdoc.who.int/publications /9241590092.pdf.

Angrist, Joshua D., and Alan B. Krueger. 1991. "Does Compulsory School Attendance Affect Schooling and Earnings?" *Quarterly Journal of Economics* 106 (4): 979–1014.

Araujo, María Caridad, Pedro Carneiro, Yyannú Cruz-Aguayo, and Norbert Schady. 2016. "Teacher Quality and Learning Outcomes in Kindergarten." *Quarterly Journal of Economics* 125 (1): 175–214.

ASER Center. 2011. "Annual Status of Education Report (Rural) 2010." Pratham Resource Center, Mumbai. http://img.asercentre.org/docs /Publications/ASER%20Reports/ASER_2010 /ASERReport2010.pdf.

Asher, Sam, and Paul Novosad. 2016. "Market Access and Structural Transformation: Evidence from Rural Roads in India." Working paper (April 20), University of Oxford, Oxford.

Attanasio, Orazio P., Camila Fernández, Emla O. A. Fitzsimons, Sally M. Grantham-McGregor, Costas Meghir, and Marta Rubio-Codina. 2014. "Using the Infrastructure of a Conditional Cash Transfer Program to Deliver a Scalable Integrated Early Child Development Program in Colombia: Cluster Randomized Controlled Trial." *BMJ* 349 (September 29): g5785.

Avram, Silvia, Horacio Levy, and Holly Sutherland. 2014. "Income Redistribution in the European Union." *IZA Journal of European Labor Studies* 3 (22): 1-29.

Baird, Sarah, Joan Hicks, Michael Kremer, and Edward Miguel. 2015. "Worms at Work: Long-Run Impacts of a Child Health Investment." Working Paper 21428, National Bureau of Economic Research, Cambridge, MA. http://www.nber.org/papers/w21428.

Baird, Sarah, Craig McIntosh, and Berk Özler. 2009. "Designing Cost-Effective Cash Transfer Programs to Boost Schooling among Young Women in Sub-Saharan Africa." Policy Research Working Paper 5090, World Bank, Washington, DC.

Banerjee, Abhijit, Esther Duflo, Nathanael Goldberg, Dean Karlan, Robert Osei, William Parienté, Jeremy Shapiro, Bram Thuysbaert, and Christopher Udry. 2015. "A Multifaceted Program Causes Lasting Progress for the Very Poor: Evidence from Six Countries." *Science* 348 (6236): 772–89.

Banerjee, Abhijit, Esther Duflo, and Nancy Qian. 2012. "On the Road: Access to Transportation Infrastructure and Economic Growth in China." NBER Working Paper 17897, National Bureau of Economic Research, Cambridge, MA.

Barnett, W. Steven, Leonard N. Masse. 2007. "Comparative Benefit-Cost Analysis of the Abecedarian Program and Its Policy Implications." *Economics of Education Review* 26 (1): 113–25.

Barron, Manuel, and Maximo Torero. 2015. "Fixed Costs, Spillovers, and Adoption of Electric Connections." MPRA Paper 63804, University Library of Munich, Munich.

Basta, Samir S., Soekirman, Darwin Karyadi, Nevin S. Scrimshaw. 1979. "Iron Deficiency Anemia and the Productivity of Adult Males in Indonesia." *American Journal of Clinical Nutrition* 32 (4): 916–25.

Bau, Natalie, and Jishnu Das. 2016. "The Misallocation of Pay and Productivity in the Public Sector: Evidence from the Labor Market for Teachers." Paper presented at the United Nations University–World Institute for Development Economics Research's Development Conference, "Human Capital and Growth," Helsinki, June 6–7.

Becker, Gary S. 1962. "Investment in Human Capital: A Theoretical Analysis." *Journal of Political Economy* 70 (5, part 2): 9–49.

Becker, Gary S., Kevin M. Murphy, and Robert Tamura. 1990. "Human Growth, Fertility, and Economic Growth." *Journal of Political Economy* 98 (5): S12–S37.

Behrman, Jere R., and John Hoddinott. 2005. "Programme Evaluation with Unobserved Heterogeneity and Selective Implementation:

The Mexican PROGRESA Impact on Child Nutrition." *Oxford Bulletin of Economics and Statistics* 67 (4): 547–69.

Behrman, Jere R., Susan W. Parker, and Petra E. Todd. 2009. "Schooling Impacts of Conditional Cash Transfers on Young Children: Evidence from Mexico." *Economic Development and Cultural Change* 57 (3): 439–77.

Berlinski, Samuel, Sebastian Galiani, and Paul J. Gertler. 2006. "The Effect of Pre-primary Education on Primary School Performance." IFS Working Paper W06/04, Institute for Fiscal Studies, London.

Berlinski, Samuel, Sebastian Galiani, and Marco Manacorda. 2008. "Giving Children a Better Start: Preschool Attendance and School-Age Profiles." *Journal of Public Economics* 92 (5–6): 1416–40.

Berlinski, Samuel, and Norbert Schady, eds. 2015. *The Early Years: Child Well-Being and the Role of Public Policy.* Development in the Americas Series. Washington, DC: Inter-American Development Bank; New York: Palgrave Macmillan.

Bhandari, Nita, Rajiv Bahl, Sarmila Mazumdar, Jose Martines, Robert E. Black, Maharaj K. Bhan, and Infant Feeding Study Group. 2003. "Effect of Community-Based Promotion of Exclusive Breastfeeding on Diarrhoeal Illness and Growth: A Cluster Randomised Controlled Trial." *Lancet* 361 (9367): 1418–23.

Bird, Richard, and Eric Zolt. 2003. "Introduction to Tax Policy Design and Development." Draft prepared for "A Course on Practical Issues of Tax Policy in Developing Countries," World Bank, Washington, DC, April 28–May 1.

———. 2008. "Technology and Taxation in Developing Countries: From Hand to Mouse." *National Tax Journal* 61 (4): 791–821.

Black, Robert E., Lindsay H. Allen, Zulfiqar A. Bhutta, Laura E. Caulfield, Mercedes de Onis, Majid Ezzati, Colin Mathers, and Juan Rivera. 2008. "Maternal and Child Undernutrition: Global and Regional Exposures and Health Consequences." *Lancet* 371 (9608): 243–60.

Black, Sandra E., Paul J. Devereux, and Kjell G. Salvanes. 2011. "Too Young to Leave the Nest? The Effects of School Starting Age." *Review of Economics and Statistics* 93 (2): 455–67.

Bleakley, Hoyt. 2007. "Disease and Development: Evidence from Hookworm Eradication in the American South." *Quarterly Journal of Economics* 122 (1): 73–117.

Bloom, David E., and Günther Fink. 2013. "The Economic Case for Devoting Public Resources to Health." PGDA Working Paper 104, Program on the Global Demography of Aging, Harvard University, Cambridge, MA.

Bourguignon, Francois, Francisco Ferreira, and Phillippe Leite. 2003. "Conditional Cash Transfers, Schooling, and Child Labor: Micro-Simulating Brazil's Bolsa Escola Program." *World Bank Economic Review* 17 (2): 229–54.

Britto, Pia Rebello, Hirokazu Yoshikawa, and Kimberly Boller. 2011. "Quality of Early Childhood Development Programs in Global Contexts: Rationale for Investment, Conceptual Framework, and Implications for Equity." *Society for Research in Child Development Social Policy Report* 25 (2): 1–30.

Broadway, Robin, Emma Chamberlain, and Carl Emmerson. 2010. "Taxation of Wealth and Wealth Transfers." In *Dimensions of Tax Design: The Mirrlees Review*, edited by Stuart Adam, Tim Besley, Richard Blundell, Steve Bond, Robert Chote, Malcolm Gammie, Paul Johnson, Gareth Myles, and James Poterba, 737–824. London: Institute for Fiscal Studies; Oxford: Oxford University Press.

Bryan, Gharad, Shyamal K. Chowdhury, and Ahmed Mushfiq Mobarak. 2014. "Underinvestment in a Profitable Technology: The Case of Seasonal Migration in Bangladesh." *Econometrica* 82 (5): 1671–1748.

Calderón, César A., and Alberto Chong. 2004. "Volume and Quality of Infrastructure and the Distribution of Income: An Empirical Investigation." *Review of Income and Wealth* 50 (1): 87-106.

Calderón, César A., and Luis Servén. 2004. "Trends in Infrastructure in Latin America." Policy Research Working Paper 3401, World Bank, Washington, DC.

———. 2008. "Infrastructure and Economic Development in Sub-Saharan Africa." Policy Research Working Paper 4712, World Bank, Washington, DC.

Carvalho, Natalie, Naveen Thacker, Subodh S. Gupta, and Joshua A. Salomon. 2015. "More Evidence on the Impact of India's Conditional Cash Transfer Program, Janani Suraksha Yojana: Quasi-Experimental Evaluation of the Effects on Childhood Immunization and Other Reproductive and Child Health Outcomes." *PLoS ONE* 9 (10): e109311.

CGAP (Consultative Group to Assist the Poor). 2011. "CGAP G2P Research Project: South Africa Report." CGAP, Washington, DC.

Chang, Susan M., Sally M. Grantham-McGregor, Christine A. Powell, Marcos Vera-Hernández, Florencia Lopez-Boo, Helen Baker-Henningham, and Susan P. Walker. 2015 "Integrating a Parenting Intervention with Routine Primary Health Care: A Cluster Randomized Trial." *Pediatrics* 136 (2): 272–80.

Chaudhury, Nazmul, Jed Friedman, and Junko Onishi. 2014. "Philippines Conditional Cash Transfer Program: Impact Evaluation 2012." Report 75533-PH, World Bank, Washington, DC.

Chetty, Raj, John N. Friedman, and Jonah E. Rockoff. 2014. "Measuring the Impacts of Teachers: Teacher Value-Added and Student Outcomes in Adulthood." *American Economic Review* 104 (9): 2593–2679.

Chioda, Laura, João Manoel P. de Mello, and Rodrigo Soares. 2012. "Spillovers from Conditional Cash Transfer Programs: Bolsa Família and Crime in Urban Brazil." World Bank, Washington, DC.

Clarke, Ronald. 2008. "Improving Street Lighting to Reduce Crime in Residential Areas: Problem-Oriented Guides for Police." Response Guides Series 8, Office of Community Oriented Policing Services, Center for Problem-Oriented Policing, U.S. Department of Justice, Washington, DC.

Clements, Benedict, Ruud de Mooij, Sanjeev Gupta, and Michael Keen, eds. 2015. *Inequality and Fiscal Policy*. Washington, DC: International Monetary Fund.

Corbacho, Ana, Mercedes Garcia-Escribano, and Gabriela Inchauste. 2007. "Argentina: Macroeconomic Crisis and Household Vulnerability." *Review of Development Economics* 11 (1): 92–106.

Crouch, Luis. 2006. "Education Sector: Standards, Accountability, and Support." In *A New Social Contract for Peru: An Agenda for Improving Education, Health Care, and the Social Safety Net*, edited by Daniel Cotlear, 71–106. World Bank Country Study Series. Washington, DC: World Bank.

Cuesta, Jose, and Mauricio Olivera. 2014. "The Impact of Social Security Reform on the Labor Market: The Case of Colombia." *Journal of Policy Modeling* 36 (6): 1118–34.

Das, Jishnu, Priyanka Pandey, and Tristan Zajonc. 2006. "Learning Levels and Gaps in Pakistan." Policy Research Working Paper 4067, World Bank, Washington, DC.

De Agostini, Paola, Alari Paulus, and Iva Valentinova Tasseva. 2015. "The Effect of Tax-Benefit Changes on the Income Distribution in 2008–2014." Euromod Working Paper EM11/15, Institute for Social and Economic Research, University of Essex, Colchester, United Kingdom.

de Brauw, Alan, and John Hoddinott. 2008. "Must Conditional Cash Transfer Programs Be Conditioned to Be Effective? The Impact of Conditioning Transfers on School Enrollment in Mexico." IFPRI Discussion Paper 757, International Food Policy Research Institute, Washington, D.C.

de Ferranti, David, Guillermo E. Perry, Francisco H. G. Ferreira, and Michael Walton. 2004. *Inequality in Latin America: Breaking with History?* World Bank Latin American and Caribbean Studies Series. Washington, DC: World Bank.

Der, Geoff, G. David Batty, and Ian J. Deary. 2008. "Results from the PROBIT Breastfeeding Trial May Have Been Overinterpreted." *Archives of General Psychiatry* 65 (12): 1456–57.

Dinkelman, Taryn. 2011. "The Effects of Rural Electrification on Employment: New Evidence from South Africa." *American Economic Review* 101 (7): 3078–3108.

Dobbie, Will, and Roland G. Fryer, Jr. 2013. "Getting Beneath the Veil of Effective Schools: Evidence From New York City." *American Economic Journal: Applied Economics* 5 (4): 28–60.

Duflo, Esther, Pascaline Dupas, and Michael Kremer. 2011. "Peer Effects, Teacher Incentives, and the Impact of Tracking: Evidence from a Randomized Evaluation in Kenya." *American Economic Review* 101 (5): 1739–74.

Duncan, Greg J., Chantelle J. Dowsett, Amy Claessens, Katherine Magnuson, Aletha C. Huston, Pamela Klebanov, Linda S. Pagani et al. 2007. "School Readiness and Later Achievement." *Developmental Psychology* 43 (6): 1428–46.

Eickmann, Sophie H., Ana C. V. Lima, Miriam Q. Guerra, Marilia C. Lima, Pedro I. C. Lira,

Sharon R. Huttly, and Ann Ashworth. 2003. "Improved Cognitive and Motor Development in a Community-Based Intervention of Psychosocial Stimulation in Northeast Brazil." *Developmental Medicine and Child Neurology* 45 (8): 536–41.

Engle, Patrice L., Lia C. H. Fernald, Harold Alderman, Jere Behrman, Chloe O'Gara, Aisha Yousafzai, Meena Cabral de Mello, Melissa Hidrobo, Nurper Ulkuer, Ilgi Ertem, Semil Iltus, and the Global Child Development Steering Group. 2011. "Strategies for Reducing Inequalities and Improving Developmental Outcomes for Young Children in Low-Income and Middle-Income Countries." *Lancet* 378 (9799): 1339–53.

Estache, Antonio, Vivien Foster, and Quentin Wodon. 2002. "Accounting for Poverty in Infrastructure Reform: Learning from Latin America's Experience." World Bank Institute Development Studies, World Bank, Washington, DC.

Evans, David, and Anna Popova. 2014. "Cash Transfers and Temptation Goods: A Review of Global Evidence." Policy Research Working Paper 6886, World Bank, Washington, DC.

Fabrizio, Stefania, and Valentina Flamini. 2015. "Fiscal Consolidation and Income Inequality." In *Inequality and Fiscal Policy*, edited by Benedict Clements, Ruud de Mooij, Sanjeev Gupta, and Michael Keen, 159–74. Washington, DC: International Monetary Fund.

Fafchamps, Marcel, and Agnes R. Quisumbing. 1999. "Human Capital, Productivity, and Labor Allocation in Rural Pakistan." *Journal of Human Resources* 34 (2): 369–406.

Ferré, Céline, and Iffath Sharif. 2014. "Can Conditional Cash Transfers Improve Education and Nutrition Outcomes for Poor Children in Bangladesh? Evidence from a Pilot Project." Policy Research Working Paper 7077, World Bank, Washington, DC.

Filmer, Deon, and Norbert Schady. 2009. "Are There Diminishing Returns to Transfer Size in Conditional Cash Transfers?" Policy Research Working Paper 4999, World Bank. Washington, DC.

Fiszbein, Ariel, and Norbert Schady. 2009. *Conditional Cash Transfers: Reducing Present and Future Poverty*. Washington, DC: World Bank.

Frankenberg, Elizabeth, James Smith, and Duncan Thomas. 2003. "Economic Shocks, Wealth, and Welfare." *Journal of Human Resources* 38 (2): 280–321.

Fryer, Roland G. 2013. "Teacher Incentives and Student Achievement: Evidence from New York City Public Schools." *Journal of Labor Economics* 31 (2): 373–407.

Gakidou, Emmanuela, Krycia Cowling, Rafael Lozano, and Christopher J.L. Murray. 2010. "Increased Educational Attainment and Its Effect on Child Mortality in 175 Countries between 1970 and 2009: A Systematic Analysis." *Lancet* 376 (9745): 959–74.

Galasso, Emanuela. 2006. "With Their Effort and One Opportunity: Alleviating Extreme Poverty in Chile." Unpublished working paper, World Bank, . Washington, DC.

Gentilini, Ugo. 2014. "Our Daily Bread: What Is the Evidence on Comparing Cash versus Food Transfers?" Social Protection and Labor Discussion Paper 1420, World Bank, Washington, DC.

Georgieff, Michael. 2007. "Nutrition and the Developing Brain: Nutrient Priorities and Measurement." *American Journal for Clinical Nutrition* 85 (2): 614s–620s.

Gertler, Paul J. 2004. "Do Conditional Cash Transfers Improve Child Health? Evidence from PROGRESA's Control Randomized Experiment." *American Economic Review* 94 (2): 336–41.

Gertler, Paul J., and Simone Boyce. 2001. "An Experiment in Incentive-Based Welfare: The Impact of Progresa on Health in Mexico." Working paper, Haas School of Business, University of California, Berkeley, CA.

Gertler, Paul J., James J. Heckman, Rodrigo Pinto, Arianna Zanolini, Christel Vermeersch, Susan Walker, Susan M. Chang, and Sally Grantham-McGregor. 2014. "Labor Market Returns to an Early Childhood Stimulation Intervention in Jamaica." *Science* 344 (6187): 998–1001.

Ghuman, Sharon, and Cynthia B. Lloyd. 2007. "Poverty, Gender, and Youth: Teacher Absence as a Factor in Gender Inequalities in Access to Primary Schooling in Rural Pakistan." Population Council Working Paper 1, Population Council, New York.

Gill, Indermit, Ana Revenga, and Christian Zeballos. 2016. *Grow, Invest, Insure: A Game Plan to End Poverty*. Washington, DC: World Bank.

Gillespie, Stuart, Judith Hodge, Sivan Yosef, and Rajul Pandya-Lorch, eds. 2016. *Nourishing Millions: Stories of Change in Nutrition.* Washington, DC: International Food Policy Research Institute.

Glassman, Amanda, Denizhan Duran, Lisa Fleisher, Daniel Singer, Rachel Sturke, Gustavo Angeles, Jodi Charles, et al. 2013. "Impact of Conditional Cash Transfers on Maternal and Newborn Health." *Journal of Health, Population, and Nutrition* 31 (4 Suppl 2): S48–S66.

Glewwe, Paul, Hanan G. Jacoby, and Elizabeth M. King. 2001. "Early Childhood Nutrition and Academic Achievement: A Longitudinal Study." *Journal of Public Economics* 81 (3): 345–68.

Grantham-McGregor, Sally M., Yin Bun Cheung, Santiago Cueto, Paul Glewwe, Linda Richer, Barbara Trupp, and the International Child Development Steering Group. 2007. "Child Development in Developing Countries: Developmental Potential in the First Five Years for Children in Developing Countries." *Lancet* 369 (9555): 60–70.

Grantham-McGregor, Sally M., Christine A. Powell, Susan P. Walker, and John H. Himes. 1991. "Nutritional Supplementation, Psychosocial Stimulation, and Mental Development of Stunted Children: The Jamaican Study." *Lancet* 338 (8758): 1–5.

Grogan, Louise, and Asha Sadanand. 2013. "Rural Electrification and Employment in Poor Countries: Evidence from Nicaragua." *World Development* 43: 252–65.

Gustafsson-Wright, Emily, and Onno Schellekens. 2013. "Achieving Universal Health Coverage in Nigeria One State at a Time: A Public-Private Partnership Community-Based Health Insurance Model." Brooke Shearer Working Paper 2, Global Economy and Development at Brookings, Brookings Institution, Washington, DC.

Haider, Rukhsana, Ann Ashworth, Iqbal Kabir, and Sharon R.A. Huttly. 2000. "Effect of Community-Based Peer Counsellors on Exclusive Breastfeeding Practices in Dhaka, Bangladesh: A Randomised Controlled Trial." *Lancet* 356 (9242): 1643–47.

Hallegatte, Stephane, Mook Bangalore, Laura Bonzanigo, Marianne Fay, Tomaro Kane, Ulf Narloch, Julie Rozenberg, David Treguer,

and Adrien Vogt-Schilb. 2016. *Shock Waves: Managing the Impacts of Climate Change on Poverty.* Climate Change and Development Series. Washington, DC: World Bank.

Hamadani, Jena D., Syed N. Huda, Fahmida Khatun, and Sally M. Grantham-McGregor. 2006. "Psychosocial Stimulation Improves the Development of Undernourished Children in Rural Bangladesh." *Journal of Nutrition* 136 (10): 2645–52.

Hanushek, Eric A., and Ludger Woessmann. 2008. "The Role of Cognitive Skills in Economic Development." *Journal of Economic Literature* 46 (3): 607–68.

———. 2010. "The Economics of International Differences in Educational Achievement." NBER Working Paper 15949, National Bureau of Economic Research, Cambridge, MA.

He, Fang, Leigh L. Linden, and Margaret MacLeod. 2009. "A Better Way to Teach Children to Read? Evidence from a Randomized Controlled Trial." Unpublished working paper, Columbia University, New York.

Heckman, James J., and Tim Kautz. 2012. "Hard Evidence on Soft Skills." *Labour Economics* 19 (4): 451–64.

Heckman, James J., Seong Hyeok Moon, Rodrigo Pinto, Peter A. Savelyev, and Adam Yavitz. 2010. "The Rate of Return to the HighScope Perry Preschool Program." *Journal of Public Economics* 94 (1–2): 114–28.

Heckman, James J., Rodrigo Pinto, and Peter Savelyev. 2013. "Understanding the Mechanisms through Which an Influential Early Childhood Program Boosted Adult Outcomes." *American Economic Review* 103 (6): 2052–86.

Hernández, Bernardo, Dolores Ramírez, Hortensia Moreno, and Nan Laird. 2005. "Evaluación del Impacto de Oportunidades en la Mortalidad Materna e Infantil." In *Evaluación Externa de Impacto del Programa de Desarrollo Humano Oportunidades 2004* (External evaluation of the impact of the human development program oportunidades 2004), edited by Bernardo Hernández Prado and Mauricio Hernández Ávila, 73–95. Cuernavaca, Morales, Mexico: National Institute of Public Health.

Hettige, Hemamala. 2006. "When Do Rural Roads Benefit the Poor and How? An Indepth Analysis Based on Case Studies." Working paper, Operations Evaluation Department, Asian Development Bank, Manila.

Hidrobo, Melissa, John Hoddinott, Amy Margolies, Vanessa Moreira, and Amber Peterman. 2012. "Impact Evaluation of Cash, Food Vouchers, and Food Transfers among Colombian Refugees and Poor Ecuadorians in Carchi and Sucumbíos." Final Report, International Food Policy Research Institute, Washington, DC; World Food Programme, Rome.

Higgins, Steve, Maria Katsipataki, Rob Coe, Lee Elliot Major, Robbie Coleman, Peter Henderson, and Danielle Mason. 2015. "The Sutton Trust–Education Endowment Foundation Teaching and Learning Toolkit." July, Education Endowment Foundation, London. https://educationendowmentfoundation.org.uk/evidence/about-the-toolkits/about-the-toolkits/.

Hoddinott John J., John A. Maluccio, Jere R. Behrman, Reynaldo Martorell, Paul Melgar, Agnes R. Quisumbing, Manuel Ramirez-Zea, Aryeh D. Stein, and Kathryn M. Yount. 2011. "The Consequences of Early Childhood Growth Failure over the Life Course." IFPRI Discussion Paper 1073, International Food Policy Research Institute, Washington, DC.

Horta, Bernardo Lessa, and Cesar G. Victora. 2013. "Short-Term Effects of Breastfeeding: A Systematic Review of the Benefits of Breastfeeding on Diarrhoea and Pneumonia Mortality." World Health Organization, Geneva.

Hoy, Chris, and Andy Sumner. 2016. "Global Poverty and Inequality: Is There New Capacity for Redistribution in Developing Countries?" Working paper, University of Sydney, Sydney.

IMF (International Monetary Fund). 2014. "Fiscal Policy and Income Inequality" IMF Policy Paper (January 23), IMF, Washington, DC.

Inchauste, Gabriela, and Nora Lustig, eds. Forthcoming. *The Distributional Impact of Fiscal Policy: Evidence from Developing Countries.* Washington, DC: World Bank.

Jamison, Dean, Lawrence H. Summers, George Alleyne, Kenneth J. Arrow, Seth Berkley, Agnes Binagwaho, Flavia Bustreo, et al. 2013. "Global Health 2035: A World Converging within a Generation." *Lancet* 382 (9908): 1898–1955.

Jensen, Robert, and Emily Oster. 2009. "The Power of Cable TV: Cable Television and Women's Status in India." *Quarterly Journal of Economics* 124 (3): 1057–94.

Jolliffe, Dean. 1998. "Skills, Schooling, and Household Income in Ghana." *World Bank Economic Review* 12 (1): 81–104.

Kane, Thomas J., and Douglas O. Staiger. 2008. "Estimating Teacher Impacts on Student Achievement: An Experimental Evaluation." NBER Working Paper 14607 (December), National Bureau of Economic Research, Cambridge, MA.

Khandker, Shahidur R., Zaid Bakht, and Gayatri Koolwal. 2009. "The Poverty Impact of Rural Roads: Evidence from Bangladesh." *Economic Development and Cultural Change* 57 (4): 685–722.

Khandker, Shahidur R., Douglas F. Barnes, and Hussain A. Samad. 2013. "Welfare Impacts of Rural Electrification: A Panel Data Analysis from Vietnam." *Economic Development and Cultural Change* 61 (3): 659–92.

Khandker, Shahidur R., and Gayatri Koolwal. 2011. "Estimating the Long-Term Impacts of Rural Roads: A Dynamic Panel Approach." Policy Research Working Paper 5867, World Bank, Washington, DC.

Kramer, Michael S., Frances Aboud, Elena Mironova, Irina Vanilovich, Robert W. Platt, Lidia Matush, Sergei Igumnov, et al. 2008. "Breastfeeding and Child Cognitive Development: New Evidence from a Large Randomized Trial." *Archives of General Psychiatry* 65 (5): 578–84.

Kramer, Michael S., Beverley Chalmers, Ellen D. Hodnett, Zinaida Sevkovskaya, Irina Dzikovich, Stanley Shapiro, Jean-Paul Collet, et al. 2001. "Promotion of Breastfeeding Intervention Trial (PROBIT): A Randomized Trial in the Republic of Belarus." *Journal of the American Medical Association* 285 (4): 413–20.

Kramer, Michael S., Tong Guo, Robert W. Platt, Stanley Shapiro, Jean-Paul Collet, Beverley Chalmers, Ellen Hodnett, Zinaida Sevkovskaya, Irina Dzikovich, Irina Vanilovich, and PROBIT (Promotion of Breastfeeding Intervention Trial) Study Group. 2002. "Breastfeeding and Infant Growth: Biology or Bias?" *Pediatrics* 110 (2): 343–47.

Kremer, Michael, Conner Brannen, and Rachel Glennerster. 2013. "The Challenge of Education and Learning in the Developing World." *Science* 340 (6130): 297–300.

La Ferrara, Eliana, Alberto Chong, and Suzanne Duryea. 2012. "Soap Operas and Fertility:

Evidence from Brazil." *American Economic Review* 4 (4): 1–31.

Lagarde, Mylene, Andy Haines, and Natasha Palmer. 2009. "The Impact of Conditional Cash Transfers on Health Outcomes and Use of Health Services in Low and Middle Income Countries (Review)." *Cochrane Database of Systematic Reviews* 4 (October 7), Cochrane Collaboration, London.

Levy, Santiago. 2008. *Good Intentions, Bad Outcomes: Social Policy, Informality, and Economic Growth in Mexico*. Washington, DC: Brookings Institution Press.

Li Ruowei, Chen Xue-Cun, Yan Huai-Cheng, P. Deurenberg, L. Garby, and J. G. Hautvast. 1994. "Functional Consequences of Iron Supplementation in Iron-Deficient Female Cotton Mill Workers in Beijing, China." *American Journal of Clinical Nutrition* 59 (4): 908–13.

Lim, Stephen S., Lalit Dandona, Joseph A. Hoisington, Spencer L. James, Margaret C. Hogan, and Emmanuela Gakidou. 2010. "India's *Janani Suraksha Yojana*, A Conditional Cash Transfer Programme to Increase Births in Health Facilities: An Impact Evaluation." *Lancet* 375 (9730): 2009–23.

Lipscomb, Molly, A. Mushfiq Mobarak, and Tania Barham. 2013. "Development Effects of Electrification: Evidence from the Topographic Placement of Hydropower Plants in Brazil." *American Economic Journal: Applied Economics* 5 (2): 200–31.

Lokshin, Michael, and Ruslan Yemtsov. 2005. "Has Rural Infrastructure Rehabilitation in Georgia Helped the Poor?" *World Bank Economic Review* 19 (2): 311–33.

Lopez Acevedo, Gladys. 1999. "Learning Outcomes and School Cost-Effectiveness in Mexico: The PARE Program." Policy Research Working Paper 2128, World Bank, Washington, DC.

Lucas, Robert E., Jr. 1988. "On the Mechanics of Economic Development." *Journal of Monetary Economics* 22: 3-42.

Lustig, Nora. 2015. "Inequality and Fiscal Redistribution in Middle Income Countries: Brazil, Chile, Colombia, Indonesia, Mexico, Peru and South Africa." CEQ Working Paper 31 (July), Commitment to Equity, Inter-American Dialogue, Washington, DC; Center for Inter-American Policy and Research and Department of Economics, Tulane University, New Orleans.

Macours, Karen, Norbert Schady, and Renos Vakis. 2008. "Cash Transfers, Behavioral Changes, and Cognitive Development in Early Childhood: Evidence from a Randomized Experiment." Policy Research Working Paper 4759, World Bank, Washington, DC.

Maluccio, John A., and Rafael Flores. 2005. "Impact Evaluation of a Conditional Cash Transfer Program: The Nicaraguan Red de Protección Social." IFPRI Research Report 141, International Food Policy Research Institute, Washington, DC.

Manuel, Trevor. 2002. "The South African Tax Reform Experience Since 1994." Address presented at the International Bar Association's Annual Conference, Durban, South Africa, October 20–25.

Martinez, Sebastian, Sophie Naudeau, and Vitor Pereira. 2012. "The Promise of Preschool in Africa: A Randomized Impact Evaluation of Early Childhood Development in Rural Mozambique." February 14, Save the Children, Fairfield, CT; World Bank, Washington, DC. http://siteresources.worldbank.org /INTAFRICA/Resources/The_Promise_of _Preschool_in_Africa_ECD_REPORT.pdf.

Martinez-Vazquez, Jorge. 2008. "The Impact of Budgets on the Poor: Tax and Expenditure Benefit Incidence Analysis." In *Public Finance for Poverty Reduction: Concepts and Case Studies from Africa and Latin America*, edited by Blanca Moreno-Dodson and Quentin Wodon, 113–62. Directions in Development: Poverty Series. Washington, DC: World Bank.

Martinez-Vazquez, Jorge, Violeta Vulovic, and Blanca Moreno-Dodson. 2014. "The Impact of Tax and Expenditure Policies on Income Distribution: Evidence from a Large Panel of Countries." *Hacienda Publica Española* 200 (4): 95–130.

Mideplan (Chile, Ministry of Social Development). 1999. "Pobreza y distribucion del ingreso en Chile, 1990–1998." Mideplan, Santiago.

Miguel, Edward, and Michael Kremer. 2004. "Worms: Identifying Impacts on Education and Health in the Presence of Treatment Externalities." *Econometrica* 72 (1): 159–217.

Mittal, Surabhi, and Gaurav Tripathi. 2009. "Role of Mobile Phone Technology in Improving Small Farm Productivity." *Agricultural Economics Research Review* 22: 451–59.

Morrow, Ardythe L., M. Lourdes Guerrero, Justine Shults, Juan J. Calva, Chessa Lutter, Jane

Bravo, Guillermo Ruiz-Palacios, Robert C. Morrow, and Frances D. Butterfoss. 1999. "Efficacy of Home-Based Peer Counselling to Promote Exclusive Breastfeeding: A Randomised Controlled Trial." *Lancet* 353 (9160): 1226–31.

Moser, Caroline, and Jeremy Holland. 1997. "Urban Poverty and Violence in Jamaica." World Bank Latin American and Caribbean Studies: Viewpoints, World Bank, Washington, DC.

Mu, Ren, and Dominique van de Walle. 2011. "Rural Roads and Local Market Development in Vietnam." *Journal of Development Studies* 47 (5): 709–34.

Muralidharan, Karthik, Paul Niehaus, and Sandip Sukhtankar. 2014. "Payments Infrastructure and the Performance of Public Programs: Evidence from Biometric Smartcards in India." NBER Working Paper 1999, National Bureau of Economic Research, Cambridge, MA.

Muralidharan, Karthik, and Venkatesh Sundararaman. 2011. "Teacher Performance Pay: Experimental Evidence from India." *Journal of Political Economy* 119 (1): 39–77.

Murphy, Cristina B., Andressa K. Peres, Elaine C. Zachi, Dora F. Ventura, Luciana Pagan-Neves, Haydee F. Wertzner, and Elaine Schochat. 2015. "Generalization of Sensory Auditory Learning to Top-Down Skills in a Randomized Controlled Trial." *Journal of the American Academy of Audiology* 26 (1): 19–29.

Naudeau, Sophie, Naoko Kataoka, Alexandria Valerio, Michelle J. Neuman, and Leslie Kennedy Elder. 2011a. *Investing in Young Children: An Early Childhood Development Guide for Policy Dialogue and Project Preparation.* Directions in Development: Human Development Series. Washington, DC: World Bank.

Naudeau, Sophie, Sebastian Martinez, Patrick Premand, and Deon Filmer. 2011b. "Cognitive Development among Young Children in Low-Income Countries." In *No Small Matter: The Impact of Poverty, Shocks, and Human Capital Investments in Early Childhood Development*, edited by Harold Alderman, 9–50. Human Development Perspectives Series. Washington, DC: World Bank.

Ndulu, Benno J. 2006. "Infrastructure, Regional Integration, and Growth in Sub-Saharan Africa: Dealing with the Disadvantages of Geography and Sovereign Fragmentation." *Journal of African Economies* 15 (supplement 2): 212–44.

Omamo, Steven, Ugo Gentilini, and Susanna Sandström, eds. 2010. *Revolution: From Food Aid to Food Assistance; Innovations in Overcoming Hunger.* Rome: World Food Programme.

Orbeta, Aniceto C., Jr., Arnelyn Abdon, Michael del Mundo, Melba Tutor, Marian Theresia Valera, and Damaris Yarcia. 2014. "Keeping Children Healthy and in School: Evaluating the Pantawid Pamilya Using Regression Discontinuity Design Second Wave Impact Evaluation Results." World Bank, Washington, DC.

Oreopoulos, Philip. 2006a. "The Compelling Effects of Compulsory Schooling: Evidence from Canada." *Canadian Journal of Economics* 39 (1): 22–52.

Oreopoulos, Philip. 2006b. "Estimating Average and Local Average Treatment Effects of Education When Compulsory Schooling Laws Really Matter." *American Economic Review* 96 (1): 152–75.

Oster, Emily. 2015. "Everybody Calm Down about Breastfeeding." *FiveThirtyEight*, May 20. http://fivethirtyeight.com/features/every body-calm-down-about-breastfeeding/.

Ostry, Jonathan, Andrew Berg, and Charalambos Tsangarides. 2014. "Redistribution, Inequality, and Growth." IMF Staff Discussion Note, International Monetary Fund, Washington, DC.

Papp, Lauren M. 2014. "Longitudinal Associations between Breastfeeding and Observed Mother-Child Interaction Qualities in Early Childhood." *Child: Care, Health, and Development* 40 (5): 740–46.

Paxson, Christina, and Norbert Schady. 2010. "Does Money Matter? The Effects of Cash Transfers on Child Development in Rural Ecuador." *Economic Development and Cultural Change* 59 (1): 187–229.

Pellerano, Luca, Marta Moratti, Maja Jakobsen, Matěj Bajgar, and Valentina Barca. 2014. "The Lesotho Child Grants Programme Impact Evaluation: Follow-up Report." United Nations Children's Fund. Maseru, Lesotho.

Pérez-Escamilla, Rafael, Leslie Curry, Dilpreet Minhas, Lauren Taylor, and Elizabeth Bradley. 2012. "Scaling Up of Breastfeeding Promotion Programs in Low- and Middle-Income Countries: The 'Breastfeeding Gear' Model." *Advances in Nutrition* 3 (6): 790–800.

Perova, Elizaveta, and Renos Vakis. 2012. "5 Years in Juntos: New Evidence on the Program's Short and Long-Term Impacts." *Economía* 35 (69): 53–82.

Ravallion, Martin. 2009. "Do Poorer Countries Have Less Capacity for Redistribution?" Policy Research Working Paper 5046, World Bank, Washington, DC.

Rebelo, Sergio T. 1991. "Growth in Open Economies." Policy Research Working Paper 799, World Bank, Washington, DC.

Reynolds, Arthur J., Judy A. Temple, Suh-Ruu Ou, Dylan L. Robertson, Joshua P. Mersky, James W. Topitzes, and Michael D. Niles. 2007. "Effects of a School-Based, Early Childhood Intervention on Adult Health and Well-Being: A 19-Year Follow-up of Low-Income Families." *Archives of Pediatric and Adolescent Medicine* 161 (8): 730–39.

Robalino, David A., Laura Rawlings, and Ian Walker. 2012. "Building Social Protection and Labor Systems: Concepts and Operational Implications." Background paper, Social Protection and Labor Strategy 2012–22, World Bank, Washington, DC.

Romer, Paul M. 1990. "Human Capital and Growth: Theory and Evidence." *Carnegie-Rochester Conference Series on Public Policy* 32 (1): 251–86.

Rosenzweig, Mark R., and Andrew D. Foster. 2010. "Microeconomics of Technology Adoption." *Annual Review of Economics* 2 (1): 395–424.

Rosero, José, and Hessel Oosterbeek. 2011. "Trade-Offs between Different Early Childhood Interventions: Evidence from Ecuador." Tinbergen Institute Discussion Paper TI 2011–102/3, Faculty of Economics and Business, University of Amsterdam, and Tinbergen Institute, Amsterdam.

Sahn, David, and Stephen Younger. 2000. "Expenditure Incidence in Africa: Microeconomic Evidence." *Fiscal Studies* 21 (3): 329–47.

Sankar, Mari Jeeva, Bireshwar Sinha, Ranadip Chowdhury, Nita Bhandari, Sunita Taneja, Jose Martines, and Rajiv Bahl. 2015 "Optimal Breastfeeding Practices and Infant and Child Mortality: A Systematic Review and Meta-analysis." *Acta Pædiatrica* 104 (S467): 3–13.

Schady, Norbert, and María Caridad Araujo. 2008. "Cash Transfers, Conditions, and School Enrollment in Ecuador." *Economia* 8 (2): 43–70.

Schultz, Theodore W. 1961. "Investment in Human Capital." *American Economic Review* 51 (1): 1–17.

Seneviratne, Dulani, and Yan Sun. 2013. "Infrastructure and Income Distribution in ASEAN-5: What are the Links?" IMF Working Paper WP/13/11, International Monetary Fund, Washington, DC.

Springer, Matthew G., John F. Pane, Vi-Nhuan Le, Daniel F. McCaffrey, Susan Freeman Burns, Laura S. Hamilton, and Brian Stecher. 2012. "Team Pay for Performance: Experimental Evidence from the Round Rock Pilot Project on Team Incentives." *Educational Evaluation and Policy Analysis* 34 (4): 367–90.

Stecklov, Guy, Paul Winters, Jessica Todd, and Ferdinando Regalia. 2007. "Unintended Effects of Poverty Programmes on Childbearing in Less Developed Countries: Experimental Evidence from Latin America." *Population Studies* 61 (2): 125–40.

Temple, Judy A., Arthur J. Reynolds, and Barry A. B. White. 2007. "Age 21 Cost-Benefit Analysis of the Title I Chicago Child-Parent Centers: Technical Report." May, Chicago Longitudinal Study, University of Minnesota, Minneapolis.

Thomas, Duncan, Elizabeth Frankenberg, Jed Friedman, Jean-Pierre Habicht, Mohammed Hakimi, Nicholas Ingwersen, Jaswadi, et al. 2006. "Causal Effect of Health on Labor Market Outcomes: Experimental Evidence." Working Paper 2006–07, California Center for Population Research, University of California, Los Angeles, Los Angeles.

Todd, Petra E., and Kenneth I. Wolpin. 2006. "Assessing the Impact of a School Subsidy Program in Mexico: Using a Social Experiment to Validate a Dynamic Behavioral Model of Child Schooling and Fertility." *American Economic Review* 96 (5): 1384–1417.

Tsibouris, George C., Mark A. Horton, Mark J. Flanagan, and Wojciech S. Maliszewski. 2006. "Experience with Large Fiscal Adjustments." Occasional Paper 246, International Monetary Fund, Washington, DC.

Tylleskär, Thorkild, Debra Jackson, Nicolas Meda, Ingunn Marie S. Engebretsen, Mickey Chopra, Abdoulaye Hama Diallo, Tanya Doherty, et al. 2011. "Exclusive Breastfeeding Promotion by Peer Counsellors in Sub-Saharan Africa (PROMISE-EBF): A Cluster-Randomised Trial." *Lancet* 378 (9789): 420–27.

UNESCO (United Nations Educational, Scientific, and Cultural Organization). 2000. "The Dakar Framework for Action." UNESCO, Paris. http://unesdoc.unesco.org/images/0012/001211/121147e.pdf.

UNICEF (United Nations Children's Fund). 2016. *The State of the World's Children 2016: A Fair Chance for Every Child*. New York: UNICEF.

van de Walle, Dominique, Martin Ravallion, Vibhuti Mendiratta, and Gayatri Koolwal. 2013. "Long-Term Impacts of Household Electrification in Rural India." Policy Research Working Paper 6527, World Bank, Washington, DC.

Vegas, Emiliana, and Lucrecia Santibáñez. 2010. *The Promise of Early Childhood Development in Latin America and the Caribbean*. With Bénédicte Leroy de la Brière, Alejandro Caballero, Julien Alexis Hautier, and Domenec Ruiz Devesa. Latin American Development Forum Series. Washington, DC: World Bank.

Victora, Cesar G., Bernardo Lessa Horta, Christian Loret de Mola, Luciana Quevedo, Ricardo Tavares Pinheiro, Denise P. Gigante, Helen Gonçalves, and Fernando C. Barros. 2015. "Association between Breastfeeding and Intelligence, Educational Attainment, and Income at 30 Years of Age: A Prospective Birth Cohort Study from Brazil. *Lancet Global Health* 3 (4): e199–e205.

Vincent, Katharine, and Tracy Cull. 2011. "Cell Phones, Electronic Delivery Systems, and Social Cash Transfers: Recent Evidence and Experiences from Africa." *International Social Security Review* 64 (1): 37–51.

Vivian, Robert. 2006. "Equality and Personal Income Tax: The Classical Economists and the Katz Commission." *South African Journal of Economics* 74 (1): 79–109.

Wagstaff, Adam, Caryn Bredenkamp, and Leander R. Buisman. 2014. "Progress on Global Health Goals: Are the Poor Being Left Behind?" *World Bank Research Observer* 29 (2): 137–62.

Wagstaff, Adam, Daniel Cotlear, Patrick Hoang-Vu Eozenou, and Leander R. Buisman. 2016. "Measuring Progress toward Universal Health Coverage: With an Application to 24 Developing Countries." *Oxford Review of Economic Policy* 32 (1): 147–89.

Walker, Susan P., Susan Chang, Marcos Vera-Hernández, and Sally Grantham-McGregor. 2011. "Early Childhood Stimulation Benefits Adult Competence and Reduces Violent Behavior." *Pediatrics* 127 (5): 849–57.

Walker, Susan P., Theodore D Wachs, Julie Meeks Gardner, Betsy Lozoff, Gail A Wasserman, Ernesto Pollitt, Julie A Carter, and the International Child Development Steering Group. 2007. "Child Development: Risk Factors for Adverse Outcomes in Developing Countries." *Lancet* 369 (9556): 145–57.

WHO (Collaborative Study Team on the Role of Breastfeeding on the Prevention of Infant Mortality, World Heath Organization). 2000. "Effect of Breastfeeding on Infant and Child Mortality Due to Infectious Diseases in Less Developed Countries: A Pooled Analysis." *Lancet* 355 (9202): 451–55.

WHO (World Health Organization) and UNICEF (United Nations Children's Fund). 2003. "Global Strategy for Infant and Young Child Feeding." WHO, Geneva. http://www.who.int/nutrition/publications/infantfeeding/9241562218/en/.

World Bank. 2005. *World Development Report 2006: Equity and Development*. Washington, DC: World Bank; New York: Oxford University Press.

———. 2009. "Supplementing Nutrition in the Early Years: The Role of Early Childhood Stimulation to Maximize Nutritional Inputs." Child and Youth Development Notes 3 (1), World Bank, Washington, DC.

———. 2011a. "Learning for All: Investing in People's Knowledge and Skills to Promote Development; World Bank Group Education Strategy 2020." World Bank, Washington, DC.

———. 2011b. "Program Keluarga Harapan: Main Findings from the Impact Evaluation of Indonesia's Pilot Household Conditional Cash Transfer Program." World Bank, Jakarta.

———. 2011c. *World Development Report 2011: Conflict, Security, and Development*. Washington, DC: World Bank.

———. 2015a. *World Bank Support to Early Childhood Development: An Independent Evaluation*. Washington, DC: World Bank.

———. 2015b. "The State of Social Safety Nets 2015." World Bank, Washington, DC.

———. 2015c. "Achieving Results for Women's and Children's Health: Progress Report 2015." World Bank, Washington, DC.

———. 2016a. "SABER: Equity and Inclusion Brief, 2016." World Bank, Washington, DC. http://wbgfiles.worldbank.org/documents

/hdn/ed/saber/supporting_doc/brief/SABER
_EAI_Brief.pdf.

———. 2016b. *Global Monitoring Report
2015/16: Development Goals in an Era of Demographic Change.* Washington, DC: World
Bank.

———. 2016c. *Chile: Distributional Effects of
the 2014 Tax Reform.* Washington, DC: World
Bank.

Yang, Dennis. 1997. "Education and Off-Farm
Work." *Economic Development and Cultural
Change* 45 (3): 613–32.

Younger, Stephen D., Eric Osei-Assibey, and Felix
Oppong. 2015. "Fiscal Incidence in Ghana."
CEQ Working Paper 35 (December), Com-
mitment to Equity, Inter-American Dialogue,
Washington, DC; Center for Inter-American
Policy and Research and Department of Eco-
nomics, Tulane University, New Orleans.